DISCARDED

CHRONICLES
OF
PENNSYLVANIA

CHRONICLES
OF
PENNSYLVANIA

FROM THE
ENGLISH REVOLUTION
TO THE
PEACE OF AIX-LA-CHAPELLE
1688-1748

BY
CHARLES P. KEITH

↑ 890845

In Two Volumes

VOL I

Select Bibliographies Reprint Series

 BOOKS FOR LIBRARIES PRESS
FREEPORT, NEW YORK

LTL LAMAR TECH LIBRARY

First Published 1917
Reprinted 1969

STANDARD BOOK NUMBER:
8369-5145-X

LIBRARY OF CONGRESS CATALOG CARD NUMBER:
72-102270

PRINTED IN THE UNITED STATES OF AMERICA

TO
MY WIFE

PREFACE

The settlement of the banks of the Delaware by Dutch, Swedes, and Quakers has been sufficiently minuted not only in printed records, but in histories which are accessible. Similarly those events of the struggle for British supremacy and of the struggle for American independence which took place within the present boundaries of Pennsylvania are too well known to require fresh narration. As to the long period not covered by these subjects, not only data as to local development, but much information as to general affairs will be found in volumes devoting most space to earlier or later times. But for the valuable contribution made by such, there would be little knowledge of men and things between the arrival of the last shipload of Quakers and the first steps in the French and Indian war. The standard works on Pennsylvania in the XVIIth and XVIIIth Centuries may be described as a panegyric upon William Penn, the *Acta* as a wonder-worker of Benjamin Franklin, or an epic about George Washington. Much matter, less vivid, but worthy of observation, even any mention of certain years, is omitted. The complete story of successive administrations and their achievements or failures, of antagonistic religions, alien immigrations, relations with aborigines, and the legislature's adherence, under repeated temptation, to the principle of not engaging in war, is, in consequence, to be hunted widely in monographs, published correspondence, and parts of a number of books, many on special lines.

A comprehensive chronicle of the most neglected period is attempted to be supplied in these volumes, detailing what took place in each year, but sometimes pursuing a topic beyond the year in question, when the bringing in of other subjects would have been bewildering. Not to include what other writers have well covered, two dates memorable in a large part of the world have been chosen, that of the English Revolution, for the starting-point, as not requiring further details of the founding of the colony than are necessary to explain later conditions, and the date of the treaty of Aix-la-Chapelle, for closing the record, so as to shut out the contention for the Ohio, which was consequent upon that treaty. It has been necessary sometimes to overstep these limits in order to treat completely a minor subject which was important or noticeable during the course of the sixty years; and the opportunity given in a book on Pennsylvania history has been used to correct misapprehensions as to matters not chronologically within its theme.

Much of what, in histories, addresses, or editorial notes, has been published relating to those who controlled or inhabited Pennsylvania, has been inspired by bitter partisanship or, at least, strong predilection. As the establishment of the colony has been the just pride of the Quakers, and as the original sources of information most accessible here until recently have been the manuscripts coming from the governing family and faction, the predilection has been usually for the side of William Penn, if not of the Proprietaries in general; but in opposition the *Historical Review of the Constitution and Government of Pennsylvania,* voicing the opinions held by Franklin, and the *History* written by Thomas F. Gordon are conspicuous. It is not easy even for the investigator, delving beneath the radical and bitter expressions, to find out what was justice in the contentions, or what was true as to the conduct, much less as to the motives, of individuals. So strong was the disposition of the men active in the politics or religion of Pennsylvania at that time to believe anything against their real or supposed adversaries that even such evidence as a contemporary letter can not always be depended upon. With no purpose of making an arraignment against venerated personages, but ready to find a plea for the poorer in estate, the followers of a different ecclesiastical use, and others animadverted upon, I have said some things which will displease, but I have tried to be impartial, and to make allowances for all parties in the clashing of interests and consciences. Investigation has led me to different conclusions from those prevalent in this part of the country, and formerly accepted by myself. I trust that no expressions, however, will be thought to indicate want of respect for the truly religious members of the Society of Friends, and it seems to me that everybody living at the present time ought to wish the world converted to the "peaceable persuasion" of the majority of the Assembly of Pennsylvania from 1688 to 1748.

It has been impracticable to cite authorities for every statement, and it has been undertaken only for such as may cause surprise. If the reader wishes to decide for himself the truth of any, and there is no closely preceding or following reference which happens to cover, he will probably find the fact mentioned in what is the best evidence, viz: the printed *Votes of the Assembly,* the printed minutes of our Provincial or Governor's Council (called the *Colonial Records*), the printed *Pennsylvania Archives,* the copied minutes and documents of the Lords for Trade and Plantations, the printed abstracts of English State Papers, the Papers of the House of Lords published by the Historical Manuscripts Commission, and the copies of deeds &ct. in the public offices in Philadelphia. As to what, not of public record, William Penn or his representatives did, we have their own written words, published in the *Penn and Logan Correspondence,* or preserved among the letters and papers in the care of the Historical Society of Pennsylvania; and the same repository holds for the student's inspection the correspondence, apparently complete, between the later Penns and their deputies.

It has seemed better to give all the dates as they appear in the original authorities, and, if alternative, then in Old Style, and, as the difference from the New Style is not always understood, to devote a page or so in the first chapter to explanation. Perhaps it is only fair to my printers to add that the spelling, punctuation, &ct. are my own except usually where I am quoting, or, as to Indian names, spelling according to the record. I have undertaken to begin with a capital, not only titles, but such words as People, Province, &ct., when meaning the political body, and also Province, when meaning Pennsylvania proper without including Delaware; and I have placed £ before a sum in sterling and *l.* after a sum in provincial currency.

CHARLES P. KEITH.

321 S. Fourth St., Philadelphia,
  November, 1916.

CONTENTS OF VOLUME I

CHAPTER I.
National Advance and Royal Charters 1

CHAPTER II.
The Ascertainment of the Southern Boundary . 30

CHAPTER III.
The Acquisition and Distribution of the Land . 60

CHAPTER IV.
The Red Neighbours 90

CHAPTER V.
The People 123

CHAPTER VI.
A Republican Feudatory 153

CHAPTER VII.
Government under the Frame of 1683 182

CHAPTER VIII.
Religious Dissension 210

CHAPTER IX.
England 243

CHAPTER X.
Failure in Government 281

CHAPTER XI.
The Church of England 327

CHAPTER XII.
Penn's Second Marriage and Second Visit 367

CHAPTER XIII.
Government by Penn's Friends 402

CHAPTER XIV.
The Anti-Proprietary Party 433

CHAPTER I.

NATIONAL ADVANCE AND ROYAL CHARTERS.

The settlement on Delaware Bay and River at the date of the English Revolution—the method of dating—Boundaries in English charters for Virginia, New England, and Maryland—Dutch and Swedes on the Delaware—English conquest and the treaties—Duke of York's control—William Penn's parentage—His application for land—Description in the charter to him.

When the English Revolution took place, white people of various nationality, but united under one government derived from that Crown which the Revolution transferred, were already scattered from below Cape Henlopen to above the Falls of the Delaware, through a depth westward from the water's edge of about twelve miles. Cultivated fields were alternating with extensive forests throughout the whole region, dwelling-houses were at the borders of the owners' plantations, perhaps more sheds than barns held crops and quadrupeds, a mill had been established to grind the corn for each neighbourhood, while primitive manufactories for lime, glass, etc., were here and there, a few meeting-houses for Quakers had been built, and two or three structures scarcely more ornate, but for more ornate worship, may have been standing. In some places, the newer houses were close to one another by a township plan, and there were a few villages representing settlements which might be called old for that part of the New World, such as Lewes, or Whorekills, New Castle, once New Amstel, and Chester, formerly Upland. New Castle had perhaps a wharf, and certainly a fort or stockade, which however had been long unused, and was in want of repair, and there were the ruins of a governor's headquarters on Tinicum Island. Up the river, several miles north of the mouth of the Schuylkill, and on rising ground, which was marked by recently inhabited caves, and divided by a creek or arm of the Delaware, were, however, the beginnings of a capital city, designed to cover the isthmus where the two rivers were bent again towards each other. A large wharf had been made, at which a goodly number of vessels were coming and going during eight or nine months of the year. Houses, quite a number being of brick, faced the Delaware on a street along the top of the slope towards the water, and there were others on both sides of the next street to the west, as also near the Delaware end of streets laid out from river to river. In the middle of the widest of the latter streets, near the top of the slope, were the market sheds and the little court house, the seat of authority. Miles away, near the rapids, or Falls, of the Delaware, was the manor-house of William Penn, Proprietary and Governor in Chief. One correction of tradition may well be made in passing: the bricks of the old buildings of Pennsylvania were not brought from England; on the contrary, clay was most abundant in the soil, and, naturally, brickmaking was early a great industry, and it is ridiculous to suppose that freight for over 3000 miles was paid for what could be obtained at or near the spot.

The Revolution was consummated when, after James II had succeeded in his second attempt to escape from England, William and Mary, Prince and Princess of Orange, formally accepted the joint sovereignty offered by the Lords and Commons assembled at Westminster, and gave adherence to the Declaration of

Right, and were proclaimed King and Queen. The
day on which this took place is that with which this
chronicling of events connected with the civilized part
of the present extent of Pennsylvania begins, viz: a
Wednesday which the English of the time reckoned as
"the thirteenth day of February in the year of our
Lord one thousand six hundred and eighty-eight," but
which most of the nations of Western Europe, including Scotland, called "the twenty-third day of February
in the year of our Lord one thousand six hundred and
eighty-nine." Those nations had adopted the Grego-
rian calendar, advancing the time ten days, and beginning the year on their first day of January, whereas
England was beginning it on what the English called
the twenty-fifth of March following. Under the English system, January and February were the eleventh
and twelfth months respectively, and March was called
the first month, although twenty-four of its days were
at the end of a year. The Quakers numbered, instead
of naming, the months, and this was directed by an
Act of Assembly of Pennsylvania, interpreted incorrectly by the editor of Volume I of the *Minutes of the
Provincial Council* as directing that the year start with
the first day of March. As was usual in private letters, the records of the colony from January 1st to
March 24th both inclusive, while giving the day of the
month according to the local calendar, generally give
the year according to both English and French style,
the last figure of the year looking like a fraction with
the English figure as numerator and the French figure
as denominator, as, for instance, $168\frac{8}{9}$, or else there
being added with a hyphen after the English year the
last figure of the French year, as in 1688-9. England
and, following her, Pennsylvania adhered to the old,
or Julian, calendar, and to the twenty-fifth of March
as New Year's day, throughout the whole period of
this history. Each date in this book being given as

stated in the authority for it, the reader may assume, unless it is otherwise declared, that it is according to that "Old Style." The only difference in the length of the months in the two calendars during the period was that the old had a twenty-ninth of February in the year 1700, while the new had not: so that the English first of March, 1700, was the French twelfth of March, 1701, and so on, the discrepancy of ten days becoming eleven days.

The year of our Lord according to the Old Style will be found in this book in parenthesis when a document dated by the year of a king's reign is mentioned; a mode of dating which would puzzle the reader, particularly as to the acts of Charles II, who dated his reign from the execution of Charles I, January 30, 1648-9, although Charles II was not restored to power until May 8, 1660, when proclaimed King, or May 29, 1660, when he entered London, in what was called the twelfth year of his reign. It may be useful to state that, counting the day of accession as the first day of the first year of the reign,

the first year of James I ended on March 23, 1603-4, O. S.,

the first year of Charles I ended on March 26, 1626, O. S.,

the first year of Charles II ended on January 29, 1649-50, O. S.,

the first year of James II ended on February 5, 1685-6, O. S.,

the first year of William III ended on February 12, 1689-90, O. S.,

the first year of Anne ended on March 7, 1702-3, O. S.,

the first year of George I ended on July 31, 1715, O. S.,

the first year of George II ended on June 10, 1728, O. S.

Although by the time with which these Chronicles start, the dream of a Scandinavian world-power had vanished, the furs of America had been diverted from Amsterdam, and the Europeans on the western shore of Delaware Bay and River had accepted the status of tenants of William Penn, it is necessary, even before studying the people, the proprietaryship, and the government, to take a retrospect as far as before the reign of Gustavus Adolphus and the voyages of Henry Hudson, in order to explain the boundary dispute which overhung a large part of the present extent of Pennsylvania during the whole period chronicled.

When there were no white people on the Atlantic Coast between Maine and Florida, King James I of England authorized two settlements to be made within certain limits by a number of his subjects in two companies, or colonies, as he called them. After one of these companies had made an establishment on the James River, the King, by charter dated May 23rd in the seventh year of his reign over England (1609), granted to those contributing, called "The Treasurer and Company of Adventurers and Planters of the City of London for the first Colony in Virginia," the Atlantic coast for 200 miles northward and southward of Point Comfort with a depth inward to the Pacific Ocean, which was not then supposed to be very far off. This charter, which was annulled in 1625, before any lots were sold north or east of the Chesapeake, is only mentioned here because this disposal of land, nearly, if not quite, up to the latitude forty degrees north, was in force when the other company also received a separate charter from the same King. The Stuart kings personally transacted the affairs of their realm: the policy during a reign was as continuous as that under a party Cabinet in later times, either changing as exigencies arose; and the theories of James I or the carelessness of Charles II affected history. James I incorporated in 1620 those who had been expected to make the other settlement, calling them "The Council established at Plymouth in the County of Devon for planting, ruling, and governing of New England in America." The charter to this Council recited the depopulation of the coast "between the degrees of forty and forty-eight," and gave the name New England to all the territory in America lying and being in breadth from forty degrees of northerly latitude from the equinoctial line to forty-eight degrees of said northerly latitude, and in length by all the breadth aforesaid throughout the main land from sea to sea. In the granting clause, but nowhere else, the word "inclusively" occurs after the words "to forty-eight degrees of said northerly latitude," but this can hardly be thought so to enlarge the description as to cover anything south of what is just forty degrees north of the equator. The parallels of latitude used by geographers mark the end or completion of just so many degrees as the number attached to them on the map, in other words the completion of just that many, starting from the equator, of the ninety parts into which the surface of the earth from the equator to the pole is divided. There has been some confusion in such expressions as "the fortieth degree," "the forty-eighth degree," etc., some persons meaning the parallels marking forty degrees, forty-eight degrees, etc., and some even meaning the space north of the parallels marking so many degrees. Early instances of the use of the expression with one or other of these meanings can be found, but, what is much in point, William Penn and Lord Baltimore, sixty years after the granting of the New England charter, were speaking of the parallel marking forty degrees as "the fortieth degree." In strictness, the later Penns were right in saying that the fortieth degree is the fortieth of the ninety spaces from the equator to the pole, the space beginning at the equator, and running to parallel marked 1°, being the first; in other words, that the fortieth degree is the space between the parallel marked 39° and that marked 40°. A description, however, like that of New England, "from forty degrees to forty-eight degrees" is obviously from where you count forty degrees complete from the equator to where you count forty-eight degrees complete. Against an interpretation that this region was to start northward from the parallel 39°, is the fact that it would then have covered a considerable part of the southern colony's 200 miles north of Point Comfort, and this could not have been intended. Although in the charter an exception was made of all land actually possessed or inhabited by other Christian princes or states, or within the bounds of the southern colony, it is most likely that the description was meant to run from as near as possible just where the southern colony ended. Therefore, the southern termination of what was meant by New England for many years after 1620, must have been the parallel marked 40°, the completion of forty degrees north of the equator.

This parallel, which will be spoken of in these pages as "the fortieth parallel," will be seen in modern maps to strike the New Jersey coast at Chadwick, about two miles south of Mantoloking, and the western side of the Delaware River at Bridesburg, and to cross Broad Street, in Philadelphia, below Clearfield Street, and the city line below Bala, and to pass through Downingtown, and south of, but not far from, Lancaster, Columbia, Shippensburg, Bedford, and Brownsville.

In the same year that James I made the aforesaid grant for the southern colony, Henry Hudson, while sailing in the employ of the Dutch East India Company, gave to the sovereign of that company by exploring both the Delaware Bay and the Hudson River a claim from the first authenticated discovery to the

8 CHRONICLES OF PENNSYLVANIA.

shores of each; and at the time when James I made the aforesaid grant of New England, citizens of Holland, etc., were trading on what they called the North River, and perhaps on the Delaware, which they called the South River. It was not long afterwards that those acknowledging allegiance to the Netherlandish Estates General came into undisputed possession of the valley of the Hudson and a large part of Connecticut and some part of New Jersey, having forts on the east side of the Delaware River, buying land in 1629 on the west side of Delaware Bay, and for a short time keeping a fort there, and even, in 1633, erecting a fort on the Schuylkill.

About 1630, Sir George Calvert, first Baron Baltimore in the peerage of Ireland, who had been one of the Virginia Company, and one of James I's secretaries of state, sought from Charles I a tract of land north of the settled part of Virginia. It is not necessary to go into the question of the King's right to convey or set off what had been granted to the dissolved company; for this did not affect the Penn and Baltimore controversy. Cecil Calvert, the second Baron, presented after the first Baron's death a further petition, describing the region desired as "uncultivated and occupied in parts by barbarians having no knowledge of Divine Inspiration." In the charter's recital of the petition the words are "*hactenus inculta et barbaris nullam divini numinis notitiam habentibus in partibus occupata.*" Under date of June 20th, in the eighth year of the reign (1632), King Charles granted to the said second Baron and his heirs and assigns, according to transcript of the enrolment of the charter, printed, with its bad spelling, etc., with the Report of Commissioners of 1872 on Boundary of Maryland and Virginia: *Totam illam partam Peninsule sive Chersonnessus jacentem in partibus Americe inter Oceanum ex oriente et Sinum de Chesopeake ab occidente a*

National Advance and Royal Charters. 9

residuo ejusdem per rectam lineam a promontorio sive Capite terre vocato Watkins' Point juxta sinum predictum, prope Fluvium de Wighco situatum ab occidente, usque ad magnum Oceanum in plaga orientali ductam, divisam, Et inter metam illam a meridie usque ad partam illam estuarii de De La Ware ab Aquilone que subjacet quadrigesimo gradui latitudinis Septentrionalis ab æquinoctiali ubi terminatur Nova Anglia: Totum que illum terre tractum, infra metas subscriptas videlicit transeundo a dicto Estuario vocato Delaware Baye recta linea per gradum predictum usque ad verum meridianum primi fontis fluminis de Pattowmack deinde vergendo versus meridiem ad ulteriorem dicti fluminis ripam et eam sequendo qua plaga occidentalis et meridionalis spectat usque ad locum quendam appellatum Cinquack prope ejusdem Fluminis ostium scituatum ubi in prefatum Sinum de Chessopeak evolvitur ac inde per lineam brevissimam usque ad predictum Promontorium sive locum vocatum Watkins' Point."

As this makes the northern boundary *"ubi terminatur Nova Anglia,"* it seems unnecessary to give any further reason why the only fair construction is that the words *"quadrigesimo gradui latitudinis"* mean the fortieth parallel, marking the completion of forty degrees, not the beginning of the fortieth space from the equator, and that the word *"estuarii"* covers river as well as bay. Thus this charter, under which the Lords Baltimore were Proprietors of Maryland until the American Revolution, relates to all land beginning at Watkin's Point on the Chesapeake, then along a line drawn to the Atlantic as the southern boundary line, then up the Atlantic coast and the shore of Delaware Bay and River to where it is crossed by the fortieth parallel, where New England terminated, and westward along said parallel—*"per gradum predictum"*— to the meridian of the furthest source of the Potomac, then due south to the Potomac, and along its southern bank to Cinquack near the mouth, and thence by the shortest line to Watkin's Point. We are confident that, had the original grantee soon put a town on the Delaware River anywhere not supposed to be above the fortieth parallel, say at League Island or the mouth of Dock Creek, all England would have thought him acting within his rights. When his heirs, notwithstanding matters to be hereafter mentioned, had persisted in claiming what is now the state of Delaware and Delaware County and a great part of other counties in Pennsylvania, the Penns found lawyers to argue for various interpretations of the charter. The Penns finally insisted that *"subjacet quadragesimo gradui"* means "lies south of the beginning of the fortieth degree," *i.e.* south of the thirty-ninth parallel. Were there no other reasons against this, it could scarcely have been Charles I's actual intention to give such a small part of the wilderness to the heir of an old public servant like George Calvert, who had spent large sums in colonial enterprises, and had asked for this grant to reimburse him. At the time the description was written, Capt. John Smith's map was the authority as to the country around the Chesapeake, and that map made Watkin's Point, the starting-place, about 38° 10′ north. To put the northern boundary at the parallel 39°, was to give only about fifty miles of width, degrees being then computed at sixty statute miles. The general notion of the English government when William Penn asked for a grant of land was that Lord Baltimore had two degrees of latitude, and it was to such dimensions that Penn desired to hold him. Watkin's Point being 38° 10′, made the traditional northern boundary at least forty degrees north. William Penn, instead of claiming that the "fortieth degree" or "the beginning" meant the parallel 39°, argued to the third Lord Baltimore that when the patent of 1632 was granted, Watkin's Point was supposed to be "in the thirty-eighth degree," Penn thus using the popular language, by which the degree is beyond the parallel marking that many degrees. Of the two lines, that at the beginning, and that at the completion of the true fortieth degree, only by using that at the completion can the figure be drawn according to Smith's map, which delineates the Potomac as having its first source about as near the fortieth parallel as the bend of that river at Hancock actually is; so that a line running south to reach the source could never start from the thirty-ninth parallel. In fact, Smith had gone up the Potomac to 39° 30', and reported the river as extending further many miles northwestwardly; so it would have appeared nonsense to talk about land at the sources of the river in a grant reaching no further north than 39°. The suggestion, once made, that Baltimore's land could not extend further north than the head of Delaware Bay would have made the description contradictory, as an east and west line therefrom would shut out the upper Potomac. In the charter for Connecticut, about thirty years later, a certain body of water is called a river, and described as being commonly called a bay. The truth seems to be that, as Argall, the English discoverer of Delaware Bay, who visited it the year after Hudson, described it as extending inwards thirty leagues, the English thought that the head of the bay might be further north than forty degrees, twenty marine leagues being a degree. To be sure, Argall said "lying in westwardly," and made the latitude of the southern cape 38° 20' north, but Hudson had more accurately made that of the northern cape 38° 54'. The Penns' final contention, from the use of the word *subjacet,* even excluded from this grant the northern part of the shore along the salt water, as not lying "under the fortieth degree." Lord Chancellor Hardwicke, in enforcing the compromise agreed upon by the Penns and Lord Baltimore, said that there was an ambiguity as to whether the grant extended to or through the degree. It would seem that any such ambiguity should have been solved according to the provision which the charter itself contained, that, in case of doubt as to the true meaning of any word, clause, or sentence, the interpretation should always be *"benignior, utilior, et favorabiliter"* for Lord Baltimore and his heirs and assigns.

There are publicists who would have settled all conflicting claims upon the broad principle that grants of political power are revocable by the supreme authority of the State, and that the latest grantee—in this case William Penn—is to supersede those prior to him. This principle, however just, and how much soever followed in reality by Councils of State and courts of law, was too dangerous to the heirs of the latest one favored to be urged by them. A solution similarly dangerous to them could be found also in treating the grants of the American wilderness, when greatly exceeding the needs or services of the recipients, as mere licenses to occupy with colonists, and as lapsing with non-user. No attempt to send colonists to the Delaware River under this charter of 1632 was made until the shores had passed under another flag, and had been afterwards freshly acquired by conquest. The main assertion of the Penns in opposition to the Lords Baltimore was that the charter of 1632 was, as to what the Penns wanted, invalid or inoperative, or had become so. Original invalidity would be recognized if some other civilized power, instead of the king who made the grant, had the rightful title. As excepted from the operation of the charter would be all land as to which the recital of its being occupied only by savages was untrue; for that recital amounted to a condition annexed to the gift, as it expressed the information on which it was based, and a royal gift based on untrue information was void. The Crown of England had claimed title by discovery to the whole region granted to the Virginia and New England companies, but James I rather appealed to early possession or a right to occupy what was vacant, and neither he nor Charles I was interfering with actual colonies of other civilized powers. Of course there was a limit to the possessions of such colonies. Unless the whole of North America was to be included in Mexico, or the northern part of the present United States was to be included in Canada, one European nation could not be deemed owner of territory beyond its effective control. Therefore the force of the charter to Lord Baltimore on the Susquehanna and Delaware respectively is to be distinguished. No European outpost had been established in that part of the region described in the charter which lay west of the watershed between the two rivers: and it was the merest pretence of Dutch influence or the boundaries of deeds to the Dutch from certain Indians which could impeach the Calverts' right in that part. Moreover, as will be shown further on, the claim had been duly prosecuted there.

As to the land drained by Delaware River and Bay, however, while it is not clear that such settlements as the Dutch had made by 1632 amounted to an occupation, the English did not really acquire the region until more than thirty years after that date. Not only did the Estates General of the United Belgic or Netherland Provinces—Holland, Zeeland, Friesland, etc.,—soon take additional points under their sovereignty, but, moreover, pursuant to the design of Gustavus Adolphus, his successors on the throne of Sweden, being also Princes of Finland, etc., sent over their subjects to both the eastern and the western shores of the Delaware. In the course of years, various Englishmen independent of Lord Baltimore, made unsuccessful attempts to trade or plant there: meanwhile the two other nations lived side by side with unsettled boundaries. William Penn very reasonably thought that, even if Lord Baltimore's patent was originally good, he had lost his right to that region by never acquiring possession, and the region had become the property of the Dutch by the treaty between Cromwell and the Estates General in 1653, yielding to the latter the land of which they were possessed at the beginning of the war. The restored English monarchy, keeping Jamaica, which was acquired through that treaty, was bound by it. Sweden, by the capture of the Dutch fort in May, 1654, secured the dominion of the Delaware basin from below Cape Henlopen to miles above the fortieth parallel; but the Dutch reconquered it in September, 1655.

Except to state title in sending commissioners to agree upon a boundary, Lord Baltimore and his representatives seem to have acquiesced in the possession by the Swedes and Dutch until 1659, when he sent an officer to New Amstel to demand the withdrawal of the settlers who were below the fortieth degree or an acknowledgment of tenure. The Dutch officials refused, and their superiors on Manhattan Island sent ambassadors asserting title under the King of Spain's right by Columbus's discoveries, and the assignment of that right to the United Republic of the Seven Provinces by the treaty of Munster in 1648, recognizing their independence, and giving up all countries conquered and seated by them. The ambassadors claimed in general New Netherland, extending along the ocean from 38° to 42°, bounded on the west by Maryland on Chesapeake Bay, as one of those countries, and in particular the South River, as having been possessed by the settlement of Hoorekill (the early spelling of Whorekill), and by various forts. A just title to the whole river and especially the western shore was furthermore claimed from purchase from the natural proprietors, the native Indians. Baltimore subsequently had an agent press his cause in Holland, but without success.

Although James I and Charles I had tried to avoid any conflict in regard to colonies with other civilized nations, Charles II in fact offered the Netherlandish possessions in North America to any Englishman who would conquer them. It has been said that he never forgave the Estates General for sending him, when an exile, away from the Hague, at the demand of Cromwell. The restored monarch did not wait for a declaration of war. Under date of April 23rd in the fourteenth year of his reign (1662), in chartering the Governor and Company of Connecticut, he granted to them a depth or extent in longitude to the Pacific Ocean, with no exceptions as to the possessions of other civilized nations. This may have been merely a careless copying of the charter for Massachusetts, or designed by the grantees to enable them to absorb the rival colony of New Haven, in which they succeeded; but such a document could have been construed as a license to seize under the old claim of the Crown of England the southern part of the Hudson Valley, and what lay west of it. The extent of the grant southward was not mentioned clearly, the description being "all that part of the King's dominions in New England in America"—as before mentioned, the land from the fortieth parallel to the forty-eighth parallel had received the name New England in 1620—bounded on the east by Narragansett River "commonly called Narragansett Bay where the said River falleth into the Sea; and on the north by the line of the Massachusetts Plantation; and on the south by the Sea and in longitude as the line of the Massachusetts Colony running from east to west that is to say from the said Narragansett Bay on the east to the South Sea"—i.e. the Pacific Ocean—"on the west with the islands thereunto belonging." Had there been no Europeans above the fortieth parallel, we may admit that, under this description, Connecticut could have sent colonists to and possessed what became Bucks County, Pennsylvania, as well as Manhattan Island, and been ultimately the greatest state in the American Union. We need not stop to examine the claim of Connecticut to the Wyoming region; for it was not brought forward until after the time at which this history closes. The recipients of the aforesaid charter of 1662 not having evicted the Dutch, King Charles, under date of March 12, 1663-4, executed a patent to his brother, who was his heir presumptive, James, Duke of York, etc., for the land from the west side of the Connecticut River to the east side of Delaware Bay. Under date of April 25th, in the sixteenth year of the reign (1664), and with a recital that complaints had been received from New England of differences and disputes as to the bounds of the charters and jurisdictions, a commission was given to Col. Richard Nicolls, Sir Robert Carre, George Cartwright, and Samuel Maverick to visit the colonies and other plantations within the tract known as New England, and hear and determine all complaints and appeals, and to provide for and settle the peace and security of the country according to their discretion and instructions. The instructions were to reduce the Dutch "anywhere within the limits of our [Charles II's] dominions to an entire obedience to our government," no man to be disturbed in his possessions who would yield obedience, and live in subjection, with the same privileges as other subjects.

The Commissioners sailed from England with a considerable force, and overawed the Dutch garrison on Manhattan, obtaining a surrender of that region without the shedding of blood; and a detachment under Sir Robert Carre was sent to summon the Governor and inhabitants on the Delaware to yield obedience to their "rightful sovereign," who was pleased to have them enjoy their real and personal property and liberty of conscience. The Swedes among the people were to receive congratulation on "their happy return under a monarchial government"! Carre was instructed to declare to Lord Baltimore's son and all Englishmen concerned in Maryland that Carre was only employed to reduce the region to obedience to the King, for whose own behoof Carre was to keep possession: if Lord Baltimore's right under his charter was asserted, Carre was to say that he was keeping the place only until the King was "informed and satisfied otherwise." Carre went up the Delaware, passing the fort at New Amstel on the last day of September; and, in the course of three days, gaining the Swedes to his side, he entered into an agreement, which was dated October 1st, with the burgomasters, who declared themselves acting in behalf also of all the Dutch and Swedes of Delaware Bay and River, that they submitted to the King's authority, and were to be protected in their persons and property. The commander of the fort, however, was true to his charge, and refused to surrender; so, on Sunday morning, the detachment under Carre opened fire, and then stormed the fort without loss, killing three of the garrison, and wounding ten. On October 24th, Nicolls was authorized by the Commissioners to go to the region thus conquered, and take care of the government, and depute such officers for the same as he should see fit.

In none of these proceedings do we find the western shore of Delaware River and Bay declared the property of the Duke. Nicolls, in various patents of 1667 and 1668 for lands there, describes himself as Principal Commissioner from the King for New England, Governor-General under the Duke of York of his territories in America, and Commander-in-Chief of the King's forces to reduce the "usurped" plantations of the Dutch to his Majesty's obedience.

By the treaty of Breda, made in 1667, the Dutch left the English in possession of these conquests, included among the places held by the English on the 10th of May of that year.

In 1668, the English officers at New York, in providing for certain persons to be Councillors at Delaware, ordered them to take an oath to the Duke of York, and established for matters of difficulty an appeal to the Governor and Council at New York. Thus the Governor commissioned by the Duke over his possessions in America took jurisdiction over what had been the southern colony or province of the Dutch, which came to be often called Delaware more than a century before that name was reassumed for the state embracing the greater part of the district. Magistrates looking to New Castle, as New Amstel was called, refused to allow Marylanders to make surveys near the bay or river, and when, in 1672, the Marylanders seized goods at Whorekill, and talked of a stronger expedition to possess the land up to forty degrees north, the commander at New Castle prepared, by order of the New York Governor, to resist what was deemed an invasion.

In the summer of 1673, the Dutch and English being again at war, the former captured New Netherland, and the people on the Delaware made submission. The treaty signed at Westminster on February 9, 1673-4, restored to each party the possessions taken by the other since the beginning of the war. William Penn spoke of this arrangement as an exchange of Surinam, which the English were actually holding, for the North American conquests of the Dutch.

Doubts could be raised whether the former grant to the Duke of York by a king not actually in possession had been valid. Apparently to set the question at rest, Charles II issued a new patent under date of June 29,

1674, to the Duke of York, again using the description running only to the east side of Delaware River and Bay. As the Duke, down to his accession to the English throne as James II, received no express grant of the region west of that river and bay, some color of title thereto was sought in the words added, as usual, in the patent: "together with all the lands, islands, soils, . . . with their and every one of their appurtenances." It would seem, on the contrary, that the patent was prepared with care not to conflict with the old grant to Lord Baltimore. However, the officers of the Duke of York assumed authority over the western shore of the Delaware in November, 1674, upon the transfer of New Netherland to the English under the treaty; and not only was this command preserved until 1681, but rents were reserved to the Duke and his heirs.

While the Lords Baltimore were losing land on the Delaware, there was a different state of affairs a few miles west of it, neither the Dutch nor the Swedes dwelling far from that water. Before the English conquest of New Netherland, those deriving title under the patent of 1632 had peopled the eastern shore of the Chesapeake, and supplanted Clayborne's Virginia colony on Palmer's Island, and perhaps elsewhere at the mouth of the Susquehanna, and the government of Maryland, by assisting the Indians in war, had extended the sphere of influence, if not the actual plantation, of its Proprietary, as far north as the limit mentioned in the patent. In 1661, troops of the Province, in accordance with a treaty of alliance with the Susquehannocks, went to Susquehanna Fort to help to defend it, and, although the English garrison stipulated for was not maintained, the Marylanders for a number of years, as appears in the records, had communication with that tribe's stronghold, which the contemporary Jesuit relations and some data collected by Eshleman indicate to have been at one time above the Great Falls of the river. Marylanders must have been familiar with the fort's location. Augustine Herman (name variously spelt), a native of Bohemia, who had decided to remove from New Amsterdam to Maryland, made a contract with the second Lord Baltimore in 1661 or 1662 to prepare a map of his province in consideration of a large grant of land. The work took long, and was very expensive, and, when finished, gave what was claimed to be a delineation of Maryland as inhabited in the year 1670. The map was published in London in 1673. It marked the boundary line as running through a large circular enclosure called "The present Sasquahana Indian fort" on the west side of the Susquehanna, at or south of "Canoage," and just below "the greatest fall," or, in other words, what is known as the Conewago Falls, at the mouth of the Conewago Creek, which also is depicted on the map. The location is actually about five miles north of the fortieth parallel, a remarkable approximation, but no parallels are shown. In carrying the line, intended to run due east and west, as far as the Delaware, in accordance with Baltimore's claims, it is inaccurately made to strike that river above where Bristol now is. The most accessible reprint of the map is in Clayton Colman Hall's book, *The Lords Baltimore and the Maryland Palatinate*. Many years afterwards, persons serving the interests of the Penns endeavored to discredit Herman's map as having been prepared and paid for in the prosecution of Lord Baltimore's claims against the Dutch and the Duke of York; and, in the lawsuit of the Penns against the fifth Lord, there was an attempt to prove that the only fort ever reached by the Marylanders was at the mouth of the Octorara, but testimony to that effect was duly contradicted by witnesses brought by the defendant. The impression received from Indians about 1700 that no white man had gone north of the mouth of the Octorara before 1682 is, at most, only additional evidence that, prior to 1632, there were no Christian colonists dwelling in the valley of the Susquehanna between the fortieth parallel and Clayborne's settlement, except possibly an isolated trader, and that down to 1680 there were none claiming possession adverse to the Baltimore grant.

There were various actions of William Penn, even connected with the boundaries, which may be condemned, but we must not think him guilty, when he applied for land, of seeking to have other people's property taken from them. He had then no intention of encroaching upon the rights of the Calverts. Nobody knew where the fortieth degree lay, but it was supposed that the parallel completing it, and marking the furthest extent northward of the claims of that family, was south, rather than north, of where modern observations have located it. As presented before the eyes of every inquiring Englishman, there was up the Susquehanna and on the western side of the Delaware a large region practically uncultivated, and to which neither Lord Baltimore's patent nor the Duke of York's patent did extend. If the great depth westward which the charter of Connecticut called for had ever been taken seriously, it was probably thought to have been legally curtailed, so that it could not embrace any part of this region.

The founder of Pennsylvania (see Howard M. Jenkins's *Family of William Penn*) was the son of an English admiral of the same name, who, after serving under the Commonwealth, favored the restoration of Charles II, and was knighted, and was the commander-in-chief under, and chief adviser of, the aforesaid Duke of York, when, in 1665, the Duke had the glory of signally defeating the Dutch; so that the Admiral and his son, both before and after the latter became a Quaker, were in close contact with the royal brothers. Charles II, after the useful Admiral died, felt regard for the self-denying son, very possibly from a similar appreciation of virtue to what that King evinced in insisting upon giving a bishopric to the prebendary, Thomas Ken, "the little black fellow that refused his lodging to poor Nelly," Ken having declined to let the King's mistress occupy the prebendal house at Winchester on the occasion of a royal visit. Admiral Penn was the son of a captain in the navy, who was at one time consul for the Mediterranean trade, and the Admiral's monument, set up by his widow, declared the family to be a branch of the Penns of Penn in Buckinghamshire. The mother of the Founder is called in Pepys's *Diary* a "Dutchwoman;" and, in Granville Penn's *Life of Sir William Penn,* her father, John Jasper, is described as a merchant of Rotterdam. This is doubtless correct as to a part of his life, and as to his origin. W. Hepworth Dixon, in *A History of William Penn Founder of Pennsylvania,* romantically narrates the courtship of the Bristol boy, afterwards Admiral, with the "rosy Margaret," who waited for him until after he received a commission, and he "ran over to Rotterdam, and claimed his bride;" but Dixon would have curbed his imagination if he had seen certain records, which, moreover, Jenkins does not notice. Margaret was a widow, and had been married to the former husband in or before 1631, the year of the date of his will, and, while we do not know about her rosy cheeks, we learn, from compensation paid her after her second marriage, that she had property. A certificate dated August 28, 1643, in the Dutch Reformed Church, Austin Friars, London, from Rev. Andrew Chaplin, who before the Irish Rebellion was minister of the congregation of Six Mile Bridge, County Clare, Ireland, tells that John Jasper of Ballycase, County Clare, lived there with Marie his wife, and that Margaret, daughter of John Jasper of Ballycase, was lawfully married according to the rites of the Church of England unto Nicasias

Vanderscure, some time of the parish of Kilrush in said County, and that said Nicasias and Margaret lived in parish of Killconrie before the Irish Rebellion. On June 6, 1643, Capt. William Penn and Margaret Van der Schuren, widow, were married at St. Martin's, Ludgate. Her former marriage does not appear to have been known to Jenkins when he wrote the genealogy. The Admiral set up a claim for money advanced to the Crown, and this, at his death, September 16, 1670, came to his executor, the Founder, who had been moved by Quaker preaching at various times, and, after engaging in various careers having no connection with Quakerism, had joined the Society of Friends about 1668, in the course of, or between, two sojourns in Ireland. A story published anonymously in London in 1682 of his immorality just before becoming a Quaker was heard by William Byrd in a twisted version, and appears in Byrd's *History of the Dividing Line* [between Virginia and North Carolina] rather as an explanation of Penn's receiving a royal grant. As such it is utterly silly, particularly when, as in Byrd's version, the mistress of the Duke of Monmouth is made to figure as the woman in the case, which certainly would never have endeared Penn to Monmouth or King Charles II (Monmouth's father) or the Duke of York. A daughter is given to Penn, of whom Byrd says that she "had beauty enough to raise her to be a duchess, and continued to be a toast full thirty years." This was Monmouth's recognized daughter, Henrietta Crofts, who married Charles, Duke of Bolton, in 1697, and died on February 27, 1729-30. Quakers, with more logic, have viewed Penn's success in obtaining royal favor as a miracle.

With the money claim against the Crown, and the general friendliness of the Duke of York, William Penn saw the opportunity to obtain what was deemed Crown land, but was occupied by the Duke rather as the Crown's agent, but really because he was heir presumptive. Penn therefore petitioned the King for a grant of the land north of Maryland, bounded on the east by the Delaware River, and extending westward as far as Maryland extended, and northward as far as plantable. It is probable that Charles II, who had once released 500 Quakers from imprisonment, and was at heart a Roman Catholic, had been made aware of and sympathized with the object of securing a land for religious toleration. When the petition had been referred to the Committee of the Privy Council for Trade and Plantations, Penn appeared before those Lords. He says in a letter of August 14, 1683, that on that occasion, he standing at the chair of the Lord President, some said that Lord Baltimore had but two degrees, whereupon the Lord President (who was John Robartes, Earl of Radnor) turned his head to Penn, and said "Mr. Penn, will not three degrees serve your turn?" and Penn replied "I submit both the what and the how to this honourable Board." The minutes say that he declared that he would be satisfied with three degrees, and would, in consideration, release the debt or part of it, and wait for the balance until the King could better pay it.

Cecil Calvert, second Lord Baltimore, had died and been succeeded by his son Charles, who had gone to Maryland before Penn made his application. The Duke of York was also away from England. Copies of Penn's petition were sent to the agents of Lord Baltimore, and to Sir John Werden, representing the Duke of York. Baltimore's agents, in answer, claimed the Susquehanna Fort—undoubtedly the one marked on the map printed seven years before—as the boundary of Maryland, and asked that Penn and his people be prohibited from furnishing the Indians with arms and ammunition. There had been war with the Susquehannocks since the printing of the map. The agents

asked that the boundary line run east from the Fort
to the Delaware River, and west from the Fort. The
Duke's agent, Werden, in his turn, stated that the land
applied for had been held as an appendix and part of
the government of New York, and, although it should
not prove to be strictly within the bounds of the Duke
of York's patent, his right was preferable to all others.
Penn was told to arrange this matter with the Duke,
and, as to Maryland, Penn agreed that Susquehanna
Fort should be its boundary, and that he be subjected
to restrictions as to furnishing arms or ammunition
to Indians. It may surprise us that the latter stipulation does not appear in the charter granted to Penn,
but the disregarding of Susquehanna Fort in framing
the description inserted was perfectly fair. Maryland
extended along the Susquehanna River or Chesapeake
Bay to the fortieth parallel, and would go beyond the
Fort, if that was south of the parallel; so, if any occupation of the site of the Fort was an encroachment upon
what the King was free to grant, Penn could ask
abandonment. Penn obtained the consent of the Duke
to a grant north of the actual colony of which New
Castle was the chief town, such grant extending northward and westward as far as the King should please,
"beginning about the latitude of forty degrees." If
Penn's land therefore ran north from 40°, he would
be clear of any claim by either Lord Baltimore or the
Duke, and need not care who had the right on the south.
A month later, having seen a description drafted by
Penn, Werden wrote that it was the Duke's intention
that the southern limits should be twenty or thirty
miles above New Castle, which distance, Werden said,
"we guess may reach as far as the beginning of the
fortieth degree." The last words "beginning of the
fortieth degree," may have been merely an awkward
rendering of the Duke's words, and intended for "as
far as the beginning spoken of by the Duke, namely,

forty degrees." Werden may have been one of those who called the space north of the fortieth parallel "the fortieth degree," having in mind that at such parallel the latitude begins to be forty degrees and so many minutes. In fact, although this is not found to have been contended, the "beginning of the fortieth degree" could mean the part of it first reached in a description reading downwards. Those who say that Werden meant the thirty-ninth parallel, that is the end or completion reading northwards of thirty-nine of the ninety spaces from the equator to the north pole, must see that in such case Werden, in explaining the Duke's intention, would be contradicting what the Duke had said; moreover, it being pretty accurately known how near Cape May was to the thirty-ninth parallel, and that it was a long distance from Cape May to New Castle, Werden could not have been looking for that parallel twenty or thirty miles above New Castle. As twenty-three miles due north of the old centre of that town would actually carry any location clearly above the fortieth parallel, we must conclude that he had the latter in mind, with remarkably accurate data concerning it, in saying twenty or thirty miles above New Castle.

Other people's opinion was more agreeable to Penn, who became dissatisfied with the amount of river frontage proposed for him, that is below the unnavigable rapids at Trenton. He was willing to leave twelve miles between his land and New Castle, and he expressed the opinion, so Werden wrote to the secretary of the Committee, that twelve miles "would fall under"—an expression similar to *"subjacet"* in the Baltimore patent—"the beginning of the fortieth degree." Certainly, it was not being urged in favor of a new starting-point that it would be south of the fortieth parallel, and so conflict with the boundaries of Maryland. Penn was meaning the same scientific line as Werden: and, after the expression "the beginning of" was finally put into the charter, it was for years deemed by everybody either as equivalent to "the extremity of" or as surplusage. Markham at Upland in 1682 had no other view; for, while the northern boundary of Pennsylvania was similarly fixed at "the beginning of the three and fortieth degree," he, according to his account, told those present that Penn's grant ran to latitude 43d 00′. There is no reason to doubt that before Werden's last mentioned letter to the secretary, Penn had been told that New Castle was much nearer the fortieth parallel than it is: in fact Lord Baltimore's commissioners eighteen months later made it out to be about ten minutes of latitude nearer. After much pertinacity, Penn seems to have convinced everybody. Lord Chief Justice North wrote a description, making, as appears from the certified copy used in the case of Penn *v.* Lord Baltimore, the southern boundary the straight line which he followed Werden by calling "the beginning of the fortieth degree," but excepting all lands in the possession of the Duke within twelve miles of New Castle. This exception was afterwards crossed out, and into the description was interlineated the fixing of the starting-point at the distance of twelve miles northward of New Castle, and also there was an alteration of the southern boundary to a circle drawn at twelve miles distance from that town north and westward "unto the beginning of the fortieth degree and thereon by a straight line westwards to the limit of longitude." Hazard's *Annals of Pennsylvania* has combined both the original and alteration as the Chief Justice's description. The interlineations and alterations appear to have been the work of Werden. On January 15, 1680-1, the boundaries with the alterations of Werden were read and approved by the Committee. It will be seen that, as the Delaware runs, the frontage thus withdrawn from the operation of Lord Baltimore's charter, *i.e.* lying between the end of twelve miles from New Castle and the fortieth parallel, was about twenty-six miles, but the agents of his Lordship, and in fact the other people in England, had no such knowledge of the course of the river and the location of the parallel as to appreciate this. If the twelve-mile circle would indeed strike the parallel, his Lordship would be losing at most a trifle of frontage not worth considering. The officials, on the other hand, were convinced that the frontage south, as well as north, of the parallel was not Lord Baltimore's, but the King's, to give to whom he pleased, or the Duke's, yielded by his consenting to the gift. As to the land west of the semicircle, or arc, of twelve mile radius, nothing within Lord Baltimore's lines was supposed to be taken from him, for that semicircle, or arc, would, it was said, reach the fortieth parallel, which would from the point of intersection be the southern boundary of the new province.

While the treatment of the words "the beginning of" as surplusage would have made Penn's southern boundary, for nearly all the length, recede from the state's present line, the northern boundary would have been recognized as running along the forty-third parallel through the present territory of New York from the point north of the source of the Delaware to the Niagara River, and the sites of St. Johnsville, Richfield, Waterville, Cazenovia, Auburn, Geneva, and Buffalo would have been in Pennsylvania with three times the frontage on Lake Erie which our Commonwealth afterwards bought. With the question of the northern boundary, this history is not concerned.

As finally issued, the patent to William Penn called for the tract bounded on the east by the Delaware River "from twelve miles distance northward of New Castle towne unto the three and fortieth degree of northern latitude," if the river should extend so far northward, but if not, then by the river to its source, and thence by a meridian line "unto the said three and fortieth degree," "the said land to extend westwards five degrees in longitude to be computed from the said easterne bounds," and "to be bounded on the north by the beginning of the three and fortieth degree of northern latitude and on the south by a circle drawn at twelve miles distance from New Castle northwards and westwards, unto the beginning of the fortieth degree of northerne latitude and then by a streight line westwards to the limitt of longitude above mencioned."

The description of the arc of the circle at the southeastern corner, viz: "a circle drawn at twelve miles distance from New Castle," plainly means, as Lord Hardwicke afterwards said, and as Penn intended, the arc of a circle having a radius of twelve miles with the heart of the little village of New Castle as a centre. Therefore, we see by our modern maps, as Baltimore and Markham saw by astronomical observations, that the boundary lines do not close together. King Charles, contrary to "he never says a foolish thing," had officially uttered nonsense.

The date of the charter, or, more properly, letters patent, was the fourth of March in the thirty-third year of the reign (1680), a day which in Scotland was called March 14, 1681.

CHAPTER II.

THE ASCERTAINMENT OF THE SOUTHERN BOUNDARY.

The third Lord Baltimore and Markham—The Duke confirms Pennsylvania, and grants Delaware to Penn—Further proceedings of the two Proprietaries—Decision of Privy Council—Advantages of the Penns in the subsequent struggle—Settlement of Nottingham—Maryland takes the offensive—Agreement of 1732, and failure to carry it out—Temporary line run—Case of Penn et al. *v.* Lord Baltimore and final determination.

In the uncertaincy of astronomical observations for latitude and longitude, it was necessary that the relation of localities to the equator and the central meridian should be settled upon by agreement. For approximations within a few miles, the statement of maps might be accepted, but when, as upon the Delaware River, there was the question of the ownership of a headland or of the mouth of a creek, nothing would be authoritative but an instrument of the latest improvement together with the latest book of calculations, and it was always conceivable that something less clumsy than the method of the time might in future be devised, and show that the determination had been incorrect by quite a distance. It would result, that, unless there was to be an intolerable shifting of boundaries, a line should be arbitrarily fixed by the parties interested, which neither side should be allowed to gainsay. A letter was issued by the King less than a month after the patent to William Penn, and dated April 2 in the

33rd year of the reign (1681), recommending Penn to Lord Baltimore's good neighbourliness, and recommending as conducive to good neighbourhood that Baltimore appoint persons to make in conjunction with Penn's agent a division according to the degree of north latitude by finding landmarks. Lord Baltimore was then residing in Maryland.

He was Charles Calvert, the 'third Baron. Ready to extend courtesy, he invited to his house Penn's deputy, Markham, who remained there ill for three weeks: and likewise this Roman Catholic nobleman later attended Penn to Friends' Meetings in Maryland, and sent military escort to wait for him. The Baron, with all his politeness, was neither easy-going nor weak, but careful of his rights, positive, spirited, expecting and receiving deference, not only in Maryland, but in neighbouring provinces also, as almost the only person of his rank then sojourning in America. He was not politic, not one to take into account that the Quaker with whom he had to deal possessed the favor of the King and the Duke of York, while he himself, although a Roman Catholic, had no influence with either.

By appointment of Lord Baltimore, made after Markham's visit to him, he and Markham were to meet at Augustine Herman's on Bohemia River on June 10, 1682. Baltimore sent commissioners, and, Markham not appearing, they took observations during the next seven days, making Herman's house "to lye in the latitude of 39 d. & 45 m." This meant that Lord Baltimore's charter called for an extent northward seventeen and a half miles further, or, as his commissioners reported, at least fifteen miles. As a matter of fact, the observation was more favorable to Penn than present calculations, which place the 40th parallel more than thirty-five miles north of the site of Herman's house. The mouth of the Octorara Creek hereafter mentioned is only about eleven miles more northerly than Herman's house. The commissioners went from that house to New Castle, about twenty miles to the northeast, and, there, on June 27, made an observation with a sextile, of six or seven feet radius, sent by Markham from New York, and belonging to Col. Lewis Morris. Lord Baltimore's Narrative (*Penna. Mag. Hist.*, Vol. VI, p. 412 &ct.) says that the latitude of the town was thus found to be "thirty-nine degrees forty odd minutes." This may mean forty minutes and a few seconds. The errors possible in observations will be seen when we read Lord Baltimore's statement that on Sep. 24, 1682, his people and Richard Noble, a Quaker, by the same sextile found Upland (now Chester), which is about twelve miles more northerly than New Castle, to be 39° 47′ 5″ N. Markham, who did not take part, quoted, in his Answer to the Narrative, Haig's notes that he was told 39° 45′. The observation, whether the minutes were 45 or 47, showed that a circle around New Castle of twelve miles radius would not come within fourteen miles at the very least of touching the 40th parallel. Nor would there have been much closer approach to it, if the twelve miles distance northward from New Castle of the starting-point on the river had been measured on a longitudinal line, and the circle had been drawn with a radius of the distance of that point from the town; a meaning which was not intended by either Penn or whoever, King or official, read the charter before it passed, but which might have been claimed, had the Duke held on to the land around New Castle. As to the thirty-ninth parallel, which in later years was claimed to be meant by "the beginning of the fortieth degree," the circle, even if carried around to the south would not have come within seventeen miles of that parallel under the most favourable elements for the calculation. In the course of a conference between Baltimore, Markham, and their attendants on the day after the observation, nobody suggested that "the beginning of the fortieth degree" was anything else than the fortieth parallel. The Maryland surveyor laughingly remarked: "His Majesty must have long compasses": the naval veteran, Markham, replied that he trusted the gentlemen would "not limit his Majesty's compasses." Well would it have been for the Calverts, if the King's compasses had been considered as marking the correct distance of the parallel north of New Castle, and the Delaware frontage had been let go!

Markham, on this occasion, suggested an interpretation of Penn's charter which made the lines of the figure meet, and which was decidedly favorable to Lord Baltimore, as it gave him in the interior the land up to the astronomically fixed fortieth parallel, the interpretation being that the circle passing through a point on the river twelve miles north of New Castle was not to be described around New Castle, but have as its centre the fortieth degree, probably meaning the point in the fortieth parallel due north of the point on the river. Thus on a map with the north at the top, the starting-point of Pennsylvania on the river would be the bottom of a circle, instead of rather below the top of one; and the shape of the Province would be pretty much a trapezoid with a bump on its southeastern corner, instead of a trapezoid with a piece bitten out. This solution, which was not agreed to, was certainly not Penn's or the Duke's interpretation, as will be seen from the Duke's deeds of Aug. 24, 1682, unknown to Americans in September, but had Baltimore agreed, the question would have been settled at once, to the saving of trouble, expense, and bloodshed; for Markham was fully empowered to act for Penn, and the latter would not have been allowed to repudiate the settlement. Markham declined to proceed up the river until the instrument should show 40°, to put the boundary there, but promised to join in ascertaining that latitude at the heads of any rivers "respecting" (*i.e.* falling into) Chesapeake Bay, apparently to run the division for that basin. Baltimore and he parted, he refusing to surrender anything on the Delaware north of twelve miles above New Castle. Baltimore went to Marcus Hook, or Chichester, and warned the people not to pay quit rents to Penn, and announced the intention of returning and taking possession. This so disturbed the people there that Markham, who had packed up to go to the Chesapeake, thought it better not to leave, and so wrote to Lord Baltimore (letter without date printed in *Penna. Archives,* 1st Series, Vol. I, p. 39), who was waiting for him at New Castle on the 26th. It appears that, after receiving this letter, Lord Baltimore, perhaps at New Castle, or carrying the instrument to the Elk River, took another observation, for subsequently he mentions one taken on the 27th. About a month later, Markham's powers ceased, Penn arriving at some point twelve miles above New Castle, and therefore within the jurisdiction, probably on October 28, if he did not, before stopping at New Castle, pass on to Upland on the 24, the date which he gives for his arrival, but which is supposed to refer to his coming within the capes—but Penn was not very accurate about dates.

Markham had declared that he was accountable only to the King and the Duke of York, not knowing that the Duke's rights had been already transferred by him to Penn. In those days, it took nearly two months for a letter to go from England to Pennsylvania, unless the ship carrying it came directly to New York or the Delaware, and the opportunities for transmission, with or without much time being taken after the end of the ocean voyage, were not frequent.

By deed dated Aug. 21, 1682, the Duke relinquished to Penn and his heirs and assigns all estate, right, title, interest, rents, services, claims, duties, payments, property, claim, and demand in the lands, islands, tenements, hereditaments, and other things comprised in King Charles II's patent to Penn "within the bounds and limits therein mentioned."

The Duke, furthermore, by two deeds dated August 24, 1682, conveyed to Penn and his heirs and assigns the territory measured by a twelve miles radius around New Castle on the western side of the Delaware and the territory to the south of that circle not occupied by Maryland. Thus did William Penn acquire what is now the state of Delaware, which was spoken of from that time until the American Revolution as "the Territories," "the Counties thereunto [to Pennsylvania] annexed," "the Country of New Castle and tracts depending thereon," or "the Counties of New Castle, Kent, and Sussex on Delaware," or, more commonly, as they were popularly called, "the Lower Counties." One difference there was between the patent for Pennsylvania and the two deeds for the Lower Counties: by the former, Penn and his heirs and assigns were to hold the land directly of the King; by the latter, they were to hold of the Duke of York as intermediate, or mesne, lord, who was to receive an annual rent of five shillings for the land around New Castle, and of a red rose and half the year's profits for the land south.

Penn says that he gave up extent to Lake Ontario, being thought to be getting a front on the Chesapeake. In the summer of 1682, he appears to have learned either from reports from Pennsylvania, or from a dependable statement of the latitude of Watkin's Point and the length of the Bay, that the latter did not extend as far north as 40°; so that if he was confined to what was north of the fortieth parallel, he was shut off from the Bay. He therefore sought the aid of the friendly King. The view was not unreasonable that, as astronomers could not come to an exact conclusion, the King could fix what should be taken as the parallel. Without some such control, Lord Baltimore seemed determined to run no line that would be a compromise. By adhering to the letter of his charter, he would, however, get more land than had been intended to be given to his father. In 1632, when two full degrees were calculated to amount to only one hundred and twenty miles, and Watkin's Point was deemed to be above north latitude 38°, the second Lord was supposed to be getting less than two full degrees, possibly one hundred and fifteen miles at most, yet by a degree being found to be seventy, instead of sixty, miles, and Watkin's Point being some miles below North latitude 38°, possession by his successor to the fortieth parallel would make an estate of no less than one hundred and fifty miles and perhaps more. The question whether the Calvert family could thus gain so much beyond the original idea, had been talked about in the Committee for Trade and Plantations when Penn's application for a grant was under consideration. Since then it was appearing that such gain by the Calverts would block Penn's colony from any front on Chesapeake Bay, which the promoter thought a necessity. To public officials, even without any desire to favor Penn, it was not hard in the circumstances, to take a view that would facilitate the planting of a new colony, and thereby the further development of England's American territory. Penn obtained in August, 1682, and took across the ocean, another royal letter to Lord Baltimore. This recommended him to fix his northern bounds by measuring at sixty miles a degree two degrees from Watkin's Point as settled upon by the Commissioners from Virginia and Maryland.

This royal letter did not mean, any more than the preceding one, to allow the Calverts any of what had been the Dutch possessions: but the third Lord Baltimore felt strongly that the land on Delaware Bay and

ASCERTAINMENT OF THE SOUTHERN BOUNDARY. 37

River to 40° north was rightfully his, and, while, in the reports in the *Maryland Archives* of his conferences with Penn, it appears as if Baltimore was contending as a preliminary for his extent on the Chesapeake and Susquehanna, yet ever and anon he and his heirs, until the final settlement, were recurring to this hopeless claim to the country of New Castle &ct.

When Baltimore and Penn first met after the latter's arrival, the former, according to his Narrative, was inclined to think reasonable, although he asked time to consider, Penn's request for an opening on the Chesapeake. When, however, in formal conference, in presence of attendants, Penn produced the royal missive, Baltimore, no doubt angered, did not flinch from insisting upon his right up to the 40th parallel, wherever it might actually be. Penn tried to induce him to be satisfied with two degrees measured at seventy miles each, or with two and a half measured at sixty. Baltimore mentions, but Penn does not, Penn's request, that, if Maryland must extend to the 40th parallel, that parallel be ascertained by accepting as true the latitude, viz: 37° 5′, so long attributed to Cape Charles, but then thought far from correct, and by measuring from Cape Charles, perhaps at seventy miles a degree. Baltimore objected to any other basis than the surest contemporary astronomical observation. On Feb. 28, 1682-3, three persons employed by Lord Baltimore took an observation on Palmer's Island with a sextant of about ten feet radius, and found the latitude 39° 44′. This was disclosed to Penn by Lord Baltimore at New Castle, when, on May 29 and 30, they had further conference. Lord Baltimore retired from that conference announcing that he would himself make further observations for the boundary. Penn sent after him in writing an offer, which he had made verbally, to join in the observations, if Baltimore would fix a "gentleman's price" per mile, at which Penn could buy the land found to belong to Baltimore north of the head of Chesapeake Bay. Had Baltimore brought himself to bargaining, he could have secured good terms from Penn, to whom some frontage on the Chesapeake and quiet possession east of the Susquehanna and along the Delaware were worth everything west of the Susquehanna. Baltimore did offer soon afterwards a Chesapeake frontage in exchange for all the Lower Counties, but this naturally was refused by Penn.

No further meeting between the two Proprietaries was held, and, in a letter of Aug. 14, 1683, to the Lords of the Committee for Trade and Plantations, Penn says that, instead of notice being sent of a day, expected to be in September, when Lord Baltimore would go to the head of the Bay, an observation had been taken, a line run, and trees marked without notice to Penn, and a demand had been made. This does not mean that the demand followed the actual marking of the line north or east of the ground demanded, and indeed the demand may have been that made by proclamation issued about the time of the conference, as to which his Lordship had prevaricated; first, on complaint made, denying the issuing of the proclamation, and afterwards, on its being proved, explaining that proclamation as but a matter of form to keep alive his claim. We learn from a proclamation made in 1722 by the Lieutenant-Governor of Maryland that an observation was taken at the mouth of Octorara Creek on Sep. 15, 1683, the latitude of that place being found to be 39° 41′ 19″, from which fact denial was made of the third Lord having ever caused an east line from that place to be run as the northern boundary. That Lord Baltimore was in that vicinity about that time, is clear from a note with his initials in the margin of the record in the *Maryland Archives* of the commission about to be mentioned, "given to my cousin Talbot when I was last up the Bay." Whether Baltimore then started a

ASCERTAINMENT OF THE SOUTHERN BOUNDARY. 39

line, and blazed trees, as one story goes, is not important, for he persisted in claiming to the parallel, which he knew must lie further north than the mouth of the Schuylkill River. He commissioned George Talbot, under date of Sep. 17, 1683, to go to the Schuylkill at the Delaware River, and demand possession of the land along said river [*i.e.* Delaware] lying south of the 40th degree, adding the words: "according to an east line run out from two observations one taken 10 June 1682, the other 27 7ber, 1682, in obedience to his Majesty's commands expressed in letter of 2 April, 1681." It may be concluded that if the second of these observations mentioned contradicted the first, Lord Baltimore took the mean, and that the mean located the fortieth parallel a little below the southern point of Philadelphia as then laid out, in other words well above the mouth of the Schuylkill, in the not very precise measurements of those years. The reason for relying on those observations was, doubtless, their having been taken after full notice to Markham, and in default of his attendance. That the line mentioned had actually been run, is not necessarily meant by the words of the commission or by Talbot's remark that he was authorized to go wherever the line took him, Penn making the point that the commission did not authorize Talbot to cross the Schuylkill. Talbot went to the City of Philadelphia, or at least east of the Schuylkill, and, on September 24, in the absence of William Penn, demanded of Nicholas More, treated as Penn's deputy, all land lying on the west side of the Delaware River and south of 40° north latitude. Penn set forth on Oct. 4 the reasons for not complying with the demand, speaking of the observations and line run accordingly as performed by Lord Baltimore and his agents only, and not by the two parties jointly, as required by the King's letter. There may have been an attempt by Talbot at a line. In January, Baltimore sent Capt. James Murfy to induce the people of the disputed region to accept tenancy. In further contention for a line which struck the Delaware far north of Naaman's Creek or the latitude of the mouth of the Octorara, Talbot, calling himself his Lordship's Commissioner for Disposal of Lands in New Ireland and the western side of Delaware River, made proclamation dated Feb. 1, 1683-4, "to all persons dwelling on the western side of Delaware Bay and River between the Creeks of Schuylkill and Whorekyll," offering all the privileges of Marylanders to those who, under their hands and seals, promised fidelity, and offering to those of them who had land by any title a confirmation by patent sent without expense at 2$s.$ per 100A, and protection from all arrears to his Lordship or any one else.

It appears to have been after this that Talbot ran or completed the line known as the Octorara line, or Talbot's line, extending from the mouth of the Octorara to the Delaware at about the mouth of Naaman's Creek. Samuel Hollingsworth, who was a boy nine years old, when, in 1682, he was brought to Pennsylvania by his father, Valentine Hollingsworth, and also John Musgrave, whom Valentine at the same time brought as a servant thirteen years old, made affidavit on June 4, 1735, that after they had lived about a year at Valentine's land on Shell-pot Creek about three miles northeast of the present Wilmington (land surveyed Dec. 27, 1683, under warrant of 12mo. 10, 1682), Talbot and George Oldfield and two or three others came to lodge there one cold evening, saying that they had come from the mouth of the Octorara, and had run a line from thence, and intended to continue it to the Delaware by Lord Baltimore's order as the division line between him and Pennsylvania, and the next day they went off to continue the line to the Delaware, and came back that night, reporting that they had done so; furthermore Hollingsworth said that the line was very plain

ASCERTAINMENT OF THE SOUTHERN BOUNDARY. 41

for years, trees being marked high up by men on horseback. Lord Baltimore, in a commission to Talbot, dated March 19, 1683 [end of year by Old Style], says "we have caused two observations to be taken at two several times and an east and west line accordingly to be run out and marked at great disadvantage to ourself being some miles south of the northern latitude of 40°."

In this later commission, Talbot was required to take as many persons as he should think convenient, and go to the Governor of Pennsylvania, and demand all the land lying on the west side of the Delaware River and Bay and seaboard to the south of the 40th degree, and more particularly that part thereof which lieth to southward of the marked line aforesaid. Talbot took a number of men, and went into New Castle County to within six miles northwest of New Castle town, and at the bridge across the Christiana built a fort on the land of the widow Ogle on the north side of that creek, raising a breastwork of trunks of trees, and palisading it. When the Sheriff and several magistrates of New Castle County demanded Talbot's authority for so doing, Talbot had the guns and muskets of the garrison levelled at them, and read his commission from Lord Baltimore, and refused to evacuate. Talbot wrote a letter to Penn on April 26, 1684, making the demand as specified in the commission of March 19. Penn does not refer to this in his declaration dated 4mo. 4, in which he commanded that no person submit to Talbot's taking possession, and levying war, as he had done and threatened to do, and that no one seat any lands within Penn's limits without his warrant, and that all magistrates, officers, and inhabitants continue as the Duke had placed them, and seize any person seducing the people of the Province and Territories from their obedience, and especially seize the persons engaged in this invasion. The fort was not maintained very long.

The line with which Lord Baltimore had offered to be satisfied, giving him the Lower Counties, except the little piece above the latitude of Naaman's Creek, was never accepted by Penn, but the western fraction of the line was made use of by Penn's representatives to confine Maryland to a part of the Susquehanna far below any approximate location of the true boundary. Baltimore's great mistake of physically marking what was tentative created a misunderstanding when the circumstances were forgotten, and gave the opposite party a fact upon which to set up the legal plea of estoppel.

The fight between the two Proprietaries being transferred to London, Penn left America in 6mo. (August), 1684.

Already measures had been taken to secure for Penn a better documentary title to what is now Delaware. The bill in equity of the Penns against Lord Baltimore states that the Duke of York obtained a patent from the King dated March 22, 1682 (Old Style, and therefore after the Duke's deeds to Penn), for the town and fort of New Castle and the land within the compass or circle of twelve miles about the said town lying on the Delaware and the islands in the river and also the tract on the river and bay beginning twelve miles south of New Castle and extending to Cape Lopin. The bill also said that the Duke, having obtained this patent for the benefit of William Penn, handed it to the latter, and that it was then (1735) in the complainants' (the Penns' custody. In a list preserved by the Historical Society of Pennsylvania of conveyances affecting the Penns' dominions, this patent seems to be incorrectly noted as a patent to William Penn, but there is noted a surrender dated April 10, 1683, and acknowledged by the Duke of York three days later before William Bevershain, a Master in Chancery, whereby the Duke surrendered the said territory to the King. This would have disposed of any right acquired under the alleged patent, subject, it would seem, to Penn's right as vassal, if such patent was valid, but the surrender may be construed as relinquishing mere possession. It was to clear the way for a valid patent, as to which the bill in equity mentions the application and subsequent proceedings. On April 17, 1683, perhaps while a project for a fresh charter to the Duke was pending, the Committee for Trade, having read a letter from Lord Baltimore, requested his Royal Highness to make no conveyance to Penn until Baltimore's bounds were settled. Early in 1683, a warrant for a patent to the Duke was issued, but Lord Baltimore's agent petitioned that such a patent should not pass the great seal until the King should be satisfied as to the extent of Maryland, because Maryland included the town of New Castle and adjacent country mentioned in the patent proposed. On May 31, the King in Council referred the whole matter to the Committee for Trade and Plantations for examination and report. The Committee, on June 12, called before them the agents of Lord Baltimore and of Penn, and the issue was raised whether in 1632 the Dutch were possessed of the land in question, which fact Penn's agent promised to prove. A year later, the Solicitor for the Duke of York appeared in the matter, and on Sep. 30, 1684, said that the proof depended upon Penn himself coming to England, where he was soon expected. The matter not having been disposed of before Feb. 6, 1684-5, when Charles II died, and the Duke of York became King, the Attorney-General and Solicitor-General in 1717 concluded that no patent to James for the Lower Counties ever passed the great seal. A *quo warranto* proceeding was begun against Lord Baltimore, inquiring into the validity of the privileges conferred upon him by the charter. While it was pending, William Penn, on account of whom, as tenant, the matter of

Baltimore's petition against a patent for the Lower Counties had been laid over, asked in August, 1685, that it be taken up, as being a question of property, and not of power, as raised by *quo warranto*. In October, the Committee decided that the land granted to Lord Baltimore in 1632 was intended to be only such as at the time was uncultivated and not inhabited except by savages, and that the western shore of Delaware Bay and River at that time had been planted and was inhabited. A very fair, a substantially just, recommendation was made on Oct. 31 to the King in Council, viz: that the land between the eastern sea and river and the Chesapeake be divided into two equal parts by a line drawn from the latitude of Cape Henlopen to the 40th degree, the eastern part to be the King's, the western part to be Lord Baltimore's. On Nov. 17, 1685, an order was made in Council approving and directing this. Nothing was said about Penn's right under James in the recommendation or order. It was afterwards claimed that this order enured to the use of William Penn as James's tenant in fee under the old deeds.

The right of James, however, at this time did not hang upon his acquirement of the land when Duke of York, and the legal conclusion must be that his true title to the west side of Delaware Bay and River, justifying the decision, came to him when he succeeded Charles as King. Was the sovereign to be bound as tiustee by his grants made when a private citizen without right to the property? or were the covenants then made for warranty and further conveyance so obligatory and beyond his royal discretion that a court of equity would afterwards presume a royal patent from him to carry them out? Was succeeding sovereigns' right, which was supposed to be for the good of the community, so to be divested? James as King did intend to give William Penn a patent for the Lower

Counties. This, moreover, as we learn from a petition of Hannah Penn of 1720, was to extinguish the rent reserved in the deeds of 1682. Logan had heard that the patent had gone through the various offices, and was ready for the great seal, when the Lord Chancellor made objection to some of the powers conferred. The Revolution prevented the final issuing.

From the livery of seisin at William Penn's first visit to America, when he entered the fort at New Castle, and turf and twig and a porringer of river water and soil were delivered to him there, and Markham, as his attorney, received similar tokens on Appoquinimy Creek, the inhabitants of the Lower Counties accepted their new master. They chose seven freeholders from each county to meet in Assembly with representatives from the counties of Pennsylvania on December 6, 1682. At that meeting, upon petition of seven persons from New Deal (Sussex), six from St. Jones's (Kent), and five from New Castle, an act of Union was passed on Dec. 7, by which those counties were annexed to the Province of Pennsylvania, and the people subjected to the same laws, and invested with the same privileges, as the people of the Province. This proceeding, which could not have force in political matters against the Sovereign, had no effect upon the disputed ownership of the soil: yet the region continued to be under the same government as Pennsylvania until the American Revolution, although with a separate legislature after 1702, and with the stipulation of the Penns in writing, whenever the appointment of the acting Governor was approved, that such approbation by the King or Queen should not prejudice the King or Queen's right to those countries. Within the region, the Penns sold and confirmed lands, and intermittently collected rents until Delaware, on July 4, 1776, was declared a free and independent State. Following that, the People decided adversely to any title having been rightfully in the Penns; for while, in divesting the Proprietaries of unsold land and of quit rents, the Assembly of Pennsylvania made exceptions, and granted a partial compensation, the Assembly of Delaware neither allowed nor paid anything.

The decision, or order, of 1685, whatever its effect as between King James and Penn, established both the eastern and northern boundaries of Maryland, and should have been accepted by the Proprietaries thereof as shutting them out from the land east of the line prescribed, and by the Proprietaries of Pennsylvania as making them in their turn recede from the land west of the line as far as the fortieth parallel astronomically fixed. The King in Council was, as Lord Hardwicke afterwards said, the proper tribunal for the determination of boundaries, even where, as in this case, the King was deciding upon his own rights, for it was presumed that he would be just. It is likely that if Lord Baltimore had accordingly yielded the great bone of contention, the Lower Counties and the river frontage above them, a line run by him or his orders according to the mean of the observations would have been accepted by William Penn as the location of the parallel. The Proprietaries of Maryland, however, tried to overthrow the decision, and the Proprietaries of Pennsylvania maintained possession of what they had far south of even an approximate location of the fortieth parallel.

Throughout the long struggle between the opposing Proprietaries, the advantage was nearly always on the side of the Penns: at the beginning, in William Penn's standing at Court, and after the Revolution of 1688, in the greater toleration of Quakers than of Papists, and, except for a very short period, in the uninterrupted possession by the Penns of the government of Pennsylvania and Lower Counties, and, except at rare intervals, in the preference of the inhabitants concerned, and almost always of the more substantial inhabitants, for the Penns, rather than the Calverts, as landlords.

In 1689, Charles, 3rd Lord Baltimore, was outlawed by the Court of King's Bench in Ireland on the charge of high treason, and this was followed in 1691 by the appointment of a Royal Governor over Maryland. Although King William III was convinced that Baltimore was innocent, and issued a warrant in 1693 for reversing the outlawry, Baltimore did not seek to avail himself of this by going to Ireland, although subsequently petitioning Parliament to relieve him; and the powers of government of the Proprietary of Maryland remained suspended during the rest of this Baron's life.

Under Royal rule, Maryland officials endeavored to have the boundary line run in accordance with the order of 1685, and Penn, on Sep. 1, 1697, ordered Markham to co-operate in doing this: but nothing resulted.

Scarcely any white people settled beyond the Brandywine except within twelve miles of New Castle until 1701. A few months after Penn ended his second visit to the Province, Cornelius Empson and others proposed to the Commissioners of Property to settle 18000 acres on the Octorara about twenty-four miles from New Castle. The Commissioners hesitated, feeling doubtful as to the Penn right so far south to the west of the line ordered in 1685, but the applicants were importunate and willing to take the risk. The Commissioners added 3000 acres for the Proprietary, and issued a warrant for the whole, dated 1, 7, 1702, the land to be adjoining on the south the barrens between the Octorara and the main branch of the North East River, and to be bounded on the south by an east and west line parallel as near as might be "to the line of the Province." The district received the name of Nottingham. It was laid out so near the latitude of the mouth of the Octorara as to be cut by the boundary as finally established. About this time, Talbot's manor, which, laid out under Maryland authority, covered the district, was offered for sale to Anthony Sharp, one of the Quaker proprietors of New Jersey, and Sharp informed Penn of this opportunity: but Penn was without ready money, and the purchase would not change the paramount lordship, but, if the land was within Maryland, would make Penn only a tenant of Lord Baltimore for it. In 1705, Empson was so little inclined to hold Nottingham adversely to that Lord that he was contemplating protecting himself by acquiring a title to it from him. Nothing of the kind appears to have been done, and, in 1718, Keith, Lieutenant-Governor of Pennsylvania, gave officials powers within that settlement, he having, however, refused to exercise authority over the settlers of New Munster, east of Nottingham, who were holding by Maryland title. To a request from Hart, Governor of Maryland, for the recalling of the commissions over Nottingham, Keith answered that, pending a settlement of the boundary dispute, each side should be allowed jurisdiction over those occupying land under grants from that side.

For a long time after the settling of Nottingham, the trend of immigration through Pennsylvania was much further north, and the agents of the Penns took care to keep their people away from the Octorara line: so Pennsylvanians generally came to believe that such line was the undoubted boundary in the region bordering on the Susquehanna.

In 1708, the third Lord Baltimore, still hoping to obtain the Lower Counties, attempted to have the order of November, 1685, set aside; but, upon report by the Commissioners for Trade, the Queen dismissed the petition. A second petition by him for the same purpose resulted in an order of June 23, 1709, that the petition be dismissed, and that the order of 1685 be confirmed, and put in execution without delay.

ASCERTAINMENT OF THE SOUTHERN BOUNDARY. 49

When Penn was old and broken by his troubles, and not long before the loss of his mind, he was ready to seize upon those stricter or more literal interpretations of the two charters which they were not understood to mean in 1681. Hannah Penn, the wife married at the end of 1695, had no knowledge to gainsay these interpretations. It is only fair to John, Thomas, and Richard Penn, who drove the ultimate bargain with the fifth Lord Baltimore, to say in this connection that they were not grown up in time to talk business with their father or even their elder brother, and came to their estate with their information derived from their mother, and in dependence upon her legal advisers.

Although the Maryland practice was to issue warrants at large, that is not specifying the locality, but allowing the surveyor to survey any land in that province at the risk of his action being void by reason of the land belonging to another purchaser; a practice likely to result in overstepping the province's boundaries: yet the preference for land convenient to the settlements kept the Maryland surveyors well south of Octorara Creek for a long time. About the beginning of 1713, surveying upon lands previously surveyed by Pennsylvanians began. Penn's Commissioners of Property, Carpenter, Hill, Norris, and Logan wrote to Charles Carroll, Lord Baltimore's agent, asserting their own observance of what they understood to have always been deemed by the Marylanders their northern boundary, meaning the Octorara line, and suggesting that all further proceedings be deferred until the boundary could be fixed by authority of the Crown following the surrender of the government of the two provinces. There had been a report that Lord Baltimore, as well as Penn, was about to make a surrender. The officers or citizens of Chester County seized the Sheriff of Cecil when executing his office upon land claimed by Pennsylvania, perhaps summoning or arresting settlers.

Carroll sent a polite reply, promising no further violence until the boundary was settled, which he suggested could be by ascertaining the "fortieth degree" by instruments, without appealing to the Crown, the degree having been already found to be much further north than any of the surveys.

It may have been only for fixing the boundary west of the eastern line decreed in 1685 that the third Lord Baltimore had been having these later observations taken. In March, 1713-4, another observation was taken, and the latitude of a place on the Upper Branch of the Elk River was calculated to be 39° 29' 17". He died about a year after this.

The fourth Lord Baltimore had, long before, become a Protestant, but, dying in April, 1715, a few weeks after succeeding to the Irish barony and the American proprietorship, did not recover the government of Maryland. He had married a daughter of Sir Edward Henry Lee, first Earl of Lichfield, but had been divorced from her after the birth of a number of children, among whom was Charles, who became fifth Lord Baltimore. Lichfield's wife, Charles's grandmother, was an illegitimate child of King Charles II, but such bastard relationship to the Stuarts exerted no influence when Charles Calvert came to his inheritance. He succeeded when about sixteen years old. Having, however, been brought up a Protestant, he was not under the cloud which had hung over his ancestors. In about a month, the government of Maryland was restored to him.

He did not grow up a man of great ability or strong character, although recognized as having some attainments in the arts and sciences. Clayton Colman Hall, in *The Lords Baltimore and the Maryland Palatinate,* quotes various opinions concerning him, including Lord Hervey's: "thinks he understands every-

ASCERTAINMENT OF THE SOUTHERN BOUNDARY. 51

thing, but understands nothing . . . is a little mad."

In 1717, Maryland surveyors went as far north as near the head of the Pequea Creek: in opposition, the Pennsylvania Commissioners of Property, on 11 mo. 2, not only awarded to a partisan some of the ground surveyed, but also offered a reward of 10 $l.$ to any person arresting such a surveyor, and delivering him to the Sheriff or proper officer. If at this time the Maryland surveyors retreated before this peril of being kidnapped, the officials of Cecil County afterwards did not hesitate to make at least a show of force to vindicate their jurisdiction, and the threatening possibilities west of the Susquehanna, remote from centres of authority, and where Indians might resent encroachments, caused in 1721 or 1722, an agreement between the acting Governors of the two colonies that no surveys for any private person should be made in that region.

Keith's steps in opposition to the putting of settlements on the western banks of the Susquehanna, will be narrated in the chapter on Confusion at the Death of William Penn. This Lieutenant-Governor of Pennsylvania accepted the views of the Penn agents and friends in the Council, that, pending a final decision by competent authority of the boundary question, the Octorara line must be recognized.

By agreement dated Feb. 17, 1723-4, between Lord Baltimore of the one part, and William Penn's widow and executrix and two of the mortgagees of Pennsylvania &ct. of the other part, it was provided that for eighteen months no persons on either side should be disturbed in their possessions, nor any lands surveyed, taken up, or granted in either province near the boundaries claimed by either side. The hope was expressed in the agreement that within the period the boundaries would be determined and settled. This hope, however, was not realized, and Marylanders and Pennsylvanians entered upon the disputed region: in fact the former, in ignorance of where the 40th parallel was, often went beyond what Baltimore claimed.

In 1731, Thomas Cresap and others with Maryland warrants took possession of Conejohela, settling at a spot in fact north of the 40th parallel, on the western bank of the Susquehanna, driving away some Indians, and burning their cabins. Depredations upon the whites of Pennsylvania allegiance, followed by resistance to arrest, brought about a border war which involved some loss of life, although during the years in which said struggle was somewhat spasmodically kept up, proceedings to settle the question, or to gain some legal advantage, were being taken by more conspicuous persons.

On July 1, 1731, Lord Baltimore petitioned the King to order the Proprietaries of Pennsylvania to join with said Lord in ascertaining the boundaries. Before this petition was disposed of, frequent interviews took place between the principals on both sides, the bill and answer subsequently filed in Chancery contradicting each other as to who made the overtures. We cannot see why Baltimore sought or suggested the compromise made, or, for that matter, why he agreed to it, even supposing that he meant the interpretation in minor details for which he afterwards contended. With the western half of the Delaware peninsula already his, it was not a case of "give and take" to accept less than he claimed to the north, or even as little, in exchange for his relinquishing claim to the old City of Philadelphia and most of its Northern Liberties, the present Delaware County, and nearly, if not all, the present state of Delaware. Even if that relinquished claim was then worthless, so that said land is not to be taken into account, he was giving away, north of the present boundary of Maryland, over 2,000,000 acres which the charter of 1632 plainly gave him, and the order of 1685 as clearly adjudged to him; acres, moreover, adjoining improved property. We can only suppose that he was not sober, or had otherwise lost his head, or had been unduly frightened by the matter of the Octorara line. With unaccountable weakness, from the consequences of which the English Court of Chancery did not let him squirm out, he, as party of the 1st part, made an agreement dated May 10, 1732, with John, Thomas, and Richard Penn, of the 2nd part, whereby it was covenanted that the circle called for by King Charles II's charter should be drawn at twelve miles distance from New Castle, that from the middle point of an east and west line to be run from the point of Cape Henlopen, lying south of Cape Cornelius on the ocean, to the western side of the Peninsula, there should be run a straight line northwardly as a boundary until it touched the western part of the periphery of the circle around New Castle, and from the point of contact a further boundary-line should be run due north to the latitude of fifteen English miles due south of the southernmost point of the City of Philadelphia, that a line due west should then be run across the Susquehanna to the western extent of Pennsylvania, or as far as requisite, viz: twenty-five English miles west of the River, so that it could be continued when those parts were better settled, that if the line running due north from the point of contact with the circle should cut off part of the circle, such part should still be in New Castle County, that seven commissioners on each side, three being a quorum, should lay out and mark the lines between October 1, 1732, and December 25, 1733, and that the party whose commissioners did not attend after any adjournment should forfeit £5000 to the party whose commissioners attended. It is rather amusing that so strongly had the Penn side been imbued with faith in the Octorara line, that Ferdinand John Paris, the Penn lawyer, in writing to Pennsylvania about the agreement, apologized for its yielding so much!

It would seem, on the other hand, that, when the prominent Marylanders heard of the agreement, they began trying to find some means of breaking it without their Proprietary becoming liable for the £5000 forfeiture, although they might have thought even that preferable to carrying the agreement out. The joint commissioners were appointed and met, but soon adjourned on a quibble raised by those from Maryland. At a subsequent meeting, the latter insisted that the circle around New Castle was to be twelve miles in diameter, instead of radius. The commissioners appointed by the Penns having no authority to run any circle but that of twelve miles radius, there was a final adjournment on Nov. 24, 1733, obviating any forfeit, but making it impossible to carry out the agreement within the time specified.

On Aug. 8, 1734, Lord Baltimore petitioned the King to grant him letters patent confirming to him in fee the Peninsula as in the charter to Cæcilius, the 2nd Lord, notwithstanding the words *"hactenus inculta"* &ct. in its recital. Richard Penn, the only Proprietary of Pennsylvania then in England, opposed this, his lawyers insisting that the agreement for adjusting boundaries was in force notwithstanding the failure to run the line within the prescribed time. A petition from several thousand Quakers of the Lower Counties against such a grant was laid before the Commissioners for Trade &ct., and the latter recommended that further consideration be postponed until the end of Michaelmas Term following, to give the Penns an opportunity to raise before a court of equity the question of the validity of the agreement. Such postponement was made by the King in Council on May 16, 1735.

The Penns filed the necessary bill in the Chancery of Great Britain on June 21, 1735. Anybody reading the bill, and not aware of the facts about the old patents as before mentioned, will get the idea that Baltimore, the defendant, was a terrible robber, a liar, if not a forger, a trickster who, after browbeating the rightful owners into his own terms, conspired to prevent their being carried out, and a sneak who took advantage of the absence of the older brothers to apply to the King. The bill prayed for equitable relief, the lawyers using every pretence of title, every accusation of bad dealing, requisite or cumulative, to make out that the agreement was reasonable, had been broken by the act of the other party, and should be specifically performed. The bill seems to have been the first formal assertion that the charter to the 2nd Lord gave him only the few miles on Delaware Bay between the cape at the entrance and the completion of the thirty-ninth degree, viz: the thirty-ninth parallel. Lord Baltimore's answer disputed the effect upon his right of orders in Council, possession, expenditure, and pecuniary loss set forth in the complaint, and denied some of the facts, and alleged that he had been imposed upon as to the location of Cape Henlopen from which the southern boundary of the Lower Counties was to be run, and set up the want of title in the complainants to the land to be allotted to him, and the want of consideration in the agreement, and defended his commissioners and their interpretations, and prayed for the cancellation of the agreement.

Before the case could be decided, the disorders on the frontiers broke out afresh, in fact the officials of the bordering counties of the two colonies seem to have promoted violence in hopes of gaining for their respective lords some small advantage. A petition was sent from Maryland to the King in 1736, reciting various offences committed, and praying some relief from the state of affairs. On Aug. 8, 1737, the King made an order in Council commanding the Governors of the two

Provinces to preserve the peace, and, for that purpose, to make no grants of any part of the land in contest, nor any part of the Lower Counties, nor permit any person to settle or attempt to settle thereon until the King's pleasure was further signified.

On petitions from both sides to the King, received after the royal order of Aug. 8, 1737, the Lords for Trade and Plantations brought about an agreement between the opposing Proprietaries as follows, viz: that settlements within the Lower Counties be permitted without prejudice to either right; that all lands remain in the possession and under the jurisdiction of the Proprietary possessing them, until boundaries be settled; that all other land in contest east of the Susquehanna, and not in the Lower Counties, and not as far as fifteen miles and a quarter south of the latitude of the most southern point of the City of Philadelphia, and all land west of the Susquehanna not as far as fourteen and three quarter miles south of said latitude, be in the temporary jurisdiction of Pennsylvania, and all land south of those distances be in the temporary jurisdiction of Maryland, that the respective Proprietaries be permitted to grant vacant lands within their temporary jurisdiction on the usual terms, subject to an accounting if such locality be finally adjudged to the other Proprietary; and that all prisoners by reason of the boundary dispute be discharged on their own recognizances to appear for trial when ordered by his Majesty. The King in Council on May 25, 1738, ordered this agreement to be carried into execution, without prejudice to either party.

The temporary boundary thus ordered between the two jurisdictions was agreed to be run by commissioners from each side, who began work on Dec. 5 by agreeing that a certain post on Society Hill was the southernmost point of Philadelphia. In the following Spring, after running due west far enough to

ASCERTAINMENT OF THE SOUTHERN BOUNDARY. 57

get away from the wide parts of the Brandywine and Christiana Creeks, and then running due south fifteen and a quarter miles along the surface of the earth with an allowance of 25 perches for altitude of the hills, all the commissioners ran the line from this starting-point thus found to the Susquehanna, and fixed the starting-point on the west side. After this, one of the Maryland commissioners being called home by a death in his family, and his colleague declining to go on without him, the Pennsylvania commissioners ran the line to the top of the most western hill of the Blue Mountain range, the limit of land purchased by the Pennsylvania Proprietaries from the Indians.

The proceedings in chancery, including the taking of much testimony in America, lasted many years. The case came finally to Lord Chancellor Hardwicke for decision by himself alone. This was pronounced on May 15, 1750. Feeling the greatness of the interests involved, he remarked that the matter was "worthy the judicature of a Roman Senate rather than of a single judge," and that it was a consolation to him that there was a judicature equal in dignity to that Senate—the House of Lords—to whom an appeal could be made, if he erred. He did not decide the dispute between the parties as it stood before the making of the agreement. Had that responsibility been upon him, it is possible that he would have come to conclusions more like those of an impartial historian as to the intentions of statesmen dead before he was born, and as to facts in which the actors had passed away. As the case was presented, he, however, saw reasonableness in the Penns' interpretation of the charters. He accepted as true the allegation of a charter to the Duke of York in 1683, and therefore thought that the Duke, afterwards King, was a trustee for Penn; but, as the Lower Counties were not to be conveyed by Penn's descendants, their title to convey needed not to be considered. The decision was: that for an agreement to compromise, it was enough that there was a doubt as to the true rights, and the settlement of the contention was a sufficient consideration. He found as a fact that, in making the agreement, Lord Baltimore was neither surprised nor imposed upon nor ignorant. There was no mistake of the intention of the parties made in the articles of agreement. So the Lord Chancellor decreed specific performance of the agreement without prejudice to any right of the Crown.

The present author is not aware that there has been any criticism of this decision by any luminary of equitable jurisprudence as bright as the one who delivered it. What is called equity by lawyers had long before that time become an artificial system very different from the justice of the old ecclesiastical Chancellors. We can imagine one of them asked to enforce such a bargain as the heir of the grant of 1632 had made: they sat partly for the very purpose of restraining any man or men who by the terms of a bargain would get an unconscionable advantage. There can be little doubt that their opinion would have been against the complainants in this case, and with the words "ils serront damnés in hell."

For an account of the carrying out of the agreement so declared binding, the reader is referred to George Johnston's *History of Cecil County, Maryland*. Suffice it to say that the boundary line or boundary lines were at last run to almost the west end of Maryland by Charles Mason and Jeremiah Dixon. They were English mathematicians and astronomers, selected by the opposing Proprietaries, and performed the work in a little less than three years, ending on Sept. 25, 1766: and the delimination was confirmed by the King in 1769. In the middle of the Nineteenth Century, the names of Mason and Dixon were in the mouth of nearly every American; for their line was marking the cleavage between the Free and the Slave States of the Union. In the uncertainty of origin, as there is for so many expressions, it is possible that Dixon has a memorial in the songster's designation of the land of the late Southern Confederacy as "Dixie."

CHAPTER III.

THE ACQUISITION AND DISTRIBUTION OF THE LAND.

The King's charter grants the soil—Europeans with anterior title—Indian rights—Swedes and Dutch purchase—Bishop Compton advises Penn to do so, and such course necessary—Regulations protecting the red men—Quit rents—Feudal position of Penn—Pennsylvania "ground rents"—The various manors—Most of Penn's first sales in small quantities—The tracts of 10,000 acres cut up—Sales by Penn after his first visit—The Proprietor's "tenths"—Uniform price of other land—Method of selling and conveying—Conditions and Concessions to the first purchasers—The "Liberties" of the great town—Plan of Philadelphia—Holme's survey—A colony and city on the Susquehanna projected—Warrants and patenting—Land Commissioners before Penn's second visit—Land legislation and disputes during the second visit—Subsequent proceedings—The Land Office—The Divesting Act.

The charter of King Charles II granted to William Penn and his heirs and assigns the soil, lands, isles, rivers, waters, &ct. within the limits or boundaries, with the fish and fishing and mines and quarries, and made him and his heirs and assigns "true and absolute proprietaries," the King retaining allegiance and sovereignty and a fifth of the gold and silver ore clear of expense, and the King reserving a rent consisting of two beaver skins, to be delivered at Windsor Castle on the first of every January. The country and islands were erected "into a province and seigniorie."

ACQUISITION AND DISTRIBUTION OF THE LAND. 61

Interfering, however, with the Proprietary's freedom to place tenants throughout the region were the rights of two kinds of human occupants: the Europeans who were already seated on particular lots of ground, and the aborigines, or supposed aborigines, miscalled Indians,—a name to which we must adhere,—who were making use of extended reaches.

It suited the purposes of England to claim that the soil on which the Swedes and Dutch had planted their North American colonies belonged all the while to her Crown by right of Cabot's discoveries, if not of acts concerning the region; but, as to all the inhabitants along the Delaware in 1664 who had not resisted the so-called recovery, justice and the King's promise and the Commissioners' stipulation forbade, while the amount of vacant land rendered unnecessary, the taking away of what a man or his father had acquired with the consent of his government, or improved by the expenditure of his money and labor. The undisposed of residue of the tracts held by rulers or political bodies was not under such immunity. In punishment for resisting the alleged rightful owner, the English confiscated the property of the Dutch Governor, the Schout, and others guilty of hostility, but, as to the other possessors of land, required merely that they surrender all old patents, and be supplied with new ones, because the old patents were upon condition of the holders being subjects of the United Belgic Provinces. Threats were made that a failure to obtain new patents would be punished with forfeiture; but a number of persons failed to comply, some hoping to avoid paying a quit rent. A rent appears to have been reserved in the old grants. This was demanded by the Duke's agents. In early patents, Nicolls reserved the quit rent to the King's use, payable yearly when demanded by the persons whom he would put in authority on Delaware River. Afterwards, the rents were often reserved to the Duke. According to Logan in 1709 (*Penna. Archives,* 2nd Series, Vol. XIX, p. 501), the government at New York fixed the rate at a bushel of wheat for every 100 acres.

Not only were claims by any one without an English patent liable to be disregarded some day by an English Proprietary, but if, indeed, the Duke of York had no title to the western bank of the Delaware, his grantees also, whether the Englishmen who came after the conquest or the foreigners who had been made subjects, were occupants without title. William Penn could not take advantage of this within the circle around New Castle and the region south of it; for there his only right was through the Duke. As to the old settlers in Pennsylvania proper, unfair as the eviction of them might be, and bad as Penn's position to attempt it would be, he having accepted from the Duke a release and confirmation of King Charles's patent, yet there was no security without a binding declaration from Penn. If a fresh contract was to be made with him, it would be upon the terms he would choose; if the old contract was to stand, he was to be the landlord, and take the rents formerly agreed upon. There were not many Englishmen within the limits of Pennsylvania at the date of King Charles's charter.

To the Swedes and very few others of foreign birth, as naturally more puzzled and fearful than the English occupants, Penn, on his first arrival, made reassuring speeches, and, moreover, he passed laws for title by seven years' quiet possession, and, in the Frame of Government of 2mo. 2, 1683, confirmed to all inhabitants of the Province or Territories, whether purchasers or others, full and quiet enjoyment of all lands to which they respectively had any lawful or equitable claim, saving only such rents and services for the same as were "or customarily ought to be reserved to me my heirs or assigns." Very early—Acrelius says that it was on June 14, 1683,—he sent for all the patents of the old inhabitants for inspection, and offered new patents. To make room for his capital city and its suburbs called "Liberties," he cut down the size, or took away the whole, of certain plantations, designating other land in compensation. His persuasiveness, mingled, perhaps, with some fear of him, accomplished a great design so beneficial to the public that it would have justified, if within his authority, acts of eminent domain. Probably also his surveyors corrected lines. All this seems the foundation of the complaint that he reduced the possessions of the older inhabitants. Rev. Israel Acrelius, Provost of the Swedish Churches in America, says, in his work generally quoted as *History of New Sweden,* that some thousands of acres of swampy land covered with water at high tide, had been used as pasturage, although not included within the old metes and bounds, and such were, upon resurveys, cut off from the adjoining plantations, and that the new patents charged three or four times the old quit rent, so that the occupants who did not surrender their deeds kept the land they were using, and did not assume increased rent. Some of those who did surrender their deeds did not take out new patents, which, besides having to be paid for, seemed sufficiently objectionable in reserving even at the old rate a rent to be paid to Penn and his heirs and assigns. An idea had spread that the old landholders, being tenants of the King, or, rather, of the Duke, whom these foreigners confused with the King, were not bound to pay rent to any one else, and were free so long as the King did not make the requisite demand. It is noticeable that the King's patent does not in so many words give to Penn the rents and reversions of lands already granted within the region: but the Duke of York's release especially conveys all the rents &ct. which he had.

The older landholders and those who had inherited

or bought from them could not be disregarded by the Assemblymen chosen by the whole body of property-owning freemen. In 1700, during Penn's second visit, it was enacted that all lands seated by virtue of letters patent or warrants under the Crown of England before the grant to William Penn except where obtained by fraud or deceit should be quietly enjoyed by the actual possessors and their heirs and assigns.

In 1709, the Swedish view was set forth in a petition to the Assembly, complaining moreover that those who had handed in their old patents never got them back. The Land Commissioners met the petitioners, and agreed to examine into any particular case of injury by taking away land, and insisted on the obligation to pay quit rent. Logan said that he, Secretary since Penn's departure, had never had any of the old patents, nor had ever asked greater quit rent than a bushel of wheat for every hundred acres. Penn, receiving notice of the complaints, represented the case, says Acrelius, to the Swedish Minister Resident in London, after transmission by whom the matter was taken up by the Royal Council of Sweden. It is possible that the malcontents were the first to approach the Minister. The Royal Council under date of June 23, 1711, warned the members of the Swedish congregations on the Delaware, if they wished further help in church matters, to conduct themselves in obedience to the laws of the country where they were living and also to Penn. Protesting that they had always been quiet and loyal subjects, the Swedes in 1713 asked a certificate to that effect from the Assembly of Pennsylvania to the British and Swedish governments, and made a long representation of grievances to the Swedish Minister. To a petition in 1721 by Swedes for an act to confirm titles, the Land Commissioners made answer that the titles of the petitioners under the Duke of York had never been called in question, as far as the Commissioners knew.

Acquisition and Distribution of the Land. 65

At the time of the Charter to Penn, the Indians had abandoned very few contiguous square miles within the present limits of the state, and, besides believing themselves entitled to the spaces between some isolated plantations, occupied the whole country from the Conshohocken range of hills to Lake Erie, receiving white visitors occasionally in the southeast, on either side of that range of hills, and French missionaries, French traders, and perhaps French soldiers in the northwest. During the whole period of this history, the Penns can not be said to have obtained possession to a greater distance in any direction than ninety miles from Philadelphia.

The general question of Indian title and Penn's attitude in relation thereto and his plan for the red man and the white man to live as good neighbours may be discussed here, leaving to the next chapter the account of particular tribes and the dealings with them before the end of Penn's second visit to Pennsylvania, and to other chapters the various episodes in Indian affairs connected with the time or subject touched upon in those chapters.

The principle being once established that discovery or occupation or cession by the discoverer or occupier gave to one Christian prince or nation the ownership as far as all Christian princes and nations were concerned, it follows that he or that nation alone of all of them could enter into relations with the barbarians inhabiting the region covered by such ownership. If another civilized power attempted to avail itself of any consent obtained from the native barbarians to a foothold in that region, it was an invasion. Moralists early doubted the right of any nation whatever to intrude where other human beings were dwelling, or even were accustomed to hunt and fish, unless those human beings gave consent, either freely or after a lawful war. Some persons had gone so far as to assert title by purchase from the natives, independent of or in opposition to title by discovery or occupation; but the general recognition by commercial and colonizing nations of title by discovery or occupation practically curtailed the rights of the aborigines of the New World by restricting the market for those rights, like some modern agreements restraining trade by apportioning territory. If wild men had any property in the soil, they could not seek in the family of Christian nations "the highest and best bidder." There was only one nation which could buy, and, under the best approved system, there was only one individual, viz: the sovereign, or his representative, either official or by license. Therefore, in discussing in the first chapter the claim of one Englishman against another, and tracing the title of one European power as against another, little has been said about any grant by the aborigines of North America. Yet it is clear that, except by absolute subjugation of these, no land within their reach could be actually and permanently acquired without license or transfer from them. In *Good Speed to Virginia,* printed in 1609, quoted in Alexander Brown's *Genesis of the United States,* there was mentioned as probably correct an opinion that the savages had no particular property in any part of the country, but only a general residence therein, as wild beasts in a forest; but, nevertheless, there was a disclaimer of any intention to take the natives' rightful inheritance by force, for, it was stated, they were willing to entertain the settlers, and had offered to yield on reasonable conditions more land than could in a long time be planted. The customs of the savages lent some support to the theory of their right being merely that of residence, and of taking sustenance. Among such nomads, no individual could exclude another from a particular piece of ground, unless covered by his hut or his hill of corn, and proprietorship even by the tribe meant nothing much beyond the villages but the right

ACQUISITION AND DISTRIBUTION OF THE LAND. 67

to hunt or fish within certain limits. Moreover, government was loose, the "kings" or sachems presiding over a democracy in which affairs were settled by "the sense of the meeting." The freedom, however, of these democracies to withhold their communal possessions from Europeans was quite early pretty generally accepted as a fact, and even recognized more than is supposed as a right.

The Swedes and the Dutch, too few to be conquerors, and looking for the furs to those experienced in hunting, endeavored to be friends with the natives, and, condoning occasional murders by them, succeeded. Before attempting to take possession of land, these Swedes and Dutch purchased it from those savages who claimed the right to sell, and, in the course of time, from successive and conflicting claimants. There was only one safe course to pursue: to buy from every Indian in sight, and if any who had sold had forgotten or doubted the scope of the transaction, then to buy over again. Whatever land acquired for the Swedish or Dutch colonies was not recognized as the property of individuals, passed to the King of England by the treaty of Westminster. The officers under Charles II or the Duke of York in dealing with the red men strove to avoid all cause of complaint through unfair trading or unjust bodily hurt. The laws published on March 1, 1664-5, at Hemsted by Col. Richard Nicolls provided that no purchase of land from Indians after that date should be a good title without leave from the Governor having been first obtained for such purchase; and that, afterwards, before a grant by the government could be issued, the sachem and right owner must acknowledge receipt of payment; and that all injuries done to Indians should, upon their complaint and proof in court, be speedily redressed gratis. Some purchases of land west of the Delaware were afterwards made by private individuals or public officers, so that by the time Penn received the charter from the King, a considerable part of the southeastern corner of the present state was covered by deeds from some Indian, much of the acreage being the private property of settlers, and much being undisposed of by the King or Duke, and so transferred to Penn. The quantity of vacant land, however, was as nothing compared to the needs of any large immigration.

We do not know how early and how clearly William Penn adopted the view, scarcely yet universally accepted, that a civilized man is morally bound to bargain and pay for land over which nomads have been merely roaming. In a letter from Philadelphia, dated Aug. 14, 1683, to the Lords of the Committee for Trade and Plantations, Penn says: "I have exactly followed the Bishop of London's council (*sic*) by buying and not taking the Natives' land, with whom I have settled a very kind correspondence." The Bishop of London from 1679 to 1713, except during a short suspension in 1686, was Dr. Henry Compton, who will be mentioned in another chapter. It would seem that this counsel, or advice, was given on June 14, 1680, when Penn, being called in, appeared before the Committee, and the Bishop, a member of the Committee, was present, that meeting being the only one attended by him when Penn's charter was considered. Although the minutes do not mention it, we must conclude that the Bishop, always very outspoken, then expressed the hope that no land would be occupied without the consent and compensation of the natives, and that Penn gave assurance that he would be extremely careful in this respect. This may not have been a new thought to Penn.

While we would not detract from the glory due to Penn and his earliest representatives for carrying out this plan faithfully in letter and spirit, and the glory due to the genuine or earnest Quakers for their whole treatment of the red man, we are quite sure, that, even

ACQUISITION AND DISTRIBUTION OF THE LAND. 69

without any humanitarian or moral ideas, Penn would have found no other course open to him than purchasing the Indian claim. The practice being so well established on both sides of the Delaware, the Indians would have driven out intruders. No leader without an army such as it was impracticable to keep, could have dared at the time to rouse in the savages a sense of being wronged.

In Penn's early prospectus called *"Some Account of the Province of Pennsylvania,"* he offered shares amounting to 5000 acres "free of Indian claims." In his early deeds, he covenanted to clear, acquit, and discharge the conveyed lands from all manner of titles and claims of any Indians, or natives of the province. This extinguishment of supposed paramount title, where not already accomplished before his time, was duly prosecuted. The district in which any of those early purchases were located became clear of Indian claims; and it continued to be a rule with him and his family and the land agents of any of them not to authorize a survey of any lot outside of what had been bought from the Indians.

Before any purchase of land from them was made by Penn or under his authority, he turned his mind to the two races dwelling together or in proximity with each other in harmony. The principle that only he could acquire the land which on March 4, 1680-1, belonged to the red men, eliminated the most important subject from the dealings of private individuals, and this was enforced by an act of 1683 punishing with fine and loss of the land involved any purchasing of land from the natives without leave from the Proprietary and Governor or his Deputy. Where there unavoidably would be contact, Penn undertook to secure fair and right dealing. In the Conditions and Concessions agreed upon in England on July 11, 1681, between him and the adventurers, the plan of selling goods in public market under public stamp was made to embrace all buying from and selling to an Indian, and affronts or wrongs to an Indian were to be punished as if done to a fellow planter, any abuse by an Indian was not to be revenged by the planter abused, but left for satisfaction to a magistrate and the King of said Indian, differences were to be decided by a jury half of one race, half of the other, the Indians were to have the same liberty as any of the planters as to the improvement of their ground and the providing of sustenance for their families.

By Penn's instructions of Sep. 30, 1681, to his Commissioners, Crispin, Bezar, and Allen, these articles of the Conditions were to be read to the Indians in their own tongue; then presents sent over for their Kings were to be given, and a friendship and league according to the Conditions was to be made, and this the said Crispin and others were faithfully to keep. The Assembly of 1683 enacted part of the Conditions in this shape: That on any damage done to the persons or estates of the inhabitants by any Indian, notice should be given to the King of the tribe to bring the Indian to trial before six freemen of the County and six of the near-by Indians; if such a trial were refused, the County Court should impose fine or other punishment: if any person in the Province or Territories injured an Indian, he should be tried by six freemen and six of the same tribe of Indians, the Indian King to be notified to be present.

Indians were allowed by an Act of Assembly a bounty for killing wolves. From 1690 until 1724, this was the same as paid to white men. Such had been the rule in the days of Nicolls.

Sale of strong drink to an Indian except by the Governor's license, and even the unauthorized giving of strong drink to an Indian, had been prohibited in the laws published by Nicolls. This not being in 1681 still in force in the Duke of York's possessions, and Penn's officers having forbidden the sale in his province, several Indians on Oct. 8, 1681, petitioned Lieutenant-Governor Markham to take off the prohibition until the sale should be stopped at New Castle, because the Indians were going down there to buy rum, and getting more "debauched" than before. Altogether the Indians were rather hypocritical temperance advocates, and rarely aided any approach towards teetotalism. Sale or exchange was absolutely prohibited in the Great Law passed at Chester after Penn's arrival. Subsequently the Governor and Council were authorized to suspend this law upon making agreement with the Indians that they submit to the same punishment for drunkenness as the other inhabitants, viz: fine or imprisonment on bread and water at hard labor. The law itself remained in force until Fletcher's time.

The Indians having been aggrieved in trade by strangers in Pennsylvania &ct., a law was proposed by the Assembly in 1693, and enacted by Fletcher, then Royal Governor in Penn's place, and was subsequently under Penn re-enacted, forbidding from trading with Indians all non-residents either on shore or aboard any vessel, except such as had come with their families with intent to settle, and forbidding the inhabitants of the Province and Territories to trade with the Indians privately in the woods, or at the wigwams or Indian towns, or anywhere but at the trader's own dwelling-house.

On 3mo. 17, 1701, Penn and his Councillors came to the conclusion that the Indian trade should be put into the hands of a company, which should take measures to set before the savages good examples of probity and candor, both in commerce and behavior, and that care should be taken to instruct them in the "fundamentals of Christianity." In further considering the matter on the 31st, it was thought that there ought to be a joint stock in which all persons, especially the old traders, should be free to share, observing rules to be laid down by the government, and that no rum be sold to any but the chiefs, and in the quantities which the Governor and Council should see fit. The Assembly failed to agree with Penn upon a bill to regulate the Indian trade further than to prohibit the sale or gift of rum, brandy, or other spirits mixed or unmixed, and to forfeit any pawn taken from the Indians for any goods, the pledging of guns, kettles, &ct. having prevented some of the red men from gaining their livelihood by hunting.

It will be shown in the next chapter that by the time William Penn ended his first visit to America he had secured from the Delaware Indians, or Lenni Lenape, or had had them confirm to him the eastern end of the present Bucks County from the Jericho Hills to the Neshaminy, and also the land at the headwaters of the Neshaminy and Pennypack Creeks and across to Chester Creek beyond the ridge called the Conshohocken hills. In 1685, his agents secured the frontage on Delaware River and Bay from Chester Creek to Duck Creek, the frontage between Chester Creek and the Neshaminy apparently having been recognized as ceded to the whites, although later some further confirmation was made. Some deeds professed to grant an extensive region even south of Duck Creek and near or on the Chesapeake and Susquehanna. During his second visit, he bought on both sides of the last named river from the ancient owners.

Penn stated late in life that he had bought the land of the natives dear. Even as to those who left to him the quantity and character of goods making up the consideration, we may judge that he did not abuse the confidence of the "untutored," for there are lists of the articles given to two of the unbusiness-like ones. Misleading is any attempt to contrast the present values of a suburban plateau and a gun; for at that time, the Indians had plenty of plateaux and few guns.

ACQUISITION AND DISTRIBUTION OF THE LAND. 73

Nor were those who sold at once shut out of the region sold: it seems that when the land was actually taken by settlers, these former owners were allowed to have their residence—the village and corn-patches—on part of what had been made a Proprietary manor.

By the course of the early officials, Dutch, Swedish, and English, and of the Quaker pioneers in dealing with the savages, not only was peace secured for the settlers, but also, at a price which it paid the European to give, and the Indian to take, land was allotted to civilized man, who, except in the surreptitious promotion of drunkenness, was useful to the uncivilized.

The land within the bounds of the King's grant not held by white men, and not still claimed by Indians, Penn undertook to sell or lease, or to cutivate by his own laborers.

In his first prospectus aforesaid, *Some Account &ct.,* he named as the consideration for a sale a principal sum and, in addition thereto, an annual quit rent starting after 1684. This disproves as far as concerns most of the quit rents the statement, made by the Assembly of 1755, that the quit rents were sprung upon the first purchasers, and were acquiesced in only upon Penn's statement that they would take the place of taxes for a salary to him as Governor. It is true, as will be shown, that there arose a question about quit rents, but only those upon lots in the City.

An old act of Parliament, beginning with the words *"Quia emptores terrarum,"* had directed that when owners of land in fee simple conveyed a piece in fee simple, the purchaser should hold feudally of the lord of whom the seller had held, but King Charles II, in the charter to Penn, authorized him and his heirs and assigns, notwithstanding this, to sell in fee simple, and retain feudal lordship of the piece sold. They were especially authorized to erect parcels of the territory into manors, and to hold courts baron or views of frankpledge, and to grant estates to be held of such manors. More than this, the Proprietaries could interpose subordinate barons between themselves and the actual owners of the plantations; for the Proprietaries' license could authorize the purchaser of land in fee from them similarly to erect it into a manor, and to hold such courts within it, and to grant in fee simple to be held of such manor; but on all further or other alienations, the lands were to be held of the lord of whom the alienor had held them. In spite of the last mentioned restriction upon subinfeudation, the Supreme Court of Pennsylvania, after the American Revolution, decided that the statute *Quia emptores* was never in force in Pennsylvania, and that our ordinary "ground rents," as we call them, are services incident to feudal tenure.

William Penn granted the power to hold manorial courts to the Free Society of Traders, whose 20,000 acres he erected into the manor of Frank, and to Dr. Nicholas More, whose 10,000 acres were to be called the manor of Moreland. The license to More was dated Aug. 21, 1682. There is a tradition that More built a jail, no doubt for joint use with the Society of Traders, he being President of the Society. Besides these and the tracts reserved for the Proprietary himself, over which, of course, he could hold court, there were several blocks of 10,000 acres, and even some smaller ones, subsequently laid out as manors for certain of his relations. Against them and his wife's brethren, the Peningtons, he did not enforce a certain article of the Conditions, hereinafter mentioned, dated July 11, 1681, viz: that no purchaser of over one thousand acres should have more than one thousand in one tract, unless he planted a family on every thousand within three years. Nor did Penn or these relations or connections suffer the loss of location by violation of another article, viz: that every one should plant, or man, his surveyed land within said period, or be obliged to move off on being reimbursed the cost of the survey. The Assembly of 1755 thought Penn himself within the rule: and he and the others probably put settlers upon these tracts ultimately. Every tract of 10,000 acres belonging to one owner came to be spoken of as a manor; and it is likely that Penn contemplated erecting as such, when peopled, even the tracts of that size of persons outside of his family: witness his direction in 1701 for a license of that kind for the Growdons' 10,000 acres or even for Joseph Growdon's 5000. In a deed of 1685 to Eneas Mackpherson alias Chatone of Inveressie in Scotland, esquire, for 5000 acres, the Proprietary erected them into a manor to be called the manor of Inveressie, with power to hold manorial courts; but claim under this deed, being made for the first time to the later Penns, was rejected.

William Penn, no doubt, could have gotten a quick return by "unloading" large shares of his province upon wealthy acquaintances, such, for instance, as those who were Proprietors of East Jersey, under whom great tracts might long lie waste, or upon those who would give considerable money to be local barons, who would make the colony less attractive to a poor man. Penn's great purpose, however, in obtaining a large territory and freedom to govern it, was to plant a colony, not to engage in real estate speculation. He surely hoped for some profit in the end; but the vision of a commonwealth based upon his ideas dominated his proceedings. Not merely was it to be a refuge for those oppressed on account of religion, although as such it would attract many, and particularly those with whom he had most influence, but it was to flourish with an industrious population. Not to interfere with the opportunities of such, he, in August or September, 1681, refused £6000—more than half the principal of the Crown's debt to his father—for 30,000 acres and a monopoly of the Indian trade from the Delaware to the Susquehanna, he to have, moreover, two and a half per cent of the profits of the trade. The Free Society of Traders had no such monopoly. Penn's first thought was to sell one hundred "shares," as he called them, of his land, each containing 5000 acres, and to let as much as he could to renters in lots not exceeding 200 acres, adding 50 acres for transporting a servant, and granting 50 acres to the servant at the expiration of the term of service. Very soon, however, the size of the lots to be sold was varied, and, in the sales of over 550,000 acres, made before 3mo. (May) 22, 1682, a tract was in some instances as small as 125 acres, and, in the majority of cases, less than 1000 acres. Besides Nicholas More, the greatest purchaser before May 22, 1682, was William Bacon of the Middle Temple. He did not remove to Pennsylvania, but soon sold his 10,000 acres in pieces. Some blocks of 10,000 acres were purchased respectively by two or more persons, so that the process of division began at once; while, with the large holdings, the descent to a number of owners, and the tempting prices early obtainable through the development of the country, brought about a break up or curtailment. Dr. More died in 1687; his widow, Mary, who married John Holmes, died in 1694. The death of two of the Doctor's children, Samuel and Rebecca, without issue tended to the concentration of the property, but, under an Act of Assembly of 1694 authorizing sale for benefit of the family, the "Green Spring" plantation, on which stood the dwelling-house (near Somerton, Philadelphia), was sold in the following year, and the heirs disposed of nearly all the other land before 1720.

The estates of the Society of Traders were sold by trustees appointed by an Act of Assembly of March 2, 1722-3. The tract of 7700 acres in Chester County, comprising the present township of Newlin, was bought by Nathaniel Newlin, who, although an agriculturist,

ACQUISITION AND DISTRIBUTION OF THE LAND. 77

had apparently no intention of keeping so much after opportunities to sell at sufficient profit. He reduced the tract somewhat, and, dying in 1729, left the balance to be divided among a number of children. The remembrance of a baronial court seems involved in the notion of residents of the locality some generations later that the Newlins would "some day come back and take away our liberties."

After Penn's return to England from his first visit to America, he made some large sales. Through some of these, Joseph Pike, a prominent Quaker of Cork, Ireland, who never resided in the Province, became owner of more than 25,000 acres, most of which he and his heirs kept throughout the period of this history. In 1699, four Londoners, probably all Quakers, viz: Tobias Collett, citizen and haberdasher, Michael Russell, citizen, mercer, and weaver, Daniel Quare, watchmaker, and Henry Gouldney, linen draper, who with their associates were commonly known afterwards as the London Company, bought from Penn nine lots in the City of Philadelphia and certain tracts and also 60,000 acres to be laid out as they might desire, 5000 acres however to be in each of the three manors of Highlands, Gilberts, and Rockland, and a single tract to be in the vacant land of each township, together with the proportion of liberty lots, if any vacant, to which they would have been entitled had they been purchasers under the first Concessions. Most of this great acreage was soon surveyed. None of the owners came to Pennsylvania, although the sales did not dispose of everything until very late in the Colonial period.

By the Conditions and Concessions agreed upon between Penn and his first purchasers, and dated July 11, 1681, he was to retain for his own use 10,000 acres out of every 100,000. The great feature of these tracts, or, as they were called, "tenths" or "manors," was that they were withdrawn from sale at the current price; and afforded the Proprietary the opportunity to reap, like the neighbouring purchasers, a profit from the appreciation of real estate in the particular district. William Penn at first did not take his full number of "tenths"; but, particularly as new regions were opened to settlers, Proprietary manors continued to be laid off until about the beginning of the American Revolution.

Upon the assumption that one acre of wild land was as valuable as another, Penn made all the sales in the earlier years at the rate of £100 principal for 5000 acres clear of Indian claim, subject to the quit rent of 1s. for every 100 acres. Such ground as differed much from the rest could, if poorer, by William Penn's fairness, or, if better, by his successors' shrewdness, or that of his or their agents, be excepted by survey as Proprietary manors. Outside of the manors, the price for frontier land asked by the Proprietaries or their agents seems to have been always uniform, although raised from time to time.

Penn's first method of disposing of land was to convey, on receipt of the purchase money, a certain quantity of unlocated acres by a lease for a year, and a release in fee dated the next day after the lease, and to have those acres laid out and surveyed under the direction of his Surveyor-General, and then to grant by letters patent the located land according to metes and bounds.

The releases, probably executed at the same time as the lease, expressed the tenure, from William Penn his heirs and assigns as of the seigniory of Windsor, and reserved a quit rent to them, and contained a covenant that they, at times appointed in and by certain constitutions or concessions, would clear and discharge the land from all Indian title or claim, and that Penn or his heirs or assigns would execute all other acts and conveyances provided for in such concessions. The pur-

ACQUISITION AND DISTRIBUTION OF THE LAND.

chasers covenanted to have the release enrolled within six months after the establishment of a registry in the Province.

As a rule, in the releases dated prior to Penn's first visit to America, and in some dated while he remained there, it was stipulated that the land should be laid out according to the Conditions and Concesssions under date of July 11, 1681, agreed upon between Penn and "the adventurers and purchasers." The latter, including those who by Penn's releases were made parties to said agreement, are known as "the first purchasers." The Conditions and Concessions required the establishment of public highways and streets before the allotment of particular lands to the respective purchasers, and provided that in the allotment two per cent of each purchase, if the ground permitted, should be within the great town or city contemplated as a capital, and ninety-eight per cent in the rural district. When such a city was decided to be impracticable, a district was set apart as the city's "liberties" to contain the two per cent, and the city proper took the small dimensions which it kept until 1854, viz: from the north side of Vine to the south side of South street, and from the Delaware to the Schuylkill. Penn gave to the holders of liberty land city lots proportionate in value and in addition thereto; but he did not divide the whole city of even nine tenths of it among these purchasers. The lots conveyed to them, like those sold later were subjected to a quit rent of appropriate amount, which thus increased what the first purchasers had agreed to pay for land partly in the great town and partly in the country. By some general assent like that obtained in "the sense of the meeting," this was arranged after Penn had made the city lots larger than he laid them out at first.

The name Philadelphia, which Penn gave to the city, had been rather a usual one for certain religious societies or an ideal community from its signification, "brotherly love": and the fashion, rather than Penn's being struck by the name in reading the Bible, probably induced his choice. Penn's city was laid out before Aug. 16, 1683, the plan being described in the *Short Advertisement* or *Account* printed with Penn's letter of that date. Along the top of the bank on each river was the Front Street, called either Delaware Front or Schuylkill Front and from river to river was a street one hundred feet wide called High, while at right angles with it, and midway between the two rivers, was another street one hundred feet wide. Streets fifty feet wide were projected parallel with one or other of the aforesaid wide streets. Upon the intersection of the wide streets was placed a public square, described as ten acres, for public buildings, while four other pieces of ground were left open as public parks like the Moorfields of London. The great difference from the present arrangement of the principal streets was in there being twenty-three streets running north and south instead of the present twenty-two in the same space, and in the Broad Street of those running north and south being the twelfth from either river. The lots on each of said Front Streets ran back to the second street from the river, but the lots on High Street did not run as far as the next street north or south. All these lots or an undivided share therein were given to the purchasers of 1000 acres or more. The Society of Traders took a strip from Delaware Front to Schuylkill Front, causing the elevated ground over which it extended about Delaware 2nd and Pine to be known as "Society Hill." Along the back streets were the lots for those who had purchased less than 1000 acres. Hardly had the scheme of streets and parks been adopted, and Holme's map of the province showing this been published, before the width of Delaware 12th street was changed. The patent dated Aug. 3, 1692, to the Society of Traders,

ACQUISITION AND DISTRIBUTION OF THE LAND. 81

reciting a resurvey, gives the property from Delaware Front, on which it extended from Spruce to Pine, thence along Spruce and Pine 320 ft., and, narrowing on the north to the width of 366 ft., and of that width, to Schuylkill Front, bounded on the south by Pine, and this patent described the block between the 2nd and 3rd streets from each river as 495 ft., and all the other blocks as 396 ft., except that between Delaware 13th and Broad, which block was 520 ft., the west side of Broad being 396 ft. from the east side of Schuylkill 8th. Probably the moving of the northwestern and southwestern parks about two blocks westward was contemporaneous with the aforesaid rearrangement of streets.

The bank of the Delaware from high water mark to Front Street was intended to be left unoccupied except by wharves, Penn leasing in 1684 for fifty years a lot to Samuel Carpenter for the latter purpose. However, some of the caves had been extended and roofed, and it took some time to make the cave-dwellers go away; after one or two had made terms to retain the better specimens of such structures, "bank lots," as they were called, began to be granted in fee, the buildings thereon being restricted to a height not obstructing the view from the western side of Front Street. The quit rent for a bank lot was not, like the other quit rents, to remain fixed, but was to be increased at the end of every period of fifty-one years to one third of the rental value as then ascertained by an appraisement.

A large part of the city remained unsold until the divesting of the Penn estates, when the Commonwealth of Pennsylvania began disposing of the lots not taken up, in many cases whole blocks. The quit rents on city lots, like those on rural property not within the Proprietary manors, were abolished by the Divesting Act, as will be mentioned.

In the rural district of the Province, according to the aforesaid Conditions of 1681, any persons whose combined purchases amounted to 5000 or 10,000 acres could have their plantations placed side by side as a township, and if possible on harbors or navigable rivers, and the list dated 3, 22, 1682, arranged the purchasers in groups of 10,000 acres; but the map of the lots as placed, probably with the consent of the purchasers who had arrived, does not correspond with this, although showing a division into townships.

A general warrant was issued by Penn under the date, 3, 22, 1682, to Thomas Holme, the Surveyor-General, to survey the lots for the purchasers in the list of that date. He accordingly cut up the available land outside of the city and Liberties, so as to place the tracts containing ninety-eight per cent of every purchase. The location was adhered to when these first purchasers or their representatives came to seat themselves, except as they exchanged their locations, or incurred forfeiture under the Conditions, or the boundaries were altered after ascertainment that they gave too many acres. Holme's map of Pennsylvania, after he had inserted tracts not in the first list given to him, but sold since, was printed in 1687.

In 1690, Penn issued a circular for the sale of the region along the eastern side of the Susquehanna, free of Indian title, and with a proportionate lot in a city to be built on that river. The project, although once or twice revived, never was carried through.

Except for the lots in the first list given to Holme, Markham, who was authorized to set out, survey, rent, or sell lands, and the Commissioners who were intrusted with laying out the city, and afterwards Penn himself and his successors and his or their authorized agents issued a special warrant to the Surveyor-General, or, if there was none, to a county surveyor, to survey in a particular place each lot agreed for. This warrant, which was as to many lots the second document necessary for a good title, was in many cases the first, the later Penns and their agents not executing deeds of lease and release. The warrant was duly returned with a description as ascertained by survey.

The patent, or deed poll of confirmation made letters patent, was signed in the absence of the Proprietary by Commissioners duly appointed by him, or, when there were none, then usually by the Lieutenant-Governor under a general letter of attorney authorizing him to make grants on the terms, methods, rents, and reservations used in the Land Office. The necessity for delivery of possession, or "livery of seisin," had been obviated. The patent otherwise followed feudal forms. The land was to be held of the Proprietary and his heirs and assigns as of a certain manor; what was within or adjoining Philadelphia or its Liberties, for instance, being granted to be held as of the manor of Springettsbury. The tenure was to be by fealty. The quit rent was expressed.

When William Penn departed from Pennsylvania, at the end of his first visit, he commissioned Thomas Lloyd, Robert Turner, and James Claypoole to grant warrants, and issue patents. Lloyd and Turner will be often mentioned in this book. James Claypoole had been a merchant in London. He was brother of the John Claypoole who married Oliver Cromwell's daughter. On 11mo. 21, 1686, Markham, then Secretary of the Province and Proprietary's secretary, was commissioned with Thomas Ellis and John Goodson to exercise those powers. An order, dated three days later, required any two of them to dispose of any tracts in Pennsylvania already taken up, but lying vacant and unseated, and most likely to give cause of discouragement to those ready to seat the same. Certain exceptions and time of grace were allowed in executing this.

A very annoying right was retained by the Proprietary so long as a patent had not been issued, viz: that of correcting wrong measurements; and this was deputed to these early Commissioners. They could resurvey lands back of five miles from the navigable rivers, and were to keep for the Proprietary's use and disposal all overplus found by resurvey, where there had not been a final grant or a patent.

Under date of 2mo. 16, 1689, Penn appointed Markham, Turner, Goodson, and Samuel Carpenter as "Commissioners of Propriety (sic)," and to act in the nature of a court of exchequer for collecting rents, and auditing the Receiver's accounts. James Harrison, as steward, had collected the rents, but Blackwell, the Governor, was made Receiver. Besides the forfeiture for not putting people on the land, and that for wrong measurement, there was, until the passage in 1693 of an act of confirmation, a forfeiture for not recording deeds. There was little complaint against these Commissioners or Penn, who superseded them by his second visit, either as to the distribution of lots or the forfeitures; but the alteration of metes and bounds by resurvey, even when fairly conducted, was deemed a hardship. In 1700, Penn and his freemen in Assembly agreed upon a law not only for quiet enjoyment of lands seated by virtue of patents and warrants under the Crown of England before Penn's charters, but also that all lands duly taken up by warrants pursuant to purchases from the Proprietary, or issued under any commission or power granted by him, except when obtained by fraud or deceit, or when interfering with others' just claims, were to be enjoyed by the possessor and his heirs and assigns according to the warrants, and that, even where no patent had been granted, peaceable possession for seven years after peaceable entry under the warrant was to give a title to such lands in such quantity as they had been taken up for. It was also enacted that future grants from the Proprietary were to be under the great seal, and to give an absolute title not to be shifted by resurvey: former grants under broad

ACQUISITION AND DISTRIBUTION OF THE LAND.

or lesser seal were to be good for the quantity of land named therein, but the land could be resurveyed within two years after the publication of the law, and the excess over the stipulated number of acres, after allowing four per cent for difference of surveys, and six per cent for roads, should belong to the Proprietary, the possessor having the refusal at reasonable rates, to be agreed upon by two arbitrators chosen by each side, any three fixing the price, or saying where the excess should be taken off, and any deficiency should be made up by the Proprietary according as he received overplus land.

The legislation, again passed in 1701, was not sufficient to satisfy the people. When the last Assembly chosen during Penn's second visit had convened, and he, in his speech, had offered to join in some suitable provision for the safety of the people in privileges and property, a number of citizens of Philadelphia presented a petition calling attention to grievances, and in a few days the House appeared before him with a request that twenty-one items be embodied in a charter. He protested that some of these concerned matters not cognizable by an Assembly, being matters between him and the individuals with whom he had dealt; and, standing on his rights, he explained that he must avoid making a precedent for control of his property by the law-making power, lest there be a Governor distinct from and independent of the Proprietary, as was threatened by a bill in Parliament.

However, he substantially satisfied the Assembly on some points; for instance, he allowed hunting and fishing on one's own land, and on that of the Proprietary not taken up, and that fees, if such as would relieve the Proprietary of the support of the Surveyor, Secretary, and other officers, be fixed by law, or left to an action of *quantum meruit*. On his promise to allow the ten acres in one hundred only for the purposes mentioned in the law, the Assembly pressed for a clearing up of misunderstanding, so that the allowance for roads and highways be made whether the lands had been already or were yet to be taken up. In a Bill of Property subsequently sent up by the Assembly, there was a clause making him supply deficiencies found on resurvey. He objected that he had never intended to be debtor where the ground was not to be had; but, as it was thought unfair that those who had ten per cent more than the deeds called for could keep it, while those who had only two per cent overplus might have to be content with that, he was willing to make up six per cent overplus to all. This the House rejected; and the law of 1700 and 1701 on the subject was not amended. He ultimately included in the charter which established a new Frame of Government the 5th item requested, viz: that no person be liable to answer in any matter of property before the Governor and Council, or elsewhere than in the ordinary courts. In one of the messages on this subject, the Proprietary said that he alone was to decide disputes about unconfirmed properties. The 8th item of the request, reciting that he had given the purchasers to expect their lots in the city of Philadelphia as a free gift, asked that they be cleared of the rents and reservations. To this he replied that the first purchasers present at the allotment seemed readily to agree to what was done, and had received more than double the frontage first promised: if those who had signed the petition to the Assembly would return the difference between 50 ft. and 102 ft., he would "be easy in the quit rents." The 9th item was that the city back of the built up portion remain open as common until the respective owners be ready to build, and the islands and flats near the city be left for the inhabitants to gather winter fodder. He said that it was a mistake to think the fourth part of the city reserved for such as were not first purchasers belonged to anybody but himself, but he was willing temporarily to lay out some land for the accommodation of the residents; yet the islands and flats had nothing to do with the city. Similarly he agreed that the bay marshes be as common until disposed of; this being in answer to the 16th item, that such marshes be commons, which proposal he took as "a high imposition," and which the Assembly did not press: whereas the Assembly adhered to the 8th and 9th items. The 13th item went so far as to ask that the land not taken up in the Lower Counties be disposed of at the old rent of a bushel of wheat a hundred. He justly replied that it was unreasonable to limit him in what was his own, or deprive him of the benefit of an advance in value which time would give to other men's property. Yet the Assemblymen thereupon voted that they "humbly move the Proprietor would further consider it as proposed." To the 20th item, that the quit rents be redeemable, he said: "If it should be my lot to lose a public support, I must depend upon my rents for a supply, and therefore must not easily part with them; and many years are elapsed since I made that offer that was not accepted." The Assemblymen unanimously adopted a retort that they humbly moved that "he would further consider it in regard to his former promises and their dependence thereon." On all these points, notwithstanding some conferences, he did not yield: the power being in his hands, the disposing of land was not changed.

On leaving the Province, at the end of that visit, Penn commissioned Edward Shippen, Griffith Owen, Thomas Story, and James Logan or any three of them to grant lots, and make titles &ct.

The law of 1701 was repealed by the Queen in Council on February 7, 1705-6, before the business of resurveying and settling for errors could be finished. Another act on the subject, passed in 1712, was repealed at the close of the following year. Very little more legislation followed, and the disposal of all unsold land was practically in the hands of the Commissioners appointed by the Penns until the oversight was taken by one of the family coming to Pennsylvania. Except when those managing the Proprietaries' property were acting under letters of attorney from the mortgagees or under the powers conferred by William Penn's will, a regular course of procedure was followed, and rules precluding favoritism were observed. In later times, the Lieutenant-Governor presided over the Board of Property, exercising any discretion usually according to the advice of the Secretary. Under that title, the chief managers from 1701 until the American Revolution were successively James Logan, Rev. Richard Peters, William Peters, and James Tilghman. As the business increased, the various executive duties were divided among a Secretary, Surveyor-General, Receiver-General, Auditor-General, and Keeper of the Great Seal, and the deputies or clerks of one or more of them, all being known as the Land Office.

The holding by one or two men of not merely the quit rents on land sold, but of the entire unsold land within the boundaries of Pennsylvania was perceived to conflict with or threaten the government of the people, for the people, and by the people inaugurated for the State at the American Revolution. So, on Nov. 27, 1779, the legislature of the new Commonwealth passed what is known as the Divesting Act, taking away or transferring to the State from the Proprietaries all unsold land except what had been acquired by them otherwise than as Proprietaries, and except what had been surveyed to them as manors or parts of manors prior to July 4, 1776; and also abolishing all quit rents except those reserved out of land within the manors. The Assembly had a free hand to confiscate or destroy. The treaty of peace with Great Britain had not been made: it prohibited for the future confiscations of the property of the Tories. The Assembly in the Act showed after all a kindly spirit. It was impossible to compensate the Penns with any equivalent: but, lest John Penn, son of Thomas, and John Penn, son of Richard, reduced to the position of well-to-do gentlemen, were not sufficiently provided for, there was voted to the heirs and representatives of Thomas and Richard Penn, deceased Proprietaries, the sum of £130,000 stg., payable after the end of the war. The money was duly paid and accepted. In consideration of the loss not thereby covered, the British government for over one hundred years paid to the representative of the Proprietaries an annuity of £4000, and then commuted it for a principal sum.

CHAPTER IV.

THE RED NEIGHBOURS.

The Lenni Lenape, or Delawares, and early purchases from them—Penn's Great Treaty: time, place, and some of the participants—Subsequent deeds—Further account of the Delawares until 1701—The Iroquoian Five Nations—The Minquas, or Susquehannocks, or Andaste—Dealings to acquire for Penn the Susquehanna Valley—Recognition of the Five Nations as Subjects of England—The Pascatoways, or Ganawese, or Conoys—The Shawnees—Treaty of 1701 with Minquas, Shawnees, Ganawese, and Emperor of Onondagas—New York Treaty with Five Nations for peace with all the English colonies—The Nanticokes—The Tuscaroras—Small expense of intercourse with Indians.

The extensive literature on the subject of those commonly called the aborigines of the northern part of the United States, particularly the *Handbook of the American Indians North of Mexico,* which is Bulletin 30 of the American Ethnological Bureau, obviates any need of filling these pages with an account of the ideas or customs of that fraction of mankind, or the movements, except in a limited time and space, of the political or family divisions thereof. Various tribes or parts of tribes had relations with the Colony of the Penns during the period of this history, some of them separated by language as widely as the Latin and Teutonic Europeans. Most of the dialects have been grouped as Algonquian or Iroquoian, and whoever spoke one of these as his forefathers' tongue has been called an

Algonquin or Iroquois, from the names of certain small tribes with whom the French came early into contact. It is more phonetic in English to spell the former name Algonkin, and more scientific to speak of the other group as the Huron-Iroquois, because the Hurons, although constantly at war with the Five Nations, were their kindred.

Between those tribes where the "untutored" of one could to some extent talk with those of another, it is hard to state the exact degree of relationship, owing to the occasional adoption of a conqueror's language, and owing to the figurative use of the titles "Fathers," "Uncles," "Brothers," "Cousins," &ct. Even when not dependent upon forefathers' tradition among such illiterate people, but set down by Europeans living near the time and place of events, Indian history presents great difficulties in the exaggeration in the talk of such poetic children of the forest, and the doubtfulness in identifying tribes migrating far, and designated by the French, Dutch, Swedes, English, Algonquins, and Iroquois respectively by names not always the translation, phonetic equivalent, or corruption of those given by others. Mere similarity of names may mean at most similarity of characteristics or of the natural features of place of residence. The variations in the following pages in the spelling of the names of individuals will show the difficulty the English scribes had in catching and representing the sound, how often soever repeated to them.

As the pioneers of Virginia had to face Algonquins forming the Powhatan confederacy, and the New Englanders had to face Algonquins called Pequots, Narragansetts, &ct., the Europeans in the intervening land, except those who contemporaneously saw the Susquehannocks, came into contact with Algonquins first as far as known. These Algonquins were such as spoke of themselves as Lenni Lenape (in some dialects Nenni

Nenape or Renni Renape, l and n and r being alternating letters), but the English called them Delawares, after the English name of their southern river or its bay. Howard M. Jenkins, in *Pennsylvania Colonial and Federal,* has given quite a description of these Indians. The reader will find annotated with a translation and a vocabulary what purports to be their epic, the *Wolam Olum,* in Dr. Daniel G. Brinton's *The Lenâpé and their Legends.*

With the northernmost Delawares, the people of the stony land or mountains, spreading to the Catskills, this history has little to do, although their name, Minsi or Munsey (hence Muncy), was preserved through later Colonial times. Their totem was the wolf. The French called the Delawares who went in the 18th century to the northwestern part of Pennsylvania "Loups," either because the advance guard of the Delawares crossing the Alleghany Mountains had that animal as their totem, or because they were classified with the Mohicans, an Algonquin tribe, formerly of New England, but afterwards mostly dwelling near the Delawares, the name Mohican resembling the Algonquian word for wolf, although Brinton suggests a different meaning. To the middle group, the dwellers in or about southeastern Pennsylvania, was given the name Unami, evidently represented in maps and records by Armewamen and Ermewarmoki; while the southernmost Lenape were called Unalachtigo, of which name some have seen Nanticokes as a form. As the Delawares have been spoken of in tradition as a confederacy, they may have been the Atquanachukes—in other words, confederates or mixed people—appearing northeast of the Chesapeake in Captain John Smith's map, while possibly a mixture of the subdivisions of the Delawares may have been the Aquauachuques, or Aquanachuques, in New Jersey in Nicholas J. Visscher's map, published before 1660.

There was a tradition that, some time in the 17th
Century, the Delawares were tricked by the Iroquois
of the Five Nations into assuming the position of
women, that is acting as peacemakers, and so becoming
non-combatants. Eshleman would fix the date about
1617. The evidence for the story does not necessarily
cover other Delawares than the Minsi; and against it,
and particularly against an early date, Jenkins shows
that down to 1680 the Minsi were holding their own
against the Five Nations, and he suggests that the submission to the latter probably took place soon afterwards, as the result of defeat, although the form of according them an honorable rank may have been followed.

Certain small tribes which appear to have been, or
have been proved to have been divisions of the Delawares, lived before the time of this history in what is
now the state of Delaware and the Pennsylvania counties of Delaware, Chester, Philadelphia, Montgomery,
and Bucks. Various items concerning them seem inconsistent with their being in subjection to any Iroquois
nation, or even being non-combatants. Capt. John
Smith placed on the extreme east of his map, within
what is now New Castle County, two villages, Chickahokin to the south, and Macocks to the north. The
Chickahokin, or Chickelaki, have been supposed to have
been then or afterwards about where Wilmington now
stands. The Ockanickon Indians in 1679 (*Penna.
Archives,* 2nd Series, Vol. VII, p. 854) claimed to be
chief owners of the land near the Falls of the Delaware.
Both names, Chickahokin and Ockanickon, sound like
Okehocking, the name applied to certain Indians who
removed from their settlements near Ridley and Crum
Creeks before 10mo. 15, 1702. On that date, a warrant
was issued to survey for Pokias, Sepopawny, Muttagouppa and others of the nation 500 acres of the Proprietary's land near the head of Ridley Creek, formerly

Griffith Jones's (Willistown Township, Delaware Co.), as promised by the Proprietary before his departure in 1701, the said 500 acres to revert to the Proprietary upon said Indians leaving it. Before 1737, the tribe removed to the Swatara Creek.

On the south hook of South River Bay (land about Lewes) in 1630, there were Indians represented by Quesquaekous, Eesanques, and Siconesius, if, indeed, these were not tribal names. The three designated by those names acknowledged a sale having taken place in the preceding year to Samuel Godyn of land on the south side of the Bay from Cape Henlopen to the mouth of the South River. In 1677, the Emperor of the Nanticokes excused himself from delivering Krawacon, who had been called a Gassoway Indian, to the Governor of Maryland, by stating that Krawacon belonged to the King of Checonnesseck, a town on Whorekill.

The *Narratives of Early Pennsylvania, West Jersey, and Delaware,* edited by Albert Cook Myers, give us contemporary mention from 1633 to 1638 of not only the Minquas, to be spoken of in another part of this chapter, but also the Sankitans, and the Indians from Red Hook, or Mantes, and the Armewamen, or Armewanninge, evidently the same as the Ermewarmoki, of which Armewamen Zee Pentor was a sachem in 1634, we being left to infer that the Minquas had caused the others to retire to the eastern side of the River and Bay; while Nicholas J. Visscher's map of New Netherland &ct. indicates about 1655 the spreading of these others far into what is now New Jersey.

Amandus Johnson, in his *Swedish Settlements on the Delaware 1638–1644,* tells us, from contemporary writings, that on March 29, 1638, certain peace sachems, acting for the Lenni Lenape entitled, sold to the Swedish Florida Company the land from Duck Creek to the Schuylkill. In 1640, Indians, undoubtedly Lenni Lenape, sold the west bank of the Delaware from the

Schuylkill to the Falls, opposite the present Trenton. The Mantas, whom Johnson suggests to have been the Minquas, but who are called in the Maryland records Mathwas or Mattawass and "Delaware Indians," soon afterwards claimed from Wychquahoyagh, or Wicacoa (afterwards Weccacoe, about Washington Avenue, Philadelphia), to the aforesaid Falls, and two of their chiefs Siscohaka and Mechekyralames, conveyed it. The sachems at Passyunk were mentioned some years before 1654, when that locality was stated to be the principal abode of those Lenape with whom the Swedes had to deal. It was from "Pesienk" that Kekerappan, hereafter mentioned, and others dated on Oct. 8, 1681, their request for the resumption of the sale of liquor in Pennsylvania.

The Maryland records tell us that Pinna, "King of Picthanomicta in Delaware Bay," on behalf of "the Passayonke Indians, now under his command," made peace with Maryland in 1661. In 1669, a league between that Province and the Mathwas nation was expected to be renewed by Capt. Carr, then at the New Castle colony, or, as it was called, "Delaware," and said treaty was to embrace with the Maryland Province its Indian confederates on the eastern shore near Choptank. The records further say that in 1677 the Mattawas "or Delaware Indians"—probably only a certain tribe of the Lenni Lenape—were embraced in a treaty of peace made by the representatives of Maryland with the Five Nations.

It was from the Unami Delawares that the English bought whatever Pennsylvania land south of the Water Gap and east of the watershed they acquired from Indians. Mamarikickan, Aurichton, Sackoquewan, and Nanneckos by deed of Sep. 23, 1675, conveyed to Edmund Andros to the use of the Duke of York in fee the land on the west side of the Delaware River from a creek next to Cold Spring, somewhat above Matinicum

Island, about eight or nine miles below the Falls, to a point equally far above the Falls, or to some remarkable point as a landmark, and all islands in front except the one commonly called Peter Alricks's Island.

By bargain arranged with Markham, a number of Indians, including two of the aforesaid four, under date of July 15, 1682, and Aug. 1, 1682, conveyed to Penn and his heirs and assigns forever the eastern end of the present Bucks County, or, as William W. H. Davis in his *History of Bucks County,* says, "all of the townships of Bristol, Falls, Middletown, Lower and the greater part of Upper Makefield, Newtown, and a small portion of Wrightstown, the line running about half a mile from its southern boundary." Part of this was included in the deed to Andros for the Duke of York, which outstanding title was assigned to Penn by the confirmation which the Duke made of King Charles's charter. In this Indian deed of July 15, 1682, were included islands in the Delaware. The consideration was not merely beads, paint, tobacco, and liquor, with some money, but also guns, axes, kettles, glasses, hoes, awls, saws, knives, scissors, needles, &ct., powder and shot, blankets and clothing—enough to make it worth the savages' while to alter the range of their roaming, enough to be a foretaste of the newcomers' fairness.

We learn from James Logan's speech to Sassoonan on Aug. 13, 1731, that, when Penn first arrived in the country, he promptly called together the chief men among the Indians, and explained his coming with a number of persons by leave of the King of England to settle among them, and that all should be brothers: a league of friendship was made, and the Indians offered their land for the settlers, but Penn insisted upon buying it. Sassoonan said that he was a little lad when Penn came, but remembered that Penn went up to Perkasie, and met the Indians, and proposed buying, and Menanget, Hetkoquean, and Tammany were present, and offered to give the land to him. Thus we find taking place at Perkasie (in Bucks Co.) the first of the conferences for making Penn's celebrated treaty with the Indians; a treaty primarily for the transfer of land, but often referred to by red men, and very famous in history, for the promises then exchanged, and in Penn's lifetime unbroken, of everlasting friendship between the races. The older members of the tribe seem to have perceived the advantage of white men with their goods and utensils being introduced into the neighbourhood: but we can conclude that time was allowed to consult those not present. Instead of the treaty being completed, as has been supposed, in 1682, no deeds from the Indians to Penn appear to have been made until June 23. A second, if it was not a third, conference was held in May, 1683. The date is fixed from the following evidence. The Provincial Council on May 24, 1683, adjourned to June 6. In connection with the boundary dispute and the interviews mentioned in Chapter II between the two Proprietaries, Penn speaks in his letter of Aug. 14, 1683, to the Lords of the Committee for Trade &ct. as having been disappointed about meeting Lord Baltimore until May, when Baltimore sent messengers to give Penn notice to meet him at the head of the Chesapeake: "but then," that is too late to reach the Chesapeake on the day fixed, Penn was, he says, "in treaty with the kings of the Indian nations for land:" however, three days later, he came across Lord Baltimore ten miles from New Castle, and took him back to that town, and entertained him, and on the following day they discussed business a little, and separated. These discussions with Lord Baltimore, including that on the day when Penn met him, took place on May 29 and 30 (*Considerations on Penn's Answer to Talbot's demand*, in *Maryland Archives*); hence the session with the Indians must have ended a day or so before May 28, 1683, if not on that very day. On the

20th of June, the Provincial Council adjourned until the 26th. On the 23rd, eleven Indians signed or witnessed deeds, apparently in pursuance of the treaty in question, the deeds perhaps having taken some time to prepare. The proceedings of the final session, which must have taken place on June 23 or within two days before, are described in Penn's letter of August 16 to the Society of Traders. He says that the Indian King asked that the Indians be excused for not complying with Penn "the last time," as it was the Indian custom to deliberate and take up much time in council, but if the young people and owners had been as ready as himself, there would not have been so much delay. The bounds and the price were then spoken of, the price being ten times what it would have been previously. When the purchase was agreed upon, Penn says, "great promises past between us of kindness and good neighbourhood, and that the Indians and English must live in love as long as the sun gave light." Two of the Indians present on June 23 lingered until the 25th, and were among the five witnesses when another Indian signed a deed. The deeds of July 14 indicate that those at the treaty who had bargained for a specific quantity of articles, sent four sachemakers to receive them, and make deeds on that day.

As to the place of one or both sessions of the conferences, it is not known how late the locality known to the Dutch and English by the Delaware name Shackamaxung or Shackamaxon, meaning "place of the Shackamakers," continued to be a meeting-ground; but it is in that part of the present City of Philadelphia that tradition has located the making of the treaty. John F. Watson, in his *Annals of Philadelphia*, after other evidence, quotes Judge Peters to the effect that Benjamin Lay, who came to Philadelphia in 1731, and could have heard from those who had spoken with eye-witnesses, used to visit a certain large elm tree, in the district, and speak of it as at the site. A monument now marks where the tree stood, by the east side of the present Beach Street above East Columbia Avenue.

Of those Indians present at the Great Treaty, the names of seventeen are disclosed, as signers or witnesses of the deeds of June 23 and June 25, 1683.

The best known of the seventeen, and, in fact, of all Delawares is Tammany, or, more correctly, Tamanen (spelt also Taminent), whose virtues James Fenimore Cooper has perhaps exaggerated, and whose name with the prefix "Saint" is borne by a political organization, of which a wag may say that the totem is a tiger. It is not to be presumed, however, that Tamanen was the presiding "King," or the speaker, mentioned in Penn's account of the conference. Tamanen with Metamequan claimed on June 23, 1683, only a piece of ground on the Neshaminy towards the Pemmapecka (Pennypack) smaller than the piece of Essepenaike and Swanpees; but, by 1697, Tamanen had acquired greater authority, for in that year, he, as a sachemaker, joining with Weheeland, his brother, and Weheequeckhon, alias Andrew, who was to be King after Tamanen's death, Yaqueckhon, alias Nicholas, and Quenamequid, alias Charles, Tamanen's sons, confirmed all land between said creeks from the River Delaware "as far as a horse can travel in two summer days," even between straight lines beyond where the creeks forked.

Menangy, or Menanget, whose presence at Perkasie when Penn spoke there to the Indians has been mentioned, appears as Menane, a witness to two of the deeds of June 23, 1683.

The Hetkoquean spoken of as being at Perkasie, evidently the same as Hithquoquean and Heteoquean, was an important chief, about the time of Penn's second visit. He would seem to have been the Idquoquequon who was one of the grantors of the eastern end of Bucks County, and the Icquoquehan who joined

Secane on 5, 14, 1683, in conveying the land lying, according to the *Archives,* along the west side of the Schuylkill beginning at Conshohocken and "thence by a westerly line" to Chester Creek. Hittoken, as the scribe set down the name of a witness to a deed of June 23, was clearly Hetkoquean.

Prominent as Menangy and Hithquoquean afterwards became, the most important grantors known to have been at the Treaty besides Tammany, were Essepenaike, Swanpisse, and Sahoppe. There are several mistakes in the printing in *Penna. Archives,* 1st Series, Vol. I, of the deed of Aug. 1, 1682, for the eastern end of Bucks County and its endorsement. The original is preserved by the Historical Society. The name of one of the right owners, misprinted "first owners," of certain land is not Eytepamatpetts, but Essepamarhatte, evidently the same as Essepenaike. Essepenaike and Swanpisse conveyed their share, greater than Tamanen's, on the Neshaminy on June 23, 1683; and Essepenaike came again in September to witness Kekerappan's deed, and was also one of the sachemakers and "right owners" who, in 1685, conveyed all the land from Chester Creek to Duck Creek, extending in depth from the Delaware as far as a man can ride in two days with a horse. Swanpisse, or Swanpees, was one of those who conveyed to Penn before the latter's arrival the eastern corner of Bucks County, bounded on the south by the Neshaminy, besides being so important a personage on the other side of that stream. Sahoppe, or Enshockhuppo, or Shakahoppoh, was another who joined in the deed for the eastern end of Bucks County. He witnessed deeds of June 23, 1683, and shortly afterwards his jurisdiction extended across both the Neshaminy and the Pennypack back of the Jericho and Conshohocken range; he joining in one grant from Chester Creek to the Pennypack and also in a grant from the Pennypack to the Delaware above

the Jericho Hills, which latter grant gave rise to the
notorious Indian Walk, to be mentioned in a later
chapter. Richard, or Mettamicont (the Indian name
being sometimes written Metamequan), joined in one
deed, and witnessed two others, of June 23, 1683, and
surrendered his land on the Delaware on both sides of
the Pemmapecca, or Pennypack, a year later.

Kekerappamand (misprinted as Peterappamand),
who joined in the aforesaid endorsement dated Aug. 1,
1682, was evidently Kekerappan (misprinted in body
of deed with l for r), described as of Opasiskunk, evidently Passyunk, who made a deed on 7, 10, 1683, for
the half on the Susquehanna side of all his lands between the Delaware and the Susquehanna, promising
to sell on returning from hunting in the following
Spring the other half as reasonably as other Indians
had sold "in this river." This he seems to have done,
in part at least, by joining in 1685 in the conveyance
of the land on the Delaware from Chester Creek to
Duck Creek.

Machaloha, whose deed to Penn of October, 1683, is
in bad preservation, and who also joined in the conveyance of the land from Chester Creek to Duck Creek,
rather exceeded Kekerappan in claims, being called, in
October, 1683, owner of the land on Delaware Bay,
Chesapeake Bay, and up to the Falls of the Susquehanna River. He seems to have been the same person
as Ocahale, or Owehela, living afterwards on the
Christiana, and, if so, is one of the few Delaware sachemakers whom Penn saw who can be traced for more
than about five years.

In 1685, four Indians, including some before mentioned, conveyed to Penn by bargain with Surveyor-
General Holme both sides of the Schuylkill above Conshohocken from Chester Creek to the Pemmapecka as
far northwestwardly as two full days journey, and thirteen other sachemakers and right owners, three of

whom have just been named, conveyed the west side of the Delaware from Chester Creek to Quing Quingas, or Duck Creek, backwards "as far as a man can ride in two days with a horse."

Apparently, such Delawares as were represented by the before-mentioned sachemakers could migrate or make peace or war as they pleased until about the time of Penn's second visit, and then bodies not small enough to be overlooked probably agreed to pay tribute to the Five Nations. Any earlier "conquest" left them quite autonomous.

A considerable number, rather from the central part of the land which had been bought by or for Penn, i.e. from nearest the capital town or its liberties, had moved up the Schuylkill to within the present limits of Berks County by the beginning of 1690, Capt. Cock and others then going thither to reassure the "chief sachem of our Indians" of the good intentions of the Pennsylvanians. Menangy, who was among the Delawares about to be mentioned as waiting upon Markham in 1694, was at the time, or became soon afterwards, the head of the Indians on the Schuylkill.

Within a few years after the purchase of the land between Chester and Duck Creeks, Penn, writing from England, if not, indeed, his Commissioners at the time of the purchase, regranted, for at least temporary occupancy, a mile on each side of the Brandywine from the mouth up to the forks, and thence up the west branch to the head. On 7, 5, 1691, six Indians, of whom the names are hard to identify with those printed as signing the deed of 1685, acknowledged receipt of full payment for the land between Chester and Duck Creeks "according to a certain deed signed by us unto William Penn," and the minutes of 7th month 19, say that on said 5th of the month, the Indians, after being paid, desired that the Brandywine Creek might be opened in order that the fish could go up, according to the contract with the Proprietary, and thereupon a letter was sent to the County Court at New Castle to take course according to law. The writing which the Indians alleged to have made the grant was destroyed in the burning of a cabin, and there was no copy. In 1706, on the Indians insisting that the grant was of absolute ownership forever, the Commissioners bought from them the lower part of the strip, as far as a certain rock on the west branch in Newlin Township for 100*l.*, paying down 73*l.* In 1725, Checohinican, or, Checochinican, was a leading sachem in the neighbourhood. In that year, several of the tribe appeared before the Assembly, and claimed part of the tract formerly of the Society of Traders, bought by Newlin, and Governor Keith issued an order for the demolition of certain dams and weirs interfering with the fishing. In 1726, the Land Commissioners, on further complaint, paid the balance of the 100*l.*, and gave Newlin some land in exchange. A law about this time was passed by the Assembly of the Lower Counties for keeping the dam of the mill on said Creek in New Castle County open during the fishing season, authorizing the Sheriff to throw down the dam: in March, 1727, on complaint of the Indians, the Sheriff was ordered to carry out the law. Up the stream, Indian privileges required attention in 1729: Checochinican complained, that, contrary to a writing by Newlin agreeing not to disturb the Indians, the land had been sold, and they were forbidden to use the timber for building some cabins, and further that the town at the head of Brandywine had been surveyed for James Gibbons and others, who were expecting a conveyance from the Commissioners of Property. This would indicate that some of the tribe had gone as far as the present Honeybrook Township. J. Smith Futhey and Gilbert Cope, in their *History of Chester County,* have located an Indian village in the present Wallace Township, where Indiantown School House stood when they wrote: they also say that another Indian village was on the north side of the west branch near the line of the Society's land, and that there Indian Hannah, last of her race in the County, dwelt for many years. Watson says that she died in 1803, nearly one hundred years old, and that about the time of the Revolutionary war she with the rest of her family, Andrew, Sarah, and Nanny, were living in Kennet.

In 1694, when the Onondagas and Senecas sent to the Delawares asking them to be "partners with them" in fighting the French, Hithquoquean, Shakhuppo, Menanzes, Tamanen, and Alemeon (possibly Alaenoh, witness to one of the deeds of June 23, 1683), and also Mohocksey, who may have been a king of the Lenape in New Jersey, came with other Delawares and two Susquehanna chiefs to see Lieutenant-Governor Markham; and Hithquoquean, on behalf of the Delawares, announced their resolve to live as a peaceable people, being but weak and very few in number. The Onondagas and Senecas had, in the message, reproached the Delawares with the very thing which tradition says that the Five Nations had long before that time imposed upon them, viz: doing nothing but staying at home and boiling the pots like women. The Lieutenant-Governor commended the visitors for not engaging in war without the advice and consent of Governor Fletcher, who, on his visit to Philadelphia for aid against the French, had secured some money, but had permitted the people of the Province to stay at home to defend it. The Delawares were assured that Governor Fletcher would take care that the Senecas should do them no injury on account of their refusal.

In 1697, a considerable body of the Delawares, enumerated as 300 men,—the small number of persons in any Indian nation must surprise the uninformed,—were tributary to the Susquehannas and Senecas around about Conestoga. Fifty were at Minquannan, mentioned as about nine miles from the head of the Elk River, fifteen miles from Christeen, and thirty miles from Susquehanna, and the rest of the body on Brandywine and Upland Creeks. All, as well as the Susquehannas and Shawnees, were said to be inclined to attach themselves to the government of Maryland, as they hunted between the Susquehanna River and the Potomac. The Delaware "King" offered that his Indians, if permitted to hunt between those rivers, would watch the movements of the Naked Indians, or Twightwees (Miamis). For some time, Owehela, or Ocahale, appears as the most prominent Delaware Indian on the Christiana. On Aug. 29, 1700, he, as "Ocahale, King of the Delaware Indians," joined with the King of the Shawnees, and with Indian Harry, representing the King of the Susquehannocks, in a treaty confirming former peace and amity with Maryland, making themselves answerable for injuries done by other Indians to the inhabitants of that province, and promising, upon damage done by neighbouring Indians, to assist against them, and pursue, and, if possible, capture and bring them for the government to deal with them.

There were Indians at Lechay, or Lehigh, during Penn's second visit, who were probably Delawares. He consulted Oppemenyhood of that place upon the law prohibiting the sale of rum.

Penn during his second visit to America gave the Delaware chief Heteoquean a belt to carry to the Five Nations. Heteoquean died soon afterwards, and the belt was not exhibited to the great men of those Nations until 1712.

The early travellers from Europe to our Middle States, proceeding into the interior, found a different race of Indians. The Hudson and the Mohawk afforded the Dutch traders access to villages inhabited by those to whom the French were extending the name Iroquois, and to whom in time they restricted that word. There were five main tribes, called by themselves respectively by a derivative of "the place of flint," "the rock set up," "top of the mountain," "where locusts were obtained," and "the great mountain." The English of New York and Pennsylvania called them respectively Maquas or Mohawks, Oneidas, Onondagas, Cayugas, and Sinnondowannes or Senecas. The Marylanders classed all as Cynegoes, or Senecas, or Jonadoes, just as some of the Dutch had confused the various names of these tribes. According to De Denonville (*Penna. Archives,* 2nd Series, Vol. VI), writing in 1685, the Sonontouans, as he called the Senecas, then outnumbered the four other tribes combined, the Anie (Mohawks) having 200 fighting men; the Oneyoust (Oneidas), 150; the Onontague, 300; the Goyoguoain (Cayugas), 200: while the Senecas were reported to have 1200.

Although certain of these tribes had continued to make war independently of the others, the five long before that year united in a confederacy, at first a loose one, and are known collectively in English history as the Five Nations, and more properly after 1712, when the Tuscaroras were added, as the Six Nations. The Onondagas had the precedency. At their castle was held the great council, called from the place of meeting "the Long House," in which much of such government as there was among Indians became centralized. Yet some "States rights," and even some conquered lands and vassals belonged to particular tribes.

The use of guns, powder, and shot introduced by the Dutch among the Indians of the Mohawk Valley gave them a great advantage over enemies armed with bows and arrows; and the Five Nations started upon a career of conquest, which their ferocity maintained after other Europeans provided the neighbouring savages with weapons, and which ended in the mastery of the interior of New York and Pennsylvania.

The policy of the Dutch at New York of amity and almost mutual aid and comfort with the Five Nations, remained, after the acquisition of that region by the English, the policy of the government 'here, so largely did the Dutch families control Indian relations, if not other affairs. This policy was necessary while the New Englanders were engaged in crushing the Algonquins in their vicinity; and when it was becoming clear that the Five Nations would dominate the border between the Duke of York's possessions and Canada, it seemed the sharpest politics to ally with the winning side.

Only straggling members of any of the five tribes lived near the parts of Pennsylvania civilized before Penn's death; but the earliest traders who went from the Schuylkill and the Brandywine to the headwaters of the Octorara and the Conestoga associated with certain Indians of the same stock. To these and to all the Iroquois, the Lenni Lenape applied the epithet Mingwe, treacherous. Amandus Johnson, in his book already quoted, gives the various forms "Mingo, Minqua, Minquaes," &ct., in which this name was used by Swedes and Dutch to denote the interior people with whom the settlers on the Delaware came in contact. There was a tribe called the "White Minquas," and one called the "Black Minquas," probably from their costume or paint. If Sir Edmund Andros was correct as to the relationship of the Susquehanna Indians and the Mohawks, the latter would seem to have been the Black Minquas, often no more friendly with the White Minquas than near blood relations sometimes are. Yet the identity of the Black Minquas remains a puzzle: they were sufficiently numerous in 1681 to be reported as joining the Sindondowannes in war. The White Minquas are supposed to have been those almost invariably meant by the simple word Minquas or Mingoes, viz: the Indians whose chief seat was on the lower Susquehanna during the days of the Swedes and Dutch. On the probability that the occupants of the region had not changed, H. Frank Eshleman in his *"Lancaster County Indians—Annals of the Susquehannocks &ct."* has traced them from Capt. John Smith's first mention of the Sasquesahanock in his *Description of Virginia:* in fact, following A. L. Guss's *Early Indian History of Susquehanna,* from Smith's mention of the Pacoughtronack in his *True Relation.* As one guess at Indian history is about as good as another, the hypothesis may be here offered, accounting for some items to follow later about the Pascatoways, that, as the syllable "pak" in Algonquian conveys the idea of division or duality, the name embracing it was used in the days of Smith and others to denote the people of a dual empire, composed of an Iroquoian and an Algonquian part, the latter being dominant, and continuing after the secession of the former to be called by the name of the whole. The dwellers on the Susquehanna, who were thus the Iroquoian part, and who, Edmund Andros in 1675 said, were "offsprings of the Maques (Mohawks)," were described as Sasquesahannock, from Sasquesahanna, the Algonquian name of the river, evidently by Algonquian-speaking Indians on the Chesapeake and the Delaware. Smith knew the great enemies of his Sasquesahanock as Massowomekes, a name remarkably like Mattawomen, that of a tribe afterwards connected with the Pascatoways: notwithstanding the usual identification with the Five Nations, the Massowomekes may have been the Pascatoways, long alternately lords and enemies. The final emancipation from them appears to have been after Lord Baltimore began the settlement of Maryland. The Susquehanna Indians called themselves, or were called by their Iroquoian kindred Ganestogas, hence our word Conestoga, and even our word "stogy" for a Pennsylvania cigar. It would seem from the creek now called Conestoga being so called in Herman's map that before its date their chief seat was near there, and may have been that marked "fort demolished" on Chambers's survey (see George Smith's *Hist. of Delaware County*). The Susquehannocks by treaty of July 5, 1652, conveyed to the Marylanders the land on the western side of the Chesapeake from the Patuxent to Palmer's Island, and on the eastern side from the Choptank to the North East branch which lies north of the Elk, except Kent and Palmer's Island, belonging to Capt. Clayborne; both English and Indians being allowed to build a house or fort on Palmer's Island. In 1744, the Six Nations testified to the greatness of the Susquehannocks' empire by acknowledging that the grantors in this deed of more than ninety years before, had the ownership of the land of which they so undertook to dispose. The printed *Maryland Archives* and the printed *Jesuit Relations* mention continuously the Indians living north of the land so conveyed, the *Maryland Archives* always giving them the same name as the great river, as did also the Duke's Governors of New York, and the *Jesuit Relations* employing apparently the Iroquoian name in the form, which may be a slight modification, "Andasto-eronnons" or "Andasto-genronons." The element "roona" was a suffix for the plural in Iroquoian. The village, or capital, appears in the *Relations* as "Andastogué." The records of the Province of Pennsylvania use indiscriminately all three names Mingoes (or Minquays), Susquehannas, and Conestogas. For a long period, these Susquehannocks, often helped by Maryland, were victorious in war against some of the Five Nations, the fortress being moved to where Herman depicted it. Eshleman quotes the *Relations,* Vol. 59, p. 251, to show that, about 1672, the Iroquois succeeded in subjugating the tribe so much feared, or, in the words of the priest, "the Sonnonlouaies have utterly defeated the Andaste, their ancient and most redoubtable foe." The government of Maryland seems to have forsaken them about this time, punishing them for offences of which perhaps none of them were guilty; and thus another Colony than New York contributed to making the Five Nations supreme as far as the Potomac. After a second defeat, called an "extermination," many Susquehannocks were taken to live with their conquerors; the relation before long became that of friends, and the conquered were believed to be stirring up the "Senecas" to depredations upon Maryland. The great war captain Harignera, on the other hand, had saved a remnant. He soon died, but his followers and other detachments were for some time strong enough to menace the whites both north and south of the Potomac. A considerable body, revenging the murder of five principal chiefs at a peace parley, raided Virginia, tomahawking the settlers, until defeated by Nathaniel Bacon, whose assumption of authority is called Bacon's Rebellion. A detachment of those who had gone to Virginia and probably some others went back to the old Susquehanna Fort, "sixty miles above Palmer's Island,"—pretty clearly the location designated for the fort by Herman's map,—and made submission to the "Senecas," but asked for peace with Maryland. After various events, peace was made between Maryland and the Five Nations and the Susquehannocks under them; after which the number of Senecas or so-called Senecas within what is now Lancaster and York Counties in Pennsylvania increased.

The Swedes had bought the claim of certain Minqua chiefs as far as the Susquehanna River. To acquire what had been beyond those chiefs' possessions or the title or good-will of those who were their lords paramount, Penn in July, 1683 (see his letter to Brockles and West, *Penna. Archives,* 2nd Series, Vol. VII, p. 3), sent William Haig (called Wm. in the letter), to be accompanied by James Graham of New York, to treat with the

Mohawks and Senecas and their allies for the land fronting on the Susquehanna. According to Rev. Jean de Lamberville's letter of Jany. 31 following—the date is Feb. 10, 1684, new style—the white people at Albany worked upon the Indians, and through Oreouahé, the Cayuga, circumvented the sale of the land of the conquered Andastogués (*Penna. Archives,* 2nd Series, Vol. VI). The Indians had much contention as to one another's rights, but appear to have agreed on one point, and to have delivered sufficient answer, even before the Indian Commissioners received a letter from the new Governor of New York, written on September 18, by the advice of his Council, to stop Penn's negotiations until his boundaries should be adjusted. Thomas Dongan, who was the Governor, was, in everything connected with these lands, guilty of treachery or double dealing or at least vacillation. Canassatego said in 1744 at Lancaster that the Governor of New York had advised the Five Nations to put the land into his hands, instead of Penn's, and promised to keep it for the Five Nations' use, but the Governor went away to England, and sold it to Onas (a quill, the translation of Penn, which they thought meant a goose's quill) for a large sum of money, and, when they were minded to sell Onas some lands, Onas said that he had bought them from that Governor, but, on hearing how the Governor had deceived the Five Nations, Onas paid them for the lands over again. The Indians, making their marks to a writing since lost, gave the Susquehanna River, i.e. the valley of it, to Dongan, as he mentions to Penn in a letter of October 10, 1683. In a letter of October 22 to the same, Dongan speaks of a second gift of the River from the Indians, adding "about which you and I shall not fall out." What the Five Nations intended, appears in the speech of the Onondagas and Cayugas on Aug. 2, 1684, in the Town Hall at Albany to Governor Dongan and Lord Howard of

Effingham, Governor of Virginia: "You will protect us from the French, which if you do not, we shall lose all our hunting and bevers. We have put all our lands and ourselves under the protection of the great Duke of York . . . we have given the Susquehanne River, which we won with the sword, to this government, . . . and will not that any of your Penn's people shall settle upon the Susquehanne River . . . we do give you two white drest deer skins to be sent to the great sachem Charles that he may write upon them and put a great red seal to them that we do put the Susquehanne River above the Washinta or Falls and all the rest of our land under the great Duke of York and to nobody else . . . and we will neither join ourselves nor our land to any other government. . . . You, great man of Virginia, we let you know that Great Penn did speak to us here in Corlear's house"—the Governor of New York was called "Corlear"—"by his [Penn's] agents and desired to buy the Susquehanne River, but we would not hearken to him nor come under his government, and therefore desire you to be a witness . . . we are a free people uniting ourselves to what sachem we please." A note in the *Documentary History of New York* says that the Falls were those in the present Bradford County, Pennsylvania; but it is evident that the claim of sovereignty extended as far south as the Falls near the Conewago.

The fact that the Cayugas were the only nation joining the Onondagas in this speech, and that about thirty-five years later the Cayugas claimed the lower Susquehanna, and that, moreover, the Mohawks, were about the middle of the XVIIIth Century deemed to have no share in the land further north sold by the Five Nations, is not easily explained. It may mean that the conquest of the Susquehannocks was chiefly the work of the Cayugas, or in pursuance of their supposed early rights.

After the Duke of York had ascended the throne, and then had fled from it, his friend Dongan, who had become Earl of Limerick, transferred to Penn what title Dongan had to the lands of the Seneca-Susquehanna Indians. Reciting his purchase from them of land on both sides of the Susquehanna River with the adjacent lakes from the head of the River to Chesapeake Bay, Dongan conveyed this to William Penn and his heirs and assigns by lease and release dated Jany. 12 and 13, 1696. A few months after this, the Susquehannas and Senecas at Carristoga (Conestoga) were reported as forty young men besides women and children. On 7mo. 13, 1700, Dongan's release to Penn having been shown to Widaagh, alias Orytyagh (Orettyagh), and Andaggy-Junkquagh, styled "Kings or Sachemas of the Susquehannagh Indians," they, in consideration of some goods, and of Penn's former expenses in making the purchase, deeded to Penn and his heirs and assigns the Susquehanna River and its islands and land on both sides of the river formerly the right of the nation called the Susquehannagh Indians, or by what name they were known, and confirmed the bargain and sale made to Dongan. In July, 1721, Civility, "a descendant of the ancient Susquehannah Indians, the old settlers of these parts, but now reputed as of an Iroquois descent," said that he had been informed by their old men that they were troubled when they heard that their lands had been given up to a place so far distant as New York, and that they were overjoyed when they understood William Penn had bought them back again, and that they had confirmed all their right to him.

James II having avowed his sovereignty over the Five Nations, and undertaken to protect them, and they having supported the English in the war carried on by William III, recognition of those tribes as English subjects was made by the French King in the following sentence in the treaty of Ryswick:

Les habitans de Canada & autres, Sujets de la France, ne molesteront point à l'avenir les cinq Nations ou Cantons des Indiens soûmis a la Grande Bretagne ni les autres Nations de l'Amerique, amies de cette Couronne. (Du Mont's *Corps Diplomatique*.)

This gave the English the foundation of a claim that the French had yielded, or recognized as belonging to England, all the territory of the Five Nations and of the tribes subject to them, such as the Delawares, Susquehannocks, Ganawese, Pennsylvania Shawnees, and the natives around Lake Erie. France, on the contrary, about the time at which this history closes, insisted that there was only a stipulation for the safety of persons, and that the territory in question followed a clause in the treaty surrendering to the parties what each had before the war, and that France had then owned, by right of discovery, all the land drained by the Ohio and the Great Lakes.

Besides the Delawares, Susquehannocks, and Five Nations, certain remnants or detachments of tribes, nearly all of them Algonquian, were to be found within Penn's boundaries before his death. The reader is referred to Charles A. Hanna's compendious work, *The Wilderness Trail,* for many items in the history of all the Indians with whom our frontiersmen came in contact, also for a presentation of evidence of much that is here written, and for narratives of the adventures of individuals, which, as mere local history, are not mentioned here.

Hanna has said very little about the Pascatoways, mentioned on a preceding page, as to whom some facts must now be given. They are usually called in the Pennsylvania records, Ganevi, Ganawese, or Conoys, from the name by which they were known to the Five Nations. The tribe is classed as Algonquian. Brinton would explain the derivation from the verb "pashk," meaning in one Algonquian language "to divide," from the old seat being on the Pascatoway, or Piscataway, Creek, where an estuary of the Potomac may be said to divide into that creek and Timber Creek. In the rapid fluctuations of power among savages, these, whatever their kinship, their locations, or their name, seem once to have been a great nation. The *Maryland Archives* furnish us with the statement of the Pascatoway speaker in 1660 that the fourteenth or earlier King, or Tayac, before the one then reigning, had come from the Eastern Shore, and commanded all the Maryland Indians and also the Patowmacks and Susquehannocks. A Virginia record, telling of an expedition in the latter part of 1623 against the Pascoticans and their associates, recognizes them as "the greatest people in these parts." The expedition revenged a murder by the Anacostans. The first settlers of Maryland found apparently in control of the Patowmacks, and very much what the leader of the Massowomekes of Smith's time might have been, an Emperor, or Tayac, of Pascatoway, who could summon 500 men with bows, and whose successor had a dominion of one hundred and thirty miles, with inferior chieftains under him. This people, Lord Baltimore took under his suzerainty, confirming the succession of subsequent Tayacs. He made peace between the Pascatoways and the Susquehannocks. Between 1660 and 1667, the former seem to have included the Anacostanck, Doags, Mikelwoman, Manasquasend, Mattawoman, Chingawawaterck, Nangemaick or Hangemaick, Portoback, Secayo, Panyayo, and Choptico Indians. The Pascatoways, although reduced in number, and the Mattawomen turned to Maryland in her struggle with the Susquehannocks in 1675 or 1676, and, after suffering at the hands of the latter and the Senecas, the Pascatoways were embraced in the peace made by Maryland with the Five Nations in 1682.

Apparently the Pascatoways immediately thereafter united themselves as a tributary nation to the great northern confederacy. When the English Revolution took place, the Protestants in Maryland became suspicious of the Indians, who had been friendly with the Lords Baltimore. Various circumstances alarmed this tribe, and caused the seeking of refuge. In 1697, the Emperor and his followers were found between the two mountain ranges of Virginia beyond the head of the Occaquan River. Although the Maryland government tried to induce them to return to that province, they, after coming back to the Potomac River, went far enough north to feel themselves within the boundaries of the Quaker jurisdiction, and preferred to trust themselves as guests or tributaries of their old enemies, the Seneca-Susquehannocks. Old Sack, chief of Conoy Town, is reported to have said in 1743 that his forefathers came from Piscatua to an island in Potowmack, and from there down to Philadelphia in William Penn's time, and that, after their return from visiting Penn at Philadelphia, they brought all their brothers from Potomac to Conejoholo,—the land on both sides of the Susquehanna for a number of miles was so called,—and built a town on the eastern side, and afterwards moved higher up to Conoy Town, the Six Nations—evidently the Senecas of the Conestoga region—saying that there was land enough, and giving permission to settle anywhere about the Susquehanna.

It is possible that the variations or derivatives of the Algonquian word for south or southern appearing quite early as the name of a tribe, like Chawons on Capt. John Smith's map, and Chowanoke in his *Description of Virginia,* may not designate the same nation which after 1688 was always meant by such attempts to represent the sound as Savino, Sabbernowle, Shevinor, Shawan, Shawanees, and finally Shawnees in English, and as Chuans and Chauonons in French. In Visscher's Dutch map before 1660, we find Sauwanoos on both sides of the Delaware at some indefinite distance above the Falls, agreeing with the tradition of the Shawnees coming to Pennsylvania before the time of this history, and of their occupying Shackamaxon, as mentioned in Rev. John Heckewelder's *Account of the History, Manners, and Customs of the Indian Nations who once inhabited Pennsylvania and the Neighbouring States.* The Shawnees who entered Pennsylvania in the period of these Chronicles came from the south or southwest, the tradition being that the nation was a branch of the Lenni Lenape which had very early split off, and gone thither. About 1688, there were Shawnee villiages on the Ohio and in Carolina and one near La Salle's Fort St. Louis, as well as probably some still on the Cumberland River, called by the French geographer in 1718 "Riviére des anciens Chaouanons," while he called the Savannah "Riviére des Chaouanons ou d'Edisto." The proximity to the French of the old homes of the Shawnees and the alliance of various bodies of them with the French made all members of the tribe within the English possessions objects of suspicion.

A statement in Volume 8 of the *Maryland Archives,* pp. 517 and 518, may mean that a party of Shawnees, fleeing from the Twightwees, passed up the Susquehanna about 1687, and joined the Iroquois. The "Sattanas" having been at war with the Five Nations, one hundred warriors of the former went on a deputation to the latter to make peace, and had reached the Delaware River—Hanna says, probably near the Falls—by August, 1692. Hanna, in the book which has been mentioned, shows how communication with the Province of New York and settlement in New Jersey followed. It is probable that the fear of the strange Indians called

Shallna-roonas felt by the Schuylkill Indians in 1693 was owing to the movement of larger bodies than the group which settled on the Susquehanna. Those Shawnees who came to the western side of the Delaware near the Water Gap about the time of, but independently of, the Shawnee immigration to the Susquehanna, had lived in New Jersey. Whether or not Martin Chartier, as Eshleman supposes, had been a trader on the Susquehanna before 1692, it is clear that Chartier, who had fled years before from Canada, and more recently from Fort St. Louis, brought a band from the Shawnee village near Fort St. Louis to the Chesapeake in 1692; in which year the Susquehanna Indians and some southern Indians, called, according to the record, "Stabbernowles," claiming to be in league with the Mohawks, who were friends of Maryland, asked permission of the government of that province for the Stabbernowles to settle on the lands of the Susquehannas, but were informed that the lands were within the limits of Pennsylvania, but that Maryland, however, would not disturb the Stabbernowles as long as they lived peaceably. They continued there, a Maryland officer in June, 1697, finding thirty "Shevanor" men, besides women and children, living "four miles below Conestoga," paying tribute to the Susquehannas and Senecas, and the *Maryland Archives* in 1696 and 1698 speaking of that Province being at peace with the Shawnees. In later generations, the officials of Pennsylvania had no knowledge of any immigration of Shawnees prior to 1697 or 1698, and did not distinguish those who came at other times or to other places from those now about to be mentioned. Lieutenant-Governor Gordon, in a letter endorsed as having been written in December, 1731 (*Penna. Archives,* 1st Series, Vol. I, p. 302), said that he had found by the records that, about thirty-four years previously, numbers of Shawnees had come to Susquehanna, and obtained leave first of the Conestogas, and afterwards of Lieutenant-Governor Markham, to settle on Pecquea (Pequea) Creek. As it was said by another authority that sixty families came in 1698 to Conestoga, it is probable that a sufficient reinforcement came in that year to raise the Shawnees in what is now Lancaster County to such number, and perhaps the reinforcements came more directly from the Cherokee country. Defeats by the Cherokees and Catawbas had stopped the spread of the nation further south. The coming to Pennsylvania has been reported as a fleeing before one of these enemies.

The Shawnees about the lower Susquehanna and the Conestoga Indians, or Seneca-Susquehannas, being on the frontier, were molested both at their homes and in the hunting grounds by the Naked Indians (Miamis, or Twightwees). In the Fall of 1699, some runaway servants, including a woman nearly related to a Twightwee King, were harbored by Conodahto, or Connodagtoh, King of the Conestogas, and Mecallona, King of these Shawnees. Mecallona conceived the project of redeeming the woman from service, and sending her to the Twightwees, as an act of kindness which must result in peace. This was frustrated by certain white men reclaiming the servants. The threats of bringing a large force, and cutting off all the Indians under Mecallona and Connodagtoh, not only brought about the surrender of the runaways, but put the two tribes into such trepidation that they did not plant corn the next Spring, and they prepared to move. The petition of the two Kings to Penn for favor and protection is dated May 1, 1700, at Brandywine, where they got a white man to write it, and is printed in Vol. I of *The Penn and Logan Correspondence,* page 1. The heading is correct, but in the body of the petition the name Savino, i.e. Shawnee, is misprinted as "Gavino." Mecallona may not have been the only king of these tribesmen; for on Aug. 29, Ophesaw (Opessa), or, as he is called in Penn's treaty the next year, Wopaththa, as King of these Shawnees, joined the Delaware King and the representative of the Susquehanna Indians in a treaty of peace and alliance with Maryland.

The Proprietary of Pennsylvania was put in the position of protector, guide, suzerain, and, moreover, monopolizer of the trade of the Indians within two hundred miles westward of the white settlements by a treaty of April 23, 1701, between William Penn for himself and his heirs and successors, and the following Indians for themselves and their successors and nations and people, viz: Connodagtoh, described in the Council Minutes as "King of the Sasquehannah Minquays or Conestoga Indians," but in the articles called "King of the Indians inhabiting upon and about the river Susquehannah in the said Province," and Widaagh, alias Orettyagh, Koqueeash, and Andaggy Junkquagh, chiefs of the said nations, Wopaththa, King, and Lemoycungh and Pemoyajooagh, chiefs, of the Shawnees, and Ahookassoongh, brother of the Emperor, in behalf of the Emperor, i.e. the great King of the Onondagas, and Weewhinjongh, Cheequittagh, Takyewsan, and Woapackoa, chiefs of the Ganawese, called in the articles "the nations of the Indians inhabiting in and about the northern part of the River Powtowmeck." There was to continue a firm peace between the Christian inhabitants of the province and the several peoples aforesaid, and no injury should be done to any one on either side; the Indians were to behave according to the laws of the government while they lived near the white people, and were to have the privileges and immunities of the laws, they acknowledging the authority of the Crown and the Provincial Government; they were not to aid, assist, or abet any one not in amity with said Crown and Government; both sides were to notify of all rumors of each others' evil designs; the kings and chiefs and their successors were not to allow any strange Indian nations to settle on the western side of the Susquehanna or about the Potomac other than those already seated, or bring other Indians into the province without the consent of the Proprietary; no person was to trade with the Indians without a license under the hand and seal of the Proprietary or his Lieutenants; and Penn, his heirs and successors were to take care to have the Indians "furnished with all sorts of necessary goods for their use at reasonable rates;" the Potomac Indians aforesaid were allowed to settle upon any part of the Potomac River within the bounds of the province; the Indians of Conestoga and upon and about the Susquehanna River, and especially their said King, Connodagtoh, should be at all times ready to confirm and make good the sale to Penn, now ratified, of the lands lying near and about the said River; and the Indians of the Susquehanna were to answer for the behavior and conduct of the said Indians, and for their performance of the articles; Penn and his heirs and successors were to assist with advice and directions—notice, not with arms—and, in all things reasonable, befriend all said Indians behaving as aforesaid, and submitting to the laws of the Province.

The Shawnees of Pechoquealon in the region known as Lechay (Lehigh), were not strictly a party to the treaty of April 23, 1701, but made some overtures for trade shortly afterwards, and seem to have been thenceforth considered as embraced within the Proprietaries' guardianship, just as, when all Pennsylvania Shawnees came to be within easier reach of one another, the Five Nations appointed one viceroy or superintendent over them all.

In accordance with Penn's suggestion, the Governor of New York, making, in 1701, a treaty with the Five Nations, made their promises of peace extend to all the other English Colonies as well as New York, and to the Indian tribes within the respective provinces.

The Nanticokes, who appear in the records of Pennsylvania a few years later, were at this time in Maryland. They are called in subsequent New York records Tochwoghs, the name by which they are mentioned in Smith's *Description of Virginia*. The *Wolam Olum* of the Delawares speaks of the Nentegoes as well as the Shawanis separating from the rest of the nation in early times, and going south. The *Maryland Archives* mention various "Emperors" of the Nanticokes. The Nanticokes who met Evans in 1707 understood English so well that no interpreter was employed. They gave the date of their peace with the Five Nations as twenty-seven years before, although the Maryland records speak of a war between them in 1681.

Among the tribes mentioned by John Smith were the Kuskarawaoks about half way down the eastern shore of the Chesapeake. They have not been supposed to be the same as the Iroquois bearing the almost identical name of Tuscaroras; but if they were the same, could they not have been the Black Minquas? The Tuscaroras, about 1701, reached in the Carolinas the southernmost point of their wanderings, and will be mentioned later. They had been enemies of the Shawnees.

The courtesies required at the Colony's hands by the Indian tribes, mostly the interchange of visits in which the Province gave more valuable presents than it received, and the maintenance of the visiting Indian families, were a small price to pay for peace. The Proprietaries paying the expense of those meetings which were for the purchase of land, the public outlay, until the treaty in 1722 at Albany, was for many years less than 50*l*. authorized in 1705 to be annually expended for treaties and messages.

CHAPTER V.

THE PEOPLE.

The small number of Swedes and Dutch—The Church of Sweden and its Ministers on the Delaware and Schuylkill—Decline of Swedish families in prominence—Welsh Tract—German Town—French settlement in Chester County—Pennsylvania practically a colony of Englishmen—Preponderance of Quakers—Early Meetings for Business—Philadelphia's oldest meeting-houses—Quaker Ideas—Jews-harps—Benjamin West—Baptists—Advantages of the Society of Friends and political importance of its leaders—Previous social rank of the settlers—Education among them—Penn's relatives and his father's companions in arms—Markham and his family—Baron Isaac Baner, Lady Newcomen, and James Annesley—Little recognition of Caste—No landed oligarchy—Sale of real estate to pay debts—Distribution of inheritance—Attractiveness of Penn's dominions as a place of residence.

A few surnames and a few churches, now Protestant Episcopal, are nearly all the vestiges in Pennsylvania or Delaware of the colonization promoted by the House of Vasa, and the name of the Schuylkill River is practically the only thing that has survived among us from the time of the authority of their High Mightinesses, the Estates General of Federate Belgium, or the United Netherlands. Moreover, there lurks in our local speech, as far as the author can recall, not a word, unless brought into it much more recently, of the language of the subjects of either of those two powers. The use of English for colloquial purposes became a necessity as soon as the immigration of Englishmen became considerable, although Swedish survived in sermons and church services for a good many years, and, in fact, Dutch was reintroduced for such uses among those whose grandfathers had spoken it. From the retirement of Dutch officials after the final surrender to England, until New Yorkers, in the days of Penn, began to come to Bucks County, there was scarcely a Dutch family in the region now called Pennsylvania, and so small a proportion were the Swedes and Dutch of its population during the period of these Chronicles that we might disregard those races, had they not been strong in the region now called Delaware, and therefore of weight in the politics of Penn's dominion. Although there was some influx of Englishmen both before and after the Duke of York's deed to William Penn, the greater part of the population of New Castle, Kent, and Sussex Counties was of other nationality than English at the Revolution of 1688, particularly if Scotland was to be reckoned a separate nation. There were even quite a number of Frenchmen.

Of the three races, Swedes, Finns, and Dutch, the Swedes were greatly in the majority on Delaware Bay and River.

The Swedish settlers and their children were not dissenters from their National Church, which, although classified as Lutheran, was, like the Church of England, liturgical, presided over by bishops, and controlled by the State; nor had the Dutch any of those peculiarities which separated some Anabaptists and the Quakers from other Protestants. When language was not a barrier, aliens who recognized the Bible as their Directory in faith and morals, not placing greater confidence in the individual conscience, whose ministers were trained, who took an oath when the magistrate required it, whose leading men wore swords, and of whom the poorer men were ready to use pikes and guns, were more congenial to the ordinary Englishman than his Quaker compatriots. There will be mentioned the likelihood of such an Englishman, at least before 1696, attending the houses of worship established by the Swedes, and partly maintained by the Dutch, where at times there ministered an Anglican clergyman.

In the year with which this history begins, the Swedes were assembling for worship at Tranhook on Christiana Creek in New Castle County (church now known as Holy Trinity, Wilmington), and on Tinicum Island (church soon afterwards abandoned), and at Weccacoe, for which the congregation afterwards built the edifice now standing, dedicated July 2, 1700, known as Gloria Dei Church (on Delaware Avenue above Washington Avenue in Philadelphia). Rev. Jacob Fabritius, living above Penn's capital town, and coming down the river in a canoe, tended all the congregations, and even went into Maryland. He had been blind since 1682, and was led about by some one who preceded him with a staff. Acrelius says that this dominie, by birth a German or a Pole, and called from New York by the non-English whites on the Delaware, preached mostly in Dutch. It may be supposed that he was never one of the clergy of the country of Sweden, although his Lutheranism was undoubted. When he was not present at Tinicum, Andreas Bengtson (Andrew Bankson) read Möller's *Postilla*.

King Charles XI of Sweden, not in the exercise of any superintendence over English subjects of Swedish descent, but out of zeal for the Evangelical religion, upon hearing of the need of ministers and books, sent over the Rev. Andreas Rudman, Rev. Eric Tobias Biörck, and Rev. Jonas Auren, who all arrived in June, 1697, when Rudman took the churches in Pennsylvania proper. He was invested with a commissaryship or vice-episcopal dignity, whereby, after he had given up his charge in Philadelphia, he presided at the ordination there by himself, Biörck, and Sandel of Justus Falckner on Nov. 24, 1703 (Sachse's *German Pietists*), Rudman had, on July 19, 1702, preached his farewell sermon in Weccacoe Church, in accordance with leave to return home; but, after laboring among Lutherans on the Hudson, he for some time served Anglican churches in Penn's dominions, and he died in Philadelphia. He had been succeeded in his Swedish charge by the Rev. Andreas Sandel, picked out by the Consistory of Upsala, and ordained by Archbishop Benzelius of that see. In Sandel's time there were enough Swedes and other Lutherans at Pennypack and Amasland and Kalcon Hook, as well as at Manatawny, as about to be mentioned, for him occasionally to preach at those places. When, in 1719, Sandel returned to Sweden, the Rev. Jonas Lidman took charge of Weccacoe and Kalcon Hook; and the Rev. Samuel Hesselius, of Neshaminy and Manatawny. Lidman, upon being recalled, left his congregation in 1730 to the care, says Acrelius, of Mr. John Eneberg, who was then preaching for the Germans. Rev. Gabriel Falk, who came in 1733, was obliged to leave Weccacoe by being found guilty of slander, and sentenced to heavy damages; but, retiring to Manatawny (of which name Molatton appears to be a variation), he for a number of years served what has since been called St. Gabriel's, Molatton (now the Protestant Episcopal Church at Douglassville). Rev. Johan Dylander came to Weccacoe in 1737, and served until his death in 1741. During the visits of Whitefield and Zinzendorf, the Church of Sweden in Pennsylvania was badly broken up. After the arrival of Mühlenberg—see a later chapter—there was an attempt to unite the Swedes and the German Lutherans ecclesiastically; but the Rev. Gabriel Naesman, who had been sent from Sweden as Dylander's successor, refused to join, as being subject to the Archbishop and Consistory of Upsala. Naesman was shepherd of the diminished flock in the year when this history ends. Under his successors, the Swedish church edifices and congregations of Pennsylvania became three in number only: Gloria Dei at Weccacoe, and what is now St. James's at Kingsessing, and Christ Church in Upper Merion (Bridgeport). In Delaware, there was Holy Trinity Church. An ecclesiastic called "Provost," sometimes the minister at Holy Trinity being appointed such, presided over all the Swedish missionaries on the Delaware, and one of the archbishops or bishops in Sweden had the general care of the mission. Pastors were sent from Sweden until after the American Revolution. When subsequent vacancies occurred, the congregations began calling clergymen of the Protestant Episcopal Church of the United States of America.

When the early purchasers from Penn arrived in Pennsylvania, they found the choicest land in the possession of those who had come under other authority, mostly Swedes. Penn, at his second visit, offered to such Swedes in exchange lands at Manatawny (partly in Montgomery and partly in Berks County on the Schuylkill), at a quit rent of a bushel of wheat per 100 A. He set apart 10,000 acres thus to be a Swedes Tract, somewhat like the tracts to be mentioned for persons of other nationalities respectively. Although Acrelius says that only a few accepted the offer, Swedes were afterwards reputed owners of that number of acres in the aggregate there. Swedes also bought considerable land from Welshmen owning the same on the western side of the Schuylkill around about the present town of Bridgeport, Montgomery Co.

In addition to Swedish ideas of public policy, there were, as have been mentioned in a preceding chapter, some Swedish grievances real or supposed; so there may be said to have been at a certain time a Swedish

Party, as well as several Swedish neighbourhoods. The sympathy, before alluded to, between the non-Quaker English and the persons of other nationality, made, independently of any personal interests, the prevailing sentiment in the Lower Counties strongly opposed to that in the Upper, or Pennsylvania proper.

While certain ideas were derived from the Swedes and Dutch, and they controlled politics in some localities, they, even in Delaware, were not the leading exponents of their views, and their importance did not outlast their relative numerical strength. It marked contrast with certain Dutch families in New York, the progenitors of some of which, to be sure, received enormous territory, and resembled Penn as landlord, but not as Governor, it is noticeable that the pioneers on the western banks of our river and bay secured no financial, social, or political advantages over those who came later. The commanders of the colony not vicegerents under an officer at Manhattan left no sons; yet there were chief men who joined Penn in inaugurating his government who left families; but their children succeeded to no political importance in the Upper Counties, and, in fact, their grandchildren, to very little in the Lower; for Delaware in good time became English, although not strongly Quaker. As a class, collection of families, or group, the Swedes and Dutch are obliterated from the history of Pennsylvania after Penn's second visit. The non-Quakers of different nationalities intermarried, and many of the most influential persons of later Colonial times had, through some female line, a strain of Swedish blood: but John Morton, signer of the Declaration of Independence, was the only person of Swedish patronymic known outside of a county court or the House of Assembly, until, in more modern times, a number of individuals have by their abilities recalled to us this old race to which they in the male line belong.

William Penn, besides his sales to the early English purchasers, made some effort to secure the taking up of tracts by persons outside of, even across the seas from, England, and in some cases indulged those of a particular nationality by putting their acres together in rather large districts apart from other people's. The earliest instance of this was for a race almost without a taint of Anglo-Saxon blood, speaking a language very different from English, but in closer political union than the Scotch or the Irish with the Crown and Parliament of England. Before coming over to Pennsylvania, Penn, according to a memorial of the inhabitants of the Welch Tract (*Pennsylvania Archives,* Vol. I, p. 108), stipulated with his purchasers from Wales and, as it elsewhere appears, certain purchasers, probably Welshmen, from Herefordshire, Shropshire, and Cheshire that they should have their lands lying together, and that within the bounds of the district thus formed, all causes, quarrels, crimes, and titles should be determined by men of their own language. On arriving, he issued a warrant for 40,000 acres, and accordingly what was supposed to be that quantity was set apart as the "Welch Tract," taking in the present townships of Haverford, Radnor, Lower Merion, &ct., where geographical names from the British principality are found to-day. About eighty settlements had been made by the latter part of 1690, when the Commissioners of Property summoned one of the purchasers to show cause why the part not portioned off or settled and improved should not be treated as forfeited, and be disposed of as other unallotted land in the province. The Commissioners wished each purchaser who had not taken out a patent under the usual quit rent, to do so, and required a speedy compliance, declaring the memorial presented by Griffith Owen and others in answer insufficient. The Welsh on 3rd mo. 2, 1691, stated their willingness to pay the future quit rent, but not the past, on the whole 40,000 acres, but this was declared not satisfactory. Thomas Allen Glenn, in *"Merion in the Welsh Tract,"* says that soon afterwards the Welsh agreed to pay the entire back rent of the whole tract, but the minutes of the Commissioners for 4, 27, 1691, speak of the repeating of the old offer. The Commissioners answered that it was too late to change the decision, and that the matter had been settled. Thus considerable land within the tract was confirmed to persons not Welsh. The racial isolation of the chief immigrants representing the ancient Britons was somewhat bridged over by their being of a social class having genealogical charts showing a line of descent from the Norman barons or kings, and thus in touch with the history of England, and, as to most of the individuals, taught the medium of communication with the people beyond the twelve shires of Wales. The tenants or servants of these freeholders and the free countrymen who followed them made the Welsh settlers quite numerous by 1700.

There was another Welsh Tract in Penn's dominions, viz: 30,000 acres, mostly within the present limits of Delaware, bought by Welsh Baptists in 1703, but this settlement was not accorded any independence of the county authority.

A more successful project of putting a foreign district in the Province was connected with the early arrival of some German-speaking persons from Crefeld or from within the borders of the Netherlands. The place for their residence was called Germantown (now within the City of Philadelphia), and the Bailiffs, Burgesses, and Commonalty of German Towne were incorporated by patent from Penn dated Aug. 12, 1689, and issued under the great seal of the Province on 3, 30, 1691, with power to hold market, impose fines, &ct., but the original settlers and those who soon joined them, although long intermarrying among themselves, were connected in trade, and sympathetic in religion, with the people surrounding the little township, and became English in everything but pedigree and, perhaps, some peculiarities of disposition.

Penn early hoped that the French Protestants in England and elsewhere would join in the colonization, and to the poorer ones among them, he was looking more particularly for renters, who might become purchasers, instead of purchasers at once for cash down. It is said that Anthony Duché came over in the ship with him. Without being part of a projected French community or separate group of settlers, others of the race, although perhaps not of the religion, followed. Among them was Charles De la Noe, of whom Penn, calling him "the French minister," speaks in 1685 as intending to come over with servants as a vigneron, and whose will, calling him "minister," is dated 7mo. 11, 1686, and was probated in the same year, giving all his real and personal estate in the Province to Jacob Pelkison of the County of Philadelphia, merchant, who may have been a religious exile. Watson, the Annalist, was inclined to identify De la Noe as the "old priest in Philadelphia" mentioned in Penn's letter of 1686 to Harrison, and to conclude from the word "priest," which Penn applied as well to the Anglican clergy, that De la Noe was a Roman Catholic. Andrew Doz was at one time Penn's vigneron.

After Penn's return to England from his first visit to America, Sir Mathias Vincent, Kt., of Islington, Middlesex, and Dr. Daniel Coxe, who was one of King Charles II's physicians, became interested in establishing a settlement of French Protestants in Pennsylvania. These two speculators, as well as Major Robert Thompson of Newington Green, Middlesex, bought 10,000 acres each, the deeds bearing date April 20, 1686. All were located within a large tract which on Holme's map is appropriated to Vincent, Coxe, Adriaen Vroesen, and Benjamin Furly, but in which Thompson's purchase took the place of those of Vroesen and Furly. The tract lies on the Schuylkill within the present Chester County, and is crossed by French Creek, doubtless so called in memory of the people early coming there, and includes the present townships of Chester County called East and West Vincent in memory of Sir Mathias. Dr. Coxe, after getting some French Protestants and perhaps other immigrants, abandoned the project for schemes in South Carolina and New Jersey, and sold out in 1691 to certain persons called the West Jersey Society. Vincent executed articles of agreement on Sep. 13, 1686, with Capt. Jacques Le Tort, and, on Sep. 18, with Gousee Bonnin. There is preserved among the MSS. of the Historical Society of Pennsylvania the certificate in French from Le Sauvage, minister, dated at London, Jany. 1, 1686 (probably N. S.), that le Sieur Jaques Le Tort, native of France, aged thirty-five years, reared in "our Religion" (Reformed), was some time member of the flock at Alençon, and at the date was desiring employment under the Elector of Brandenburg. Apparently on failing to obtain this employment, or diverted by the opportunity of a career in the New World, he, when making the agreement with Vincent, was bringing over, at the suggestion of Coxe, a number of French Protestants. Several families of them settled on Vincent's land. Nicole Godin, a native of London, whose father had come from Paris, was brought over "with a French gentleman who came hither upon the account of Dr. Cox (*sic*)," probably Le Tort. Possibly Peter and Richard Bezellon (often spelt Bizalion) were brought over at the same time. It is stated that the emigrants led to the region by Le Tort deserted, but that he remained until 1696. On a voyage to England, he was captured by the French, but he came back to the Province. The sons and executors of Vincent and of his wife conveyed on Dec. 30, 1698, the 10,000 acres to Joseph Pike, subject to the aforesaid agreements with Le Tort and Bonnin, and to 10*s*. quit rent. Le Tort and his son of the same name, as well as Godin and the two Bezellons, figured for many years as traders with the Indians. Although a Protestant and a native of London and son of an English mother, Capt. James (Jacques) Le Tort the younger, was at times an object of suspicion because his father had been French.

When Penn received the charter for Pennsylvania, the scattered residents north of what is now Delaware included a number of natives of the British Isles. So great was the stream of people immigrating under him, and in it so largely did the Anglo-Saxon element predominate, that by 1688 Pennsylvania was already a colony practically of Englishmen. For thirty years longer, this stream was replenished from England proper: so that afterwards the population of the thickly settled part of the Province was so thoroughly English that it could not be affected by the Scotch Irish or the Germans, commonly called the "Pennsylvania Dutch," when those semi-Scots and those Palatinates and Swiss took possession of the mountainous region. Separate chapters will be devoted to such: we will now confine ourselves to the condition and ideas of the element dominant throughout the time of this history.

Penn had contemplated as his holy experiment a Quaker colony, within which all religions should be tolerated. While he made laws with the latter object, freeing the planters from tithes, and from any requirement to frequent or maintain any worship contrary to their own mind, and permitted any Christian to hold office, he induced to immigrate from Europe such numbers of his co-religionists as gave them an enormous preponderance during the rest of that century, whether or not we include after 1692 the Separatist Quakers. Meetings for worship had been held on the Delaware before Penn received the royal grant. Those worshipping at the Falls of the River and at Chester united in a Monthly Meeting at the latter place before his first arrival in the Province. A Monthly and a Quarterly Meeting at Philadelphia were established in 1682, and, under the latter, there were started in the following year Monthly Meetings at Radnor and Abington. Bucks Quarterly Meeting started with Falls and Middletown Monthly Meetings and in 1684 Darby and Concord Monthly Meetings were established under Chester Quarterly Meeting. The Quarterly Meetings within Pennsylvania associated with those in New Jersey and Maryland in a Yearly Meeting, which, first held in Burlington on 6, 31, 1681, was arranged in 1685 to alternate at Philadelphia and Burlington, and finally in 1760 was fixed at Philadelphia.

The earliest meeting-house erected within the limits of the capital city of the Province was on Delaware Front Street about 60 ft. N. of Arch, and was probably what was known as the "boarded meeting-house," from its material: a brick building, known as "Bank Meeting" or "Meeting on Delaware Side," was soon put on its site. A meeting-house at the Centre, presumably on the lot intended by Penn for it at Twelfth and High Streets, was commenced in 1685, completed in 1689, and torn down after 1700. The "great meeting house" of the period of this history was at the S. W. cor. Market and Delaware Second streets, begun in 12th month, 1695, and used from 6th month following, and pulled down in 1755, to give place to a larger structure (George Vaux's article on *Early Friends Meeting-Houses* written for centennial of Fourth and Arch Meeting).

By the time of the English Revolution, the "Children of the Light," as they first called themselves, or "Quakers," as they were nicknamed, or "Friends," as they themselves came to speak of those composing their

Society, had been gathering together for about forty years, and had had an organization for more than half that period. The distinguishing doctrine was as to the Inner Light, and led those confident of or seeking direction by that Light to shut themselves off from the distractions of the world, such as music, the fine arts, bright colors, the flattery paid to rank, luxury, etiquette, &ct., and to reject sacraments, priesthood, ritual, and even to some extent the Protestants' dependence upon the Bible. Rather as afterthoughts came the peculiarities most popularly known: the refusal to take an oath, the non-support of ministers, the avoidance of bloodshed, and the wearing of a certain garb. All these peculiarities seem to have been pretty generally adopted among the Quakers by the year 1688. The garb of course has been changed from time to time, the Quakers of that year, at least in America, probably wearing the dress of English tradespeople with an avoidance of ornament. Penn had soon found that wearing a sword, as was the fashion among men of his station in life, made him unpleasantly conspicuous at the meetings, and his wig is described as a small circle to cover the baldness resulting from imprisonment without a barber, and later as an inexpensive article to keep head and ears warm.

How far was carried the discouragement of music and painting is shown in two instances. The Philadelphia Monthly Meeting of 8th month, 1696, hearing that Walter Long had sold Jews-harps, sent to admonish him to take them back, refund the money, and return the Jews-harps whence they came. The Meeting sent also to speak to the widow Culcop to hand over those which she had bought from Long. Long agreed to sell no more, and take back those sold, and stand half the loss. About fifty years later, when, in boyhood, Benjamin West, who was born near the site of Swarthmore College was showing a talent for painting, it was a serious question among the Quakers influential with his parents whether it would be right to permit the exercise of his skill. Fortunately the weightiest appreciated that the talent was God-given. Perhaps the world owes to the Quaker predilection for the matter of fact rather than the imaginative the revolution which West made in the portrayal of modern battles, when he refused to dress General Wolfe and the Indians as Roman soldiers.

Before the Keithian separation, to be narrated in a special chapter, there was no lasting congregation assembled in Pennsylvania outside of the Society of Friends and the Church of Sweden, except two little groups—hardly congregations—of Baptists, one being at Cold Spring, Bucks County, which was established under Rev. Thomas Dungan from Rhode Island about the year 1682, and the other on the Pemmapecka (or Pennypack) Creek in Philadelphia County, of which latter group Samuel Jones and some persons named Eaton had come about 1686 from the Baptist Congregation of Rev. Henry Gregory in Radnorshire followed by John Baker from the congregation at Kilkenny, Ireland, and Samuel Vaus from England. Elias Keach, son of the celebrated English Baptist, Rev. Benjamin Keach, was ordained by Dungan, baptized John Watts and several others, and became in Jany., 1687-8, minister at Pennypack, afterwards going to England, and taking charge of a congregation there. John Holmes, said to have been from Somersetshire, and some time in the West Indies, and to have arrived in Pennsylvania in 1686, who married the widow of Dr. Nicholas More, seems to have been the most conspicuous Baptist layman in the colony before 1700.

The cost of maintaining non-Quaker services was deterring. Quakerism had financial advantages independent of numerical strength. The Quakers felt no call to set apart a place for hallowed uses, and could meet in private houses until those attending were too numerous to be so accommodated, and too numerous to feel the cost divided among them of buying and building and occasionally warming: and the Quakers paid no salaries to their ministers. When the Society of Friends had the only religious gatherings in a locality, in fact when Quaker meetings were the only gatherings of any sort, the Society was likely to gain accessions. Also we must notice the fact that Deists and Roman Catholics would find it less troublesome to masquerade as Quakers than as any other Protestants, being required only to sit still in meetings, where no sacraments were administered, and rarely, if ever, a chapter in the Bible was read. When the civil authorities relaxed the persecution of Quakers, or when public opinion was tolerant of them, as was not the case with either those who denied Christ, or those who acknowledged the supremacy of a foreign ecclesiastic, some infidels and Papists, no doubt, let themselves be supposed to be Quakers, there being no formality involving a profession of faith. The remark applies more particularly to the growth of Quakerism in other regions than Pennsylvania, and is not to be understood as impugning the sincerity of any of the ministers here or elsewhere.

From 1688 to 1692, the Monthly and Quarterly Meetings in Pennsylvania itself, although it was not so in Delaware, were practically the organization of the Province ecclesiastically as much as the Governor and freemen represented in Council and Assembly were the organization secularly. During those years, and for some time afterwards, the leaders in the former organization were leaders in the latter. It was natural that the spiritual relationship through which the emigrants had first known of one another should be so reflected in their civil government as to make it a theocracy. By popular choice, the Quaker ministers took a more important part in the temporal business of the infant commonwealth than by custom or statute the bishops did in England. This union of capacities in the same individuals, whereby retributive justice was to be enforced by those who were to preach and exemplify meekness, long suffering, and forgiveness, was very awkward for them. Even when the ministers were seldom members of the Council or Assembly, but those bodies were largely, sometimes entirely, composed of those who had scruples against war, the reference of the question of participation in military measures to those bodies worked badly for the group of British colonies, and for the empire of which this community was a part.

The Society of Friends had been recruited from those social classes which were considerably above George Fox, its recognized Founder, a shoemaker, and considerably below Robert Barclay, its great Apologist, almost a noble, descended in the female line from the Gordons and the first King James of Scotland. It became the Pennsylvania Assembly's boast, as expressed on Dec. 18, 1706, that "this Province was not at first settled, as some others were, either at the charge of the Crown or of any private man; nor was it peopled with the purges of English prisons, but by men of sobriety and substance, who were induced chiefly by the Constitution which by contract with the Proprietary was to be established as that the purchasers and adventurers were to have greater privileges than they enjoyed in their native countries." Of course, there were persons brought over at other's expense and even without their own volition, as some of the servants and sailors, but a number who came as servants or sailors were very shortly afterwards to be described as property-holders or officers. When, in 1685, a large number —Penn says, about 1000—of Monmouth's rebels were to be transported, Penn, before Oct. 2, begged and obtained twenty as a present from King James. It would be interesting to identify these. It may be confidently asserted that they welcomed the diversion to Penn's dominions, and obtained with their safety a fair position in life: and the same may have been the fate of several runaways, who came certainly "to have greater privileges" than where they had been residing. So the exceptions to the Assembly's generalization were few.

On the other hand, Fox's only visit to the Delaware was in 1672, Barclay never saw it, Penn can not truly be called a settler, and, as a rule, the wealthiest and the most important Quakers did not transfer themselves to this "land of promise;" in fact, as we learn from Hugh Roberts's letter to Penn (*Penna. Mag. Hist.*, Vol. XVIII, p. 205), many Friends disapproved of the movement. The richest of the Quakers who came were probably Robert Turner, some time a merchant in Dublin (ancestor of the Rawle family), Samuel Carpenter, some time in the West Indies, and Edward Shippen, some time a merchant in Boston. Turner and Carpenter were among the first purchasers, and came in the earliest years of William Penn's rule: Penn agreed in 1690 to sell to Shippen for 100*l*. about 250 acres adjoining Philadelphia on the south, nearly all of which afterwards descended to his family, but he did not come until in or after 1693, in which year it is said that a meteor had been seen in Boston, and had been interpreted by some inhabitants as a Divine warning to be more active against Baptists and Quakers, so that Shippen felt that it would be pleasanter outside of Massachusetts. Turner was perhaps less rich than Carpenter or Shippen: Carpenter was ultimately obliged to sacrifice much property: while Shippen, "the biggest man," and afterwards celebrated for "the biggest house and the biggest coach," was hardly exalted much above ordinary men of property by the fortune of 10,000*l*, which he is said to have brought on arrival, multiplied as was in those days its present purchasing value. Thomas Lloyd, for whom a royal descent has been traced, had no prestige on account of it. In prominence as an apostle of the doctrines, George Keith alone of the settlers could be classed with Fox, Barclay, and Penn. Thus there came men who had lived at one time under the English Commonwealth, pious, self respecting, and, except when indentured as servants, independent, all, including many of their "help," sprung from early surroundings of no great variety, none looked up to except for their "gift" of the ministry, and such really of secondary importance in the sect at large. To be sure, counting both the Quakers and non-Quakers, the settlers of Pennsylvania in Penn's day above the grade of day laborers averaged as high in the matter of original worldly station as the emigrants above the grade of day laborers to other parts of the United States. A different impression may have been received from particular items, and from the talk about the "cavaliers" of "the Old Dominion" and the lords of manors in the land of the "Knickerbockers" and the religious exiles among the progenitors of the Carolina "chivalry:" but it should be borne in mind that nearly every lord, baronet, and knight who went to Virginia died without issue male, that the prefix "van," which looks so much like the aristocratic "de" or "von," was used in America as a rule to introduce the name of the place from which the immigrant came, instead of the estate of his ancient ancestors, and that the Huguenots who crossed the ocean except a few petty "seigneurs" were tradespeople or mechanics. It can be shown that the immigrant ancestor of nearly every one of the first families of those colonies where subsequently there was a following of fashion, had his equal among those contemporaries whose children or grandchildren came to the region of Quaker plainness. Yet the summary can be made that the emigrants from the British Isles hither, except some Welsh gentlemen of little or no estate, nearly all came from a worldly station one or more degrees below the poorer gentry.

Thanks to the political and religious excitation in every British community and the number of schools partly free within reach, mental development and literary information were not engrossed by those in higher station. A lower class had produced John Bunyan and Cardinal Wolsey; while Shakspeare could not, if Bacon could, be said to have belonged to a higher. No small number of polemic and didactic pamphlets came from the ranks of the Quakers; and even such a mere local celebrity as Caleb Pusey, in an answer to George Keith, wrote like a great theologian. The first printing press in the part of the world between Massachusetts and Mexico was set up in Philadelphia, before this history opens. The printer was William Bradford, a Quaker from Yorkshire, who had worked for Andrew Sowle in London. In Bradford's pamphlets appear Greek and Hebrew letters. While many of the Welsh who came over were physicians, a number of the English were schoolmasters, and it was a time when Latin and Greek and Hebrew were more commonly studied in schools than at present. Of course, there were not the same number of matriculates of English colleges as had gone to New England as Puritan divines two or three generations before. Nevertheless, some of the early Friends in Pennsylvania, were graduates of colleges in the British Isles, and had been ministers of non-Quaker congregations. An ex-monk, John Gray, alias Tatham, of the Benedictine congregation at St. James's, came over, and joined Charles Pickering and others in obtaining a survey of ore lands. The King ordered Gray to return. Penn declared the survey irregular, perhaps because contravening the rule to keep the ore land for the Proprietary. Penn was accused, by those who wished to prove him a Papist in disguise, of having the aforesaid ex-monk kidnapped and taken over to England, to be delivered to those whom he had forsaken. However, he declared Penn not guilty, and returned to Pennsylvania before Oct. 20, 1688, and was afterwards an important man in New Jersey, where he lived with a wife Elizabeth. A son survived him. While the Established Churches of the Old World had institutions of learning, and the anti-prelatists of New England had Harvard College, the Society of Friends did not train young men for the profession of preaching; so the scholars in divinity in Pennsylvania and Delaware were to be looked for among non-Quakers. In fact, the immigrants or sojourners from Continental or Scandinavian Europe included most of the men who had taken any University course.

The Quakers, moreover, tried to adjust disputes between one another, the Meetings hearing and acting upon complaints against a member, even by persons not in good standing in the Society, and it was a violation of Gospel order to obtain satisfaction at law, unless private appeal to the delinquent and the decision of examiners appointed by the Meeting had been in vain. So the Quakers rather looked askance at those who argued in court. We know of a Welsh attorney, Griffith Jones, in Kent County, with the reputation of an orator, evidently the person of that name who headed a petition to Sir Edmund Andros (*Penna. Archives,* 2nd Series, Vol. VII, p. 815), closing with the words: "That age may crowne your Snowy haires with Cæsar's honours and with Nestor's yeares." There was contemporary with him another Griffith Jones, a merchant in Philadelphia, who was a Quaker. When, in 1695, the Churchmen of the province got up a petition to have the services of a minister and the right to arm for defence, the Welsh attorney Griffith Jones was supposed to have written the petition, so he was probably

a Churchman. At that time there seem to have been
but two other lawyers in Penn's dominions, viz: John
Moore, a Churchman, and David Lloyd, who had read
at the Temple, and who, Gov. Gookin relates, had been
bred under Lord Jefferies, but, marrying in Pennsylvania, had turned Quaker. Burton Alva Konkle has
prepared a *Life of David Lloyd,* to which the reader
is referred when the account in this book of Lloyd and
his political party and their labors does not seem exhaustive or sufficiently laudatory. What grade Moore
or Lloyd had in their profession at home, we do not
know. About a half a dozen persons trained to the
law came over about the time of Penn's second visit.
Finally, Acts of Assembly made provision for a body
of attorneys admitted by the courts to practise.

Those non-Quakers who might have claimed to be the
patricians of the immigration in Penn's time were
mostly his relatives or connections or the companions
in arms of his father, glad to get public office or a cheap
habitation. Of the Quakers or non-Quakers who came
before 1688, several had been captains in the navy:
William Markham, the first Deputy Governor, William
Crispin, one of the three commissioners appointed on
Sep. 30, 1681, and Thomas Holme, the first Surveyor-General. There was also Major Jasper Farmer from
Ireland (see early editions of Burke's *Landed Gentry*).
Farmer, who is said, probably incorrectly, not to have
reached our shores, died in 1685. He and his son
Jasper, who had bought together 5000 acres, received
a patent in 1684 for land fronting upon the Schuylkill,
covering the greater part of what is now Whitemarsh
Township, Montgomery County. Having brought over
a number of servants, the family long lived there. About
the time of Penn's second visit, Robert Assheton, of
Salford, Lancashire, whose mother was Penn's near relation, and whose father was a Deputy Herald, was induced to come to take a court clerkship. Capt. Samuel

Finney, Robert Assheton's kinsman, is said to have accompanied Penn on this second voyage. Finney had become rich in Barbados, and, after returning to England, had built Fulshaw Hall in Cheshire about 1684, and had raised a troop for the Prince of Orange, and had afterwards been a merchant at Chetham Hill near Manchester. His son and heir-apparent, Captain John, who had been cornet in Captain Samuel's troop, and had afterwards served in Flanders, accompanied him to America, apparently from political ambition, which was doomed not to be fully satisfied. Samuel Finney and several of his children made Pennsylvania their permanent home, but John, after being one of the Governor's Council, returned to England, and died at Fulshaw Hall in 1728.

How such patrician stock except the Asshetons soon sank in importance is illustrated in the posterity of Markham, so long the head of the Colony. He used as a seal, with an impalement which has not been identified, the ancient arms borne by those of his name. His father's first name and career, we do not know, but the mother was a sister of Admiral Penn. Apparently older than the Founder, Markham had begun service in the navy before the taking in 1658 of Dunkirk, being in the fleet which rode before it on that occasion, and subsequently had been six years with Sir John Lawson, and in the fleet which brought Charles II back to England, and at the attack on Algiers, and in the Dutch wars of 1665-6 and 1672-3. Evidently his career had not only betokened ability, which seemed to fit him to organize Penn's government, but had given him some acquaintances and influence, causing him to be sent back to England in the summer of 1683 as Penn's agent in the boundary dispute. Later pages will give Markham's official career after his return. He married twice at least, an early wife being apparently the Mrs. Markham mentioned in Pepys's *Diary* as twice in

THE PEOPLE. 145

Pepys's company at dinner or supper in 1666, and first figuring thus: "Aug. 6, 1666, . . . Nan at Sir W. Pen's lately married to one Markeham, a kinsman of Sir W. Pen's—a pretty wench she is." This does not necessarily mean that she had been a servant. William Markham had a daughter Ann, who in January, 1699-1700, is spoken of as his only child, and whom he, probably when coming to America in 1681, left in the care of William Penn, for she was seven years one of Penn's household. Late in life, Markham married Joanna —————, a widow, whose daughter married Jacob Regnier, a lawyer in New York. Joanna Markham had a nephew Theodore Colby. Ann Markham married a sea captain, James Brown, who will be mentioned as suspected of piracy. They had three children. Markham leaving what property he had to the stepmother, and the latter removing to New York, and Brown dying, Ann followed to that city, and tried to support herself as a midwife. Her claims made against certain property after her stepmother's death being rejected, the Proprietaries, out of compassion, granted something to this relative. Two of her children died at an early age without issue; the survivor, Joanna, married John Barker, but appears to have been the last of Markham's family, when, about 1767, the Proprietaries pensioned her. Her board being paid to Penelope Healy, Mrs. Barker was still living at the beginning of the American Revolution. A social club in Philadelphia and one or two unimportant railroad stations perpetuate the name of Markham.

To persons of higher social rank than those whom we have mentioned, a frontier inhabited by such serious, utilitarian, and disapproving people as the Quakers, afforded no attractions, and could only be a place of refuge. Acrelius tells us of Baron Isaac Baner, a Swede, who, after being in the service of William III of England, settled in Philadelphia in 1695, and afterwards removed to the Lower Counties, where he tried to support himself at first by keeping a small store, and where he married, had children, and died in 1713, leaving a destitute family. His relatives in Sweden, a Lieutenant-General and a Royal Councillor, sent for the children in 1727, and, Deputy Governor Gordon escorting them to the ship, they sailed by way of London. The wife of Sir Robert Newcomen, Bart., unhappy in her married life, came over in 1702, and, under the name of Mary Phillips, boarded with Penn's cousins the Asshetons. She was a daughter of Arthur Chichester, 2nd Earl of Donegal, by his Countess, who had married, 2ndly, Penn's cousin Richard Rooth. Incognito, Lady Newcomen set no fashions, and on the delay of her remittance had the prospect of doing ironing— however, Sir Robert ultimately allowed her £50 sterling per annum. She went back in 1712. She had six children by Sir Robert.

When it became common for the needy, the criminal, or the troublesome to come or be sent over, and to reimburse those who transported him or her by being sold as a laborer for a term of years, there was, as an involuntary resident, James Annesley, his assertion of noble parentage and of relatives' knavery being disregarded. A book called *The Memoirs of an Unfortunate Young Nobleman returned from a thirteen years slavery in America,* published in London in 1743, tells, with some disguise of names, a marvellous tale of his early experiences, his life in Penn's dominions, the suicide of an Indian girl in love with him, the behavior of his master's daughter, &ct., all of which is condensed in the *Gentleman's Magazine,* Vols. XIII & XIV. Neglected by the profligate Arthur, 4th Lord Altham, who was pretty surely his father, the subject of the memoir, by the agency of his uncle Richard, who assumed the title, was taken from squalid surroundings at the father's death, and decoyed, being about thirteen years old, into going aboard a ship which sailed for Philadelphia on April 30, 1728. Consigned to the captain to be disposed of as a servant, Annesley, on arrival, was bought by a farmer. In an attempt to escape from drudgery and privation, Annesley fell in with a man and woman eloping from her husband, attended by a servant, and was captured with them, and was sent to the pillory. Annesley, reclaimed by his master, finally, in 1739, escaped to Jamaica, and there, in September, 1740, enlisted as a common sailor on a man-of-war. Through a lieutenant, who had been a schoolmate, the identity was revealed to the Captain, and through him to Admiral Vernon, who released Annesley from his enlistment, and sent him to England to recover his rights. His uncle, meanwhile, at the death of a cousin, had taken the additional titles of Earl of Anglesey in the peerage of England and Viscount Valentia in that of Ireland, which titles, as well as that of Baron Altham in the peerage of Ireland, should have gone to James, if, as he claimed, he was the son of Lord and Lady Altham. James Annesley was welcomed by many people in Ireland, and his uncle was disposed to compromise with him, and had him taught French; but, on James killing a man in "chance medley," the uncle strove to have him convicted of murder, as a way of getting rid of him; but he was triumphantly acquitted. James brought ejectment for certain Irish property, and, although the evidence given rather pointed to his having been the 4th Lord's bastard, the verdict of the jury on Nov. 25, 1743, was in his favor; but, lacking the money to prosecute his claims thoroughly, and in face of legal obstructions, he never obtained wealth or title. He died (*Gent's Mag.*) Jan. 3, 1760, leaving children, but his two sons died a very few years later and presumably without issue.

Being settled at a date in the history of the Anglo-Saxon race when class distinctions and privileges had weakened to a considerable extent, and by persons among whom there were no great inequalities of birth, and because of the brotherly feeling of a band of religionists, and still more because of the sentiments of the sect, Pennsylvania was less affected than other colonies by the idea of caste. The Quakers were levellers. They had wished to get rid of the vain distinctions of the world. While we need not credit family traditions of a Quaker ancestor taking up a humble trade, as a matter of religion, when belonging to a class thought to be considerably above workers at such trade, yet it is a fact that among Quakers there was not a social stratification according to business occupation. They were not communists or socialists or equalizers of private wealth, or such as scrupled at the laying up of treasure; and the natural tendency of a Quaker estate when once fairly started was to grow faster than that of a less ascetic owner. Sydney George Fisher has well said that a consistent Quaker could not spend a large fortune except in charity. At the same time, the Meeting supervised a man's conduct in business with the penalty of disownment, quite severe when there were none but Quakers to associate with; and thus extortion, non-payment of debts, reckless speculation, and some tricks of trade were eliminated as sources of riches. By the discountenancing of luxury and show, the difference between the rich and the poor was less observable. It was a long time before Pennsylvania had anything like a "submerged tenth" or pauper class. The industry characteristic of the disciples of Fox, and the rich soil obtained by the purchasers from Penn, combined to provide nearly every settler with enough and to spare. Poverty came only through failure of crops, losses by sea, or bodily injury. A member of Meeting who had lost by misfortune was again started in life, and measures were taken that the children of the poor should have from education and care their chance with others. When into the colony were introduced persons of all grades, habits, and principles, inequalities came inevitably: but as a rule, the rich, however well satisfied with their own or their fathers' moral superiority, were not inclined to assume the appearance of an aristocracy deriving consideration from "carnal" ideas.

The formation of a landed oligarchy was not facilitated in Penn's dominion. Mention has been made how small were the tracts of the first purchasers from William Penn, and how, by the regulations, the retention of a location depended upon its being peopled, and how the tracts of over 5000 acres before very long were cut up.

A resident country gentry conspicuous in respective neighbourhoods by number of acres and mode of life was not established. Except Dr. More, before mentioned, and the Growdons at "Trevose," Bucks County, and one or two others, the first purchasers of as many as 5000 acres, and those who afterwards bought plantations of that size, did not reside upon them. The wealthy men of the province lived in its city with in later times a country place near by, but in size very different from the landed estate of a rural grandee of New York, Virginia, or South Carolina.

The laws of Pennsylvania interfered with the unfairness by which many landed estates have been preserved and increased. In the first place, as to being withheld from creditors, "the Laws agreed upon in England" made all lands and goods liable to pay debts except where there was lawful issue, and then all the goods and one third of the land. This was changed by the Great Law passed at Chester so that, in case of issue, all the goods were liable and half the land, in case the land was bought before the debt was contracted. By various temporary laws and a permanent one of Fletcher's time, all lands were subjected to sale on judgment and execution against the defendant or his heirs, executors, or administrators, but the messuage and plantation on which the defendant was residing was not to be sold until the last, and not until a year after the judgment. When Penn was on his second visit to Pennsylvania, a clause was adopted requiring the personalty to be sold first. In Fletcher's time was introduced the liability of all the real estate as well as personalty of any decedent to sale for payment of debts by the executor or administrator under approval of a court, or by judgment and proceedings of court except where the personal property was sufficient.

There was a remedy, too, against an inheritance increasing in value while the family starved. Following a temporary law of earlier date, Fletcher enacted in 1694 that the widow or administrator of an intestate might, in case of considerable debt or charge of child or children, sell such part of the intestate's lands as the Council or County Court should think fit for paying the debts, educating the children, supporting the widow, and improving the rest of the estate to their advantage.

In the next place, while the English common law tended towards the monopoly of land, the statutes of Pennsylvania almost always required the division of what a man left at his death. By the charter of Charles II, the laws of England were to govern the descent of land and the succession to personalty in Pennsylvania until altered by the Proprietary and freemen. The first enactment to curtail the unfair benefit of primogeniture went into force in April, 1683, providing that the whole estate in the Province and Territories, unless an equal provision had been arranged for with property elsewhere, should go, after payment of debts, one third to the wife, and one third to the children equally, and the other third as the decedent pleased; if his wife were dead, two thirds to the children equally, and one third as he pleased, his debts being first paid, whereas if he died intestate, the estate should go to his wife and children, but if he left neither wife nor child, then to his brothers and sisters or to the children of his brothers and sisters; if there were none, one half to the parents, and the other half to the next of kin; if no parents, the half should go to the Governor, and if no kindred claiming within three years, the other half to the public. This same law, as we see, interfered with the power of a parent to aggrandize one child by disinheriting the rest. As the words of the law did not say what the division should be between wife and children in cases of intestacy, chapter CLXXII, passed in 3mo., 1684, fixed it thus: one third of the lands to the wife during her life, the rest to the children, the eldest son taking a double share: if there were no child, half of the real estate to the wife for life, the rest to the intestate's kin. The limitation upon the right to dispose by will was removed in 1693, when also the right of the children of deceased relations to take their parents' share was recognized, and it was explained that, except where the eldest son was concerned, the division among relations in equal degree should be equal. The right of children of deceased brethren to take the share which their parent would have taken if living, was allowed by act of 1700.

The act of Jany. 12, 1705-6, made the children share the land equally, the widow taking the same share as a child. There was nothing said to limit her interest to a life estate, and apparently she was always allowed to have a fee simple until the act of February 4, 1748–9, prescribed a different construction of the aforesaid law.

There were good reasons why the Quaker province attracted, besides the Quakers and the separatists wishing to be undisturbed in religion, those who were not sure of the means of support at home. Here was good soil, cheap land, a well behaved population, public sentiment in favor of the simplest style of living, no danger from the aborigines, no military service, nothing to pay for a military or ecclesiastical establishment, a government run at the least cost possible, there being no handsome houses provided for the acting Governors, and such acting Governors as received salaries other than occasional sums drawing their pay from William Penn until the XVIIth Century closed. If a man wished to get drunk, or break Sabbath, or have certain sports, he found the laws decidedly "blue;" but it was the era of "blue laws." On the other hand, if his necessities drove him to some small theft, the punishment was lighter than at home: however, it was only after the colony had been in existence a number of years that Pennsylvania was to any degree a resort for persons looking forward to crime.

In due time, among the immigrants of English or Welsh birth or ancestry, the non-Quakers outnumbered the Quakers. Differing from the latter in matters of religion, and at times in earnest dispute and bitter anger against them over certain measures of civil government, yet these non-Quakers attempted only sporadically to lessen the Quaker's share in legislation, and largely combined with them on questions not interfering with the Church of the one or the conscience of the other, and made lasting the impression upon the community of the social and political principles of the co-religionists of the Founder of the Colony.

CHAPTER VI

A REPUBLICAN FEUDATORY.

Powers granted by Charles II—Penn's attitude as to war—Penn's claim to greatness—His suggestion of Union of the Colonies and of a Parliament of Europe—His character and abilities—Covenant for a Democracy—Delaware taken into Union—Naturalization—General Suffrage—Frame of 1683—Religious freedom—All Christians eligible to office—The theological tests in England—"Solemn promise" of witnesses—Unsettled laws—Absentee rule by the Penns—Thomas Lloyd and other deputies—Fortune inherited by William Penn and his first wife—Too small for his undertaking—Philip Ford—Receipts and indebtedness—Penn very prominent in England—James II and the Quakers—Penn at the time of the Revolution.

The Charter of King Charles II not only made William Penn and his heirs and assigns feudal lords of the soil, but added an authority in him and his heirs like that of Viceroy. The clause directly granting powers of legislation did not extend them to his assigns, although the clause providing for certain laws of England to be temporarily in force, said that they should be so until altered by him, his heirs and assigns, and by the freemen, their delegates or deputies or the greater part of them. Penn or his heirs or his or their Deputies and Lieutenants could ordain and, under his or their seals, publish any laws for raising money or other public or private purpose with the consent of the majority of the freemen or of their deputies, whom Penn and his heirs were authorized to assemble in such way as to them would seem best. The laws were to be consonant to reason, and as near as conveniently could be to those of England, and were to be transmitted within five years after enactment to the Privy Council in England, and, sitting in Council, the King was to have the right within six months to declare the law void as inconsistent with his prerogative or the faith and allegiance due to him. This was liberally construed in practice as to both the time which the English government would take in examination of a law, and the grounds on which the Sovereign would reject it: the Acts of Assembly were often sent in the first place to the Lords and others forming the Committee or the Board for the affairs of trade and plantations, and by them referred, in whole or for certain questions, to the Attorney-General or other law officer, and the King's decision was made after the formal presentation to him, upon the receipt of the law officer's long delayed opinion, and upon the completion of a representation by the aforesaid Committee or Board; and the rejection would take place for any matter of form or of policy that did not commend itself to these examiners. Thereupon remedial legislation would fail until a new act avoiding the obnoxious phraseology or details could be passed. There would be uncertainty for several years. The time consumed in communication in those days between the colony and England was but a part of the period during which the colonists were obliged to wait. Penn told his people once that the laws lay unreported upon by the Attorney-General for want of a big fee to induce him to take them up. On the other hand, a law was to be in operation until rejected by the King; so the local enacting powers took advantage of the allowance of five years for presenting an act. often passing one to be in force for only a year, or for less than five years, or repealing and reenacting one, so that the five years would begin to run from the last reenactment, and sometimes, when an act had been disallowed by the Sovereign in Council, it was passed afresh, and put in execution, and the process repeated after a later disallowance. Richard West, one of the King's law officers, being asked for his opinion, advised the Commissioners for Trade on March 25, 1719, that there was nothing in the Charter to Penn to prevent the reenactment by the Province of disallowed laws. West also advised to the effect that the six months to which the King was limited for examination and disallowance of laws were to be computed from the day on which they were delivered to the Privy Council, but not from their being delivered to the Board of Trade, unless simultaneously duplicates were delivered to the Privy Council.

Upon emergencies, when the freemen could not be gathered together, the Royal Charter allowed Penn and his heirs or their magistrates and officers to make ordinances for the preservation of the peace and better government of the people, consonant to reason, and, as near as might be, agreeable to the laws of England, but not affecting any person's life, limb, or property: the laws of England as to felonies, and regulating property and the descent of lands or succession to goods and chattels, were to remain in force until altered by Penn, his heirs or assigns, and the freemen, as before stated.

Penn and his heirs were to execute the laws made with the consent of the freemen. Penn and his heirs and his or their Deputies and Lieutenants had the power to appoint judges, magistrates, and officers, including those for probate of wills, and granting of administration, and to administer justice by tribunals subject to an appeal to the King, and also to pardon all crimes except treason and wilful murder, and to grant reprieves in those cases until the King's pleasure were known. The appeal from the decisions of courts and the reprieve of condemned murderers seem never to have taken place. Penn and his heirs and assigns could divide the region into counties &ct., incorporate cities and boroughs, constitute fairs and markets, and fix the only ports of entry.

There was one power granted to the Proprietaries by the King which it seemed inconsistent for a Quaker to accept, and which had much to do with the willingness of the Founder and his family to govern through a non-Quaker deputy: William Penn and his heirs and assigns, acting by themselves or their captains or other officers, were authorized to muster soldiers, and make war on the King's enemies, and put them to death by the laws of war, or save them at pleasure, and act as a Captain-General. The Frame of Government granted by Penn in 1683, hereinafter mentioned, was silent as to the exercise of this power, except in prohibiting the acting Governor from performing any act relating to "safety" without the consent of the Provincial Council. It was apparently without waiting for such consent that the Founder of Pennsylvania, the most illustrious politically of all Quakers, ordered the fort at New Castle to fire upon the Marylanders coming in force to demand possession. He did not stop to think that, if bloodshed by princes was abominable, it seldom had less excuse morally than his own claim to the land in question.

It should here be said, throwing light on many acts of William Penn, that he was not a rigid moralist on the subject of war. He believed it contrary to the spirit of Christianity, and he did not, like some Quakers, make a distinction between offensive and defensive use of "the carnal weapon," and he sacrificed bright prospects by withdrawing from the career of a soldier, and he wrote about the advantages of turning the population to the arts of peace; but there have not been found by the present writer any utterances by Penn that killing in battle is murder. Penn was, some will say, too practical, others will say, too illogical to view all participation in a national struggle as sinful. It might almost be said that his writings justify the Quakers' refusal to bear arms very much on a par with their peculiarity of saying "thee" and "thou." He conformed to the practice of his peaceable sect, but he did not follow out the theory as many others did. He seems to have had no objection to non-Quakers fighting for him. His bringing the Delawareans into political union with the Pennsylvanians may have been with the astute policy of having a "fighting half" among his people: he subsequently spoke regretfully of the loss of this by the disunion.

This difference in view between Penn and the ordinary Quakers, as the world associates the latter with non-resistance, brings up the whole personality, character, abilities, and ideas of the first Proprietary, of which there was some disclosure in the preceding chapters; and an estimate of him and his career, such as is generally given after noting the death of the person in question, may be allowed at this point. William Penn is to be called great without reference to qualities or manifestations of the soul, but by a mundane criterion, viz: the affecting of the lives of many others, a criterion which does not insist upon martial deeds or the surmounting of obstacles, and which does not presuppose any natural superiority of intellect, and which considers the holding, however fortuitous, of a position of power. Although the position and achievements of other persons have prevented Penn from being the greatest man in American history, he is at least the greatest among the founders of English or Dutch colonies. Far more than any other of them, he had an importance in the Mother Country, independent of connection with the New World, a connection which, in his case, has caused his name to be known where the prelates, jurists, statesmen, and generals, possibly even

Marlborough, who were his contemporaries and acquaintances, have been forgotten.

While not the founder of a sect or of a school of thought, Penn was one of most active missionaries and controversialists for a set of religious ideas which spread much more widely than is popularly supposed. The actual result of his labors in this line can not be measured. His learning must have conveyed an impression in intellectual classes outside of the Society of Friends. His defence at trial tended to break down repressive measures against the attendants of Meetings. There is no point in detailing here his work as a preacher and elder: it is of as little general interest as the administration of a particular diocese by Wolsey or Richelieu, with which political ecclesiastics, in the broad meaning of the term "ecclesiastics," Penn is to be classed. His religious views are the least striking thing about him, except as sometimes denying what had been considered Orthodoxy: he generally used the expressions common to spiritually minded Christians. His sufferings for conscience make no tragic scene, unpleasant as were expulsion from Oxford and imprisonments, even if short. Except opportunities in some lines, he lost little by his religion. His closing years were pathetic, but most of his tribulations were from political and financial causes.

The distinction of Penn is in secular affairs. While he was not a forceful ruler, he had remarkable influence over a widely extended variety of human beings, and, while in some matters, like slavery, he was not ahead of his time, he was profound in establishing principles which have come to be recognized as the true bases upon which to build a nation. He gave a code, and held a lordship, in which many abuses in English jurisprudence and property rights were avoided. To be sure, in the actions from which he has received most credit, viz: paying the Indians for lands and allowing freedom

A REPUBLICAN FEUDATORY. 159

of worship, he was scarcely a free agent. It has been shown that, in buying instead of taking the land, he followed the advice of Bishop Compton and the practice on the Delaware. Some secret understanding, too, may have bound Penn, as much as his kindheartedness, to leave the Roman Catholics unmolested; as to Protestants, the Church of Sweden could not be uprooted, the Church of England could not be excluded, and there seemed no point, when he had land to sell, in refusing the money of Presbyterians and Baptists. In details, he gained the Indians' confidence and love. He carried out so well the plan of giving all religious denominations a fair chance that he ultimately failed in his object, a commonwealth under the control of Quakers. Only his care safeguarded, and only he could have safeguarded such a colony as he created, imperilled as it was successively; and the advantages which he gave to the settlers, combined with the goodness of the soil, were the reason that his colony outstripped others. Exactly what measures or Royal actions in England are to be traced to him except the sparing of certain lives, we do not know: but Macaulay describes how this untitled Quaker had the ear of at least one occupant of the throne. Harley, who became Prime Minister, sought through Penn the votes of Quakers at the elections.

The unfollowed suggestions of Penn should give a high notion of his genius. In the line of toleration, which was with him a theory of rightfulness, and no mere expedient, he suggested in James II's reign a division of the royal patronage into thirds for the Anglican Churchmen, the Roman Catholics, and the Dissenters respectively. The share for the King's co-religionists was too great, but any distribution was rejected because the Protestants felt that they were in a life and death struggle.

Penn in 1696 proposed a union of the British colonies in North America, submitting to the Commissioners for

Trade and Plantations a scheme, according to which two delegates from each colony, making twenty persons, would meet once in two years during peace, and oftener in time of war, should be under the presidency of the King's Commissioner, and would adjust differences between Provinces in cases where persons removed to avoid paying debts, where offenders fled justice, of injuries in the matter of commerce, and of ways and means to support safety against public enemies, fixing the quotas of men and expense, and the King's Commissioner would be General or Chief Commander of the forces formed of the quotas. Shall we call Penn the projector of the United States Senate?

His greatest dream—to some extent materialized in the Hague Tribunal, and essentially what we have heard suggested very recently—was a Parliament, or Diet, of Europe, to which disputes between the Powers were to be submitted, and the decisions of which were to be enforced by the other Powers. Thus war would be abolished, except as between the general police force and a delinquent. Co-operation of this kind for this purpose had been suggested previously—see Thomas Willing Balch's pamphlet on *Eméric Crucé;* and it is too much to claim that such a reader as Penn was unaware of this. His own suggestion appeared, and in detail, in 1695 in his *Essay towards the Present and Future Peace of Europe.* The representation in the Parliament was to be based upon a census of the wealth of the countries represented, and it is interesting as showing the relative importance of those countries that he tentatively supposed that the Empire of Germany would have 12 members, France 10, Spain 10, Italy "which comes to France" 8, England 6, Portugal 3, Sweden 4, Denmark 3, Poland 4, Venice 3, the Seven Provinces of United Netherlands 4, the Thirteen Swiss Cantons "and little neighbouring sovereignties" 2, and the Dukedom of Holstein and Courland 1; and if Tur-

A REPUBLICAN FEUDATORY. 161

key and Muscovy were taken in, they each would have 10. The representatives were to sit in a circular chamber, and the presidency should rotate, to preserve equality. The decision was to be by a three fourths vote or at least seven more than half. The vote was to be by ballot, that no potentate inclining to resort to bribery could be sure of getting a bribed member's vote! No power could refuse to submit to this arbitration, and, if any were maintaining an army dangerous to the others, the question could be raised, and the necessary reduction of the army enforced.

Penn urged free trade between all the colonies, in connection with which his letter to the Commissioners for Trade &ct. written in 1700 speaks against the law about transporting wool from one to another, and tells how it was avoided by the purchasing of a thousand sheep with the wool on, and the shearing of them in the province needing the wool, after which the sheep were sold. The matter had little reference to Pennsylvania, where, there being more money than elsewhere in British North America except Boston and New York. the people were already too luxurious to be satisfied with American wool and woolen goods.

In September, 1700, Penn, as Governor of Pennsylvania, met in New York Gov. Nicholson of Maryland, Gov. Hamilton of New Jersey, and the Earl of Bellomont, who was Gov. of New York, Massachusetts, &ct. Penn then suggested as desirable in the colonies: 1st, one standard for foreign coin, so that Boston would not call a piece of eight—i.e. a Spanish "dollar"—six shillings, when New York called it six shillings nine pence, New Jersey and Pennsylvania called it seven shillings eight pence, Maryland, four shillings six pence, and Virginia five shillings; 2nd, a mint for small silver to the denomination of six pence in the City of New York; 3rd, an impost in England on foreign timber, to encourage the exportation of timber from the colonies;

4th, such adjustment of the boundary with the French on the north as would give the English the south side of the St. Lawrence and of the Lakes; 5th, for prevention of runaways, rovers, and fraudulent debtors coming from one province to another for shelter, all provinces to make a uniform law with the same restrictions and penalties; 6th, foreigners coming daily, especially Dutch, Swedes, and French, to inhabit the colonies, a general naturalization law passed in England to allow such of them as declared freemen by Act of Provincial Assembly to enjoy all the rights and liberties of English subjects, except being masters or commanders of vessels; 7th, no appeal to England under £300; 8th, the allowance of expenses and part of the prey to those capturing pirates. The 7th suggestion was or had been adopted. The 6th was observed as calculated to people Penn's own dominion.

If, to have a man's ability recognized, it must be shown that he labored under disadvantages, the reader will see that Penn had a number; and when there is an occasion to criticize his later acts, it must be remembered that he was always short of money.

The character of William Penn, as we see him turn from a Moses into a William the Conqueror, saving, to be sure, the bloody war, and, finally, into a King John Lackland, is the most interesting one made prominent by the Colonial history of the original United States: other characters, which, to be sure, have not been questioned like Penn's, have been exhibited as simple and solid specimens of good or bad qualities with some extraneous setting, which is negligible; but Penn's character requires study because of many sides, complexity, and contradictions. Whatever may surprise those looking for a maltreated innocent, his piety was sincere. He had, indeed, the Christian virtues of forgiveness and taking trouble for others to a degree that made him friends even among former enemies. Becoming a preacher, he remained, when required to meet or correspond with men highly placed, a gentleman, dignified, courteous, punctilious, although independent of his class in opinion, and dressed in a different fashion. In those days of dying feudalism and young and lusty "graft," an "esquire," as a knight's eldest son was called, a lesser noble, as he was classed in other countries, had in England prerogative, leadership, the right to other men's service, &ct.; and we find Penn, as troubles beset him, disinclined to forego, or endeavoring to resume this. Like a feudal baron, he asked his people to come to his financial assistance. His religious career shows activity, determination, and at last a settled responsiveness to the call to seriousness. There had been an interval of gaiety and pleasure, to use no harsher word: but there has been nothing found in his private life after he had been several years in the Society of Friends to brand him a hypocrite. As to financial transactions with individuals, could the acts and plans of all men be disclosed as we are able to see Penn's in the records and in his confidential letters, it is doubtful whether the acts and plans of many would look as clean. No one who reads the list of articles which Penn or his agents gave to the Indians will echo any flippant remark that he got Pennsylvania from them for a few beads. In public affairs, rather than an ideal Quaker, he was something like a Stuart king, due allowances being made for difference in sphere, power, and surrounding sentiment. Starting with the sagacity of James I of England and the early leaning of him and his three successors to religious toleration and the disinclination of nearly all of them to war, Penn kept unworthy or unpopular men in office, strove for taxes, contributions, and loans, sought to change what had been agreed upon, and thought himself the Lord's chosen vessel. As a sufferer for ecclesiastical ideas, Penn would be too much honored by being classed with Charles I, who lost his life, or James II, who lost his crown. Yet if giving up much for one's religion entitles to canonization, Penn has claims. He sacrificed, along with his ease and comfort, a greater position in his day than that of a mere English gentleman. Had he accepted the opinions of the majority, his abilities might have led him to the highest offices. There is a tradition that the Admiral, owing to his son's religion, declined a title of nobility, that of Viscount Weymouth being mentioned. Succeeding to this, his son would no doubt have risen to a higher title: but, outside of the peerage, with the capacity he had shown as a soldier, a law student, a politician, a scholar, and a preacher, and with the "back door" influence he possessed to give him a start, it would be too much to say that a great military command, the lord chancellorship, a seat in the King's Cabinet, or an archbishopric would have been beyond his reach. Living in a corrupt and bellicose age, he was constrained to follow paths for the carrying out of his projects, or for his own safety, which have been thought dark and dirty by good people not so tempted. Intimacy with a Roman Catholic king caused Penn to be suspected of being a Jesuit, and, although he was not of Loyola's Society, the reader has seen an attitude taken in the matter of the boundary explicable only as unscrupulousness for the attainment of a noble and, in Penn's thought, a holy end.

Following the career which he chose, or felt called upon to follow—for he believed himself Divinely sent forth—and meeting the obstacles which nature, society, and church presented, and making the false steps which we can see, he may be summarized as more of a statesman than a saint, a better preacher than a business man, a rather weak ruler, but, considering the people he had to deal with, including kings, Quakers, and Indians, and his general success, we ought finally to say, the greatest of the long line of Pennsylvania politicians.

We can not call him self-seeking: he seems actuated, when asking for power and money, by a sense of duty to others. The reader of history must take to himself the Psalmist's address to the Deity:

"If thou . . . wilt be extreme to mark what is done amiss, . . . who may abide it?" —Prayer Book version of the *De Profundis*.

Later chapters will show how the veto power given to Penn and his heirs and their Deputies and Lieutenants was used as a weapon to protect the Proprietary interests, and how the patronage became an asset of commercial value, both of which effects King Charles II intended in giving the Charter: but in this chapter the reader will see a great exhibition of altruism, an abnegation of power because of belief in human rights, or of desire to do kindness, and somewhat because of broadminded recognition of what would make a colonial project attractive. Penn, after closer acquaintance with kings, found monarchy practicable, thought Charles II a great man, saw what was good in James II, advised the Crown's ministers, and finally acted as a petty duke of an empire: but before all this, Penn had accepted Republican theories. At the end of 1680, he took the power in legislation and as executive with the purpose of making it, or soon afterwards he chose to make it, a conduit pipe through which his colonists would govern themselves. It seems to have been politically necessary to make the government seigniorial in form. Charles II scarcely intended to have a republic set up. He felt that he knew William Penn, and was willing to confide a territory to his discretion, the freemen's consent being necessary for taxes and new laws. Early Penn must have determined to curb his own power. On 2mo. 12, 1681, thirty-nine days after the date of the King's letters patent, Penn expressed to Robert Turner and others his intention: "For the matter of liberty and privilege, I promise that which is extraordinary, and to leave myself and successors no power of doing mischief, that the will of one man may not hinder the good of an whole country. But to publish these things now, and here, as matters stand, would not be wise; and I am advised to reserve that till I come there. . . . let Friends know it, as you are free." The letter is printed in Samuel M. Janney's *Life of William Penn*. The postscript lets us infer that he had similarly expressed himself to "the most eminent Friends here-away," i.e. about London. Perhaps the representations of possible settlers may have carried him later further than he first intended. Rather to excuse him, Markham wrote to Fletcher in 1696 that Penn was obliged to grant the Charter of 1683, or, in other words, the popular features which were copied into it from the charter of 1682, being compelled by "friends"— perhaps Markham meant Quakers—who, unless they had received all they demanded, would not have come to the country. This corroborates the Pennsylvania Assembly as to the object in coming of such substantial people as the English settlers of the Province, viz: the enjoyment of privileges which they could not have at home.

The Charter dated 2mo. (April) 25, 1682, prescribing a form of government, was very much a covenant that Penn and his heirs and assigns would hold their authority to and for the use of a democracy. As near as possible, there was to be direct legislation. The freemen were to send seventy-two of the small number which there would be of them to a Provincial Council, which, among other powers, had the origination of all laws: all the freemen were to appear in their own persons on 2mo. 20, 1683, and pass or reject said laws; afterwards the freemen were annually, on the 20th of 12th month, to choose representatives not exceeding two hundred, but as the population increased, then up to five hundred, to form the General Assembly, or lower house of the legislature. All that the Governor, whether the Proprietary or his deputy, was to have, was a vote equal to three members in the Council. The Council was joined with the Proprietary in the executive functions, giving judgment on criminals impeached, settling ports, &ct., the Governor or his deputy having always the treble vote; a small return, surely, for the surrender of power, a small recognition of Penn's or his appointee's superior wisdom. Two thirds of the whole Council were to be the quorum in important matters, and the consent of two thirds of such quorum was to be necessary. Three more than said two thirds thus could compel action against the Governor's wishes. Even in the appointment of Judges, while Penn himself picked out the first ones, and they were to serve as long as they behaved well, the successors, as well as the successors of the similarly appointed County Treasurers and Master of the Rolls, were to be selected by the acting Governor from two persons nominated by the Council. The first Sheriffs, Justices of the Peace, and Coroners were also picked out by Penn. Their successors were to be selected by the acting Governor from a double number of persons nominated by the freemen in the County Courts when erected, and by the Assembly until the erection of such Courts. The Governor's consent, as well as the consent of six sevenths of the Council and the Assembly, was necessary to change the Charter.

This system of government was accepted in the first of a series of laws agreed upon on May 5, 1682, by certain persons, then in England, who had bought lands from Penn, the second law declaring practically all purchasers, renters, and tax payers to be freemen. By another of these laws, no tax, custom, or contribution was to be levied upon or paid by any of the people except by a law made for that purpose, and when this was reenacted at Chester, Pennsylvania, it was added that no tax should continue longer than one year. These Laws Agreed upon in England were to be changed only by the same consent as in the case of the Frame of Government.

As a preliminary to putting in force this Charter, William Penn, having received title, such as it was, to what is now called Delaware, and, by virtue of the assignment of the Duke of York's powers, taken the designation of Governor of those Territories, issued writs for the choosing of seven deputies from each of the three counties into which the same had been divided, New Castle, St. Jones, and Deal, to meet the freemen from the Pennsylvania counties of Philadelphia, Bucks, and Chester on Dec. 6, 1682, for the common good of the inhabitants of both the Province and Territories. By the Assembly of these deputies, the laws and privileges of the inhabitants of Pennsylvania were extended to the inhabitants of the Territories, as stated in the chapter on the Ascertainment of the Southern Boundary. An Act of Naturalization, passed at the same meeting, took into the category of freemen all foreigners inhabiting either region holding land in fee in freehold who within three months thereafter promised on record in the County Court fidelity and allegiance to the King of England and fidelity and obedience to the Proprietary. A Great Law of many chapters, enacting, with or without modifications, or supplanting, the laws agreed upon in England, was also passed in this preliminary Assembly, or, more correctly speaking, Congress. By Chapter LVII, it was made necessary that the land to qualify for voting or holding office should be not merely unlocated acres, but such as had been seated, a freeman being defined thus: an inhabitant who had purchased and seated one hundred acres, a person who had paid his passage, and taken up one hundred acres at 1d. per A., and seated the same. a person who, formerly a servant or bondsman, had become free of his service, and taken up and seated 50 A., or a resident paying scot or lot to the government. In these general terms, it might be supposed that women were included, but probably this was never contended.

When Penn attempted to set up the governmental machinery devised, most of the people of both Province and Territories, busy with private concerns, seem, even the Quakers, to have lost political ambition, objecting to forsaking their habitations to make rules, and not well able to spare what money they would be obliged to spend or lose in doing so: so those meeting on the 20th of 12th month (February), 1682-3, to elect the first members of the Provincial Council, declared that the twelve men then chosen from each county were enough to attend to public business, and accordingly petitioned that three of the twelve be accepted as Councillors for one, two, and three years respectively, and the nine others stand for the whole body of freemen of their county for the first regular General Assembly. The nine from each county meeting at the same time as the Council, the proposition was agreed to, and was confirmed in an Act of Settlement, with a promise by the freemen to do nothing in prejudice to the just rights of William Penn and his heirs and successors, who were thereby acknowledged true and rightful Proprietaries and Governors of the Province and Territories. By this Assembly, the laws made in the preceding December at Chester were ordered to stand in force until the end of the first session of the next Assembly, except as altered by a number of laws at this session passed. Among these was an act of indemnity for offences previously committed, and a specification that certain laws be fundamental, i.e. not to be altered, diminished, or repealed without the consent of the Governor, his heirs or assigns and six sevenths of the freemen in Council and Assembly met. All laws passed at this session, except that of indemnity, and that prescribing the fundamentals, were to continue in force until the publication of the laws of the first session of the next Assembly.

On 2mo. 2, 1683, with the unanimous consent of these representatives of the people, a new charter was substituted, whereby the freemen of each county were to elect, on the 10th day of every first month thereafter, one Councillor to serve for three years, and six Assemblymen to serve for one year, the treble vote was not given to the acting Governor, and he was prohibited from performing any act of state relating to justice, trade, treasury, or safety, without the consent of the Council, but, as a sort of compensation for some of the powers taken from William Penn, there was a postponement until after his death of the Provincial Council's participation with the acting Governor in the erection of courts, and of the Council's nomination to him for Judges, Treasurers, and Masters of the Rolls, and of the Assembly's annual nomination of Sheriffs, Justices, and Coroners. As in the former charter, the Governor and Council had the preparation of all laws: the quorum of the Council in this and certain other business was two thirds, and a two thirds vote of that quorum was required. The Assembly had in legislation mere assent or rejection, for which, as well as the nomination of Sheriffs, Justices of the Peace, and Coroners for appointment by the Governor, a quorum of two thirds was necessary. The Assembly had the power of impeachment; the Provincial Council, the trial of the officials impeached.

In Penn's letter of 12mo. 1, 1686, hereafter mentioned, when he was much irritated, particularly by the Councillors' neglect to attend the meetings of the Council, he threatened, as if he were a modern Czar, to dissolve the Frame of Government. Nevertheless, it remained the written Constitution of Pennsylvania and Delaware until April, 1693, and, after an interim of about two years, may be deemed to have continued such until 1700, although for a time the tentative Frame of 1696 was followed.

Before we enter upon the story of administration, there should be noted certain of the Laws Agreed upon in England as early enacted and made fundamental, establishing the principles and judicial arrangements long followed in the colony. Carrying out Penn's great idea, his dominion was made a place of opportunity for the ecclesiastically oppressed. No person who confessed one Almighty God to be creator, upholder, and ruler of the world, and professed to be obliged in conscience to live peaceably and justly in civil society, was to be in any way molested or prejudiced for religious persuasion or practice, or to be obliged to frequent or maintain any religious worship, place, or ministry; any person abusing or deriding another for different persuasion or practice in religion being punishable as a disturber of the peace; but all persons were to abstain from labor on the Lord's day, and not to swear or curse in conversation, and not to speak loosely and profanely of Almighty God, Christ Jesus, the Holy Ghost, or the Scriptures of truth: the officers under the government, the members of Council and Assembly, and all who had a right to elect such members, were to be such as professed faith in Jesus Christ "to be the son of God, the Saviour of the world." In contrast to the breadth of this eligibility, the tests required in England, and insisted upon by the opponents of James II, included, as to members of both Houses of Parliament, by statute of 30 Car. II st. 2: "I do solemnly and sincerely in the presence of God profess, testify, and declare that I do believe that in the sacrament of the Lord's Supper there is not any transubstantiation of the elements of bread and wine into the body and blood of Christ at or after the consecration thereof by any person whatsoever; and that the invocation or adoration of the Virgin Mary or any other saint, and the sacrifice of the Mass, as they are now used in the Church of Rome, are superstitious and idolatrous." When, by the English act of 1 W. & M., c. 18, Dissenters were tolerated, such as would not take an oath were required, besides making the aforesaid declaration, to profess faith in the Trinity, and to acknowledge the Holy Scriptures of the Old and New Testament to be given by divine inspiration. Under the laws passed at the inauguration of Penn's government, process in civil actions was to be by summons on the complainant declaring that he believed his cause just; judgment was to be given for want of an appearance. Certain rights to bail and trial upon criminal accusations were established. Court proceedings were to be in English. As dictated by Quaker scruples, witnesses from the first were to qualify simply by solemnly promising to speak the truth, the whole truth, and nothing but the truth. This method seems to have been observed by non-Quakers and Quakers alike until the coming of Fletcher. He reenacted it, changing the word "shall" to "may," thus permitting the Quakers and Mennonites to give testimony in that way, but restoring apparently the use of the oath by Swedes and the few others who preferred it. Not until 1696 could testimony without oath be accepted in England: the Statute of 7 & 8 Wm. III, c. 34, permitting this, expressly limited it to civil actions. Even in such matters, there was a distinction between the early Pennsylvania law and the English statute, for, by the latter, the affirmant was obliged to acknowledge that he spoke "in the presence of Almighty God the witness of the truth of what I say."

The laws made before and for some time after 2mo. 2, 1683, were not laid before the King, but, apparently treated as tentative only, were usually reenacted with amendments at each Assembly, to stand in force until the end or twenty days after the end of the first session of the next Assembly. A short period to permit pub-

lication, ultimately fixed at twenty days, after the end
of the Assembly was allowed before new laws went
into effect. The Assembly of 1686 and that of 1687
failed to continue the laws or enact new ones.

Penn claimed one strange right, not meeting with
expostulation in the early days, but declared unfounded
by lawyers in later times. By the letter of 12, 1, 1686,
before mentioned, of which Edward Blackfan was
bearer, Penn directed those named in the commission
mentioned in the letter, to declare to the Assembly his
abrogation of everything done since his leaving, and
of all the laws except the fundamentals, and then to
dismiss the Assembly, and call one again, and pass the
laws afresh with any alterations. He also enclosed a
proclamation exercising the power in the King's
Charter of making ordinances. These instructions seem
to have been disregarded, owing to the non-arrival of
the commission spoken of; but, in a letter dated 4mo.
6, 1687, they were inferentially confirmed by the Proprietary's remark that he had little more to say than
he had communicated of his mind already "in a former
letter by Edward Blackfan." In 1688, a law was passed
that all the laws formerly passed continue in force until
twenty days after the end of the first session of the
next Assembly, and no longer, except the fundamental
laws, and certain additional laws were passed to last
during the same or a shorter time.

The first visit of the Founder of Pennsylvania to the
shores of the Delaware lasted twenty-one months and
a half, and the only other visit twenty-three months.
During the ninety and more years of rule by the Penns
except during those visits, and even during the visits
of the Founder's sons, John and Thomas, the power left
by the subsisting frame of government to the chief
executive was in the hands of the Council of the
Province or of Commissioners or of a Deputy with the
title of Lieutenant-Governor selected by the Governor-

in-Chief. The Lieutenant-Governors were seldom equal to the requirements of the position, and were never fully empowered to speak for their principals: so, even when the person holding the Proprietaryship was not missed for his abilities, there was always a great disadvantage in his being three thousand miles away.

Under date of 6mo. 7 (?), 1684, William Penn, saying that he was "not knowing how it would please God to deal with him on the voyage" back to England, appointed Thomas Lloyd, James Harrison, and John Simcock, of whom the first named was to preside, guardians of the heir, Springett Penn, and, if he died under age, then of his successor, until of age, the surviving guardians to fill any vacancy happening by the death of a guardian.

At the end of William Penn's first visit, he left the whole Provincial Council to act in his place, excepting, however, in his commission to the body, which was read on 6mo. 18, 1684, any power to make laws diminishing his interest. Thomas Lloyd was made President. He also was appointed by Penn Master of the Rolls and Keeper of the Great Seal during good behavior. Probably not paternally related to David Lloyd, spoken of in a preceding chapter as a lawyer, who had not yet arrived in the province, Thomas Lloyd was a younger brother of Charles Lloyd of Dolobran in Wales, one of the few gentlemen of landed estate who joined the Society of Friends. Thomas had matriculated at Oxford, and was probably the person of the name at Jesus College, who was graduated B. A. on Jany. 29, 1661. The President had practised medicine in England, and did so somewhat in America. To the position accorded to him of a minister among Friends, he had the further claim upon their consideration of having lain in prison many years for the cause, and he was credited with some share in bringing about the repeal of the ancient law for burning heretics, with the execution of which law some persons had threatened the Quakers. When Lloyd's term as a Councillor was about to expire, Penn signed a commission authorizing Lloyd, Dr. Nicholas More (before mentioned as owning 10,000 acres), James Claypoole (brother of Oliver Cromwell's son-in-law), Robert Turner (before mentioned), and John Eckley, under the title of Commissioners of State, or any three of them, to represent the Governor-in-Chief, but reserving to himself the confirmation of what they might do, as well as his peculiar royalties and advantages. This was the commission, which seems never to have arrived, or at least not until superseded, as mentioned in Penn's letter dated 12mo. 1, 1686. A commission of later date appointed as Deputy or Lieutenant of the Proprietary: Lloyd, Turner, Arthur Cooke, John Simcock (name eventually so spelt, although one signature is Simcocks), and Eckley or any three of them. These were serving at the arrival of Blackwell. When Penn was looking about for somebody to make sole Deputy in their stead, Lloyd and other Quakers declined. This was perhaps on account of the military duties contemplated in the King's Charter. After Blackwell, Lloyd, as will be mentioned, was Lieutenant-Governor of Pennsylvania, the only Quaker ever appointed such by the Penns.

It was a pity both for Penn's colony and for himself that, after his first coming to America, he could not stay the rest of his life. Even if the colony did not need his wisdom, his influence would have smoothed away difficulties in government, where his representatives showed want of tact. Except when he sent Markham as aforesaid to take possession, and even including the latest commissioning of Markham, every appointment of a Lieutenant-Governor by William Penn was unfortunate. The support of such an official was an item of the Founder's heavy expenditure, and, when it was borne by the taxpayers, it was hard upon them. For the

Founder himself, residence in his colony would have saved him money, liberty, and a better name than stern critics have allowed.

William Penn had not been brought up a business man, but a knight's son, to be courtier and soldier, while bailiffs, solicitors, and agents drew up his papers, and handled his money. The usual means of livelihood or of increasing an estate for persons of his class were public office and marriage with an heiress. From the former, William Penn debarred himself by his ecclesiastical attitude. His first wife, Gulielma Maria (Posthuma was an additional part of her Christian name), was not without patrimony. She was the only child of Sir William Springett of Sussex, and came of knighted ancestors on the maternal side as well, her mother, who married, secondly, Isaac Pennington (name then so spelt), being the daughter of Sir John Proude by his wife Anne Fagge (since Fagg). Although connected rather closely with Lord Culpepper and Sir John Fagg (created a baronet in 1660), and others of worldly station, William Penn's wife, being a Quakeress, avoided the superfluous expenditure of the fashionable, which might have made her relatively poor. After Penn's death, somebody in the family employ swore that he had heard that Gulielma had brought Penn an estate of £20,000, which he put into the Pennsylvania venture. One or the other part of the story is an exaggeration. Worminghurst, which is spoken of as descending from her to her son, appears to have been bought for her by Penn with £4500 of her money. She also had the property worth about £3000 which was mortgaged at the time of his first coming to America. In part recompense for this, some land in Pennsylvania was granted by Penn to her younger children.

Penn's father left him a good estate, without counting the money claim against the English government; but William Penn, instead of husbanding his property, followed the career of a minister among Friends, which, involving trials and punishment and travelling and putting forth books, engrossed his attention, and devoured his income as much perhaps as the diversions of the worldly would have done.

From the day, or before the day, when Pepys speaks of Admiral Penn's coach being better than the King's, until the careful John and Thomas Penn grew up, the Penns were extravagant; but free expenditure in religious work, or in maintenance of a Quaker family, would not have piled up indebtedness for William Penn. His great real estate speculation and his part in English public life, with what grew out of both, brought him to such financial straits as changed him from a philanthropist to a spoilsman and at times a lobbyist.

In the matter of principal business agent, or steward, William Penn was very unfortunate. He employed about the time of the Admiral's death, a Quaker named Philip Ford to look after the Admiral's affairs. Ford, who may have been the Philip Ford of Buckinghamshire in 1666, as well as the Philip Ford of Mary Le Bow Parish, London, in 1677, mentioned in Joseph Besse's *Sufferings of the Quakers,* was subsequently styled as of London, merchant, and became in fact until his death banker to the first Proprietary.

When the sales to the "first purchasers" were in progress, practically all the cash was paid by them to Ford: it amounted by Aug. 23, 1682, to £5652 9s. 11d. Ford bought the goods to be sent to America, and paid other expenses of the undertaking, with probably sums to Penn and the officers under him, until, as Penn was at Deal, about to set sail the first time for America, Ford appeared with an account making Penn in debt to him £2851 7s. 10d. Penn, having no time to look into this, marked it correct. Then, to secure Ford, he gave him, intended as a mortgage, a lease and release, dated Aug. 23 and 24, 1682, for 300,000 acres in Pennsylvania, and a bond, dated Aug. 24, to pay £3000 on Aug. 26. These and the subsequent instruments executed by one to the other were not to interfere with Penn's making sales, and his giving good title to surveyed lots, but were merely to protect Ford, and were accordingly kept secret during his life.

Over and above the debt which Penn relinquished to the Crown, the actual expenses of starting the colony, including Penn's living there two years, took all the money from the sales until after his return from his first visit; and then, for a long period, the sales were few. He had secured as quit rents an annual income for the future of about £400, exclusive of what the Swedes and other old inhabitants would pay. The quit rents were not promptly paid, and in many cases were years in arrears. The Assembly had, in March, 1682-3, been so complaisant as to grant him 2d. per gallon on all rum, wine, brandy, and strong waters imported, 1d. per gallon on all cider, and 20s. on every £100 on all merchandise except molasses. How much was ever collected, we do not know: but, although intended to be permanent, and so reenacted until 1690, this aid to him was repealed in that year.

On Penn's return from his first visit, Ford said that £1000 were owing to the latter, while the account, or the copy of it preserved by the Historical Society of Pennsylvania, has a further credit of £1858 12s. 4d. received by Ford for lands to 1mo. 21, 1684-5. Ford's wife was not satisfied with the security, and, although £518 12s. more came from sales, Penn was continuing to get advances; so, under date of June 10, 1685, he made, in place of the lease and release, a long term lease to Ford, following a method at one time much in vogue in England to make land disposable as if not real estate. This lease from Penn to Ford was for 5000 years, and covered all quit rents and 300,000 acres, including the manors of Pennsbury, Springton, and Springfield and city lands, making exceptions, it appears, of what had been already sold. There was a clause for annulment on repaying the consideration expressed, viz. £5000. On 2, 24, 1686, before going to Holland, Penn wrote to friends in Pennsylvania that to raise money was hindering his return to the province—perhaps the King contributed to the journey to Holland. Penn told these friends that he had spent £3000 since he saw London, besides paying some bills drawn before leaving America. So the long term lease to Ford was replaced two years after its date by one covering also the town of New Castle, and representing £6000.

Brought by the Baltimore claim into closer intercourse not only with the court officials, but with James, who was Duke of York at Penn's return to England, but succeeded as King a few months later, William Penn, until the authority of that monarch was at an end, had great prominence and power in the realm as one of the King's personal friends. Attached to him by gratitude, and seeing in his endeavors to break down the Established Church a chance for general religious toleration, Penn pursued a political course, which, however beneficial to the Quakers and to others, has not made him popular with English historians. The Quakers should rather revere the memory of the Stuart, who, in his attempt to reconcile England to Rome, relieved their early co-religionists and other Dissenters. His "merry" brother, Charles II, although at first inclined to toleration, had yielded to the party insisting upon conformity to a Protestant liturgy, and had relinquished an idea of reestablishing Romanism, and had not stirred himself to interfere with the prosecution of the "Children of the Light:" at least he left at his death about 1200 of these non-militant persons in jail for not taking an oath, or not attending their parish church. James, by proclamation dated March 15, 1685-6, released them, and remitted their fines, and he stopped further process and indictment. It is not strange, therefore, that, as a messenger from James, William Penn, about two months later, on a religious visit to Holland, sought William of Orange, who, failing the Princesses Mary and Anne, was heir to the British throne, to get his support for James's proposal to abolish the religious test for holding office. William would not agree, although expressing himself opposed to penal laws against faith and worship. Penn is said to have thought that a declaration of indulgence founded on a royal claim to dispense with statutes would be a mistake; but, after James, on April 4, 1687, issued his famous declaration suspending the laws against non-conformity, and dispensing with the tests which had excluded all but members of the Established Church from seats in Parliament and offices, the Yearly Meeting, on 3, 19, 1687, adopted an address thanking the King, and praying God to preserve him and those under him in so good a work, and assuring him that it was well accepted in the counties from which the attendants came, and hoping that its good effects would produce such a concurrence from the Parliament as would secure it to posterity; and Penn, at the head of a delegation for the purpose, presented the address.

Penn's right to make laws for more than Pennsylvania proper, being of even greater doubtfulness than his title to the soil of the Lower Counties, and a patent for the latter being in preparation after James II ascended the throne, a suggested form for the patent, which is preserved by the Historical Society, relieved Penn from all liability for allowing religious toleration in those parts.

When James II, by headlong disregard of the advice of Penn and other loyal and honest observers, had lost his hold upon his subjects, and nearly every one was serving the plans of the Prince of Orange, Penn did not even go to the country, and assume an appearance of neutrality. On the day preceding that on which James, throwing the great seal into the Thames, made the first attempt at flight, Penn was walking in Whitehall, and the Lords of the Council sent for him, and took security in £6000 for his appearance to answer any charge which might be made against him. Thus, having overspent so much, he was, at the accomplishment of the Revolution, poor, in debt, and under suspicion. On Feb. 20, 1688-9, the Committee for Trade and Plantations, having called him and Lord Baltimore before them, ordered the two Proprietaries to proclaim William and Mary in Pennsylvania and Maryland respectively, and both Penn and Lord Baltimore promised to obey any order of the Committee. Three days afterwards, a letter from the Privy Council, dated the 19th, with the form of a proclamation to be used in Pennsylvania, was handed to Penn. By the infrequent, slow, and perilous communication with America in that century, this did not reach Pennsylvania until a year and six months all but a few days had elapsed. Before the end of February, 1688-9, the Council ordered Penn's arrest, he being then at his seat, Worminghurst; but, writing to the Earl of Shrewsbury, Penn protested his innocence of any part in any conspiracy against the new government, and his not knowing of any, and requested that the new King allow him to remain at his house in the country, and attend to pressing business relating to America, being under the aforesaid heavy bail. The King allowed this. At Easter Term, nothing being alleged against Penn, he was cleared and discharged by the Judges.

CHAPTER VII.

GOVERNMENT UNDER THE FRAME OF 1683.

Insignificance of the acting Governors of Penn's colony and the explanation—John Blackwell—Quakers hard to manage in political affairs—His high notions of government—Control of the press—Penn partly responsible—Obstruction of business by Thomas Lloyd and others—Assembly contends for member's privileges—Question of any laws being in force—White's arrest—All laws passed before Penn's departure declared in force until he could be heard from—William and Mary recognized, and debate in Council upon arming the colony for defence against France—Blackwell relieved of the governorship, the Council succeeding with Lloyd as President—Impost for Penn discontinued—The people of the Lower Counties dissatisfied with the Pennsylvania Councillors—Failure of justice in Lower Counties—Split in Council on choice of new commissions for the Deputyship—Lloyd chosen Lieutenant-Governor—Delawareans choose Cann as President—The borough Philadelphia chartered as a City—Capture of a river pirate—Penn commissions Lloyd, and makes Markham Lieut.-Governor of the Lower Counties.

While the Governorship of some of the colonies, being a rulership directly under the Crown, was often, even in pioneer days, held by a person distinguished by title of nobility, by family relationship, or by the command of expeditions, the reader will look in vain for such, unless one baronet will answer, among those who before 1776 administered the affairs of Pennsylvania

Government Under the Frame of 1683. 183

and Delaware. They with the exception of William Penn himself and Benjamin Fletcher were merely Lieutenants of a Governor-in-Chief, and so of lesser dignity. As a rule, the Penns appointed some inhabitant of the colonies or an inferior military officer. Without the prestige of a Governor-in-Chief, or "King's Governor," or "Royal Governor," and involving practically banishment from civilization, and with a stipend providing for mere daily living, the office long was what no resident of the Old World in good circumstances would accept. Edward Randolph, in 1695, making objections to all Proprietary governments, pointed out that the actual governors in such were mere stewards of the Proprietaries, and were persons of indifferent qualifications, parts, and estates, with inconsiderable maintenance and precarious tenure. The dominions of the Penns and the dominions of the Calverts alone remained subject to rule by Proprietaries after pioneer days, being in fact so subject until the American Revolution. Occasionally, matching the said Lieutenant-Governors in inferiority of designation, the actual governors of some colonies under Crown rule, as Robert Dinwiddie in Virginia, were only Lieutenant-Governors, an absentee being titular Governor. The earliest Governors of Virginia were knighted upon appointment, if not already knights or higher in precedency. The dullness of Philadelphia to a non-Quaker has been spoken of: the parsimony of those who were expected to pay the stipend will appear in the early part of this history. These respective characteristics were slow in yielding to the influence of neighbouring example. Besides all this, the task of conducting the affairs of Pennsylvania was, as will be seen, peculiarly difficult; and, even when the colony equalled or exceeded some of the Royal ones in population and wealth, and furnished to a satisfactory official a good income, the situation of the Lieutenant-Governor, who otherwise might have been contented with the title, surroundings, and remuneration, was very disagreeable. He had to serve three masters, to whom his conduct was reported by independent officers, by business agents, or by intractable politicians respectively; the three masters being the King, chiefly in matters of war, customs revenue, and trade regulations, who could force his removal, and otherwise punish him, the Proprietary, who appointed and could supersede him, and the People, or, at least, the freemen represented in Assembly, who paid him. To the difficulty of harmonizing the requirements of the King and the freemen, was added the obligation to protect the interests of the Proprietary, and, lest gratitude or fear of removal might not be sufficient to induce the Lieutenant to follow this obligation, instructions and limitations of power were put upon him. William Penn himself, not only, as we have seen, made reservations capable of great extension, but also began the giving of instructions.

In the matter of previous career, more can be said of John Blackwell than of most of the other Lieutenant-Governors. He, as Captain John Blackwell Junr. from Mortlake, Co. Essex, had been a Treasurer of the Army in the time of the Commonwealth, and afterwards had refused a great office in Ireland under Charles II and James II because its emolument was derived from perquisites. Blackwell had married General Lambert's daughter, and was a Puritan, of whom Nathaniel Mather wrote in 1684 (*Mass. Hist. Coll.*): "For serious reall piety & nobleness of spirit, prudence, &ct., I have not been acquainted with many that equall him." He was residing in New England, when, without solicitation, Penn selected him, hoping that, while Blackwell's conscience would leave him free to perform military service, his high character would command the respect of the Quakers, and that thus there would be an administration satisfactory both to the King and to the colonists. Penn does not appear to have taken into account the antipathy between a Puritan and a Quaker, who had scarcely anything in common but opposition to the Church of England, and were inclined to tolerate one of its adherents rather than each other. Blackwell, rather as a favor to Penn, to whom or to whose father he may have felt gratitude for something in those perilous times, accepted with the expectation of being soon relieved by the return of Penn to America. The collection of the quit rents was also given to Blackwell, and the percentage allowed to him with the fines and forfeitures accruing to the Governor seems to have been his entire or the chief part of his remuneration. He thus being an interested party, when he had sat as magistrate in trials where fines or forfeitures might be found due, the Assembly, but not by unanimous vote, took a stand for the impartiality of the judiciary, and declared such a course a grievance. He arrived in Philadelphia on Dec. 17, 1688, before news had come of the landing of the Prince of Orange in England. Blackwell's first act, on assuming office on the 18th, was, it happened, the setting apart, according to an order received, of a day for "solemn thanksgiving to Almighty God for His inestimable blessing to his Majesty's kingdoms and dominions by the birth of a Prince," the poor little baby who in later history was commonly known as the Pretender, who on the thanksgiving day was in France for safety.

The Councillors when Blackwell arrived were the following: from Philadelphia County, Turner and Carpenter and Samuel Richardson; from Bucks, Cooke and Joseph Growdon and William Yardley; from Chester, Simcock and John Bristow and Bartholomew Coppock; from New Castle, John Cann, Peter Alricks, and Johannes De Haes; from Kent, William Darvall, ex-Lieutenant-Governor Markham, and Griffith Jones, a Quaker, evidently identical with the Philadelphia merchant, and from Sussex, William Clark and Luke Watson, there being a vacancy owing to the dismissal of William Dyer, who was a son of the Quaker martyr, Mary Dyer, put to death in Boston. Besides Jones, Clark and all those from the Upper Counties were Quakers. If the Jones whom Blackwell so much favored was not the Welsh attorney, but the Councillor, the latter was not one of the former Quaker officeholders, and consideration shown to him rather excited their jealousy.

A Quaker community in the time when nearly every member had experienced a call to seriousness was more moral probably than the same number of persons of any other religious denomination, although the number of accusations in the early records of Pennsylvania, as well as those of the Territories Annexed, surprises us. Physical violence was utterly inconsistent with Quaker habits, so that in this respect, under Quaker influence, at least Pennsylvania proper was law-abiding. Politically, however, the Quaker freemen were hard to manage, apart from any question of obeying God rather than man, as they felt on the subject of war and oaths. A characteristic of the Children of the Light was not docility. They had begun by the adoption of theories and practices in the face of all ecclesiastical tradition known to them, and of the customs of their neighbours; and the tendency of such reformers was to be opinionated, censorious, and intractable. Years of subjection to persecution had hardened their character, had accustomed them to the status of rebels, and had made them fearless. Disputations had sharpened the wits of their leaders, and embittered their language. It will be seen, particularly at the attempts to enforce privileges, perquisites, and impositions which landlords and rulers had usually exacted, and which elsewhere had been agreed to as matters of course, how far the Quakers of Pennsylvania were from being a flock of sheep uncomplainingly allowing themselves to be fleeced.

Blackwell was dignified and fairly courteous, but very exacting of deference, unflinching in following what he deemed his duty, and requiring everybody to observe the letter of the law. His participation in the Civil War had made him more military than republican. Perhaps he was afraid of not appearing thoroughly loyal to the monarchical régime: he had narrowly escaped attainder as an accessory to the putting to death of Charles I, having, in the course of business as Treasurer, paid for building the scaffold. Commissioned, it appears, as Governor, instead of Lieutenant-Governor, by Penn, Blackwell had high ideas of the prerogative with which the appointment invested him. When he examined William Bradford on the charge of printing without authorization the Frame of Government, and, finally, on Bradford's declining to accuse himself by acknowledging the printing, bound Bradford in 500*l.* to print nothing without the Governor's "*imprimatur,*" Blackwell remarked: "I question whether there hath been a Governor here before or not, or those which understood what government was, which makes things as they now are." It is most probable that until his arrival he was not aware how Penn's charter embodying the Frame of 1683 had neutralized the seigniorial powers conferred upon the Proprietary by the King: and Blackwell doubted the validity of such neutralizing. Blackwell was either very astute in raising legal questions, or appreciative of points, suggested, perhaps, by Griffith Jones the lawyer.

Perhaps Penn expected Blackwell to set things right, a sentence of some instructions telling him to "rule the meek meekly, others that will not be so ruled, rule with authority." Moreover, Penn had given to Blackwell, so the latter told Bradford, a particular order for "suppressing of printing here, and narrowly to look after your press." This we have from an old manuscript account of Bradford's examination. Before the Council, Blackwell said that Penn had declared himself against the use of the printing press.

With Blackwell, on his part, feeling, as might have been expected, no predilection for the Quakers, and putting Jones in the commission of the peace for at least three counties, making Patrick Robinson pro-Register-General, and naming Markham as first among the Justices of all the counties, the conduct of the leading Quakers, on their part, was not such as to win Blackwell. Contention filled the time of his administration. Lloyd, from the first, interposed his own judgment in matters where it seemed to be his duty to obey orders. Blackwell, being referred by his commission to such instructions as had been sent to the President and Council, or to the Commissioners of State, called for "the letter sent by the hands of Edward Blackfan," and secured resolutions from the Council—those present being four Quakers and Darvall and Markham—that all original letters and instructions either to Commissioners of State or President and Council should be delivered to the Secretary, and such parts of other letters to any of them as gave instructions should be transcribed, and the transcripts certified for the Secretary. Perhaps Lloyd and those in his confidence had been concealing Penn's threat, in the letter of 12mo. 1, 1686, to dissolve the Frame; perhaps they thought it injudicious to publish his order to abrogate the laws, deeming such order illegal, or not representing his later wish, or in fact obsolete. At any rate, Lloyd allowed Blackwell to read only some parts of the letter, and then Lloyd took a month to consult the others to whom this and other letters were addressed as to complying with the request for delivery to the Secretary. Apparently Cooke and Eckley felt the same way as Lloyd, who made answer that the original letters had been duly considered by those lately Commissioners, and they knew of none which might now be of service, that such as contained instructions had been delivered to view, and were transcribed, and that most of the letters remained in his own custody with the assent of those to whom they were directed. It was at last agreed unanimously in the Council that attested copies of the letters and of the parts of private letters should be delivered.

Lloyd also claimed the right to refuse the great seal to documents which he deemed improper, a right which would have made him a chancellor or a court to declare acts unconstitutional or a superior governor, and which would have resulted in such confusion that Penn can not be supposed to have intended it. Lloyd's first refusal was in regard to a certain commission for Justices of the Peace and holding of a County Court for Philadelphia County, the form of the commission being disapproved of by him. On his intending to visit New York, the Council, six being present, asked him to leave the seal for the accommodation of public business, the Quakers on this occasion adopting Blackwell's motion, Simcock saying that the Keeper should not be allowed to go away. Lloyd, in writing, declared that the action of the Council was an arbitrary disposing of the most eminent estate for life yet given in the government, that he had been unkindly dealt with, and that, being done by a minority of the members, and by vote instead of ballot,—the Frame requiring ballot in the choosing of officers and all other personal matters,— the act was unwarrantable by law and charter; and he asked that either the order be erased from the Council book, or his paper filed as a protest. Blackwell had gotten over the difficulty about the County Court by deciding to issue under the lesser seal the commissions in the form which he had chosen, and to refer the matter to the Proprietary. But it was not easy to do without Lloyd in the matter of the Supreme Court, or, as it was called, the Provincial Court, which alone could try capital crimes. The law passed while Penn was in the colony provided for five Judges appointed by the Governor under the great seal. There had been passed in 1685 a provision for a special commissioning, not requiring that seal, of three Judges by the Governor and Council, but, even if this was not abrogated by Penn's letter of 1686, it appeared to be an infringement of his right by the King's patent to appoint all Judges, and therefore void as within the exception to the power under which in 1685 the Council had represented Penn in making laws. Cooke asked that Lloyd's advice be sought, and, this being refused, Cooke left the meeting; Clark, Darvall, Jones, Coppock, Turner, and Markham remaining, it was carried unanimously to commission under the older law, and according to a form then read by Blackwell. This being sent to Lloyd, he declared it not proper for the seal, and "more moulded by fancy than formed by law, the style insecure, the powers unwarrantable, and the duration not consonant to the continuance of the laws upon which it should be grounded." The Governor and Council having removed David Lloyd from the Clerkship for Philadelphia County, Thomas Lloyd, claiming the right to appoint the Clerk, commissioned David as such on 1mo. 1, 1688-9. It was resolved by the Council that this was an usurpation of the Governor's authority; and David surrendered the records in due time.

Richardson (ancestor of Gov. Samuel W. Pennypacker) offended Blackwell's punctiliousness by criticising both in and out of Council a resolution of the body, and his pride by repeated declarations that Penn's deputy was not Governor, for Penn could not appoint one. Cooke, expressing himself more mildly, scrupled at any title but Deputy-Governor. Blackwell moved that Richardson be ordered to leave while the

Council debated the question. Richardson declared: "I will not withdraw, I was not brought hither by thee, and I will not go out by thy order; I was sent by the people, and thou hast no power to put me out." The others thought he should withdraw; and, when he had done so, it was agreed, seven members being present, that he should acknowledge his offence, and promise more respect in future, before he could be allowed to sit again.

The imperative business in the Spring of 1689 was the making of a new set of laws, the act of 3mo. 10, 1688, having provided that, except the fundamental laws, no law passed previously, or at that session, should remain in force longer than until twenty days after the end of the first session of the next Assembly. Accordingly, the Governor and Council were bound in duty to propose, as prescribed by the Frame, a code, to be published and affixed in the most public place in each county by the 20th of the 2nd month, i.e. twenty days before the meeting of the Assembly which was to accept or reject them. The election held in 1st month, 1688-9, resulted in the continuance of Simcock and Clark in the Council and the choice of John Eckley, Lloyd, William Stockdale, and John Curtis, in the place of Turner, Cooke, Cann, and Darvall, and the choice of John Hill for the vacancy from Sussex.

Questions as to right to seats prevented the Council from getting to work in time for legislation. On the ground that fifty or sixty inhabitants of the Welsh Tract had voted in Philadelphia, whereas that tract had been actually taken into Chester County, Eckley's election was declared void. The Lieutenant-Governor, pursuant to the suspension of Richardson, issued a writ for an election in his place, as well as for an election in Eckley's. As to Lloyd, Blackwell proposed articles of impeachment. Richardson came to the Council meeting to take his place, justifying his former language, and refusing to withdraw; so that the Governor adjourned the sitting until the afternoon. Then the question was raised whether the Council could exclude a member chosen by the people, Blackwell standing on the privilege of all courts and corporations to judge of the misbehavior of their members, and saying that he would not suffer such affronts from any person sitting at the board, and would so notify the Proprietary. Markham, the Secretary, writes this minute: "Many intemperate speeches & passages happend, fitt to be had in oblivion." The question of Lloyd's impeachment being then taken up, there arose warm debates, his friends objecting to framing any charges. At the next meeting, Lloyd walked into the room, saying that he had come to take his seat. The Lieutenant-Governor told him that nothing was expected from him until he answered the charges. He, replying that he had as good a right to be there as Blackwell had to be Lieutenant-Governor, accordingly refused to withdraw. Blackwell then asked the other members to follow him to his lodgings. Some stayed to reason with Lloyd, among them Markham, the Secretary, but such were the "sharp and unsavory expressions" used by Lloyd, which the Lieutenant-Governor heard, he having gone no further than outside the door, that Markham induced him to return. Lloyd was again commanded to depart, and the other members followed the Lieutenant-Governor to his lodgings. On arriving there, eleven members voted to proceed with the preparation of the laws for the Assembly's action: four Quakers, Carpenter, Growdon, Yardley, and Bristow, voted no, being apparently unwilling to act without Lloyd, Richardson, and Eckley. On the 8th of 2nd month, at the election ordered by the Lieutenant-Governor to fill Eckley's and Richardson's places, the freemen decided to take no ballot, although the Frame required it. In Chester and the Lower Counties, the ballot had been frequently by black and white beans in a hat. On this occasion, by majority vote or voice, Eckley and Richardson were sent back. On the same day, there was an agreement reached in Council as to what laws were fundamental: but, it having been pointed out that the laws, to be valid under the King's letters patent, were to be published by the Proprietary or his Deputy under the seal of the Proprietary or Deputy, and it not being clear that any but the Act of Union had been passed under the great seal, a question arose whether any of the fundamentals had been legally established.

The Councillors were turned from the subject the next morning by the Lieutenant-Governor finding fault with Growdon for promoting the printing of copies of the Frame of Government. It was this printing which caused the proceeding against Bradford, as before related. Blackwell expressed a fear that, if it were known outside of the province, that Penn had granted certain privileges, it might result in a questioning of the Proprietary title. Growdon declined to retire during the discussion, and demanded the admission of the three excluded members. Blackwell maintained the disqualification of Lloyd and Richardson, and the nullity of the second election of Eckley, although politely regretting that it was not legal to admit one so fit as the last named. Blackwell refused to let the Councillors ballot upon this point, declaring it unsafe to let men who were under such factional influence vote secretly. The Quakers generally being indisposed to go into the consideration of the laws with three representatives of their element of the population excluded, the Lieutenant-Governor, then excusing from attendance all the Councillors except those required for routine business, let all legislation fail.

After the adjournment on that day, Simcock, Growdon, Yardley, Curtis, Carpenter, Coppock, and Stockdale wrote a complaint to Penn—Bristow had gone before it was signed—of Blackwell's actions against Lloyd, Richardson, and Eckley in opposition to the Councillors' wishes, and of the putting of a stop to legislation. These seven told Penn that Blackwell rather watched them for evil, taking down in short hand every word they said, and preparing, when they were gone, the minutes for his servant, a Frenchman, to transcribe, and, although in many things keeping "near to the truth," frequently omitting or denying what was material, that he represented them and "the best people" as seditious &ct., for asserting in moderation their just rights, and appearing unanimous in choice of representatives, and standing together against their known enemies, and that Blackwell, instead of taking the advice of those previously intrusted with the government, consulted with Jones, Robinson, and Markham. The wish was earnestly expressed that Penn return to America. "We now see the difference between an affectionate and tender father whose children we know we are and a severe hard hearted father-in-law who hath no share nor lot nor portion among us."

The Assemblymen met in no good humor. Not only were the excluded Councillors high in the estimation of some, in fact of most, of the Quakers attending, but John White, chosen a representative of New Castle County in the Assembly, had been committed to jail, and was detained there. Blackwell for several days telling the messenger of the House that there was no quorum of the Council, the House unanimously resolved that the exclusion of members of the Council from that body was a grievance of the country; and it also was unanimously resolved that the detention in prison of any person chosen to the Assembly during the time of its session was a breach of privilege, and that such person with the charge against him should be brought before the House, that the House could judge whether the charge amounted to treason or felony. Therefore the House issued a writ to the Sheriff of New Castle to bring before it the body of John White, and the cause of his detaining. Five members, however, Joseph Fisher, Edward Blake, Luke Watson, Jr., Samuel Gray, and James Sandelands, protested against such a writ.

On the 14th of 3rd month, Blackwell addressed the Assembly at length, reciting the Proprietary's direction to drop all laws except the fundamentals, the doubt whether laws already passed or to be passed could be valid without the great seal, the difficulty in getting Lloyd to affix the great seal—according to Blackwell, the Keeper "refusing to allow the use of it in any cases by my direction,"—and the uncertainty of the Proprietary's position in the state of affairs in England, and the danger to him and the colonists of passing such laws as they wished, and the Proprietary's reservation of the confirmation or annulling of any laws passed in his absence, so that their execution must be postponed until his pleasure should be known; so Blackwell announced his intention of observing as Proprietary instructions what had been enacted while Penn was in the province, unless contrary to the laws of England, and of supplying any defect therein by the laws of England. The House, by Arthur Cooke, who had been elected Speaker, appears then to have presented its resolve as to the grievance of not admitting the three Councillors. Blackwell adjourned the Council to his lodgings, against the wishes of certain members, who set up a joint power to appoint the place of meeting. His answer was that by his commission and the charter and laws, they were to attend him; not he, them. One affirming that they were not dealt with fairly, Blackwell reproved him, saying that he, Blackwell, was sorry that the member did not understand things better. Three days later, he submitted to a quorum of the Councillors the question of issuing a declaration for continuing the laws formerly passed by the Proprietary himself until word should come from England. Simcock and Clark feared, that, even with such a declaration, justices would not feel safe in doing anything after the expiration of twenty days from the end of the Assembly's session. Blackwell said that all action by the justices would surely be confirmed by an act of indemnity and confirmation, as government was a necessity. Growdon suggested to keep the laws alive by agreeing to the Assembly taking a recess, while Stockdale and Carpenter said that the Assembly could, by its own power, take such a recess; but Blackwell said that this was in no way countenanced by the Charter, the instructions, or the laws. Bristow thought it would be well for the Governor and Council and the Assembly to join together in a declaration to the magistrates that the laws made and confirmed from the beginning and practised, continue in force until further order from the Proprietary. This pleased Blackwell, but was not followed by the Council.

The Assemblymen, adopting on the day of this debate in Council an answer to the Lieutenant-Governor's speech, said that they were credibly informed that William Penn had changed his mind about letting the laws drop, and, as far as they knew, all those passed since his departure had been sent for his refusal, and none had been declared void by him; no higher sanction was required than what had been accepted up to that time by the colony; it was hoped that no law would be imposed upon them as being made and published under the great seal by the Proprietary and Governor with the consent of the freemen, instead of as made "in the stipulated way of the Charter and Act of Settlement;" the representatives conceived all laws not adjudged void by the King under his Privy Seal to remain in force; and they deemed inconsistent with the constitution the Deputy's expedient of governing, unless with the concurrence of the Council, by such laws made be-

Government Under the Frame of 1683. 197

fore the Proprietary returned to England as Blackwell should think not contrary to the laws of England, because how far the laws of England were to be the rules had been declared by the King's letters patent.

The Sheriff of New Castle did not obey the writ of *habeas corpus* issued by the House, but allowed White to escape. So he came to Philadelphia, and, on the 17th, took his seat. Yet Richard Reynolds of New Castle, perhaps under a warrant from Markham as Justice, rearrested White, while, it seems, in the Assembly room, and would not take bail, but left him when the House again unanimously resolved that the arrest of a member or attendant during the session except for treason or felony was a breach of privilege. At 10 o'clock that night, John Claypoole (James's son), Sheriff of Philadelphia County, under a warrant from Markham and Jones, broke into the room in Benjamin Chambers's house where White was going to bed, and took him away. The next morning, Joseph Fisher of Philadelphia, James Sandelands of Chester, and John Darby and Edward Blake and Richard Mankin of New Castle, and five of the six members from Sussex, the other member not having attended at all, refused to attend, apparently in expectation of the petition which their fellow members adopted asking the Governor for justice.

Two days later, there being less than the quorum of two thirds, the attending members of Assembly passed censures upon Markham, Jones, Claypoole, and Reynolds, and also upon Robert Turner, who was reported to have signed the last writ aforesaid, as violators of the privileges of the Assembly and betrayers of the liberties of the freemen. The members also ordered a writ, which, however, was never made out, to bring these censured persons before the House. A number of the Assemblymen went before the Governor and Council, and presented several papers, probably including the speech in reply to Blackwell's, one apparently being upon the non-admission of the three Councillors, and another being that as to White's imprisonment. Blackwell told the Assemblymen that they were not judges of the membership of the Council, and bade them take back their papers: Growdon told them not to. Blackwell then put the papers in his pocket to keep until he could be certain whether the Assembly was legally in being, inasmuch as it might be said to have fallen by the non-attendance of a quorum. After Growdon had whispered to his fellow Quakers, Yardley stood up, and said that it appeared to him that the Assembly had not ceased to be. Then, speaking of himself and a number of the Councillors, and saying that they were of a mean education, whose speech sometimes appeared very rude, and memory weak, he offered some views in a folded paper, which Blackwell, supposing it to have emanated from Thomas Lloyd, did not wish to receive. Some debate arising, Lloyd, Eckley, and Richardson came walking in. The Lieutenant-Governor rose, and asked what was their pleasure. Lloyd replied that they came to pay their respects to him, and to sit in the Council. Blackwell told them that they could not take their seats, until he and the Council were satisfied. Lloyd refused to withdraw, and, after some little hubbub, Blackwell declared the meeting adjourned. No further attempt to meet was made by the Assemblymen, whom Blackwell spoke of as *felones de se,* or suicides. On 3rd mo. (May) 23, the Councillors present except Carpenter agreed to the issuing of a declaration, which was drawn up by a committee consisting of Markham, Clark, and Yardley. Simcock and Growdon were absent. The declaration was adopted and signed by Blackwell and nine Councillors, Carpenter voting no, and not signing. Coppock, Clark, Jones, and Yardley, signers, were Quakers. It denied all intention of subverting the Frame and the laws, and declared the laws passed by

GOVERNMENT UNDER THE FRAME OF 1683.

the Proprietary and Council and Assembly before his going to England to be in force until orders from England should be received, with the proviso or exception, however, that the Governor might issue commissions to the Provincial Judges under the lesser seal.

News had come about midnight of the 23rd of February of the great events in England up to December 23, when the person bringing the news had sailed out of the Downs. Little more was known for some time. In April, documents bore date "in the fifth year of the reign of King James the Second." After hearing of the accession of William and Mary, the people of New Castle became dissatisfied that the new rulers were not proclaimed, but the Governor said that he had no orders for proclaiming them, and did not know how it was to be done, having never seen a proclamation for that purpose, and feared that he might exceed or fall short in giving the proper titles, which would be treason in either case. The Council, on 6mo. 29, unanimously agreed with the Governor.

On October 1, the Governor received a letter, dated Whitehall, 13 April, 1689, signed by the Earl of Shrewsbury, announcing, by the King's command, preparations for a war with France. The Councillors, after a long notice, were brought together on November 1st, to consider what was to be done, and then decided that it was time to make an acknowledgment of the authority of William and Mary, and to profess readiness to proclaim them upon receipt of orders or a form of proclamation. The next day, a declaration was signed by Blackwell and ten Councillors, acknowledging the new sovereigns, commanding all Justices and officers to act in the new names, and process to be so issued, and continuing all officers except Roman Catholics, and continuing all process previously issued. Then opened a debate upon arming the Province. The non-Quakers thought notice should be given to the people to get arms and powder and shot. The first Quakers who spoke, wished to await further news before putting the people to such expense, or said that there was no danger except from bears and wolves, or feared that the neighbouring Indians might take fright when they saw the population in arms, and might start hostilities: then Samuel Carpenter explained that he was not against those who would undertake to defend themselves, but, it being against the judgment of a great part of the people and his own, he could not advise it, or express approval of it, the King must know the judgment of Quakers, but, if they must be forced, he, Carpenter, supposed, that, rather than do it, they would suffer. Coppock agreed with him. Jones proposed it be left to the Governor's discretion. Simcock and Carpenter prevented such question from then being put, saying that it would be prejudicial to them to be otherwise than passive. At the next meeting, Blackwell gave his opinion as to the Frame limiting the Governor in the care of the safety of the Province by making him dependent upon the consent of the Council: he argued that, by Acts of Parliament passed in Charles II's reign, the King had the command of the militia, and not the Parliament, and much less could the Provincial Council of Pennsylvania claim command, when the King by letters patent had vested his authority in William Penn. Penn's Charter of 1683 to the people was in its very words limited "as far as in him lieth:" as it was not in the Proprietary's power to subject part of the King's dominions to the chance of being captured, therefore the said Charter of 1683 could not be so construed that the Governor without the Council could not use arms to defend the colony; furthermore his levying of troops and making war was a condition of the grant, and a failure to do it might work a forfeiture. Blackwell also reminded his hearers of the power in the Governor on sudden emergencies to make ordinances. All this, which could be stretched to a complete nullification of the Frame of government, and which might have caused a long argument at any other time, opened a way of escape to the Quakers, when Blackwell proposed that it be left to his discretion to execute the military powers conferred by Charles II upon the Proprietary as near as possible according to the laws of England and the laws of the Province made under the Duke of York. The five Quakers forming the majority present, did not question the Governor's power, Simcock saying: "It is a thing too hard for us to meddle with, and so we leave it." They expected the Governor to follow his conscience: they would follow theirs; and they declined to take such a part as voting. Carpenter, who was then or afterwards the richest man in the colony, said: "I had rather be ruined than violate my conscience." The Governor now said that, as the matter seemed left to him by the general voice of the Councillors, he would act in the best manner he could for the preservation of the whole, without further pressing them on this occasion.

Blackwell had early asked to be relieved of office, and would have liked to go home before the end of the Summer, but awaited the convenience of the friend who had appointed him. At last, in 10th month, a number of belated letters and documents came from Penn. One, dated 6mo. 12, was to the Councillors, saying that he had thought fit to throw everything into their hands, and directing them to let the laws they might pass hold only so long as he should not declare his dissent. If they would prefer to have a Deputy-Governor, they were to name three or five persons, fixing on a proper salary, and the Proprietary would appoint one of them; this, however, not to be a precedent. This was modified by a letter to Blackwell inclosing two commissions dated 7, 25, 1689, explaining to Blackwell that the Councillors should choose whichever they preferred. One was empowering the Council to present three names to the Proprietary, and, until his choice were known, the person having most votes or first chosen was to act as Deputy according to the power and limitation of former commissions. The other was appointing the whole body as Deputy according to the power and limitation of former commissions, the body to elect a President. The Council, on 11mo. 2, accepted the latter of these two alternatives unanimously, cancelled the commission for choosing a single Deputy, and chose Lloyd as President. Penn's feeling towards Lloyd had been expressed to Blackwell thus: "I would be as little rigorous as possible, and do desire thee by all the obligation I and my present circumstances can have upon thee to desist ye prosecution of T. L. I entirely know ye person both in his weakness and accomplishment, and would thee end ye dispute between you two upon my single request and command and that former inconveniences be rather mended than punished. Salute me to ye people in generall, pray send for J. Simcock, A. Cook, John Eckley, and Samuel Carpenter, and let them dispose T. L. and Sa. Richardson to that complying temper that may tend to that loving and serious accord yt becomes such a government." Blackwell remained some time in the province after leaving office, his age and constitution making it unfit that he should take at that season of the year so long a journey as to Boston. On 1mo. 31, 1690, Lloyd was unanimously reelected President, the Council having been changed by the election of Griffith Owen, Arthur Cooke, John Blunston, John Cann, John Brinckloe, and Thomas Clifton, in place of Carpenter, Growdon, Bristow, Alricks, Markham, and Hill respectively, and by the election of Thomas Duckett, in place of Eckley, who had died. Blunston declining, William Howell was elected on 2, 22, 1690, but declared himself incapable, and appears never to have served. The Council succeeded in having laws passed, and undid what they could of Blackwell's work. Nevertheless the feeling of the Quaker leaders against those who had acted against White and Lloyd, or had not supported the measures proposed in the House, was not appeased. The resolutions as to breaches of privilege were passed in 1690: while the acts complained of, being committed by those representing Delaware sentiment, had something to do with the breach of the following year.

The impost granted to William Penn in 1683, being 2*d*. per gal. on strong liquor, 1*d*. on cider, and one per cent. on all other goods imported, had met with opposition from those who were to pay it, and on 11, 2, 1689-90, a letter was read from the Proprietary mentioning that there was 600*l*. due to him which had been neglected or refused to be paid, and asking that the sum be made up by the colony building a house for him on his city lot, or putting stock to the extent of 200*l*. on each of the three plantations for his children. The impost was discontinued in 1690, Samuel Carpenter, John Songhurst, Griffith Jones, and others undertaking to pay the lump sum of £600 as a composition. This, however, failed to be paid.

The persons and descendants of persons who had settled on the Bay and River before Penn received his title, had stood by Blackwell, and were disgruntled by the reestablishment of the Quaker clique at the head of affairs, and perhaps were alarmed for the safety of the colony with non-resistants in control. The Quakers of the Lower Counties, moreover, were estranged, like the other inhabitants living so far from Philadelphia, by the want of consideration for them. The Pennsylvania Councillors, when the appointment of officers for the Lower Counties came up, voted for and elected whomsoever they saw fit, without regard to the wishes of the members present from the locality. The expense and loss of time in coming to Philadelphia often caused the absence of Councillors from a distance. The coming to Philadelphia to attend court was also onerous. Penn had wisely provided a Supreme Court for the whole dominion to hear appeals, and try capital offences, with five Judges, of whom two were to go every Spring and Fall into the five counties, besides three of the Judges holding two sessions a year in Philadelphia. At the next Assembly after his departure, the Court for hearing appeals and trying murders &ct. was made stationary at Philadelphia, so that some persons would be obliged to travel one hundred and forty miles. Most of the representatives of the Lower Counties had opposed this, but it had been carried, it was said, by the influence of a leading man of the Upper Counties. In May, 1690, the going of the circuit by any two of five Provincial Court Judges was ordered by Act of Assembly: The appointment of the five Judges, however, was delayed in Council; so that no court was held in the Lower Counties that Fall, although there was at least one person suspected of murder in each of these Counties. By the trouble in constituting courts and neglect by authorities, and probably by some inclination in Quakers to pity, and a shrinking on their part from putting anybody to death, a widow in Sussex Co., committed to prison in 1688, but bailed, on the charge of murdering her bastard child, was not brought to trial, and about a year later, being suspected of murdering another, still remained at large and untried, and was employed as a servant when, in February, 1690-1, she was delivered of another bastard, which also died apparently by her hand. Somebody reproached Thomas Lloyd for the failure of justice, and reasoned with him as follows: if she had suffered for the first murder, she would not have committed the two last; if she had been cleared of the first, she could then have been at liberty to marry and live honestly and bring up children, as she did in her husband's lifetime, which would also have prevented the two last murders. Certain Councillors from the Lower Counties decided to remedy the want of Provincial Judges in that region, and on 9, 21, 1690, without having a meeting formally called by President Lloyd, because in a well attended Council the Pennsylvanians were likely to make a majority, Clark, Watson, Jones, Brinckloe, Cann, and De Haes met at New Castle, and ordered two commissions of five Judges, the names being the same in each, but one commission, covering Pennsylvania, naming Simcock first, and the other, covering the Lower Counties, naming Clark first. On application to Lloyd as Keeper, he refused to affix the great seal, and a meeting attended by Pennsylvanians declared the proceedings void. The matter was compromised by the Council adopting the plan of a Pennsylvanian and a Delawarean heading the Court in his respective half of the dominion. So strong was the feeling in the Lower Counties that no representatives from the same were chosen to the Assembly of 1691, although Richard Halliwell, George Martin, and Albertus Jacobs were chosen to the Council.

On 1 month 30, 1691, there were submitted for the Council's choice two new commissions from the Proprietary, one for the Council to name three persons from whom Penn would appoint a Deputy-Governor, the person having most votes to act until Penn's pleasure were known, the other commission for Lloyd, Markham, Turner, Jennings, and Cann or any three of them to act as Deputy. It is said that Penn indicated his preference for the latter arrangement. He also gave notice that if a single Deputy were decided upon, the colony was to bear his support. If neither commission were accepted, the government was to remain in the whole Council. The members from Pennsylvania were unanimous for a single executive, but those from the Lower Counties declared against it, being unwilling to charge their people with a salary for such an officer, particularly one who would reside in Philadelphia. They perceived a design of the others, who were a majority of those in attendance, to choose Lloyd, giving to that self-willed individual the power to put in and turn out what officers he saw fit. The five Commissioners were more agreeable to the Delawareans, Cann being one of themselves, Markham very acceptable to them, and Turner not under the control of Lloyd and Jennings. The Delawareans asked, if that arrangement were not chosen, then that the authority of the whole Council be continued, otherwise they would secede. On this day, David Lloyd, Clerk of Philadelphia County, issued a writ in an action for a debt against one of the Councillors from the Lower Counties: his fellow representatives thought this a scheme to prevent his attendance. At the next meeting, ten members being present, Thomas Lloyd in the chair, Growdon suddenly called for those in favor of nominating Lloyd, Cooke, and John Goodson for Deputy-Governor to rise and say "yea." Whereupon the Delawareans, protesting that the charter required two thirds as a quorum and a two thirds vote in "affairs of moment," withdrew. The others made the nomination aforesaid, and, after some hesitation by Lloyd, he, being the one having most votes, was proclaimed Deputy-Governor on April 2. On the 4th, Cann, Clark,—who, the reader will note, was a Quaker,—Brinckloe, Halliwell, Hill, Martin, and Jacobs, claiming that the governorship was still in the Council, met at New Castle, and chose Cann as President. Lloyd tried to win these back, offering that the pay of himself under the commission should not be a charge upon the Lower Counties until desired by their representatives; but in vain, the seceders not only disliking the influence of David Lloyd upon all Judges whom Thomas Lloyd might appoint, but being now incensed at being stigmatized as traitors, and charged with wishing to throw their territory into the hands of

New York. The latter thought, they disclaimed in a letter to Penn.

On petition of the "inhabitants and settlers" of the town of Philadelphia, "being some of the first adventurers and purchasers within this Province," the said town was erected into a borough—if the charter of 1691 means that there had been such action previously. Lloyd as Deputy Governor, with the advice and consent of the Provincial Council, on 3mo. (May) 20, 1691, erected said town and borough into a City to extend to the limits and bounds as it was laid out between the Delaware and Schuylkill. This charter appointed until the first annual election Humphrey Morrey as Mayor, John Delaval as Recorder, and David Lloyd as Town Clerk and Clerk of the Courts to be held within the City and Liberties, and Samuel Richardson, Griffith Owen, Anthony Morris, Robert Ewer, John Holmes, and Francis Rawle Jr., then Justices, who were citizens and inhabitants of said City, as the Aldermen, and Samuel Carpenter, Thomas Budd, John Jones, John Otter, Charles Sanders, Zechariah Whitpaine, John Day, Philip Richards, Alexander Berdsley, James Fox, Thomas Pascall, and Philip James, as the Common Councilmen, with power to acquire and sell real estate, the Mayor, Recorder, Aldermen, and Common Councilmen to choose annually from the inhabitants persons to fill said offices. The Mayor, Recorder, and Aldermen were to be Justices of the Peace and Oyer and Terminer in the City and Liberties, and the Mayor, Recorder, and one Alderman were to hear and determine all causes arising therein civil and criminal except treason, murder, and manslaughter, reserving appeal according to the King's patent and the laws of the Province. Power was given to make and enforce laws, ordinances, &ct. for the government of the City not repugnant to the laws of England or Pennsylvania, and to impose fines, and keep the same for the use of the corporation.

In the time of Lloyd's presidency occurred the first and for a long time greatest employment of force by Quaker rulers. Caleb Pusey, in *Satan's Harbinger Encountered,* minimizing the charge of inconsistency, relates that Peter Babbitt with some accomplices stole a sloop, and took her down the river; then three magistrates issued a warrant in the nature of a hue and cry; and, Samuel Carpenter, the owner of the sloop, stood on the wharf, and encouraged the volunteers by offering 100*l.* reward; so Peter Boss and a party of men started in pursuit, and captured both the vessel and the robbers, although it was said that Boss and party had neither "gun, sword, or spear." That a minister and two other Quakers acting as magistrates gave a commission to fight, will be shown in the next chapter to have caused animadversion.

The Assemblymen chosen from Philadelphia, Bucks, and Chester Counties were convened in 7th month, 1691, under a law referring all matters not otherwise provided for concerning the Province to the Governor and freemen thereof. This Assembly continued the laws until the next session.

Penn received the letters of both the Pennsylvania and the Delaware Councillors in 7th month; and, on the 11th, within a day or so of the time when he is alleged to have escaped to France, he wrote to the whole number of Councillors, begging them to forgive each other, and to choose again in a full meeting. Taking up the grievances, he said that it was not well to reject petitions, it was not discreet knowingly to arrest David Lloyd, the Assembly's clerk, but that body by the Frame had no clerk other than the Clerk of the Provincial Council, and it was wrong in the Council to choose the Deputy without a quorum of two thirds. This letter went by way of Maryland, enclosed to Richard Johns, and was sent by Ralph Fishbourn to

Government Under the Frame of 1683. 209

those for whom it was intended, and reached them on April 12, 1692.

About the beginning of 1692, however, Penn commissioned Thomas Lloyd as Lieutenant-Governor of Pennsylvania, and Markham as Lieutenant-Governor of the Lower Counties; so that this division lasted until the arrival of Governor Fletcher. The representatives of all six counties united in 1692 in one Assembly, but that body had a conflict with the Council of Pennsylvania, and none of the laws suggested by the Councillors presided over by Lloyd and Markham respectively were passed. For the years 1691, 1692, and 1693, the minutes of the Council are wanting. The following new members appear to have been among the representatives of Pennsylvania proper: William Jenkins, Samuel Levis, William Biles, Hugh Roberts, and Richard Hough, while the *Pennsylvania Archives,* Vol. I, show the election of Richard Wilson in 1st mo., 1692, from Kent, and Samuel Gray appears in that year as a Councillor from the Territories, probably from Sussex.

CHAPTER VIII.

Religious Dissension.

The Quakers without a standard of belief—George Keith—His contentions with members of the Society—Separate meetings—Written judgment against him and replies thereto—Arrest of Bradford and McComb, seizure of Bradford's tools, and proclamation against Keith—The Yearly Meeting of 1692—Liability of Keith to punishment under the civil laws—His arraignment with that of Boss, Budd, Bradford, and McComb—Hat incident—The rest of the Court proceedings—Relief granted by the Governor under the Crown—Keithians issue exhortation against negro slavery—The Yearly Meeting in London disowns Keith—His services in the Turners' Hall, London, and decision to join the Established Church—Subsequent course of various Keithians—Welsh Baptists—Lower Dublin—Seventh Day Baptist burying-ground in the city—Trinity Church, Oxford—Upper Providence Keithians and rival congregations formed among them—Philadelphia Keithian Meeting—Thomas Rutter—Dispute as to the property—The Lloydians—Triumph of Orthodoxy in the Society of Friends.

The Society of Friends had never promulgated articles of religion to be subscribed, or a catechism to be taught. Peculiar tenets and practices, which presupposed the truth of much of what Western Europe believed, were recognized as Quakerism: but the prefatory and even basic dogmas, while they might be gathered from writings like Barclay's, were left to the individual conscience, directed by an inner revelation. There was no insisting upon even those creeds which have been called the symbols of Christianity, and which Fox and the majority of his followers had accepted together with the historical statements of the Gospels. Fox had flouted at training-schools for ministers, even at making them familiar with Hebrew, Greek, and Latin. Thus, with hearers ignorant of, or with no predilection towards, what was agreed upon by Roman Catholic, Calvinist, Lutheran, Greek, and Anglican, there was a diversity of teaching in the bond of fellowship, which is delightful in the view of many people of to-day. There does not seem to have been any considerable movement to give a Unitarian interpretation to the New Testament. John Gough's *History of the People called Quakers* says that George Whitehead, William Mead, and other English Friends, on examination before Parliament, gave satisfactory statement of their belief in the Trinity as well as Holy Writ, so that the profession of faith required by the Act of Toleration then passed was put in the words suggested by them—a strange way, indeed, of stating the Trinity —viz: "I, A. B. do profess faith in God the Father and in Jesus Christ his eternal Son, the true God, and in the Holy Spirit, one God blessed for evermore; and do acknowledge the Holy Scriptures of the Old and New Testament to be given by Divine Inspiration." Yet there had been, and there lingered in that body of exalters of their personal intuition a tendency to make figurative or to forget the Bible's story, and, from the expressions of some prominent members, it seemed at times that they were lapsing into Deism. The great opposition which Christian theologians, Presbyterians, Episcopalians, and Congregationalists, made to the Society of Friends in the last third of that Century was more conscientious than a desire for soldiers, for tithes, or even for observance of the sacraments: it was loyalty to external Revelation. The reproaches cast upon the Society that its teachers, if, indeed, they did not reject, at least failed to hand down, their deposit of truth, seemed to many people to be justified by the events now to be mentioned, when a party taking a stand for Orthodoxy declined to hold meetings with the majority of the ministers at Philadelphia, and when, moreover, the Yearly Meeting in London expelled the leader of that party.

George Keith, one of the most eminent preachers and controversialists of the Society, long felt the need of some sort of confession of faith, probably almost as much to answer the jibes of non-Quakers, as to control or teach Quakers. In fact, the occasion of his urging the matter in the Philadelphia meeting was the accusation made by Christian Lodowick in Rhode Island that the Quakers, giving another sense to the words of Scripture, denied the true Christ. Keith had gone to Rhode Island to assist other Friends in disputation. No impression seeming to be made by the spoken avowal of positive or literal faith, Keith and others, in 4th month, 1691, wrote a declaration of the belief of the Friends in certain points of elementary Orthodoxy as to our Lord Jesus Christ of Nazareth. Apparently it was another one of Keith's productions, printed in 1692, which he submitted to the Philadelphia Monthly Meeting of 11th month, 1691, and approval of which was expressed at the next Monthly Meeting by three of the six appointed to examine it. The Rhode Island Meeting directed the printing of the aforesaid confession, and it was printed by Bradford in Philadelphia. The leaders in Penn's great town went so far as to find fault with Bradford for doing this, they never having authorized the publication of that much of a creed.

It is necessary not only to mention the Keithian schism, because it was an important incident in the history of the colony, but to go into considerable detail, because, with the exception of Gough, the Quaker writers and those who have echoed them, have told little except of the bad temper, violent language, and self-will of Keith. He certainly had the natural indignation of a zealot, he was habituated to the bitterness of expression of that age, in which the Quakers had been about as bitter as others, and he carried out the sectarian idea of separating from those teaching what is false. The schismatics from whom he separated, by that time, however, had formed themselves into what they believed to be a Church, and thought schism from it to be a sin; and their preachers had begun to be separate as clergy from the laity. Gough's account is not entirely accurate in details, apart from being pretty much a sermon upon two texts put at the end, viz: the statement that, on 1mo. 16, 1713-4, Keith, as he lay sick in bed, said that he did believe that if God had taken him out of the world when he went among the Quakers, and in that profession, it had been well with him; and the statement that, a couple of years later, to a Quaker visiting Keith, when on his death-bed, he said that he wished he had died when a Quaker, for he was sure that it would have been well for his soul— remarks which were, after all, different from saying that he had done wrong in leaving the latitudinarians controlling the Society of Friends, and did not even involve the unimportance of the sacraments, for he had received them, water-baptism, as he mentions, and almost as certainly the bread and wine before becoming a Quaker. Both Robert Barclay and he had shown themselves not wholly satisfied with the Quakers' discontinuance of a religious—we may say eucharistic, but not sacramental—feast; and, before Keith received the Communion from the Church of England, he practised the rite, as well as that of baptism, among the seceding Quakers who attended him. Some of the Scotch Quakers were then practising a feast.

Keith was born in the vicinity of Aberdeen, Scotland, and graduated at Marischal College, intending, it is supposed, to be a minister of the Scottish Kirk. He was converted to Quakerism in or before 1664, when he suffered the first of his many imprisonments in its cause. He assisted Robert Barclay in disputations, succeeded Christopher Taylor in the school at Edmonton, and was Surveyor-General of East Jersey. Bp. Burnet, acquainted with Keith at College, claimed that he was the most learned member of the Society of Friends. He came to Philadelphia in 1689, and for over a year had charge of the school chartered by Penn, retiring from it on 4mo. 10, 1691.

Keith, who, by his far superior prominence in the Society at large, could without presumption aspire to the leadership of the members in America, first ruffled his new neighbours by projects for changing their discipline. Gough says that Keith proposed some regulations to the ministers at the Yearly Meeting, but, on the latter wishing to ask the Yearly Meeting in London, decided to let the matter drop. He then undertook to correct by Orthodox standards the loose preaching which he was hearing at Meetings. In attempting to restrain the tendency to allegorize the New Testament, he overhauled William Stockdale for preaching "Christ within" to the exclusion of the historic Christ. Going beyond this elementary reform, Keith insisted on doctrines well accepted by contemporary theologians, but of which probably his fellow ministers present had never heard, while he indulged in speculations which perhaps they did not comprehend. Jennings reported afterwards to the Quakers in England that the question on which so many took the negative was the universality of the need of faith in the historic Christ for salvation. Keith had formerly taken the negative, but, changing, suggested at one time that the heathen might acquire that faith in some future state, and suggested at another time that the "inner light" could give an unconscious faith. In short, Keith undertook to direct in doctrine and procedure the Friends of Pennsylvania. How troublesome certain of them were in secular affairs, this history elsewhere shows; while as to Jennings, who had recently moved from West Jersey, his course there may have been conscientious, but he was once elected Governor of that province, and his election declared by Quaker arbitraters an infringement of Byllinge's right. It was difficult enough to teach a group of the most independent religious thinkers. Those with whom Keith was concerned, were the most important part of the Society of Friends politically, and felt themselves a chosen people. At their head as Clerk of the Quarterly Meeting of Ministers, enabling him to mould the expression of the sense, was Jennings; and nothing could be done among the Philadelphia Friends which did not commend itself to Thomas Lloyd, while any confession of faith would abridge the liberty, or contradict the views, of some old preacher or "martyr." Lloyd (see Roberts's letter in *Penna. Mag. of Hist.*, Vol. XVIII, p. 205) did not antagonize Keith until he insisted upon a declaration of faith. There were some leaders who actually had cast aside many of the older and widely prevalent beliefs. In the *Reasons and Causes of the Separation,* written by Keith or his friends, it is said that the doctrine of Christ's being in Heaven in the true nature of man, and of faith in Him being necessary to our perfect justification and salvation, and of His coming again, outside of us, to judge the quick and the dead, and of the resurrection of the dead and day of judgment were called by some "Popery," and by others "Presbyterian and Baptist principles." With the leaders, the resentment excited by Keith's various propositions, and, with the more docile, the feeling that he was troublesome, obscured the greater issue which was raised when he criticized theological expressions, and was met with statements and questions which until some time in the Nineteenth Century, would not have been tolerated in any so-called Christian Church. Some of those who refused to follow Keith, including Lloyd, had no intention of committing themselves to Rationalism, particularly after a letter was received from George Whitehead, Patrick Livingston, and other London Friends deprecating disputations upon subjects not tending to edification, and affirming salvation through Christ to those who never heard of Him, but urging all not to reject Jesus Christ's outward coming, suffering, death, resurrection, ascension, and glorified state in the heavens.

Those who had been reproved by Keith, attacked him in return. Stockdale criticized Keith's speaking so much of Christ within and Christ without as preaching two Christs, or as letting people infer two distinct Christs. *The Plea of the Innocent,* in contradiction to the Quarterly Meeting of the following year about the violation of Gospel order, says that Keith did privately deal with Stockdale, and then laid the matter before twelve of the ministers, who, except John Hart, and except John Delaval, rather excused Stockdale. Calling Stockdale an ignorant heathen, Keith asked judgment against him for making the criticism, or charge, and, receiving no answer, laid the matter before the Yearly Meeting held in Philadelphia in 7th month, 1691. Keith afterwards made a great point that that assembly of preachers of the Gospel debated for about ten hours one day, and at five subsequent "meetings," i.e. sittings, whether preaching Christ without and Christ within was preaching two Christs, and then came to "a slender and partial judgment," of which they made no record. Nevertheless, a declaration was made that Stockdale was blameworthy, because Keith's doctrine was true. On 11mo. 29, 1691, at the Monthly Meeting, Thomas Fitzwater charged Keith with denying the sufficiency of the light within for salvation. This insinuated that Keith could no longer be properly classified as a Quaker. Gough is not accurate in his account of the Fitzwater episode. At the next Monthly Meeting, 12mo. 26, 1691, to which Fitzwater had promised to bring his proof, Stockdale came forth as a witness in support of Fitzwater, but other Friends testified that Keith had denied the sufficiency "without something more," meaning the death and mediation of Christ. After Jennings, the Clerk, and other opposers of Keith, had retired from the assemblage, those remaining, including Fitzwater, unanimously agreed to adjourn to the next day at the 8th hour at the school house, the usual place of holding meetings in winter. Lloyd and Cooke, but not Jennings, attended this adjourned meeting, as did Fitzwater. However, there being strong contention, all three went away. Stockdale was sent for, but declined to come. Those present, numbering about sixty, including ministers and "those in the habit of attending monthly meetings," then unanimously agreed to a judgment signed by J. W. (*Qu:* Joseph Willcox?), whom they constituted Clerk, to the effect that Fitzwater should forbear to preach until he gave a writing condemning his charge against Keith, and satisfying as to his own true faith and belief in Christ's resurrection and Christ's being in Heaven in his glorified human nature; and also to the effect that Stockdale forbear to preach until he condemn his unrighteous charge against Keith of preaching two Christs. Furthermore, the opinion was given that the book vindicating the Christian faith of the Quakers of Rhode Island was for good, and for the service of truth, and that Bradford should not be discouraged for printing it. With a misprint giving date of the meeting as 2nd month instead of 12th month, the names of "some of the Friends that gave the aforesaid judgment," to the number of forty-five are in print, viz: George Hutcheson, Thomas Winn (evidently Dr. Thomas Wynne, Speaker of the Assembly) Thomas Budd, Paul Saunders, John Hart, Thomas Hooton, John Lynam, Anthony Taylor, Thomas Paschall, Ralph Jackson, Abel Noble, Humphrey Hodges, Phillip James, Nicholas Pearce, Henry Furnis, Richard Hillyard, John Furnis, Anthony Sturges, John Redman, Robert Wallis, Thomas Peart, John Williams, Thomas Jenner, Thomas Tresse, Ralph Ward, William Davis, John Loftus, William Dillwyn, Francis Cook, William Harwood, John Duploveys, Henry Johnson, James Chick, John Budd, Joseph Walker, Thomas Morris, William Bradford, Hugh Derborough, John McComb, William Paschall, William Say, John Hutchins, Joseph Willcox, William Hard, and James Cooper.

At the Quarterly Meeting held at the beginning of March, 1691-2, a few days after this, it was asked that this judgment be recorded in the Monthly Meeting book, but the other party denied that those who gave the judgment constituted a legal Meeting, inasmuch as there was no precedent for an adjourned Monthly Meeting, and as the Clerk had gone, and few ministers were present. Moreover, this party asserted that, as the subject of the charge against the ministers Fitzwater and Stockdale was a matter of doctrine, it could not be judged by a Monthly Meeting, but only by a meeting of ministers. However, it was agreed that the adjourned meeting was legal, but that an appeal had been taken from its decision. Keith was then told that he should submit to a judgment by the present Meeting. This curtailment of the right of private judgment, so much talked of by Protestants, was denied by Keith, as giving the ministers the teaching powers of a sacerdotal order. He would say only that he would submit to the judgment "of the spirit of truth in Friends." When asked to leave pending discussion, he refused to do so, unless about seven or eight of his opposers also absented themselves, and, they not doing this, the subject was not taken up. As the policy of the leaders was to smother discussion, and to shield comrades whose views the majority themselves thought erroneous, there was really no inaccuracy in Keith's remark, made at this time, that the ministers opposed to him had "met together," that is had come intending, "to cloak heresies and deceits."

The subject at bottom was and is, however, one as to which Patrick Henry's words at the beginning of the American Revolution are appropriate, even if some readers would emphasize the first word: "Gentlemen may cry, peace, peace—but there is no peace." These criers of "peace" undertook to silence Keith's tongue. Accordingly, two members were appointed to admonish him to retract at the next Quarterly Meeting; but, when they visited him, he, feeling himself a champion of the truth, said that there were "more damnable heresies and doctrines of devils among the Quakers than among any profession of Protestants," and that he trampled "the judgment of the Meeting under his feet as dirt."

At the Monthly Meeting held on March 25, 1692, some of his opponents proposed to change the hour and place of meetings for worship established for the Winter. This was objected to by several of the Keithian faction, but was agreed to by the majority, and declared adopted. Although Lloyd and his party accordingly went the next morning to the meeting-house at the Centre, the followers of Keith, claiming that the change contravened the principle of unanimity by which all Quaker proceedings were to be conducted, met at the usual time and place, and did not unite with the others in the afternoon at the Bank Meeting House (Front above Arch), a few of them holding a private gathering at Keith's house. Subsequently they attempted to go to the house on the bank in the morning, but found the doors locked against them.

With the fair claim that the others were the aggressors, but on the broad basis of duty not to unite in worship with those who rejected the truth, arose the "Christian Quakers," as they called themselves, or "Separatists," or "Keithians," as the others called them. Out of the sparse population of the country and the small number of dwellers in the great towne, hundreds flocked to hear Keith, wherever he was expected to preach. Persons of other religious antecedents joined these Separatists, so that Keith prepared a confession of faith. Outside of Philadelphia, the sense of many of the regular meetings was Keithian: and Joseph C. Martindale, M.D., in his *History of the Townships of Byberry and Moreland,* asserts that, at one time which he does not clearly indicate, Keith's followers had the ascendency in sixteen out of thirty-two Meetings. Apparently the latter number covers the Meetings previously established for worship on one or both sides of the Delaware.

Yet the Keithians, soon after the beginning of the separation, put themselves on record as attempting an accommodation. Fifteen made in writing an offer for restoration of unity and the oblivion of all hard words, if the others would bring their erroneous ministers to a confession of error, and would declare certain fundamental doctrines. Through the influence of two visiting Friends from England, a conference was held on 3mo. 14, between the ministers then in town and an equal number of Keithians, but, the matter not being settled, T. B. and W. B. (Thomas Budd and William Bradford) wrote the next day to T—— and A—— (evidently Thomas Lloyd and Arthur Cooke), for another meeting. This brought no reply, and Keith did not help the cause of harmony, but was thought a disturber, by going to the afternoon meeting on the 22nd, and expressing a desire to have the breach healed. Two of the opposite side came to Keith's meeting, and declared their testimony against him. The Monthly Meeting of 3rd mo. 26, 1692, controlled by Keith's enemies, disposed of the Fitzwater matter by letting him off with an apology for his "rash spirit in making the charge" against Keith of denying the sufficiency of the Light Within without something more, which charge Fitzwater, however, said was true; and no affirmance of belief was made in the paper given forth.

The ministers in Quarterly Meeting judged Stockdale on 4mo. 4, 1692; the paper signed by Jennings as Clerk reproved him for "uttering new words offensive to many sound and tender persons," but blamed Keith for violating Gospel order in not dealing with Stockdale alone before prosecuting the complaint, and for his "indecent expression" to Stockdale. Keith not appearing to retract what he said about "cloaking heresies and deceits," and the persons sent by the last Quarterly Meeting to admonish him reporting his words about "doctrines of devils," and about trampling "the judgment of the Meeting under his feet," a second committee was sent to him, and the Meeting adjourned for a fortnight. The second committee, obtaining no satisfaction, prepared a testimony, to be published after he should have an opportunity to read it, for which they were obliged to wait four or five days later. The Meeting, on reconvening, forbade him to preach, and the declaration was published against him, dated 4mo. 20, 1692, and signed by the twenty-eight "public friends" following:

Thomas Lloyd
John Willsford
Nicholas Waln
William Watson
George Maris
William Cooper
Thomas Thackory
William Biles (printed "Byles")
Samuel Jennings

Thomas Duckett	John Delaval
Joshua Fearne	William Yardley (printed "Yeardly")
Even Morris	
Richard Walter	Joseph Kirkbride
John Symcock	Walter Fawcit
Griffith Owen	Hugh Roberts
John Bown	Robert Owen
Henry Willis	William Walker
Paul Sanders	John Lynam
John Blunston	George Gray.

Certain of these twenty-eight signers went from Meeting to Meeting to deliver the judgment. On 4mo. 27, Lloyd, Jennings, and Delaval with Samuel Richardson went to Frankford Monthly Meeting to give countenance to the reading of the judgment, Lloyd speaking against Keith for "imposing unscriptural words," i.e. asking belief according to theological terms. This judgment could not have been received at Frankford Monthly Meeting with unanimous satisfaction; for Martindale's *History* says that John Hart controlled the constituent First Day Meeting at Byberry in Keith's favor, and in time drove the opposing attendants of Byberry to secede.

The friends and followers of Keith in Philadelphia were not overawed. In protest against the judgment, Peter Boss wrote two letters to Jennings. The first receiving no notice, Boss kept a copy of the second, to insure an answer to it. It was clearly scurrilous in saying that the twenty-eight would have been better employed in inquiring whether Jennings or Simcock had been drunk on certain occasions, and also it was scurrilous in Quaker eyes in similarly insinuating that Jennings had once made a bet on the speed of his horse. The letter was not put in print until after Boss had been tried for defaming a magistrate. Keith and Thomas Budd wrote a *Plea for the Innocent*, signing it on behalf of themselves and other Friends of their

Religious Dissension. 223

Meeting. Extenuating and justifying Keith's use of bad names to his opponents, and telling of the bad names which they gave to him, the *Plea* was very severe on Jennings, and said much more besides calling him "an ignorant, presumptuous, and insolent man" and "too high and imperious both in Friends meetings and worldly courts"; expressions for which Keith and Budd were indicted as contravening an Act of Assembly that no words of defamation be spoken against a magistrate. An answer to the judgments was issued "on behalf of brethren who are falsely called the Separate meetings at Philadelphia," maintaining that, by the first judgment of Monthly Meeting, those making it had declared themselves no true believers in Christ Jesus, and so the answerers could not own them as Christians, nor join with them in worship. This answer was dated 5mo. 3, 1692, at a meeting at the house of Philip James, and signed by

Richard Dungworth	John Loftus
John Wells	John McComb
Phillip James	James Chick
Henry Furnis	John Bartram
James Shattuck	Abel Noble
James Cooper, Sen.	Joseph Walker
William Davis	Thomas Paschall
Robert Wallis	Richard Hilliard
James Poulter	William Waite
Nicholas Pierce	Anthony Sturges
Thomas Budd	Ralph Ward
John Barclay	Thomas Peart
William Bradford	John Chandler
James Cooper, Junr.	Peter Chamberlain.

This answer was followed by an Appeal to the Yearly Meeting. The Appeal was signed by Keith, Budd, Dungworth, George Hutcheson, John Hart, and Abraham Opdegraves, and offered to have tried by two or three impartial men twelve questions, whether Keith's "reviling words" were not true, and whether the expressions and certain practices of his enemies were not condemnable. The 9th of these questions was based upon the use of force against Babbitt and his men, as mentioned in the last preceding chapter, and inquired whether the twenty-eight condemners of Keith had not better have condemned some of themselves for hiring men to fight, commissioning them, as one preacher had done, and so, by force of arms, recovering a sloop, and taking privateers. There will be little doubt that the hiring of men to fight, and the providing of Indians with powder and lead to fight other Indians, against which practices the 10th question was directed, was inconsistent with the peace principles of Friends. Question No. 11 was whether it was according to the Gospel that ministers should pass sentence of death on malefactors, as some had done, "preaching one day not to take an eye for an eye, . . . another day taking life for life?" In this connection, it may be remarked that the bishops in the English House of Lords do not adjudge matters of treason or capital crime. This 11th question, which may have been suggested by Opdegraves, a former Mennonite, brought forward the difficulty in conscience which had induced Quakers elsewhere and all Mennonites to keep aloof from administering secular government. Bradford, the printer, having taken side with Keith, printed this Appeal.

Thereupon began proceedings which amounted to religious persecution by indirection, although it took the form of prosecution for slander, and for unlicensed use of the press, and could be justified if the acts of some modern judges of our own day in punishing for contempt of court can be. Those whose conduct had been animadverted upon in this published Appeal, who probably had previously, in another situation, contended for liberty of conscience and of the press, now persuaded themselves that bitter words against magis-

Religious Dissension.

trates uttered in religious controversy, and questions whether their executing offices was consistent with their principles, tended to overthrow the government. They proceeded against the printer. A warrant was signed by Samuel Richardson and Robert Ewer, Justices; and the Sheriff and a constable entered Bradford's shop, and seized all the copies of the *Appeal* which could be found, and took Bradford before the Justices. John McComb, who was alleged to have circulated two copies, was also arrested. Refusing to give security to answer at the next court, Bradford and McComb were committed to jail by warrant dated Aug. 24, 1692, signed by Justices Cooke, Jennings, and Humphrey Morrey, as well as Robert Ewer. On another warrant, Bradford's house was searched, and his type taken away. The day after the commitment of Bradford and McComb, Justices Cooke, Jennings, Richardson, Morrey, Ewer, and Anthony Morris asked the only Justices who were not Quakers, viz: Lasse Cock, a Swede, and John Holmes, a Baptist, to join in taking steps against "the seditious and dangerous," but Cock and Holmes told their five colleagues that the whole matter was a religious difference, and did not relate to the government. Holmes asked them to send for Keith, and offered to join them if it then appeared that Keith struck at the government. This not being done, Cock and Holmes withdrew. The others then issued a proclamation describing Keith as a seditious person and enemy to the King and Queen's government, in that Keith had publicly reviled Thomas Lloyd, the Deputy-Governor, calling him an impudent man, telling him that he was not fit to be Governor, and that his name would stink, and in that Keith had misrepresented the industry, care, readiness, and vigilance of some magistrates and others in the proceedings against some privateers. The point was made in the document that to grant that it was inconsistent for ministers of the gospel to act as magistrates, would render the "Proprietary incapable of the powers given him by the King's letters patent, and so prostitute the validity of every act of government more especially in the executive part thereof to the courtesie and censure of all factious spirits." After explaining that the procedure against those in the Sheriff's custody, and what was intended against others, respected only the tendency to sedition and disturbance, and did not relate to difference in religion, the proclamation warned against giving countenance to any contemners of authority, and against further publishing of the pamphlet called the *Appeal*. It is declared in *New England's Spirit of Persecution Transmitted to Pennsilvania* that Keith never spoke the aforesaid words except in Monthly Meetings and religious controversies, and that Lloyd had several times said that he would take no advantage of what was being said.

Bradford and McComb asked for a trial at the approaching term of Court, but the case was continued until December, and McComb's license to keep an inn was revoked. Meanwhile Bradford retired from his employment of printing for Friends. The restraint upon the two was indeed relaxed by the Sheriff: McComb's wife lying ill, he was let off daily, and even at night, to visit her, and afterwards both he and Bradford were allowed to go about their business, on giving their word to appear. But they or their advisers saw the dramatic effect of their writing a statement from prison, so, having prepared a statement to the public, they went to the Sheriff's house, which served as jail, and which communicated by a common entry with the house adjoining, and, the Sheriff being out, so that they could get in no further, they signed their names in the entry. With more frankness, to show the unfairness of the claim that the Appeal was subversive of government, the three judgments complained of by Keith, the

Religious Dissension. 227

Answer, and the Appeal were then printed in one pamphlet. The *Appeal* was set up on posts in Philadelphia nine days before the time appointed for the Yearly Meeting.

The Yearly Meeting was held that year in Burlington on the 4th, 5th, 6th, and 7th days of 7th month. It is evident that those who gave the judgment appealed from, were not willing to submit the subject to the general company of Friends attending: Keith, if given the opportunity to make a speech, was to be feared. He and his supporters conferred together in the Court House, and sent to the Meeting a paper asking for an answer to the *Appeal,* or requesting their adversaries to allow a fair hearing before impartial Friends an hour after the close of the meeting for worship on the second day of meeting. The messenger found the door of the meeting-house crowded, with the object, he supposed, of keeping out the Keith party; whereupon the messenger got up into the window, and stood there while he read, probably both letter and Appeal, nor did he desist when Thomas Janney started to pray, which the Keithians believed to be an expedient to stop the reading. It is not necessary here to examine the question, who had the standing to be considered in adjourning the sittings, or taking the action of Yearly Meetings. Many who claimed impartiality, as not having been concerned actually on either side, met at the time Keith desired for a hearing. Lloyd and his party were then sent for, but refused to come, and those in attendance adjourned until an hour after the public meeting the next day. Then Lloyd and his party again refused to come. Then or on the previous day some ministers came to offer a hearing on the last day of the Meeting, but these were sent away, because Keith would not agree: he knew that the large attendance, on which he depended for victory, would not continue so long. The following, who may have included a number of New

Jersey ministers, then declared Lloyd and his party in default, and proceeded to hear Keith, and decided in his favor:

Robert Turner	Andrew Smith
Elias Burling	William Hixon
John Reid	John Pancoast
Charles Read	Henry Burcham
Thomas Coborne	Thomas Hearse
Harmon Updengraves	John Jones
Thomas Powell	Joseph Willcox
Nathaniel Fitzrandal	Thomas Godfrey
Joseph Richards	John Budd
Edmund Wells	Roger Parke
Thomas Kimber	Caleb Wheatly
Edward White	Abraham Brown
Thomas Gladwin	John Hampton
Thomas Rutter	Daniel Bacon
Edward Smith	Joseph Adams
Benjamin Morgan	Edward Guy
Joseph Sharp	Bernard Devonish
William Thomas	Samuel Ellis
John Bainbridge	Thomas Cross
John Snowden	James Moore
William Black	Thomas Jenner
William Snowden	John Harper
Nathaniel Walton	Robert Wheeler
Robert Roe	Emanuel Smith
Peter Boss	Peter Daite
Thomas Bowles	Richard Sery
William Budd	George Willcox
James Silver	William Wells
Samuell Taylor	Isaac Jacobs Van Biber
Griffith Jones	Cornelius Scivers
William Righton	William Snead
Thomas Kendall	David Sherkis
Samuell Houghton	John Carter
John Neall	Henry Paxon
Anthony Woodward	Thomas Tindal.

They signed as from the Yearly Meeting, on behalf of themselves and "many more Friends who are one with us herein," a declaration that Keith and his friends were not guilty of the division leading to the setting up of separate meetings, that Lloyd and the rest of the twenty-eight should recall their paper of condemnation, and condemn the same in writing, and that the public Friends charged with misdemeanors and ill behavior should forbear speaking in public meetings until they cleared themselves. The declaration, or decision, with the signatures was printed: a reprint of the whole is in Mrs. Thomas Potts James's *Memorial of Thomas Potts*. We are more familiar with other forms of some of the surnames, such as Fitz Randolph (now Randolph of Phila. and N. J.), Updengraff, van Bebber, &ct. A Confession of Faith, probaly the one prepared by Keith, as before mentioned, was also issued under date of 7mo. 7, 1692. It was subsequently printed by Bradford. It appears that those remaining in attendance at the meeting-house either treated Keith's appeal as not prosecuted before them, or formally confirmed the judgment against him, the latter action being mentioned by Gough. A contrite letter dated 11, 31, 1692, from Caleb Wheatly, aforesaid signer in favor of Keith, saying that he had been blinded by fond, foolish affection for Keith, is printed by Gough.

As hinted in the Justices' proclamation, Keith could be caught under Chapter XXVIII of the Great Law of 1682, that any person convicted of speaking, writing, or any act tending to sedition or disturbance of the peace should be fined not less than 20s., or else under Chapter XXIX, that any person convicted of speaking slightingly or carrying himself abusively against any magistrate or person in office should suffer acording to the quality of the magistrate and nature of the offence, but not less than a fine of 20*s*. or ten days imprisonment at hard labor. Both of these statutes allowed much latitude to the judges imposing sentence, although Chapter XXVIII did not admit of imprisonment, except as resulting from non-payment of a heavy fine, whereas Chapter XXIX contemplated a severe punishment when the magistrate in question was the highest officer in the Province, as was Thomas Lloyd. It seems straining the meaning to say that putting to death was authorized. Overt acts of sedition, rioting, &ct. seem to have been so punishable, by the laws of England in this regard not having been superseded. As to one who had done more than print or circulate a pamphlet, or write a scurrilous letter, it was to be expected, from the tone of the proclamation, that in some process or proceeding emanating from them or other members of their party invested with the authority, there would be the formal charge of sedition. We can not suppose that there was any likelihood of Keith suffering death, but the possibility of it was not only set forth by him, some years later, apparently as a claim to hearing and consideration, but, indeed, was mentioned by his old antagonist, Rev. Cotton Mather, before Keith's statement, at least the one known to the present writer, appeared. Mather said in his *Decennium Luctuosum,* printed in Boston in 1699 (reprinted in *Narratives of Indian Wars 1675-1699*) : " 'tis verily thought that poor George would have been made a sacrifice to Squire Samuel Jennings and the rest of the Pennsylvania dragons [is there an allusion to St. George and the dragon?]; and that since a crime which their laws had made capital was mentioned in the mittimus whereby Keith was committed, they would have hang'd him, if a revolution upon their government had not set him at liberty." Keith's statement was "I was presented by a grand jury at Philadelphia, and the presentment would have been prosecuted if the government had not been changed, and I had been accused for endeavoring to alter the government, which is capital by their law, and they would have found me guilty of death, had they not been turned out of the government, tho' I was innocent, and when I objected against the jury, they would not suffer one of the jury to be cast.'' Perhaps he meant the Grand Jury.

The actual proceedings in the County Court, as far as ascertained, were as follows. Boss, Budd, Keith, Bradford, and McComb, having been indicted by the grand jury of Philadelphia County, were arraigned for trial in December, 1692. The Justices sitting through the proceedings were Jennings, Cooke, Richardson, Ewer, Henry Waddy, and Griffith Owen, Quakers, and Holmes, the Baptist, but Turner, a Keithian, attended on the 10 and 12th of the month, and Cock, the Swede, and Anthony Morris attended on the 12th. When Bradford and McComb, apparently the first ones to be tried, appeared, a Justice upraided them for "standing so before the Court." McComb said "You can order our hats taken off." Probably the Quaker Justices did not proceed to such inconsistency. About thirty years after this, when, as Chancellor of the Court of Equity, Sir William Keith —no near relative of George—ordered John Kinsey's hat to be taken off, strong exception was taken to such interference with Quaker custom, and, on the next day, the Chancellor made an order that thenceforth, in the Courts of the Province, every man should remain covered or uncovered according to his persuasion. We may here recall the story which Miss Strickland, in her *Queens of England,* tells of King James II, when, for the first time after his accession, receiving William Penn. Penn came with his hat on, whereupon the King took off his own, and, on Penn being surprised, naïvely remarked that it was the custom in that place for "only one man to wear a hat."

The vindication of the dignity of Lloyd and the

Quaker ministers in the judiciary was not left in the hands of impartial men, and, in the proceedings in Court, there was a neglect of the proprieties which only the scarcity of lawyers, judges, and jurors disconnected with the controversy can, as to some points, excuse. The public prosecutor, or Attorney-General, John Moore, being an adherent of the Church of England, David Lloyd was appointed to conduct the prosecution. Jennings sat on the bench with the other Judges, even in the trial of Boss, although refraining from joining in the judgment, or the fixing of the fines. Keith made a speech, but declined to plead in form, and was marked "Nihil dicit;" the others, particularly Boss, putting themselves on trial, excepted to the Quakers on the jury as prejudiced, some especially so, against Keith and all who favored him, but the majority of the Judges would not allow the exceptions, although the Baptist Judge wished to; and one of the twenty-eight who signed the paper of condemnation against Keith, and against whom Boss's letter was written, actually sat on this jury. However, to the credit of Quakers be it spoken, the jurors, or at least enough to control the verdict, were rather scrupulous, and gave a verdict satisfactory to the prosecution only in the case of Boss, whom they found guilty of transgressing the XXIXth Chapter of the Law. He was accordingly fined 6*l.*, in default of paying which he remained a prisoner until after the change of government. In Budd's case, the jury, after sitting all night, found him simply guilty of saying that Jennings behaved himself too high and imperiously in worldly courts. It was claimed that this was no conviction on the indictment. However, Budd was fined 5*l.* Bradford, denying that the *Appeal* was seditious, asserted the advanced principle that the jury must find both that it was seditious, and that he had printed it. This protection to liberty was not allowed: a majority of the Judges declared that whether it was seditious was a question for the Judges, and that all the jury had to do was to say whether he had printed it. To prove that fact, his printing frame was sent to the jury after he had retired, without it being exhibited in open court. The jurors in this case remained out forty-eight hours, and then came in to ask a question, and were sent back, according to the barbarous method of forcing a decision,—it was Winter,—without meat, drink, fire, or tobacco. In the afternoon, they returned and said that they could not agree, and were discharged. McComb appears to have been acquitted or discharged; for Gough says that he afterwards was so just as to give a true state of the case. Budd and Keith asked for an appeal to the Provincial Court, but this was denied. They then asked for an appeal to the King and Queen under the Vth article of the Charter to Penn. This, too, was denied, Justice Robert Turner dissenting, as he had done on several points. However guilty the various accused had been of discrediting the civil government, and even if the circumstances had not mitigated their offence, there is no wonder that, reading the report of these trials in *New England's Spirit of Persecution transmitted to Pennsilvania,* and even before hearing of any danger to the life of Keith, people outside of the Province felt, that, if such were Quaker methods, no man could trust his liberty or property to a trial by Quakers. Whether the law had been stretched too far or not, the fact remained that both liberty and property had been taken away judicially by the opposing party in a religious dispute. Should a case arise where the legal penalty clearly involved loss of life, would not the Quakers vindicate their authority in the same way as the Congregationalists of New England? This suspicion had nothing to do with the assumption, described in the next chapter, of the government by the Crown. That change had already been ordered. What was the occasion of the letter of Lloyd and others to Keith shortly after the Court adjourned, is not known.

The indictment or a fresh one was pending against Keith when the new Governor assumed authority. Keith, in his aforesaid statement about being accused of a capital offence, goes on to say that this representative of the Crown "ordered them to let fall the indictment, and I was cleared by a public writ signed by the Deputy Governor Col. Markham and the Council." The only record found bearing on this is the minute of Fletcher's Council for June 20, 1693, Markham presiding, that George Keith (printed "Seith" in *Colonial Records,* Vol. I.) exhibited a letter to Keith dated 10th month 26, 1692, from Thomas Lloyd, Samll. Jennings, Arthur Cooke, and Jno. Delaval, charging him with being crazy, turbulent, a decrier of magistracy, and a notorious evil instrument in Church and State; whereupon Fletcher's Council issued a certificate of Keith's good behavior. The fines against Keith and Budd, which the Quaker government had not attempted to collect, were remitted, as well as Boss's, by Fletcher, who released Boss from prison, and caused Bradford's tools and type to be returned to him.

It was the Keithian Monthly Meeting which, at Philadelphia, on 8mo. 13, 1693, gave forth "an exhortation and caution to Friends concerning buying or keeping of negroes." This, except what was expressed at a gathering in Germantown in 1688, was the first antislavery declaration of the Quakers.

Keith and Budd went to England about the end of 1693. Jennings and Thomas Duckett went about the same time, to circumvent them. Keith and Budd attended the next Yearly Meeting in London, where Jennings and Thomas Duckett appeared against them from America, and were supported by the visiting Friends, Thomas Wilson and James Dickenson. The Meeting declared that Keith had done ill in printing and publishing the differences, and asked him to call in his books, or publish something to clear the body of Quakers. Thomas Ellwood submitted on the 2nd day an epistle warning against him, and obtained leave to print it. Keith being no more inclined to submission than most reformers, the next Yearly Meeting, on May 25, 1695, after hearing him through, disowned him, explaining that this was not for doctrine, but for his unbearable temper and carriage and refusal to withdraw his charges against the Philadelphia Quakers.

Keith then hired the Turners' Hall, Philpot Lane, London, and there, in Quaker garb, he preached and administered baptism and communion. Köster the Pietist (see chapter on the Germans), or more likely his biographer Rathlef, misunderstanding him, strangely accounts for the Keithians of Pennsylvania delaying to practise these ordinances from Keith's Anglican misgivings about a layman doing so, misgivings which Köster as a Lutheran did not have. The Keithians of Pennsylvania, we are told, being twitted with not practising what they showed their belief in, several of them who had not been baptized in infancy induced Köster to immerse them in the Delaware River. It was a few years after this, and when various Pennsylvania Keithians had gone different ways, that Keith entered the ministry of the Established Church. He gave his reasons for so doing in a farewell sermon at the Hall on May 5, 1700, and was made deacon by the Bishop of London seven days later. Keith's further career will be mentioned in connection with the Church of England.

Although it has been stated that some of the Keithians reunited with the regular organization of the Society of Friends, no instance has been found of any prominent one doing so. Robert Turner and others of those who were inhabitants of the City are recorded in the list kept by William Hudson of persons deceased "not Friends." Nor did a movement back to the Society break up the Keithian meetings at Southampton, Lower Dublin, or Providence. Equally untrue is the idea that Christ Church, Philadelphia, the Mother of the Episcopal Churches of the City and the Province, was started by or absorbed most of the Keithians. The greatest trend was towards the Baptists, but a number, after being immersed, were keepers of Saturday as the day of rest and worship, and joined the Seventh Day Baptists.

According to Rev. Morgan Edwards's *Materials towards a History of the Baptists in Pennsylvania,* William Davis and Thomas Rutter in 1697 were immersed by Rev. Thomas Killingworth, a First Day, or regular, Baptist minister from Norfolk, England, who had a small congregation at Cohansey, New Jersey. Davis joined the Pennypack Baptist Church, but was expelled on Feb. 17, 1698, for heresy as to the Divine and human natures in Christ. John Hart seems to have led the non-seceding members of his First Day Meeting to the house of John Swift in Southampton Township, where they joined other Keithians. To these Hart preached. He was immersed by Rutter in 1697. For a while at least, Hart and his followers were among those convinced of the obligation to keep Saturday as the Sabbath, but he, in 1702, and most of the other Keithians of Southampton sooner or later joined Pennypack Baptist Church. Evan Morgan was also immersed by Rutter in or about 1697, and became a minister in 1706.

Perhaps it should be here noted that the Pennypack Church bid fair to become flourishing, a not inconsiderable number of Baptists from Pembrokeshire and Carmarthanshire, who had organized in 1701 at Milford, came over that year to Philadelphia with their minister, Rev. Thomas Griffiths, and went to the Pennypack. However, they insisted upon the ceremony of laying on of hands, and so could not be in fellowship with the others, and, in 1703, bought 30,000 acres, since known as the Welsh Tract, in New Castle Co., and removed thither. From the Welsh Tract Church, missions and perhaps emigrants founded several congregations, among them that of the Great Valley (in Tredyffrin Township, Chester Co.), instituted in 1711 with Rev. Hugh Davis, an ordained minister from Wales. The Pennypack Church died out, and the views and practices of the Welsh Tract people spread through the Baptist denomination of Penn's colony.

Either before or after aligning themselves with Keith, certain Friends about Frankford and in Lower Dublin built a meeting-house on land belonging to Thomas Graves. Among them was John Wells, a signer of the answer to the judgment of Lloyd and others. Wells on Sep. 27, 1697, became a Baptist. Davis, upon his expulsion from the Pennypack Baptist Church, joined the Keithians of Lower Dublin, who before long began to separate rapidly. In 1699, David Price and wife, Abraham Pratt and wife, Richard Wells, Richard Sparks, and others were baptized, and formed a congregation with Davis as minister. Davis adopted Sabbatarian views, in which he was joined by a number, including Pratt, at whose house meetings were at some time held, and it appears that others seceded. In 1703 and 1704, there was a dispute, mentioned in the records of the Sabbatarians of Westerly, Rhode Island, before whom appeared Davis and Pratt—Sachse quotes the record "Abraham ———." Davis went in 1710 to take charge of the Sabbatarians at Westerly. Richard Sparks, above mentioned, died in 1716, having left a lot in Philadelphia on the east side of 5th below Market as a burial-place for himself and other Seventh Day Baptists. It is now included in the pavement in front of the Bourse, the remains that could be found having been removed to the Cemetery of

Seventh Day Baptists at Shiloh, Cumberland Co., N. J.

It is claimed, however, that most of the "Christian Quakers" of Frankford and Lower Dublin, including Graves, as the fruit of Anglican preaching, and independently of Keith, went over to the Church of England in 1699 or 1700. Graves conveyed the meetinghouse and lot of three acres by deed dated Dec. 30, 1700, to Joshua Carpenter and John Moore "for the use and service of those in communion with our holy mother the Church of England and to no other use or uses whatsoever." The congregation since known as Trinity Church, Oxford, worshipped for a time in the meetinghouse, and before Nov. 5, 1713, erected on the lot its present church edifice, the meeting-house becoming a stable, and afterwards being taken down. Before our civil courts undertook to enforce theological trusts, there were several instances, where, as a result of change in religious opinion or the impracticability of keeping to the old design, the majority of a congregation or the holders of title to church property took it into another ecclesiastical connection. These instances seem to us, where they were not the nearest possible carrying out of the trust, fraudulent conversions to new uses: but the persons who gave the ground, or built the edifice, may have said to themselves that their primary intention was to provide a place for themselves to worship in, and that they were not to lose the use of it, because of some obstinate associate, or of somebody with whom they once agreed in opinion.

There is a tradition mentioned by Sachse, but not by Edwards, that Abel Noble, visiting Jersey, had been baptized by Killingworth. Perhaps it was in Rhode Island by Stephen Mumford of Newport. Noble had devoted himself very much to the Keithians of Upper Providence. When these became impressed with the obligation of baptism and the Lord's Supper, and were left to their liberty by those in association with them in Philadelphia, Thomas Martin was selected to baptize them, but first to be baptized himself by Abel Noble, who had been already baptized. Edwards gives the date of Noble's baptizing Martin as June 28, 1697. Afterwards, the members nominated Thomas Budd, Thomas Martin, and William Beckingham, and, lots being drawn, the choice fell on Martin to administer the Lord's Supper. Edwards says that Martin did so on Oct. 12. An offer was made to receive such friends in Philadelphia as thought their baptism when infants sufficient, provided there was nothing else against them, but these refused, and the others soon felt relieved, the record saying: "we account it a providence, and acknowledge our shortness in giving away the Lord's cause." This Upper Providence congregation split on the question of the Sabbath, and dissolved. However, those who favored keeping Sunday were gathered together about 1715 by Rev. Abel Morgan, and, in 1718, built a meeting-house in Birmingham Township. In 1742, a second place of worship for part of the same congregation was built in Newlin Township, bearing the name of Brandywine Baptist Church. The Sabbatarians, on the other hand, united at Newtown. In 1717, a number took up considerable land between the Brandywine and French Creek, and, reinforced by some seceders from the Great Valley Baptist Church, this congregation, called Nantmeal, became a strong one.

The Keithians in the City of Philadelphia had a wooden meeting-house on the west side of Second below Mulberry (Arch) street. The lot had been conveyed to Thomas Budd, Thomas Peart, Ralph Ward, and James Poulter in trust for the use of the Christian people called Quakers subscribing the articles of faith, for a meeting-house or place of worship, and such other uses as the major part of the Meeting should appoint, and to convey to such persons as the major part of the

Meeting should appoint. The meeting-house was lent to the Church of England congregation, while its building was in course of erection.

Thomas Budd died, his burial being on 12mo. 15, 1697-8. His antecedents or inclination, at least the ecclesiastical destination of his family, was Presbyterian.

Rutter baptized nine persons, among whom was Thomas Peart, and these nine, with Rutter as Minister, united for meetings on June 12, 1698, and they continued apparently to be included under the name of Keithians, and doubtless, through Peart being a trustee, occupied the meeting-house, or perhaps shared it, even at first, with those who attended a different preacher. The chapter on the Church of England will mention the removal thither of the regular Baptists. Rutter resided a while in Germantown, and then at Manatawny, where he began making iron in 1716 or 1717, being the first to start an iron works within the limits of Pennsylvania.

We learn, from the statement prepared in 1730 in favor of Christ Church's claim to the Keithian meetinghouse property (*Penna. Archives* 1st Series, Vol. I), that those who paid nearly two thirds of the original purchase money, including Thomas Peart and Ralph Ward, joined Christ Church congregation, but, as before said, they were not among its earliest members. Logan speaks in 1702 of some Keithians, including McComb, greatly opposing Keith at that time: but either before or later, as their Society died out, Nicholas Pearce and Thomas Tresse were among those who became Churchmen. The tombstone of the former is in the floor of the present edifice of Christ Church. The statement tells that in 1723 Thomas Peart, as surviving trustee, conveyed the meeting-house property to certain Churchmen in trust for a school for all Christians without any violence to their consciences. About this time,

Joan Lee, who, with her husband, William Lee, had joined Christ Church, forsook it for the Baptists: She and two other Baptist women, former members of the Keithian Meeting, and John Budd, heir of Thomas Budd, and William Betridge and his wife Frances, heiress of James Poulter, as representatives of deceased members, made a deed to the Baptists in 1725. After some years dispute, Christ Church surrendered to the Baptists all claim in consideration of 50*l*.

For some time, the name "Lloydians," after Thomas Lloyd, was given to those Quakers who had adhered to him. The word is misprinted as "Hoytians" in the letter of Rev. Thomas Clayton published in Perry's *Collections*, as will be shown in the chapter on the Church of England.

In the remnant of the Society of Friends on the Delaware remaining after the Keithian secession and the subsequent propaganda of various denominations, Orthodoxy triumphed; perhaps because of the death of certain radical opposers of Keith, perhaps because of the influence of the positive teaching of the religious bodies surrounding—but there is here no intention to deny that it was the work of the Spirit. There was early a readiness in prominent adherents to profess their faith in the Trinity, and to acknowledge the Scriptures to be divinely inspired. Within four years after the Philadelphia Quarterly Meeting's condemnation of Keith, five signers of the declaration against him, viz: Waln, Maris, Simcock, Blunston, and Biles, and prominent men like David Lloyd, Richardson, Shippen, Morris, and Carpenter, and also Caleb Pusey, who then or afterwards wrote against Keith, had subscribed the declaration and acknowledgment set forth in the English Act of Toleration. The Frame of Government of 1696 was not designed to exclude the leading Friends from office, nor was it objected to as having such effect; yet it prescribed the making and signing of such profession and acknowledgment as the alternative for taking a certain oath for qualifying to serve as Councillor, Assemblyman, or any officer, and the Assembly chosen in 1705, composed almost entirely of Quakers, passed bills, which became the permanent law of the Province, not merely requiring that profession and acknowledgment for eligibility to office, but also insuring liberty of conscience only for those whose belief was represented in the Parliamentary phraseology. It is not likely that there were at the time any number of Pennsylvania Quakers left unprotected by such curtailment of toleration. Going, however, beyond this outline of faith, the following, under date of 3mo. 20, 1696, signed, in a petition to King William III, their recognition of Jesus conceived miraculously by the Holy Ghost, born of a Virgin, giving his life on the cross a sacrifice for man's sins, rising again, ascending into glory, and living to make intercession for men, as the Son of God and Saviour of the World, viz:

David Lloyd	Samuel Preston
William Harwood	Jno. Symcocke
Thomas Makin	Hugh Roberts
Nathan Stanbury	Samuel Carpenter
Edward Shippen	Alexander Beardsley
Samuel Richardson	John Linam
Isaac Norris	Caleb Pusey
Abra. Hardiman	Robert Ewer
James Fox	Walter Faucett
Antho. Morris	George Gray.

Following this lead, it came to pass and continued throughout the rest of Colonial times and into the Nineteenth Century that American Quakerdom in the greater notes, if with some minor elisions, joined in chorus with Rome, Geneva, Augsburg, Constantinople, and Canterbury.

CHAPTER IX.

ENGLAND.

Position of England among European powers in 1688—War—Opposition to William and Mary in the British Isles—James II's invasion of Ireland—Attitude of Penn—Directions to proclaim William and Mary in Pennsylvania and Maryland—Proceedings against Penn—The Preston Conspiracy—Penn's frustrated plan to sail—Forbearance of William III, and insufficiency of evidence of overt acts by Penn for James—Foolishness of Charles II's grant of Pennsylvania—The Province and Territories placed under the Governor of New York—Fletcher's commission, arrival, and early proceedings—His debate with the Quakers as to money for the war—Promise it should "not be dipt in blood"—Confirmation of laws named in a Petition of Right—Vote of money "towards the support of this government" "as a testimony of our dutiful affections" to the King and Queen—Post Office—Fletcher advises union of Pennsylvania with New York, the Jerseys, and Connecticut under one Assembly—The Philadelphia market place—The Pennsylvania Assembly of 1694—Penn's friends among English public men—Royal permission to go and come—Restoration of the government—Markham appointed Governor with Goodson and Carpenter as Assistants—The customs—England's regulation of Trade.

The throne, calling the headship over England and Scotland one throne, which William and Mary ascended, had not then the exalted position in the World which the throne of Great Britain and Ireland had at the accession of George V, when the millions upon millions of Hindus were recognizing it as an imperial seat, when the continent of Australia, half of North America, and the lower end of Africa were bowing before it, when Gibraltar and Malta and Weihaiwei were garrisoned by its soldiers, when Egypt was administered by its agents, when the politics of Europe awaited the casting voice uttered in its name. When the fourth Stuart King of England was superseded, and his infant son passed over, the Hapsburger at Vienna was still called the successor of Augustus and Charlemagne, the Hapsburger at Madrid was still the greatest beneficiary of Columbus. Besides the suzerainty over Germany, powerful and unrestrained and rebellious as some of its greater princes were, and besides the direct control over Austria as Archduke, and over Bohemia as King, Leopold I held the kingdom of Hungary: Carlos II, who was also King of the Two Sicilies, and lord of what is now Belgium, ruled, as King of Castille, Aragon, &ct., over California, Texas, Mexico, Central America, Cuba, and practically all of South America except Brazil. The Sultan of Turkey had the most extensive dominion in the Old World. France, controlling Canada and much of what was recently called by people in the United States "the Great West," was the greatest nation of Christendom. Portugal was a world-power, owning Brazil, and being one of the European nations having considerable foothold in Asia and Africa. Poland and Lithuania, united under an elected king, played an important part in European politics, and had just stemmed the tide of Ottoman advance in coming to the relief of Vienna. Sweden, while possessing no colonies, bid fair by conquest to hold a great realm southeast of the Baltic. Whatever promise of being the equal or superior of any of these powers England had given under the Tudors, or when it came under one king with Scotland, however widely the

British people had been extended by colonies planted under James I, Charles I, and Cromwell, or by the acquisition of New York and Tangiers and Bombay, England sank into a contemptible position in the latter years of Charles II, and exerted little influence on the main Continent of Europe. The short reign of his successor was taken up with a domestic struggle.

In one of the intervals when Charles II had not been under French control, he had bound himself, in one of the treaties made at Nimeguen in 1678, to aid the United Netherlands, if, after the peace then about to be made, they should be attacked by France. So that England was already burdened with the support of the independence of that small confederacy, and was more securely fastening that burden upon herself when she accepted the Stadholder, William, as her king. There was very little net gain in the contribution which he brought, viz: the co-operation, if not merely friendship, of the United Netherlands, rich in colonies, but not as powerful as before the loss of supremacy at sea and the loss of possessions in North America. There was an alliance, which had been entered into in 1685, between the Estates General, the supreme authority, and the Elector of Brandenburg and the King of Sweden; and the latter, still possessor of Pomerania and Bremen, had united with the Emperor and various rulers of the German states in the League of Augsburg, signed June 21, 1686, for the purpose of maintaining certain treaties, which Louis XIV seemed preparing to violate. Louis conquered the Palatinate in 1687, and it was apparently to support Germany that William gathered the army with which, the next year, he invaded England. Before William reached London, Louis declared war against the Netherlands, and so England, under the treaty of Nimeguen, became liable to furnish aid to them.

Thus, as soon as England and the Netherlands had

been brought together under a master mind,—for, at the transfer of the English Crown, William was designated as the actual ruler,—they were embroiled in a Continental war. A league was concluded at Vienna on May 12, 1689, between the Estates General and the Emperor, binding them to prosecute the war until France had been driven back to the boundaries fixed by treaty in 1659.

Very powerful would have been the whole combination, or even England and the Netherlands without others, if the population of the British Isles had been unanimous, as William and Mary's bloodless triumph in England seemed to indicate. But a great number of Englishmen, including many of the higher clergy of the National Church, still believed James to be their lawful king, while with others there was before long some reaction against William and Mary, and a jealousy of the Dutch. Scotland, the ancient kingdom of the Stuarts, had been brought, largely by its Presbyterian party, to accept the new sovereigns; but there were great lords and fierce clansmen attached by interest, nationalistic sympathy, or a common religion to James (the seventh James Stuart who had been king of that country): while throughout Ireland the Roman Catholics, greatly in the majority, rose against the Protestants, drove them to seek shelter in certain towns, and asked James to leave his place of retirement, St. Germain-en-Laye near Paris, and to come and reign at Dublin. Provided by Louis XIV with a French fleet, with arms, ammunition, and money and some French officers, commanded by Lieut.-Gen. Conrad de Rosen, Comte de Bolweiller, and with De Mesmes, Comte d'Avaux, as French Ambassador, James landed at Kinsale on March 12, 1688-9, and entered Dublin on March 16 (O. S.).

There is no reasonable doubt that William Penn, while unresisting to the powers in possession, and not following James to France, or joining him in Ireland, wished him restored to the throne: a different sentiment in Penn would have involved not only the disregarding of his interests, but also an ungrateful hardening of his heart: nor was it likely that he saw, far beyond the contemporary scattering of his friends and glorification of a liturgical and title-taking Church and participation in a foreign war, that withal, under intruding sovereigns, England would be ultimately better off. What he did towards the fruition of his wishes, or in line with his feelings, is a subject of dispute. When examined as to the letter about to be mentioned, he said that he had never had any correspondence with —i.e. had never written to—King James since the latter left England. This plea does not cover any later date than July or August, 1689.

Certainly James had a high opinion of the abilities of his Quaker favorite, and would have liked to use him in the project of a restoration. By some authorities it is said that the letter from James to Penn with which Penn was confronted, which is spoken of as having been intercepted, but which may have been received and lost or stolen, was written before James left France for Ireland. It asked Penn to come to James's assistance, and to express the resentments of (the services possible in return for) his favor and benevolence. It certainly did not contradict Penn's denial by containing an acknowledgement of the receipt of any letter from Penn, or confer any authority upon him, from which those finding the letter could prove his previous undertaking to perform any acts. Yet there is evidence for an historian, even if it does not amount to proof, that, subsequent to the writing of the letter, and before Penn's examination concerning it, two things happened which were inconsistent with Penn's neutrality. About two months after James's arrival in Dublin, Comte d'Avaux, saw a letter from "M. Pen," possibly without signature, but of which the writer must then have been mentioned truthfully but perhaps indistinctly to Avaux. The letter gave news which Avaux copied or translated for "le commencement" of "Memoire des Nouvelles d'Angleterre et d' Escosse," which he sent to Louis XIV, with a letter dated June 5, 1689, printed in full with the "Memoire" in W. Hepworth Dixon's *History of William Penn Founder of Pennsylvania.* The beginning of the "Memoire" is: "Le prince d'Orange commence d'estre fort dégoutté de l'humeur des Anglois, et la face des choses change bien viste selon la nature des insulaires, et sa santé est fort mauvaise." The "Memoire" goes on to speak of "Un nuage qui commence à se forme au nord des deux royaumes," where "le Roy" had many friends, and of the anxiety of William's partisans, who apprehended an invasion from France and Ireland, in which case the dethroned King would have more friends than ever, also of the jealousy which the English had of the Dutch, and of the belief that if James would arrive with an army, even Parliament would declare for him. Macaulay, when he wrote his much attacked *History of England,* believed that "M. Pen" was the author of most of this encouragement of civil war, and was identical with the eminent disciple of peace, our Founder: but, if more than the opening sentence of the "Memoire" came from "M. Pen," and if our Founder's sweeping denial of having communicated with James is not deemed conclusive, there is the great improbability that a shrewd man, already put under heavy bail, took such a risk, probably before his discharge from bail in Easter Term, as writing to the exiled monarch at all, and particularly any seductive matter. Dixon has made the excellent suggestion that "M. Pen" was Neville Payne, the well known plotter. His activity a few months later, if not that early, is stated in the *Account* by the Earl of Balcarres, or his

letter to King James, known as Balcarres' *Memoir*.
Dixon's identification is strengthened by Dr. Bromfield's connection with a trial of Payne some years afterwards. There still remains, accounting also for the other fact for which there is evidence, the hypothesis that our Founder, with what may be called his mania for putting pen to paper, wrote the aforesaid letter, not to James or any officer acompanying him, but innocently to Dr. Bromfield, who was reputed to be a Quaker. John Lunt, whose information, given in 1694, appears in Part IV of Appendix to 14th Report of the Historical MSS. Commission, swore that about the end of May, 1689, Dr: Bromfield came over to Dublin from England, and brought an account of conditions there and the readiness of his friends, Papists and Jacobites, and desired from King James commissions for persons of quality with blanks for inferior officers, which accordingly the King caused to be issued, and which Lunt carried across the Irish Sea, arriving near Lancaster about beginning of July, 1689; that Lunt gave to one Jackson two bundles of commissions with a royal declaration and two other papers sealed up with each, one of which bundles was to be delivered to "Sir William Penn the Quaker" (in other copies of the information it is "Mr. William Penn the Quaker"); and that Lunt supposed that Jackson delivered them, for he took coach in Lunt's presence. Lunt figures in Macaulay's *History* with reference to statements as to others as a betrayer betrayed, and may be discredited, but the corroborative force of Lunt's story could not have been known to persons concocting it, for the people of England in 1694 were unaware of Avaux having quoted any Pen, and there was no object in inventing a lie against William Penn, when his friend Trenchard was Secretary of State and the actual examiner of Lunt. No notice was then taken of the reference to Penn. In *The Jacobite Trials at Man-*

chester in 1694, published by the Chetham Society in 1853, the date of Lunt's landing in England in 1689 is proved to have been June 13. Under date of June 22, 1689, a warrant was issued (see *Calendar of State Papers*) for apprehending William Penn, suspected of high treason. It is possible that the alleged letter entrusted to Jackson for Penn, which Lunt supposed to have been delivered, fell into the hands of William III's officials before Penn's appearance under this warrant, and that such letter was indeed the one upon which Penn was examined, but, if so, it certainly gave him no directions, and was not found accompanied by blank commissions. Narcissus Luttrell in his Diary, printed as *A Brief Historical Relation of State Affairs,* says after the date June 29, 1689, "William Penn the famous Quaker and one Scarlet another busy fellow pretendedly a Quaker have been lately taken into custody for some practices against the government." The examination of Penn upon a letter from the exiled King to him is mentioned in *General History of Europe* compiled in 1692 from Monthly Mercuries. Under date of August, 1689, or taken from the *Mercury* then issued, is the statement that several persons had been released that were suspected of holding correspondence with King James, but Mr. Penn, who had been under the same suspicion, was still under restraint, that he denied ever having any correspondence with King James after he left England, confessed himself greatly beholden to the latter, and willing to be serviceable to him so long as it was not to the prejudice of the Protestant religion or present government, and justified that King James's writing to Penn could not make Penn a criminal, because it was not in his power to hinder it. From the Quaker historians, we learn that he was asked why the dethroned King had written to him, and that he made the obvious answer that is was impossible for him to prevent any man from writing. Questioned as to what the "resentments" were, Penn said that he did not know, but that he supposed that James meant for him to make endeavors for James's restoration. With boldness and nobleness of heart, Penn avowed that he had loved James in prosperity, and could not hate him in adversity, had loved him for many favors, and would repay him with any private service, but would observe the duty to the State incumbent upon all its subjects, and had never thought of endeavoring to restore to James the Crown which had fallen from his head. It is further said that King William, who was present at the examination, was inclined to let Penn go; but, at the officials' suggestion, he was to be within reach.

On Aug. 31, 1689, Penn and Lord Baltimore were ordered to prepare duplicates of the orders they had sent, or were assumed to have sent, to their provinces for proclaiming the new Sovereigns, a messenger to be appointed by the King to go and return at their expense.

On 9ber. 20, actually eighteen days after Blackwell had proclaimed William and Mary in Pennsylvania, Edward Blackfan wrote from London a letter to the Secretary of the Council of Pennsylvania enclosing the duplicates of the orders and drafts which Penn was to send for such proclamation. The packet was carried to Philadelphia by Richard Morris, master of the ship "Philadelphia Merchant," and arrived there eight months later.

The collection now in progress of Penn's letters and other writings may be expected to clear up at least the chronology of his career in England. Until that great work be finished, we can not use all the information extant. He appears to have been in the custody of a jailor or messenger on Oct. 24, 1689, the second day of the term of King's Bench, when, Luttrell tells us, a habeas corpus was obtained. On the next day, Penn was admitted to bail in a recognizance for £1000 with four sureties in £500 each. Pursuant to this, he appeared on Nov. 28, the last day of the term, and was discharged.

Queen Mary in 1690, administering the government in King William's absence, was alarmed by the defeat of the English at sea. As, it is claimed, a precaution against enemies at home, warrants were issued against Penn and others on a charge of high treason, perhaps without fresh evidence in Penn's case. They, not being found at the usual abodes, were deemed to have fled from justice. On July 14, a royal proclamation was issued reciting their conspiring to destroy the government, and their adhering to the enemy in the present invasion. Penn, among the others, was commanded to be seized, taken to the nearest Justice of the Peace, and by him committed to jail until delivered by law, the Justice of the Peace to notify the Privy Council. Penn wrote to the Secretary of State before July 19, offering to surrender, and asking to be admitted to bail. Penn was discharged on Aug. 15 on recognizance to appear in Court at the next term, Michaelmas. A news-letter of the 18th speaks of his being on bail. Luttrell mentions that on Oct. 23, the first day of the term of Court, Penn, being on recognizance, appeared before the King's Bench, when his case was continued to the end of the term. There being no real evidence at hand against him, he was discharged on coming into Court on Nov. 28, the last day.

Some time in or after April of that year, William Fuller, who had been a short time in France, and who was one of the chief witnesses against Crone for treason, and reaped reward thereby, went to Ireland, and, there spending the Summer and perhaps Autumn of 1690, gave testimony along with one Fisher and an Irishman, whose name is not mentioned in Penn's biographies or published letters, on the strength of which testimony Penn was indicted there for high treason. He not being found in that jurisdiction, where he had not been within twenty years, his estate was sequestered, and put up for rent, and the indictment and its incidents hung over Penn, it appears, until he had it discharged on his going to Ireland in 1698. Fuller, trying to live by the trade of informer, was unanimously voted an imposter and false accuser by the English House of Commons in 1691.

There is little doubt that Penn's powers of observation caused him to be consulted, and his interest in politics caused him to dabble in matters from which he should have stood aloof; and a conspicuous instance was at the time of Preston's Conspiracy, so called after Sir Richard Graham, President of the Council in James's reign, and created by him Viscount Preston in the peerage of Scotland. For the interesting and pretty well attested details here omitted of this conspiracy, the reader may consult Macaulay's *History*. There had been, according to a report found among the papers carried by Preston and his companions, a conference between some Tories and Whigs, agreeing that it would be possible to restore James II, if neither he nor Louis XIV came as a conqueror, but that James must accord the English a Protestant administration, with no other privilege for the Catholics than liberty of conscience, and must show a model of this at St. Germain's by preferring the Protestants about him to the Catholics, and must encourage seven or nine Protestant lords and gentlemen then in England to come to him, as a standing Council, and that the King of France must allow the English Protestants in that country to have chapels—all of which seems such a solution of the state of affairs that we could not blame Penn if he had proposed it. Furthermore, a declaration had been suggested for James to issue, viz: that the army brought with him would be sent back as soon as the Dutch were sent away from England. Various persons had written letters, which, under disguises, urged James to make a speedy invasion. It is not necessary to traverse Penn's denial of being at any formal conference, or of knowing what was on foot: but his letter without date to Viscount Sidney, as will be seen, means that Preston, in the latter part of December, had a conversation with Penn, and Preston's report in his confession may be relied upon as showing that they canvassed the "state of mind" of various prominent personages, and that Penn—let us suppose not knowing the use to be made of it—expressed the opinion that the Earl of Devonshire, Lord Steward of the Household under William and Mary, and Earl Dorset, the Lord Chamberlain, and a number of others would be glad to see James back under certain conditions. It is not clear, but it is possible, that Penn even was the Mr. P. who is down in Preston's memorandum as giving him a commission for Flanders: the next words may have no connection with this, but are "hinder Eng. and D. from joining;" then comes "two vessels of 150l. price for Pennsylvania for 13 or 14 months." With the various letters and some information about the defence of the coast, Preston and John Ashton with a more innocent companion, Edmund Eliot, left London on December 31, 1690, in a fishing smack, hired to take them to France, ostensibly for smuggling. They were overhauled and captured, and the papers seized. Convicted of high treason, Ashton suffered death, but Lord Preston saved his life by a confession. Viscount Sidney wrote on Jany. 20, 1690-1, to the King that Preston had been tried on the preceding Saturday, and would endeavor to deserve his life at the King's hands, so that Sidney favored suspending the execution, and what Preston could say against Lord Clarendon, the Bishop of Ely, and Mr. Penn was of great importance. Sidney added that neither the Bishop nor Mr. Penn was to be found, and that Penn was as much in the business as anybody, and that two of the letters were certainly of his writing. So probably on this account, rather than by reason of anything which Fuller had said, had an officer been sent to arrest Penn at George Fox's funeral, which took place on January 16, 1690–1, at Bunhill Fields, London. Making a mistake as to the hour, it is explained, the officer was unsuccessful. Dixon, from mistaking the date of the subsequent proclamation for that of the warrant, has contradicted Macaulay's statement of this plan to arrest; but it is found in the Quaker biographies of Penn, who himself says in a letter of 4 mo. 14, 1691, to Thomas Lloyd, printed by Janney: "That night, very providentially, I escaped the messenger's hands." Although the Marquess of Carmarthen said on Feb. 3 that Preston was the only witness against Penn, a proclamation, dated Feb. 5, 1690–1, was issued for the capture &ct., as in the proclamation of July 14 preceding (both proclamations printed by American Antiquarian Society), of Francis, late Bishop of Ely, William Penn Esq., and James Grahme Esq., as having, for procuring an invasion by the French, &ct., held correspondence with Preston. Warrants against them for high treason were recited, as well as their absence from their abodes, and fleeing from justice. Penn had been making preparations to sail in the following April to Pennsylvania with a large number of settlers, and the Secretary of State had appointed a convoy to protect the vessels, but this, in fact everything but hiding, was now impossible.

After the discovery of the Preston Conspiracy, King William sailed from Gravesend for Holland on Jany. 18, and was not again in London until March. About Feb. 19, through arrangement made by Anthony Lowther, Penn's brother-in-law, and, with consent of Queen Mary, allowing freedom from detention, Penn had a secret interview with Viscount Sidney, the Secretary of State. Sidney's letter to the King is reprinted by Dixon from Dalrymple's *Memoirs of Great Britain and Ireland*. Penn protested loyalty, and that he knew of no plot, and believed in none but what Louis XIV had laid, and of the bottom of which Penn thought that James II knew as little as other people; also Penn said that William had many enemies, and some who came over with him, or soon joined him, were more dangerous than the Jacobites, among whom, Penn declared, there was no man who had even ordinary ability, that, if William would trust Penn, the latter would tell all he knew that would be for the King's interest to know, otherwise he would very unwillingly leave the kingdom; but that he could not appear as a witness, being unable to take an oath. On King William's return, and Preston's repetition in his presence of the confession, that crowned politician, knowing his precarious situation on the throne, was disinclined to ferret out the disaffected, and arouse their violent hostility. Two letters of this time from Penn to Henry Sidney, then Viscount Sidney, are printed as being to Lord Romney, the title of Earl of Romney being conferred on Sidney three years later. One, dated 22 A, 90 (April 22), to show to the King, asks permission to live quietly in England or America. In the other letter to Sidney, Penn offers to appear, if he will be believed, but says that he can not come out of retirement, and put himself in the power of his enemies: he denies all knowledge of invasions or insurrections or men, money, or arms therefor, or juncto or consult in order thereto, and says that he never met any of those named as conspirators, or prepared measures with anybody for Lord ———. [Janney queries, Sunderland? but evidently Preston is meant] to carry with him as one sense or judgment, nor did Penn know of his, said Lord's, being sent for any such voyage, and adds: "If I saw him a few days before by his great importunity, as some say, I am able to defend myself from the imputations cast upon me, and that with great truth and sincerity, though in rigour, perhaps, it may incur the censure of a misdemeanor, and therefore I have no reason to own it without an assurance that no hurt should ensue to me." This letter is undated, but, from the answer, we find that it was written as King William was hurrying to Holland, whither he went in May. Neither Penn's story nor his body for punishment seems afterwards to have been sought. There was a report, which Macaulay can not be blamed for accepting, that Penn fled to France. Robert Harley, writing to Sir Edward Harley on Sep. 15, says: "William Penn got safe into France last week." This accords with Luttrell's *Brief Relation,* which, noting events of that month, says "Wm. Penn the quaker is gott off from Shoreham in Sussex and gone for France." It seems, however, that he stayed in London. Otherwise, some notice of his having been at St. Germain would have been taken by officials in the course of the years next following.

We may conclude that there was no proof before King William's officials, at least before those not particularly Penn's friends, to convict him of knowingly aiding James. Had there been, Penn would have been deprived, if not of life, certainly of property, and probably of both. It would have been necessary to make an example of him. There would have been no mercy shown to please such a weak body as the Quakers. His wealth would have added to the means of satisfying the adventurers in William's train; and statecraft, in the interest not only of the new party, but of the empire at large, was demanding the revocation of the grant of Pennsylvania.

John Wilmot, Earl of Rochester, lost some favor with Charles II by writing the following, over the latter's bedchamber door, it is said:

"Here lies our Sovereign Lord the King
"Whose word no man relies on;
"He never says a foolish thing,
"Nor ever does a wise one."

Surely no public act could have exceeded in folly the grant of Pennsylvania to William Penn. Some economies, perhaps greater than the withholding of some of the jewels scattered on ladies of the court, would have enabled the debt of the Crown to his father to be paid. Yet, instead of this, there was sacrificed—a worse bargain that the Indians made for tracts of the land —something like 45,000,000 acres. Charles, to be sure, was ignorant of their mineral wealth, which, could the ore land have been retained until our day, would have made the Admiral's present heir-at-law the richest man in the World. What was then more to be considered, and should have been plain to any statesman, the frontier approaching the French, and the middle of the strip of territory which England owned in America, was to be peopled with non-resistants, was to be made smooth for the advance of an enemy designing to cut the territory in two! And the danger might remain even if relations with France were friendly: the Spaniards in Mexico could send an expedition without crossing the ocean, and no one could be sure that Sweden or Holland, possibly recovering the strength so recently lost, would not again secure footing on the shores of Delaware Bay. Even in the unhoped for contingency of the Proprietary and his tenants being willing to take up arms, military considerations called for a single strong colony in the space between New England and Virginia, instead of several under independent and disagreeing governments. New York, which protected New England on the west, was weakened by the creation of a rival with charter boundaries enclosing the seats of those Indians who had been New York's allies in war, as well as purveyors of New

York's chief article of commerce. We need not lay stress on the agricultural productiveness of the region formerly claimed by, and thus taken away from New York; for such was not then known. It was seen, however, by Gov. Dongan shortly after the grant to Penn, that the loss of the beaver and peltry trade would deter Europeans from settling in the Hudson Valley, if, indeed, it would not cause the departure of the whites; while the Indians in question, who had saved New England in the preceding Indian war, and could bring 3000 or 4000 warriors to decide a conflict, threatened to remove to the other side of Lake Ontario, rather than live under any government south of it other than that of New York. Dongan proposed that a line be run at the latitude of 41° 40′ from the Delaware to the Susquehanna, which line, he understood, would strike the falls in what is now Bradford County, Pa., and that Penn be content with what was below that line. The attitude of the Five Nations has been mentioned in the chapter on the Red Neighbours. The authorities of the City of New York addressed the King as to the injury done to it. Governor Sloughter, appointed over New York by William and Mary, wrote that, to defray the charges of government, and for maintaining the war, it would be necessary to bring Connecticut, East and West Jersey, and Pennsylvania under New York, and, on Aug. 6, 1691, after Sloughter's death, the next Governor and the Council said that no step could be more conducive to the safety of their Majesties' subjects in America.

In time of peace, even, the direction of a great empire was interfered with by having an enormous district to which a uniform system of administration could not extend, where a feudal baron was at least to be notified, and the tenantry owing him allegiance, and perhaps under his influence, could nullify what the majority of the race or nation favored. Witness the question of Admiralty courts in Maryland and South Carolina as well as Pennsylvania.

When war was declared by William and Mary against France, the Proprietary of Pennsylvania was a non-resistant suspected of treason, the Proprietary of Maryland was a Roman Catholic, the Proprietors of South Carolina included a Quaker and an aged ex-soldier under James. On May 16, 1689, the Committee of the Privy Council for Trade and Plantations decided to represent to the King that the relation in which those three provinces stood to the government of England should receive the consideration of Parliament for bringing them under a near dependence on the Crown.

The needs of New York for assistance from her neighbours, and the accusations against Penn, singled out Pennsylvania for attention. It was argued by many persons that all powers granted by royal patent, being subject to the King's sovereignty, could be resumed by the King, if, by dereliction on the part of the grantee, the latter forfeited them, or if, by any circumstances, there was imminent danger of that part of the realm being lost. Some lawyers went further, and thought that the powers of government granted to William Penn, involving the revenue of the Crown, legislation, life and death, arming the subjects, and waging war, were part of the *regalia* of the Sovereign, and that Charles II's alienation of them was valid during that monarch's life only. No judicial decision was sought by the government. There were sufficient complaints of failure in the administration of justice, the Proprietary was not able to perform personally the duties of Governor, there was clearly danger of foreign conquest, to justify, under the less radical theory, a measure necessary for protection. On March 9, 1691-2, the Committee for Trade agreed to report to the Privy Council that a temporary commission should be granted to Colonel Fletcher, Governor of New York, to command and lead out of the Jerseys as many as 700 of the militia thereof for the defence of New York and Albany, in case of any attempt by the French and Indians, also for Col. Fletcher to take the Province of Pennsylvania under his command. It was several months before the commission for these purposes was put in shape. Under date of Oct. 21, in the 4th year of the reign, Benjamin Fletcher was constituted Captain-General and Governor-in-Chief of the Province of Pennsylvania and Country of New Castle and all tracts of land depending thereon, with like powers as in his commission of March 18 preceding as Captain-General and Governor-in-Chief of New York, and was commanded to act according to instructions given then or afterwards, and according to such reasonable laws and statutes as were then in force, or as he might agree upon with the consent of the Council and Assembly of Pennsylvania and New Castle, he to appoint over the region a Lieutenant-Governor and not exceeding twelve Councillors from the principal freeholders and inhabitants, three to be a quorum. The commission for New York gave him a negative in the making of laws, and power, with the advice and consent of the Council, to appoint Judges and officers. He was to exercise certain military authority. His governorship &ct. of Pennsylvania &ct. was to continue during their Majesties' pleasure, and in case of his death or absence, the powers were to be exercised by whoever might for the time being be Commander-in-Chief of New York, and in the absence of such, by the Council of New York.

Penn, in 9th month, wrote to Robert Turner that it was a pity that the Delawareans had not remained united in civil affairs with the Quaker Province; for they could not only defend the whole of his possessions, but also resist this commission. He added: "I expect a firm adherence to the patent, my freehold and inheritance." He instructed his officers to object to Fletcher exercising his commission, and if he did not desist, then to draw up exceptions, and lay them before the Lords of the Committee for Trade, and also before "Friends concerned in the province here," who would appear before the Committee. Finally, Penn expressed confidence that the courts at Westminister Hall or the House of Lords on appeal would do him justice. This seems like bluster in a man who may be considered lucky that he was allowed to live; but boldness was perhaps the best policy. Penn also warned Fletcher not to interfere with the deputies commissioned by Penn.

We do not find that there was any attempt in America to carry out Penn's plan of campaign against the appointee of the Crown; and it is noticeable how little anybody seemed to care for Penn's claims. The people of Delaware probably rejoiced at the change. We would have expected the Indians to say something nice about their great friend: on the contrary, some "from the upper part of the river," coming to ask Fletcher's protection from the Senecas, complained of the Quakers, because they never encouraged or assisted them to fight. Over one hundred inhabitants of Philadelphia County signed an address acknowledging the favor done to them by the King and Queen. The Keithian Quakers were glad to escape subjection to Thomas Lloyd; while Lloyd welcomed removal from an office which was an expense to him.

After notice to Lloyd, Fletcher, between 11 and 12 o'clock in the forenoon of April 26, 1693, arrived in Philadelphia with a military escort. The Sheriff of the County went to meet him, and conducted him to the market place, then Front and Market Streets; and there, although the leading Quakers did not countenance by their presence the transfer of authority,

Lloyd slipping away when the commission was about
to be read, the royal commission to Fletcher was read
to the public without protest. Penn was displeased at
the acquiescence shown by Lloyd and others, who
merely held aloof from the new government. Afterwards Penn realized that they could have done nothing
more.

Fletcher at once showed courtesy. He immediately
sent for Lloyd, and offered him the first place in the
Council. Lloyd refusing, as Fletcher was confident he
would, that place was given to Markham, who the next
day was nominated Lieutenant-Governor. The others
whom Fletcher had chosen as Councillors, viz, Andrew
Robeson, Robert Turner, Patrick Robinson, Lawrence
(or Lasse) Cock, and William Salway, unanimously
approved of the appointment of Markham. Afterwards, William Clark, George Forman, and John Cann
were taken into the Council, and, later still, Charles
Sanders, Griffith Jones (probably the lawyer), and
John Donnaldson. In order to have an Assembly meet
on May 15, 1693, writs, under resolution of the Council
of April 27, were issued for the election of four
Assemblymen from Philadelphia County, four from
New Castle County, and three from each of the other
Counties. This caused a letter to be presented to
Fletcher by seven of Lloyd's Councillors, in behalf of
the freemen, asking that no other method of calling
their legislative power be used than that prescribed by
the received laws. The letter was addressed to "Benjamin Fletcher, Esqr., Captain Generall and Governor-in-Chief &ct.," but, by not naming Pennsylvania
and Country of New Castle, did not express a recognition of his authority over the region. Fletcher's Council decided that, with such an address, it would not be
consistent with his commission to pay any attention, or
give an answer to the letter. Fletcher offered to reappoint Jennings, Cooke, Ewer, Owen, and Morris as

Justices, but all except Morris declined. Samuel Carpenter declined appointment.

The Lloydian Quakers, but not Thomas Lloyd himself, undertook to maintain their privileges before Fletcher, who, however, was more powerful than Blackwell, being armed with authority from the King and Queen, not hampered by instructions, and not required to fight his Councillors, of whom, although two, Markham and Turner, had been friends of the Proprietary, none were followers of Lloyd. The Quakers were driven back to the Assembly, holding fourteen out of the twenty seats filled at the first election. David Lloyd was one of the members from Chester, and, being the only lawyer in the body, is to be largely credited with what was accomplished at the session. For about thirty years afterwards, he was the leader of the democracy of the Province. Unlike Blackwell, the bluff, downright, and energetic Fletcher made no stand on the etiquette due to him, and, to secure the main point, was willing to come to an accommodation in minor details. As an act of grace, with the stipulation that it was not to be treated as a precedent, he allowed the Quaker members to serve without taking an oath, but the declaration of faith and test was presented to and subscribed by them. Complimenting Growdon, who was elected Speaker, Fletcher laid before the House a letter from Queen Mary, dated Oct. 11, 1692, signed by the Earl of Nottingham, directing the Governor of Pennsylvania to send such assistance in men or otherwise as the colony could furnish, for the defence of Albany, upon application from the Commander-in-Chief of New York, and to join with the Governors of New England, Virginia, and Maryland in fixing upon the quota of each colony. Fletcher told the Assembly: "If there be any amongst you that scruple the giving of money to support war, there are a great many other charges in that government for the support thereof as officers' salaries and other charges that amount to a considerable sum: your money shall be converted to these uses, and shall not be dipt in blood.'' He then argued to them that the walls around their gardens and orchards, the doors and locks of their houses, the mastiff dogs which they made use of to defend their property against robbers, were the same as forts, garrisons, and soldiers, which their Majesties made use of to defend their kingdoms and provinces and all their subjects, including those whom he was addressing. The House, replying with a preamble that the King and Queen had appointed him to supply the want of the Proprietary's personal attendance, asked that the procedure in legislation be according to the usual method and laws founded on the late King's letters patent, which the members conceived to be yet in force, and that the same be confirmed to them as their rights and liberties. Fletcher, pointing out how inconsistent the Frame of Government was with his commission, plainly told them that they could not keep the former, it having fallen at Charles II's death, but, if the Assembly would propose any laws for the convenience or safety of the colony, he, the Governor, would concur therein, if consistent with the trust reposed in him. The House then resolved unanimously that it could act in legislation with the Governor, and added a proviso that the People could be governed under the laws and constitution as far as consistent with Fletcher's commission. Fletcher replied that certain of their laws, being repugnant to those of England, he would not reenact. The Assembly in a Petition of Right, presented on May 24th, taking care to omit the laws to which Fletcher objected, set forth that 203 laws, passed under King Charles's Charter, and which, according to the Petition, had been transmitted to the King, and not disapproved of as the Charter provided, had not been repealed, and were still in force, and asked the Governor to cause them to be executed. Fletcher asked for a certified copy of them, doubted their presentation to the King, and argued that the seal of Penn or his deputy was essential to their enactment, but, the House having made a codification into 86 chapters, Fletcher, on June 1, ordered the code to be enforced until their Majesties' pleasure were known. Thirty other laws were passed, by one of which the representatives of the People expressed their humble submission to the King and Queen's pleasure in taking the government into their own hands, and presented to them, "as a testimony of our dutyful affections towards them," a tax to be spent by the Governor for the support of the government, asking their Majesties to allow one half to Governor Fletcher himself. The rate was 1d. per l. of the valuation (to be fixed by the Assemblymen from the county with the assistance of three substantial freeholders) of all real and personal estate over and above the owners' indebtedness, and 6s per head on certain freemen not worth 100l., with an exemption in favor of those who had a great charge of children, and were not worth 30l. The Proprietary and his late deputies were exempted, which was not unreasonable in the case of Thomas Lloyd, who had been at considerable expense as Lieutenant-Governor. One act of Assembly is worthy of note, and Fletcher had done the colony a service in suggesting it, viz: that for the extension to Pennsylvania and Territories of the post office inaugurated by Andrew Hamilton (subsequently Lieutenant-Governor). The act fixed the rates for private letters and packets, that for carrying a letter from New York to Philadelphia or in the reverse direction being 4½d.

Fletcher refused to pass a law offered by the Assembly, disqualifying a man getting drunk from voting or being elected, which Fletcher declared the freeholder's birthright as much as his name. Fletcher said "I will give you leave to banish me out of the government

when you shall find me drunk." He expressed his
readiness to impose fine or corporal punishment, but,
not flatteringly, said that he believed, if the proposed
bill were applied to the present Assembly in the strictness of it, there would be but a thin House.

A quarrel with the Council was the last event of the
session. The Assemblymen proposed a bill giving 6s.
a day wages to themselves. The Governor asked why
not also for the Councillors, particularly Lieutenant-
Governor Markham? The Assemblymen were unwilling, and the Councillors rejected the bill. Fletcher, de-
parting on the day or the day after the Assembly was
adjourned, left Markham at the head of affairs. The
impossibility of securing any appropriation directly
for war, induced Fletcher about this time to urge upon
the King the union of Pennsylvania (including the
Lower Counties), New York, the Jerseys, and Connecticut under one Assembly, which Assembly could
not be controlled by Quakers. It is said that William
III personally favored this.

In the year 1693, the Lieutenant-Governor, with the
advice of the Council, moved the market from Delaware Front and High Streets to the middle of High
Street where Second Street crossed it, and ordered the
market to be kept on Wednesdays and Saturdays after
the ringing of a bell, and provided that all provisions,
viz: flesh, fish, tame fowl, butter, eggs, cheese, herbs,
fruits, roots, &ct, brought to town for sale be sold in
the market place, even if not coming to town on market
days. Fees were established for killing animals in the
market.

Another Assembly for Pennsylvania and Territories
was called to meet on April 10, 1694, the Councillors
doing their best to have tractable members selected:
but those returned from Philadelphia, Bucks, and
Chester were all Quakers, besides one from New
Castle and one from Kent. David Lloyd was made

Speaker. When it was proposed for the Lieutenant-Governor to adjourn the session until Fletcher, who had been detained by military affairs, could reach Philadelphia, a remonstrance was voted maintaining the Assembly's right to adjourn itself. It was finally agreed by Markham, his Council, and the Assembly that the adjournment be to May 22. Fletcher met the House on May 23, and asked, if the members would not carry arms, or levy war, would they not feed the hungry, and clothe the naked, that is, supply the Indians of the Five Nations, now poor, naked, and cut off by the war from hunting, with such necessaries as would influence them to continue in friendship with the English? He himself, having given those Indians one hundred days from the day of his conference with them to consider their answer, would meet them with the sword in one hand, and presents in the other. It was ascertained that the tax granted the preceding year would amount to about £500 sterling with salaries for collection taken out. The Governor, on June 1, sent a message asking for an answer to the Queen's letter, which had not been referred to in the law imposing the tax. The Assembly declared the law a compliance with the letter as far as the religious convictions of the majority would permit, and furthermore looked upon the amount as the colonists' full share, and complained that, at the conference which Fletcher had held with the Indians at Albany, the former Assembly's action had not been properly set forth: if the expenditure of money upon the Indians would be accepted as a compliance with the order to assist New York, the Assemblymen were willing that any sums voted for support of the government be applied in that way. They offered, among other laws, another tax of 1d. per pound, 200l. of the amount raised to be allowed to Col. Markham, 200l. to remunerate Thomas Lloyd for his late services, and the balance to be spent in presents for the Indians. Fletcher and his Council refused to pass this, saying that the proper form was to grant the sum to the King and Queen, and pray them to allow the sums to Markham and Lloyd. A further objection was that the bill appointed the Receiver-General of the proceeds, instead of leaving the appointment to the representative of the Crown; and, in fact, it was rather a reflection upon Robert Turner, who had acted as Receiver of the preceding tax. Finding no likelihood of a satisfactory bill being passed, Fletcher dissolved the Assembly on the afternoon of June 9, 1694, allowing some laws, and disapproving of one for giving Assemblymen 6*s.* a day, instead of the old allowance of 3*s.*, and also disapproving of a new system of county levies, whereby the Justices and Assemblymen of the County were to fix them, even for the purpose of paying debts, perhaps twelve years old. The general practice in England and the colonies was for the grand jury at the Quarter Sessions to make presentment of the amount to be raised. Fletcher went away on June 26, having asked his Council to decide whether he should not, as a compliance with the Queen's letter, array the whole colony, and detach at least 50 men for the assistance of Albany.

Let us not dispute any Quaker's belief that for Penn's escape from death on the scaffold and the colony's retention of whatever advantages it had under the Charter to him, there was a special interposition of Divine Providence. In no contradictory humor, there can be pointed out for a secondary cause, that Penn, with or most frequently without any ulterior end than the disconnected act which he was promoting, had so used his opportunities in the preceding reigns, and conducted himself since, as to place in his hands wires which ramified far, in fact almost, at some time or other, everywhere, in the complex and changing jumble of political affairs. His activities had made him, if not the associate, and even if sometimes an opponent, yet an acquaintance at least of everybody. What anger he had felt, did not prevent a readjustment of relations. His personal charm and his lofty sentiments predisposed in his favor those who were not leading partisans in opposition to him. With his influence with James II, great enough to do individuals a good turn, Penn had followed the injunction

"Cast thy bread upon the waters:"

and the promise

"for thou shalt find it after many days"

was fulfilled in the recovery of not only his life and liberty, but also his viceregal powers. It was not merely the chance to escape some mild trouble, or to make money, or to rise, that he had given to men who afterwards, some quite unexpectedly, were in a position to make some return to him. At the bureaus, the Council boards, and the Cabinet ministers' desks were those who owed to Penn their very lives. One instance will suffice. A few months before the Revolution, Penn, in his own coach, drawn by four horses, took Sir John Trenchard to Windsor, where, leading him into the King's presence, Penn secured Trenchard's pardon, notwithstanding his complicity in the Monmouth and Lord Russell affairs, and his having been exempted from a general offer of pardon. After the Revolution, Trenchard speedily helped Penn financially by buying the four horses: but this had scarcely left Trenchard quit of obligation. After Penn was deprived of the government of his province, Trenchard became one of the Secretaries of State.

In a letter, undated but written probably in October, 1693, to the Earl of Rochester (Laurence Hyde, the Queen's uncle, created Earl in 1682), Penn spoke of a desire to go to Pennsylvania, but said that he would not accept liberty on condition of going, so as to be looked upon as "an articled exile," and he must go to Ireland to settle his almost ruined estate, and to take off the prosecution against him begun upon Fuller's evidence, and therefore the departure for America could not be before the following Spring. On Nov. 25, Rochester and the Earl of Ranelagh, who was an Irish peer, and Viscount Sidney went to the King, and represented Penn's case as a hard one, there being no evidence against him, except that of imposters, fugitives, or those who since their pardon had refused to stand by their first assertions, whereas these lords had known him long and favorably for many good deeds; furthermore these lords explained that he might have gone abroad two years before, had he not been unwilling to seem to defy the government, and now he was waiting for leave to go about his affairs. King William replied that Penn was also his old acquaintance, and should be allowed to follow his business, as there was nothing to say to him. By the King's command, Secretary of State Trenchard, on the 30th, discharged Penn. Penn went from the Secretary's to the Friends Meeting, and spoke for the first time for nearly three years. Dixon is probably right in identifying the Mr. Penn who was reported as saying about this time that James II had the most favorable opportunity for an invasion, as being Neville Payne. On 12mo. 4, William Penn wrote to certain Friends in Pennsylvania for a large loan, on receipt of which he would sail thither, God giving him health, in three or at most six months. This loan was not made; but some of the Quakers decided on the plan, as Fletcher says in a letter of Aug. 18, 1694, of sending delegates to England to secure power to act under their former commissions, or, if they could not accomplish Penn's restoration, to have the government annexed to that of Maryland.

We would have expected Penn to be glad that he was relieved during a war of a position where he by himself or deputy would be obliged to perform military duties, and moreover against his former king: but to the natural desire to resume place and authority which had been arbitrarily taken away, was doubtless added the conviction that the powers of government granted by King Charles's patent were necessary for both the protection of the Proprietary's real estate rights and the happiness and prosperity of the colony. Penn persisted in claiming that the King and Queen were misinformed, when they superseded him on the ground of failure of justice and danger of capture in the war. However objectionable proprietary governments were, they had been too long settled in the colonial system of England to be declared illegal. Offices and franchises were private property, which could be taken only by judicial process or the fiat of King, Lords, and Commons in Parliament. In the absence of William III, in the Summer of 1694, the Countess of Ranelagh took up Penn's cause with Mary II, left as usual as sole sovereign, and, when Penn petitioned for restoration of his government, she was favorably disposed. The petition coming before the Privy Council, was referred on July 12, 1694, to the Committee for Trade and Plantations. The next day, the Attorney-General and Solicitor-General made a report justifying the appointment of Fletcher in the emergency, for the reasons set forth in his commission, but finding that, when the occasion ceased, the right of government belonged to the grantee of Charles II and assignee of the Duke of York. Penn, waiting outside the room where the Committee was sitting, was called in to be heard. The promises he then made do not show him a martyr to the principles of peace. He said that if her Majesty would be pleased to restore him to his property according to the grant, he would with all convenient speed go to Pennsylvania, and take care of the government, and provide for the safety and security of the region, as far as in him lay, and he would transmit to the Provincial Council and Assembly all orders from her Majesty for supplying quotas of men, and defraying share of expense, and—here was a strange statement for him to make—he doubted not that they would be fully complied with. Perhaps he thought that he could arrange for a non-Quaker majority in Council and Assembly, or obtain volunteers and contributions sufficient. To prove the colonists' loyalty and readiness to do as desired, he then exhibited a copy of the Act of Assembly of 1693, expressing submission to their Majesties' pleasure in taking the government into their hands, and moreover levying a tax to be spent by the Governor appointed by the King and Queen. We must remember that Penn had not heard of the proceedings of the Assembly dissolved in June, nor probably of the small yield from the tax. The Lords of the Committee, after these stipulations by Penn, referred the Act levying the tax and the other laws passed in 1693 to the Attorney-General. The Lords decided that, on learning what the Queen fixed as Pennsylvania's quota for the safety of New York, they would recommend, on the strength of Penn's assurances, the restoration of the government to him. On July 27, they, probably to prevent Penn from appointing a Quaker, extracted from him a promise to continue Markham as Lieutenant-Governor; and Penn also stipulated to submit the direction of military affairs to their Majesties, if the Assembly of Pennsylvania would not comply with the orders transmitted. The validity of the laws of 1693, passed without the Proprietary's participation, being questionable, his consent in writing was exacted for the execution of those not already rejected by their Majesties in Council. Certain laws were disapproved, but most were left until future Assemblies would have the opportunity to repeal them.

On August 20, William and Mary, reciting that they had thought fit to restore William Penn to the administration of the government of Pennsylvania and New

Castle and Territories, annulled the appointment of Fletcher as Governor of the same. By letter dated the next day, addressed to the Proprietary, or, in his absence, the Commander-in-Chief, the Queen fixed the quota of Pennsylvania and New Castle, to be furnished on the demand of the Governor of New York, at not exceeding eighty men with their officers.

Thomas Lloyd died Sept. (7 mo.) 10, 1694, perhaps without Penn hearing of the fact before arranging the restored government. The subsequent prominence of Lloyd's sons-in-law, grandchildren, and other posterity by blood or marriage, made him the patriarch of the most important family connection of Colonial Pennsylvania, and three Presidents of the Supreme Executive Council of Revolutionary times, Wharton, Moore, and Dickinson, married descendants.

Penn, on Nov. 24, while in Bristol on a preaching tour, constituted Markham "Governor," but, as simultaneously Penn appointed two Assistants, viz: John Goodson and Samuel Carpenter, both moreover Quakers, and charged Markham in all things to govern with the advice and consent of at least one of them, the action was scarcely a compliance with the promise to the Committee. The explanation, as given in the document addressed to Goodson and Carpenter, was the frequent indisposition of Markham. Penn wrote on the same day to Friends in Pennsylvania, saying "We must creep where we can not go," and asking them not to take it amiss that he could not follow what was his inclination as well as theirs, but hoped to do so in a short time. He would at once, and probably did, write to the Assistants to consult them in the advice and consent they might give to his cousin Markham. In December, Penn induced William Ford to write, as Ford did on Dec. 14, to Secretary Blathwayt to get him to make the Lords understand and allow that Markham's investment with the military power answered the substance of the promise made to them, and that the civil affairs be in the hands of "those more suitable to the mind and improvement of the colony."

England, notwithstanding the restoration of the government to William Penn, retained or subsequently imposed her control over his dominions in several ways quite annoying to the colonists. In the first place, by King Charles's Charter, the Proprietaries and their Lieutenants and Governors were bound to admit to all ports the officers appointed by the Commissioners or farmers of the Customs, and to allow to the Crown such impositions and customs on merchandise laded and unladed as then or later appointed by Act of Parliament. The Charter authorized carrying from England to Pennsylvania under the customs due by any law or statute of only such articles as not prohibited by the law and statutes to be carried out of the kingdoms, and the produce of the country was to be carried first to England, and, if afterwards any further, then under the same duties as the subjects in England paid, and under the directions of the Acts of Navigation and other laws.

Various Acts of Parliament either regulating trade or for other purposes were made by their very terms to extend to the American Colonies.

The policy of the Mother Country in dealing with the American colonies was to subordinate their interests to hers. Perhaps it was not yet feared that if they were commercially able to do without England, they would become politically independent; but it was planned that they should supply the material, while the depots and factories and markets should be in England. Ireland, Wales, and the little English possession, Berwick upon the Tweed, were usually included in the measures for Protection, so as to share with England the monopoly.

Scotland, although her King was King of England,

was until the Act of Union of Queen Anne's reign a separate realm, with distinct officers, nobility, and Parliament; and the inhabitants north of the boundary between the two countries were not admitted to the rights of Englishmen except by special naturalization or letters of denization, and as to some privileges seemed excluded by not being "native born."

An Act of the English Parliament passed very soon after the Restoration of Charles II, *i.e.* 12 Car. II, c. 18, for the encouraging and increasing of shipping and navigation, commonly called the Act of Navigation, provided that after Dec. 1, 1660, nothing should be imported into or exported from any lands, islands, plantations, or territories belonging to or in possession of the King in Asia, Africa, or America (New Netherland being included, for the Act covered future possessions) in any other vessels than those belonging to the people of England, Ireland, Wales, or Berwick, or built in and belonging to the people of any of said plantations, and whereof the master and three fourths at least of the mariners were English. The penalty was loss of goods carried, and of the vessel and its guns, furniture, tackle, ammunition, and apparel.

It was further provided that no alien, or person not born within the allegiance of the King or naturalized or made a free denizen, should after Feb. 1, 1661 (query, 1661–2?), be a merchant or factor in any of said places, on pain of forfeiture of his goods. All Governors of plantations and all future Governors appointed by the King were, before entrance into the government, to take an oath to do their utmost to have these two prohibitions observed, and were, upon proof of negligence, to be removed. No goods or commodities of the growth or manufacture of Africa, Asia, or America were to be imported into England, Ireland, Wales, Guernsey, Jersey, or Berwick upon Tweed in any other vessels but such as belonged to people of

England, Ireland, Wales, or Berwick or the plantations, and whereof the master and three fourths at least of the mariners were English. No Governor of any plantation should allow any foreign built vessel to load or unload any commodities until a certificate were produced to him or person appointed for the purpose by him, that the owners had taken an oath that said vessel was bought for valuable consideration, and that no foreigner had any interest, nor until examination were made whether the master and three fourths of the mariners were English.

It was further enacted that after April 1, 1661, no sugar, tobacco, cotton-wool, indigoes, ginger, fustic, or other dyewood of the growth or manufacture of the plantations should be carried to any other place than the other plantations or England, Ireland, Wales, or Berwick, there to be laid on shore. Every vessel sailing from England, Ireland, Wales, or Berwick for any English plantation was required to give security to the chief officers of the Custom House of the port to obey this law on the return voyage. For all ships from any other port or place with which any of said plantations were permitted to trade, the Governor of a plantation, before such ship was to be permitted to load there any such commodities, was to take bond that the vessel carry the goods to an English plantation, or to England, Ireland, Wales, or Berwick on Tweed, and if any load were taken before giving bond, the bond should be forfeited.

In soon afterwards arranging for a monopoly for English built vessels, Ireland's dealings with the colonies was restricted. By act of 15 Car. II, c. 7, no commodity of the growth or manufacture of Europe was to be imported after March 25, 1664, into any of the plantations unless shipped in England, Wales, or Berwick, and in English built shipping or shipping bought before Oct. 1, 1662, and of which the master and three fourths at least of the mariners were English, and unless carried directly to the plantations, under penalty of loss of goods and of vessel, guns, &ct., except that the wines of Madeira and the Azores and servants and horses from Scotland or Ireland and victuals from Scotland could be taken in. The Governors of the plantations were, before entrance upon their governments, to take an oath to do their utmost to have this act observed.

Scotchmen had evaded the provision requiring masters of vessels to be English by coming over as supercargoes and merchants, although often they directed as if masters; and Randolph, claiming that the law should be strictly construed against Scotchmen, said on Dec. 7, 1695, that many Scotchmen had been engaged in trade, *i.e.* as merchants, in America for many years, as being persons "born within the King's allegiance." Upon the incorporation by the Parliament of Scotland of the trading company for India, Africa, and America, which resulted in the Darien fiasco, England became alarmed, lest her trade and navigation except with Europe would be destroyed. Her Parliament addressed the King, particularly representing that when the Scotch would be settled in plantations in America, England's commerce in tobacco, sugar, &ct. would be utterly lost. The King's answer favored a vigorous execution of the English laws for the security of the plantation trade, and for making England the staple of the commodities of the plantations, and of the commodities from other countries and places for the support of the plantations.

On May 15, 1696, in place of the Committee of the Privy Council for Trade and Plantations, Commissioners were appointed "for Promoting the Trade of our Kingdom and Inspecting and Improving our Plantations in America and Elsewhere;" and it was made part of their duty to promote the supplying of England

with naval stores from her colonies, improving and
settling in them such other staples and manufactures
as England was obliged to obtain from the subjects of
other princes and states, and to ascertain what may
be best encouraged in the plantations, and "what
trades are taken up and exercised there which may
prove prejudicial by furnishing themselves and our
other colonies with what has been usually supplied
from England, and to find out means of diverting them
from such." John Locke, who largely owed his life
to Penn, was one of these Commissioners.

An act, 7 & 8 Wm. III, c. 22, passed for preventing
frauds and regulating abuses in the plantation trade,
allowed no goods after March 25, 1698, to be imported
into or exported from the plantations, or from one part
to another of the colonies, or to England, Wales, or
Berwick, in any ship or bottom but of the build of
England, Ireland, or the colonies, wholly owned by
people thereof, and navigated with master and three
fourths of the mariners English. All the Governors and
Commanders-in-Chief of any of the English colonies
were before March 25, 1697, and all afterwards appointed were before entrance upon the government, to
take an oath to do their utmost to have this and the
preceding acts observed, and said officers were to give
security upon notice. The jurors in all actions upon
any statute concerning the King's duties or the forfeiture of ship or goods were to be natives of England or
Ireland or the plantations: and all places of trust in
courts of law were to be filled by native born subjects
of England or Ireland or said plantations. No persons
claiming propriety in tracts of land in America by
charter or letters patent were to sell to other than
natural born subjects of England, Ireland, Wales, or
Berwick without consent of the King signified by
order in Council first obtained. All Governors appointed by any of such proprietors who were author-

ized to nominate such, should be allowed and approved of by the King, and before entering on government take oaths like Governors of other colonies. No vessel should be deemed qualified to carry to or from the plantations, as built in England &ct. or the plantations, until the persons claiming property registered it by proof upon the oath of one or more owners of the vessel.

Those who wished to discriminate against Scotland experienced a defeat when the Attorney-General and Solicitor-General gave an opinion that Scotchmen were qualified to be owners, masters, and mariners in America. All the restrictions upon them in trade and navigation were removed by the Act for the Union of the Two Kingdoms of England and Scotland, 5 Ann., c. 8.

CHAPTER X.

FAILURE IN GOVERNMENT.

Question as to resuscitation of Frame of 1683—Councillors chosen under it—Requisition for troops—Councillors leave defence of Penn's dominions to Markham's conscience—Assembly offers 250*l.* "for the support of the government" in answer to the requisition, but demands first the confirmation of the Frame with some changes—Markham refuses, and dissolves both Council and Assembly, and rules without any for about a year—Deterioration of the colony in morals—Illness and complacency of Markham—Wide-spread disinclination to punish—Difficulties of enforcing laws regulating trade—Rapid increase of population with loss to other colonies—Size of Philadelphia and population of town and country about 1697—Pennsylvania drawing foreign silver—A bank—Linen, woolens, and wine—Trade—Randolph suggests annexation of Lower Counties to Maryland and union of Pennsylvania and West Jersey under Royal Governor—Markham appoints a Council, and summons an Assembly like Fletcher's—A would-be pirate employed for defence, and protected against a naval force sent to arrest him—Appropriation of 300*l.* "for the relief of the distressed Indians," as the reply to the requisition for troops—Precaution against fire in Philadelphia and New Castle—The Frame of 1696—Taxation disproportionate and without representation—Opposition to the Frame—Assembly refuses to send further money for the war—Admiralty Court with Quary as Judge—Penn's arguments and suggestions to a Committee of the House of Lords—Instructions from the King and requirement to give security—Markham's correspondence with Capt. Daniell—Penn urges the suppression of forbidden trade and vice in his colony—The licensing of drinking places put in the county Justices' hands—Penn's plea as to Markham—Pirates—Every and men from his vessel—Pennsylvania Act relating to trade—Interference with Admiralty and Customs officers—Replevin—Lloyd's insult to the seal with the King's effigy—Plunder of Lewes by Frenchmen—Legislation and other proceedings of the provincial government—Captain Kidd.

The correct legal opinion, and that held by a number of persons, was, that at the end of the suspension of Penn's government, all the privileges and institutions derived from Penn, and particularly those created by the Charter of 1683 establishing the Frame of Government, sprang again into full force. Certain fundamental legislation amounted to a covenant between Penn and the People, to destroy which was to the interest of neither party. Upon the laws establishing a constitution depended the People's great share in political authority: on the other hand, upon the Act of Union and Act of Settlement under the first Frame, as legally replaced by the Frame of 1683, depended what was a great advantage to Penn, as well as to the dual colony, viz: the integrity of the dominion from below Lewes to the headwaters of the Delaware. If that Act of Union was void, while the Charter from King Charles authorized Penn and the freemen of Pennsylvania proper to make laws for that Province, there was really nothing to bind any inhabitant of New Castle, Kent, or Sussex except the common law of England, and, if the representatives of what is now Delaware were to meet to tax themselves, they could insist upon being an independent House. William and Mary had recognized the vitality of the old order of things in the Province of Pennsylvania and Country of New Castle and all the Territories and tracts of land depending thereon; for the letters patent saying that their Majesties had seen fit to restore Penn to the administration of the government, did not contain any words making a grant to him, but merely a decree that the appointment of Fletcher with his powers over the region should cease. As part of the covenant between Penn and the People, he and the representatives of both Province and Territories had agreed, in Article 24th of the Frame, that no act, law, or ordinance should thereafter be made or done by the Proprietary and Governor or freeman in the Council or Assembly to alter, change, or diminish the form or effect of that Frame, without the consent of the Proprietary and Governor or his heirs or assigns and six sevenths of the freemen in Council and Assembly. Such consent to alter or annul had never been given: a transcendent authority had imposed its will, but had since relinquished its hold, had even undertaken to execute such reasonable laws as were in force at Fletcher's taking charge, although providing means for further legislation, and had, on yielding the government again to Penn, asked his consent to the laws passed meanwhile.

Markham in Philadelphia received his commission from Penn about seven months after William and Mary's patent restoring the government, and took the oaths on the second day of the new year, *i.e.* March 26, 1695. He acted at once upon the theory that the old Frame was in force, issuing in a few days writs for the election of Councillors as prescribed in the Frame. As the old succession had been broken, he could not fill the body, and preserve the rotation in office, except by having one Councillor chosen from each county for three years, one for two years, and one for one year. For these terms respectively, Philadelphia County chose Carpenter, Richardson, and Anthony Morris, Chester County chose David Lloyd, Caleb Pusey, and George

Maris, Bucks County chose Joseph Growdon, Phineas Pemberton, and William Biles, New Castle County chose John Donnaldson, John Williams, and Richard Halliwell, Kent County chose John Brinckloe, Richard Willson, and Griffith Jones (apparently not the person of the name in Fletcher's Council), and Sussex chose Clark, Thomas Pemberton, and Robert Clifton. All the Pennsylvanians and Jones and Clark were Quakers, as appears by their subscribing the declaration of fidelity and profession of the Christian faith and the test, while the others took the oath required by Act of Parliament, and subscribed the test.

Most persons wanted the guarantee of privileges and the limitation of Penn's powers; but most of these Councillors desired changes in the Frame. The first business of the Council, except some judicial and administrative matters, was to go over the laws, so as to propose such alterations and additions as were to be submitted at the meeting of the Assembly. On May 25, the grand committee, into which the Council had been resolved for the aforesaid purpose, presented to Markham a bill for remodelling the government; but, after several days spent upon it, an agreement could not be reached, and the subject was dropped.

Fletcher had written, on April 15, for the full quota of 80 men with their officers, which he stated to be a captain, two lieutenants, four sergeants, four corporals, and two drummers, to be at Albany as soon as possible, and for their arms, ammunition, and pay for one year to be provided also. The Council advised that an Assembly be called, but postponed its meeting until the 9th of September, declaring that it would be the ruin of many families for the men to be away from home during harvest. Markham, expressing the hope that the delay would not be looked upon as a refusal, mentioned Penn's assurances to protect the country as far as in him lay, and asked, if an enemy made any attempt upon it, were the Councillors willing that the Governor should defend it by force of arms? Some said that they were willing; others, that they must leave every one to his liberty; some admitted that Governor Penn's instructions were to be followed; finally various Quakers declared that it was the Governor's business, and they had nothing to do with it. Carpenter being probably among those unwilling to meddle, Markham asked John Goodson, the other Assistant, whether he was dissatisfied with anything that had been done; he expressed himself satisfied.

Fletcher, making a change in the number of sergeants and corporals from four to three, asked, on June 12, that the troops or money to maintain them be sent to New York by the 1st of August. The Councillors to whom this second letter was read, whether Quaker or not, still saw no use in drawing the representatives of the People away from harvesting, as not until Winter would the crops be paid for, and the inhabitants have any money to pay a tax.

The Sheriffs were commanded to hold elections for six Assemblymen from each county, the number mentioned in the Frame. The Assemblymen chosen, of whom Shippen was made Speaker, were all Quakers except four of those from Sussex.

The Council having failed to promulgate bills twenty days before the meeting of the Assembly, no legislation was possible consistently with the Frame. This may have made the leaders of the People more determined to get rid of the Frame: and there was a purpose to obtain greater concessions in a new Charter. Somebody, perhaps Lloyd, suggesting that the old was void, the opportunity seemed to have arrived. A third request for the quota of troops or money followed a meeting of Fletcher with some of the Mohawks, and was laid before the Assembly. A resolution was carried that legislation might be proceeded with, in the present emergency, without the previous promulgation of bills. A committee of Councillors and Assemblymen made a report, in which was set forth the present made in 1693 to the King and Queen for support of government, upon Fletcher's assurance of supplying the friendly Indians with necessaries, and there was expressed the opinion that the money then raised or now to be raised "for the support of government," and not otherwise expressly appropriated, ought to be taken instead of the assistance asked, and as an answer, as far as conscience and ability allowed, to the Queen's letters, and that the said money might be appropriated as the Governor or his Deputy for the time being should see fit. Markham, welcoming any chance for a substantial aid, desired the representatives to go on as they had begun, and give an effectual answer by raising money. The Committee also made a report as to an Act of Settlement. There was a unanimous vote of the House that the old Frame was dead; certain alterations were decided upon to be embraced in a new law reviving it, to be passed by the Proprietary's Deputy with the consent of the freemen in an Assembly. An Act of Settlement, following the adoption by the House of that report, was presented along with a bill levying 1d. per l. and 6s. per head on persons not otherwise rated, 250l. of the proceeds to be for the support of the government as before mentioned, 300l. to go to Markham for his services, and the balance to pay the debts of the government. Markham offered to pass the money bill to answer the Queen's letter in any manner, or under any "title," meaning the phraseology to avoid ostensibly appropriating for war, and desired his own name to be entirely omitted from the bill, rather than that the Queen's letter remain unanswered. He wished the Act of Settlement left for further debate, and refused to pass any bill before the money bill. One Councillor pointed out that Parliament always had their privileges granted first, and voted the money last. Several members said that there was nothing in the Act of Settlement but what the Proprietary had formerly granted. Markham reflected that, if the Frame binding Penn and his heirs, and curtailing their powers, was indeed dead, as asserted by the very beneficiaries of it, the Deputy would be unfaithful to his principal in binding him again. Markham accordingly declared that he could not, in honor or justice to the Proprietary, pass the Act of Settlement. As for the People's privileges, he never had attempted, or would attempt, to diminish them. Despairing of any answer to the demands of the Governor of New York, unless a Charter of Privileges were granted, Markham dissolved both Council and Assembly. If he was Deputy of a Governor bound only by the Charter from King Charles or the usual customs of the British colonies, this action was perfectly valid. Apparently Markham had the consent of his Assistants, one or both of whom refused to agree to his calling an Assembly in the way it was done in other colonies. With the Assistants' consent, he administered the government without Council or Assembly for a year all but two days, writing to Penn for a solution of the dilemma, but the letters being captured by the French.

The English provinces of North America, at least some of them, were not at this period filled with God-fearing or law-abiding people. Nicholson, when he complained of the loose government of Pennsylvania, drew a sad picture of the low state of religion and morality in Maryland, his own province, where there were men with two wives, and women with two husbands. Pennsylvania might have been expected to be a bright spot, from the character of Penn's first settlers, most of whom were still living, but the Keithian movement, overturning, like all reforms, something beneficial in the old order of things, had destroyed the influence of those who might have kept the public, even with increasing additions of non-Quakers, to a high moral sentiment. Having no regard for such monitors, the many persons who for other than religious reasons had come to the western shore of Delaware Bay and River were on the average no better behaved than those who were residing elsewhere away from home. Moreover, black sheep in the diminished Quaker flock were visible, and it was even alleged that its ministry furnished enough cases of immorality to seem to be no more like angels than the clergy of other bodies have shown themselves to be.

While examples and ideals were becoming insufficient in many cases to restrain conduct, the government was ceasing to be a terror to evil doers. Markham was in failing health, Randolph calling him "very infirm." Penn writing on 3mo. 7, 1700, pleaded this as an excuse for "slips," Markham "having been so rudely handled with gout, he has not the use of his legs, and but little of his hands, he can not even ride, and is prisoner to his own chamber." Uncertain as to what Charter he was acting under, in trepidation at the Assembly's non-compliance with the royal order for troops, without any fund at his disposal, or guards at his command, and depending on the rough characters to do the fighting which might be required for the dominion, and naturally politic and easy-going, Markham was not energetic in correcting irregularities. It is even noticeable, that, although the Act of Navigation gave to the Governor of the plantation—in this case Markham or Penn—one third of any vessel or goods seized there, Markham showed no avidity in making seizures. In fact, while Penn in England was sanctimonious, Markham adopted the policy for making Penn's dominion prosperous of having a "wide open" town. No ordinary or drinking place being allowed without the Governor's license, Markham seems to have granted licenses to all who would pay to him the fee for the same. Randolph, Surveyor-General of Customs, repeated stories of Markham receiving large sums from illegal traders and pirates, whom he allowed to reside unmolested. Against such complaints and Penn's insinuations covered by the word "avarice," Markham, in the course of two letters in the Spring of 1697, said: "I have been a slave to this Province many years and never saw a penny of their money. . . I have had as many opportunities since I have been here to have bettered my fortune as those that have made use of them, but I have always been governed by such principles whether out of religion or honor I will not say that I fear will always subject me to the character [of being impecunious] Randolph gives of me. In short I have served you faithfully but desire not to be a burden. I have trusted Providence hitherto and tho' it may be hard with me being a cripple, yet can not beg an alms tho' at the door of those I spent my strength for." A few years later, Penn, in a letter referring to Markham having set apart a certain lot for a meeting-house for the Friends, spoke of him as having lived "corruptly and lavishly" upon him: but the angry language may have been too strong. If, to be sure, this complaisant Governor did not take as much blackmail or presents in the nature of blackmail as some Governors of other colonies, he by that very circumstance added to the attractiveness of Pennsylvania and the Lower Counties for bad characters.

Although the Quakers in their Address to King William of 3mo., 1696, spoken of in the chapter on Religious Dissension, attributed misrepresentations of them to revenge for their magistrates' strictness against disorders and night revels, there was, contemporary with the coming of men of bad character among the non-Quaker residents or sojourners, a dislike widely spread among the religious people of the use of anything but moral suasion to control a fellow man's conduct. This was independent of any worldly motives. Not only were the Mennonites principled against coercion by force, and the Keithians had reproached their enemies with readiness to fight to enforce the law, but many who thought about human rights justified unkindness to anybody only when necessary to protect others in life, freedom, and lawful property. Retribution, as an object apart from prevention, seemed to them not man's affair. The disinclination to punish naturally increased with the severity of the punishment, and, as well as legal obstructions, left grave offences unatoned for. Except the persons benefitted by fines or forfeitures, and not even Markham or Penn among such, few wished to see any man suffer very much in person or estate for a breach of the laws giving England a monopoly of trade. Although this remark seems to be at variance with the Vindication sent by the Council and Assembly to King William in 1698, two years later than the Address already spoken of, and although the word of those who signed may be worth more than the word of Edward Randolph, yet in this matter the Vindication need be taken as proving only that the leading men were neither conspiring nor wishing to foster prohibited trade.

Along such a water frontage, where vessels could escape observation in a wide bay and in creeks, in days when a deep channel was not required, no Governor except with numerous revenue cutters could prevent smuggling. Goods could be landed, and, while kept away from New Castle, Chester, and Philadelphia, could be disposed of among the country people, and in some cases carried over to Maryland. Similarly, even tobacco could be put on board by stealth. One vessel said to have been owned by a Netherlander did its work by night. As required by the law to prevent exporting except to England, the acting Governor duly exacted bonds with sureties for proceeding thither from the masters of vessels leaving Penn's dominions. When on the high seas, a master would sometimes change the course, and carry his cargo to Scotland or the Netherlands. Hearing of vessels which had not reached their ostensible destination, Markham did not sue out the bonds, and when Randolph expostulated with him, gave Randolph no satisfaction. Nearly every case in the list made out by Randolph is explained in the Vindication aforesaid, the vessel as a rule being captured by the French: but in March, 1696–7, Penn was obliged to raise the point before the Committee of the House of Lords that Proprietary officers could not be expected to sue out the bonds, in which contention he was unsuccessful.

While Markham and the Deputies of Proprietary Governors generally co-operated less with the Customs officials than did Governors directly under the Crown, judges and juries outside of Penn's dominion were apparently as unwilling as those within it to enforce the Trade and Navigation Laws, and perhaps were less disinterested in their motives. By December, 1695, when Randolph made the statement, he had never gained a case in the courts of any colony against any vessel. He may have brought his suits without sufficient evidence, but, as the judges in America were often merchants, the unvarying acquittal looks more like partiality or affiliation, and led to the belief that justice to the King's side in such tribunals was not obtainable. In the case of the ship "Dolphin," Randolph asked Markham for a special court at Philadelphia, but the trial was ordered to be at Chester, and, on April 30, 1695, there was a verdict for defendant with damages and costs, and Randolph was arrested and imprisoned for £46, and, although an appeal was allowed, the ship was not detained.

The population along the western side of Delaware

Bay and River increased rapidly during the fifteen years following the grant to Penn. To the causes mentioned in the chapter on the People, there were added towards the close of the Century, to attract from other colonies, greater employment for labor and gentler exercise of authority. Better wages and, according to Governor Nicholson, the chance of booty offered by piratical captains, induced such desertion of sailors to Pennsylvania that the vessels in Maryland could not be manned. He, in June, 1695, did not doubt that one hundred had run to Pennsylvania from the Virginia and Maryland fleet. There was another cause for emigration from Maryland; in that colony, people were caned and clubbed. As to New York, the burdens of the war with Canada were mentioned in September, 1696, as having induced two hundred or three hundred families to leave, some going to New England, but most to Maryland or Pennsylvania. Philadelphia became nearly as large and possessed of nearly as much trade and riches as the city of New York, which was much older. Penn told the Commissioners for Trade in 1697 that he thought it possible that Philadelphia comprised 1500 houses, and that the inhabitants of town and country together numbered 12,000.

Pennsylvania had bid for actual money by passing a law in 1693, with the consent of Fletcher, that all Peru pieces of eight weighing not less than 12 dwt. and all Lion dollars (coined in the Netherlands) not clipped should pass for 6$s.$, and all pillar, Mexico, and Seville pieces of eight should pass, if weighing 13 dwt., for 6$s.$ 2$d.$, and, if weighing 14 dwt., for 6$s.$ 4 $d.$, and, if weighing 15 dwt., for 6$s.$ 6$d.$, and, if weighing 16 dwt., for 6$s.$ 9$d.$ and, if weighing 17 dwt., for 7$s.$ This had operated to draw both silver and trade to the Delaware: Hartwell and other Virginians complained on Oct. 20, 1697, that, by appointing the piece of eight weighing 12 dwt. to go for 6$s.$, Pennsylvania was draining all the money from Maryland and Virginia, the best piece of eight being in Virginia 5s., and in Maryland 4s. 6d.

Nicholson, in a letter of June 14, 1695, to the Duke of Shrewsbury, said that there was a bank in Penn's dominion of £20,000, most of the people, even the tradesmen and farmers, being concerned in it, the farmers putting in their grain. On this subject, nothing further has been found except that on 12mo. 7, 1688-9, Robert Turner, John Tessick (Tysack?), Thomas Budd, Robert Ewer, Samuel Carpenter, and John Fuller, by petition to Governor Blackwell and Council, set forth said petitioners' design to start a bank for money, and asked to be encouraged, whereupon Blackwell told them that he himself had, when in New England, proposed such a thing to Penn, and the latter's answer might be expected by the first ship from England. Nevertheless, Blackwell explained that he saw no reason why they should not give their personal bills, as merchants usually did bills of exchange, to anybody who would take such bills to pass as money. He warned as to the danger of counterfeiting. If Nicholson, who had only recently arrived in the adjoining province, was correctly informed, there was thus an association distinct from the Society of Traders, and apparently unchartered, warehousing and marketing much of the agricultural product.

Nicholson also mentioned the Germans in Pennsylvania employed in linen and woolen manufacture, and that more were expected, "which," he added with true English feeling, "will be very prejudicial to England." Two years later, Penn, before the Committee of the House of Lords, spoke of the possibility of America furnishing wine for England, saying that in Pennsylvania both Germans and French were then making white and red wine every year.

The other colonies, and particularly Maryland, were

jealous of Penn's, and jealousy fostered suspicion that the commerce of the latter was illegal. Nicholson heard and, in the aforesaid letter, communicated the gossip that Penn's colony, having many Scotchmen engaged in trade, was sending tobacco to Scotland and other unlawful European destinations, also to Curaçoa and Surinam, in casks with only flour and bread visible at the ends. The story continued that the vessels contrived to reach Curaçoa and Surinam in time for the arrival of the Dutch fleet from Europe, so as to buy goods from it, which were then brought back and sold in Pennsylvania as cheap as in Holland. Nicholson said further that twelve or fourteen sloops, brigantines, and other vessels were then being built in Pennsylvania, *i.e.* Penn's whole dominion. After much suspicion had been cast upon the trade to Curaçoa, a Dutch possession, Francis Jones, a sea captain, in his letter hereinafter mentioned, explained that as it was not to the interest of merchants to bring Dutch goods to the dual colony, but that provisions, a legitimate export, were sent to Curaçoa, payment was made in Spanish pieces of eight, otherwise dollars, at 4s. to 4½s. per piece, and these were used to buy salt to bring back. As to a charge of shipping tobacco to forbidden places, Jones did not believe 1000 hhds. were grown in Penn's dominion, the inhabitants chiefly growing corn. Maryland discriminated in 1695 against Pennsylvania by laying an impost for three years of ten per cent. on all European goods imported thither through Maryland ports and across country, although not exposed to sale on the way; yet Maryland, without paying a similar impost in Pennsylvania, got most of her European goods through its ports. Goods for New York and Virginia were allowed to pass through Maryland free.

Randolph, being in England in the latter part of 1695, laid before the Commissioners of Customs an account of the state of the North American colonies with reference to the Scotch act incorporating an East India Company, and also some suggestions for preventing illegal traffic between the tobacco plantations and Scotland. He spoke of a possible design of the newly incorporated Scotch East India Company to purchase a settlement in one of the Lower Counties on the Delaware, and suggested the annexation of those Counties to Maryland, and also of West Jersey to Pennsylvania under a Governor to be appointed, more active than Markham. The act of 7 & 8 Wm. III, c. 22, aimed at the dangers spoken of by Randolph, has been mentioned in the chapter of this book just preceding. Randolph represented that in Proprietary colonies, there was every encouragement for illegal trading, and various persons in office were Scotchmen, and naturally inclined towards their countrymen. He said that in Pennsylvania several well known pirates were engaged in trading, chiefly with Curaçoa, and that nine vessels had lately sailed directly for Scotland. He urged that the Crown establish a court in the colonies for cases concerning the revenue and trade.

Benjamin M. Nead, in his excellent *Historical Notes* published by the State as an Appendix to the *Duke of Yorke's Book of Laws,* speaks of the dissatisfaction of the representatives of the People with Markham's dissolution of the two legislative houses, Council and Assembly, in 1695, and with his not issuing writs in 1696 for elections to be held at the time fixed by the old Frame, and also says that Markham dissuaded the freemen, who were planning to hold elections.

A circular from the English government for the vigorous enforcement, really against the Scotch, of the laws of Trade and Navigation, and a copy of a letter from the Committee for Trade and Plantations for the publishing and carrying out of the Act of 7 & 8 Wm. III, c. 22, and a letter from the said Committee, dated April 20, requiring the inhabitants to put themselves in a posture of defence against the French, convinced Markham that circumstances required an organized government. Therefore, like the Governors of other colonies, he established a Council appointed by himself, admitting thereto on Sep. 25, 1696, Shippen, Morris, David Lloyd—said three being Quakers—and Yeates, Halliwell, Brinckloe, John Hill, and Robinson—said five taking oaths. On the 28th, Markham again took the oaths, and subscribed the test: he thought it necessary to do so, because there had been "some alteration in the frame of government." He asked the Councillors to administer the oaths to him, but some of them answered that, being unable to take an oath, they could not administer one, and so Patrick Robinson administered the oaths. By unanimous advice, Markham summoned an Assembly, issuing writs for the same number of representatives as under Fletcher's rule.

About this time, a French privateer took several vessels out of New York harbor, and a sloop belonging to Philadelphia with a valuable cargo off Barnegat; then the privateer came into Delaware Bay, sending part of the force to plunder on shore. A brigantine commanded by John Day came to New Castle under clearance papers from South Carolina for England, with a crew so large that he was supposed to be intending a piratical expedition. Markham hesitated to avail himself of the authority and opportunities to arrest him: there was no force, even if there was any pretext, to restrain Day's men, who might therefore, if they lost their commander, plunder the land, or themselves take the vessel on a piratical cruise. There was some military organization for volunteer defenders of the dominion. John Donnaldson, the Councillor, as Major, had been put in charge at New Castle, where there was a fort with seven guns. Pemberton, doubtless the Thomas Pemberton who had been a Councillor, was Captain of the Lower Precincts by Markham's appointment. Markham is called "Colonel" from Fletcher's time. Day offering to sail down, and to fight the privateer without any expense to the government, merely for the chance of getting such a prize, Quary advised Markham to commission Day, and to give him 30 or 40 men from the Lower Counties, and let him ambuscade such French as had landed. Markham gave Day the commission, and he got ready. Francis Jones, before mentioned, some of whose men had deserted to Day, could not induce Markham to attempt to recall him. So, in great anger, Jones appealed to Governor Nicholson in Maryland, where there was a fleet under Captain Wager. Two lieutenants of Capt. Daniell's ship with about sixty men, landing at French Town on Elk River, marched over to New Castle without asking Markham's leave, and there seized Day and most of his officers on shore, but were confronted on the vessel with Markham's commission. The lieutenants could not refuse to recognize the military authority of Donnaldson, who told them that he would have prevented their entering the town as they did, if he had known that they were coming. They, finding that their followers were getting drunk, made these deliver their arms into Donnaldson's custody for the rest of the stay. Donnaldson protected the brigantine with the guns of the fort, the sails moreover being in the fort. When, without a drop of blood having been shed, the invading force started home, several of the men did not appear. To the great annoyance of Capt. Daniell, these deserters were not found and surrendered to him. Day, who was indeed a rascal, was allowed to proceed on his voyage. The French privateer appears to have put to sea, and to have escaped him. Day went to Curaçoa, and there sold the brigantine, and disappeared, for a time at least, to the defrauding of the owners.

On October 26, 1696, the day appointed for the meeting of the Assembly, Donnaldson and Clark were admitted to Markham's Council, and Goodson retired from the office of Assistant. It was then learned by Markham that Arthur Cooke had had in his possession for about eighteen months, and had been forbearing to use, two commissions from Penn, one appointing Markham as Lieutenant-Governor to act acording to the laws and Charter, viz: the Frame of 1683, and the other appointing Cooke and Jennings as Assistants. Cooke therefore took Goodson's place. Markham still did not feel free to reenact the Frame, if that was necessary to its validity. The Assembly met, and elected John Simcock as Speaker. Then Markham presented the last message for the quota, and said, that, while he had received no authority to reenact the Frame, and had called the House under the Charter of Charles II and the usages of neighbouring Provinces, he would agree that nothing done at the session should prejudice any claim or right to the Frame. It was finally arranged by a committee of conference that a money bill be passed, and also an act for a Frame of Government with a proviso that, if the Proprietary disapproved, it should be null and void, without prejudice to him or the People in relation to the validity or invalidity of the old Frame, and that Councillors and members of Assembly meanwhile be chosen on the 10th of the following 1st month (March). Markham himself presented the heads of the new Frame, somewhat altering the old. As finally agreed upon, the new Frame was passed on November 7, 1696, with the seal of the Province affixed, as the first of five laws made at the session. By the second law, a tax of $1d.$ per $l.$ and $6s.$ per head was levied to manifest affection to the King as well as "readiness to answer his expectations in supporting the said government as far as in conscience we can:" $300l.$ of the proceeds to go towards the relief of the distressed Indians above Albany in alliance with the Crown, late sufferers from the French; $300l.$ to Gov-

FAILURE IN GOVERNMENT. 299

ernor William Markham for his services; and the net balance to paying, under the order of the Governor and Council, the debts and necessary charges of the government, the Council accounting to the Assembly. In advance of the collecting of this tax, 300*l.* were borrowed at interest, perhaps from the aforesaid bank, and sent to Fletcher, who reported that the same had been expended in contingencies to feed and clothe the Indians.

One of the laws of this session was for the safety of Philadelphia and New Castle from fire: no one was allowed to clean a chimney by burning it out, or to leave it so dirty that it would flame at the top; every owner of a dwelling was to keep therein a swab twelve or fourteen feet long and a bucket or pail always ready; and no person was to smoke tobacco in the streets day or night, and out of the twelve pence fine for doing so, one penny was to be employed in providing "leather buckets & other instruments or engines agt. fire" for the use of the town. Apparently the fine was not expected to be absolutely prohibitive.

The Frame of 1696 did not arrange, like that of 1683, for the exercise of the appointing power after William Penn's death. Besides the limitation of offices and legislative seats to those of Trinitarian faith, as mentioned in the chapter on Religious Dissension, the other important changes were: the reduction of the number of Councillors to two from each county and of their term of office to one year, and the reduction of the number of Assemblymen to four from each county, and the permission for the Assembly, as well as the Council, to originate laws, and the allowance as wages of 5*s.* for each day's attendance to the Councillors and the Speaker of the House, and of 4*s.* per day to the Assemblymen, and of 2*d.* per mile for travelling to and fro to Councillors and assemblymen, and, finally, the limitation of the franchise of electing or being elected Councillor or Assemblyman to such inhabitants only as were free denizens resident for two years before the election, aged twenty-one years or more, and possessing 50*l.* clear wealth; fifty acres of land, ten of them seated and cleared, being taken as 50*l.* wealth. The charge was a departure from popular government: while the shortening of the term of the Councillors made them more likely representative of the current feelings of the voters, the number of voters appears to have been cut down considerably by the disqualifying of those who merely paid "scot and lot."

This would indicate that, perhaps owing to the changes in the population, there now was less liberalism among the politicians in control, in fact an instinctive tightening of the reins by the well-to-do Quakers. The Assembly had proposed three years as the time of residence necessary for voting or being elected, but Markham and his Council, there being present Shippen, Morris, Lloyd, Brinckloe, Clark, Hill, and Robinson, had it amended to two. Those imposing the tax at this session took care of the interests of the property holders, and showed no inclination to be munificent to the man living from hand to mouth. The tax was to be at the rate of one penny per pound on the appraised value of the capital, or in other words about four tenths of one per cent., a moderate charge when only occasional. The tax was to be on both personal and real estate, but the personalty was to be exclusive of all debts and of household goods and implements in use. Both personal and real estate were to be valued by the Assemblymen serving from the respective counties with the assistance of four or more of "the most substantial freeholders:" and we may presume that unproductive land, nothwithstanding the inevitable enhancement for which it was being held, was not appraised very high by such assessors. The rate was kept down somewhat by there being no exemption of any male inhabitant over twenty-one years old who had six months previously finished his servitude. More than this, every such male inhabitant whose estate was less than seventy-two pounds contributed six shillings, the same as if his estate amounted to seventy-two pounds, the tax being changed at that sum to a rate per pound. He who had not seventy-two pounds thus paid more in proportion than he who had. Fletcher's law of 1693 imposing 1d. per l. had been different, allowing the taxpayers worth less than one hundred pounds to get off by paying six shillings. The only estates exempted by the Act of 1696 were the Proprietary's and his Deputy-Governor's. The poorer inhabitants lifted no voice against the Frame and the tax law, passed by representatives chosen by more general suffrage than was to choose their successors. When, in after times, in fact down to the American Revolution, those appointed by a small electorate passed tax laws largely copying this one, there was "taxation without representation" in Pennsylvania.

It was not with the inequalities of taxation bearing upon the poor, but with the changes in the constitution that discontent showed itself. John Goodson had protested. The day for election of Councillors and Assemblymen being the same as under the old Frame, voters in Philadelphia County not aware of the alteration in the government, appeared, and three fourths of those present chose according to the old Frame, and two days afterwards drew up a remonstrance to the Governor, asking for their rights, but the three Councillors chosen were not admitted. According to the minutes of the Council for May 10 and 12, 1697, the Sheriffs returned that the following were chosen as Councillors: Carpenter and Shippen from Philadelphia, Growdon and Phineas Pemberton from Bucks, Simcock and Pusey from Chester, Alricks and Halliwell from New Castle, Griffith Jones and John Curtis from Kent, and Clark and John Hill from Sussex. Griffith

Jones (apparently the one elected Councillor from Kent), Francis Rawle, Robert Turner, and Arthur Cooke, four important men, who could scarcely be said to represent a single faction, wrote to Penn on 2mo. 9, 1697, for redress of grievances, complaining of the failure to observe the forms of the old Frame in making the alterations, speaking of the promulgation of bills to be passed as "a privilege we could hardly sufficiently value," and declaring the change in number of representatives and in the qualification of voters a departure from fundamentals, and reporting as illegal the collection of the tax before Penn's ratification of the act. Jones refused to qualify as a Councillor, unless he could be admitted under the old Charter.

In reply to a representation from Fletcher that the charge for Pennsylvania's quota for a year would be 2000*l.* and upwards, and that he needed fifty men for the forces required at Albany, and his request for twenty-five men or the proportionate sum, the Assembly, which on May 12, 1697, chose John Blunston as Speaker, unanimously on the following day adopted a report prepared by a joint committee from Council and Assembly, that, as the former 300*l.* had not been collected and paid to those who had lent the sum, the Assembly could not raise any more money.

A letter from Secretary Blathwayt desiring an article of association to be signed, it was on May 24 signed by Markham and the members of Council and Assembly free by their religious principles to do so. The Quaker members presented a declaration of their loyalty to the King.

Randolph, who had a great friend in Sir Robert Southwell, one of the Commissioners of Customs, reiterated the complaints against the colonial, and particularly the Proprietary, governments. While the King's advisers were very slow in moving towards the suggested abolition of Proprietary authority, Randolph, in spite of the Proprietaries' claim that their Lieutenant-Governors should be Vice Admirals, achieved the erection of Courts of Admiralty in each colony, with the Judge, Register, and Marshall and an Attorney-General, all appointed by the Crown; and, upon Randolph's recommendation, Robert Quary was made Judge for Penn's dominions and West Jersey. Quary, formerly of South Carolina, but at this time residing in, or occasionally visiting Philadelphia for purposes of trade,—his title of Colonel being an honorary one, connected with his public office in Carolina—is the subject of much animadversion in the published *Penn and Logan Correspondence,* but, against the idea of Quary's character to be obtained therefrom, it must be remembered that he was the representative of the King's rights, and had a duty in antagonism to Penn's interests.

The House of Lords having, on Feb. 10, 1696-7, appointed a Committee to consider the state of trade, Penn appeared before it several times, maintained his right to appoint a Governor over New Castle, as the Duke of York had done, announced that the late act relating to the plantation trade had been put in execution, made excuses for Markham, and suggested a series of regulations for preventing illegal trade, and that there be free trade between the colonies, without such imposts as Maryland had laid on goods destined for Pennsylvania. Presenting on March 4 some proposals for the advancement of trade in America, Penn was asked what objection he had to Randolph's suggestion that Proprietary governments be abolished. Penn replied that the soil would be worth nothing to him the moment after he lost the government: he and his family would be ruined; for he could not then sell an acre of land. He proposed that Markham, whom he had formally nominated, be approved as Deputy-Governor, and give security; but the House of Lords, in addressing the King to have the Proprietary Governors receive the same instructions as Royal Governors, and to make the Proprietaries answerable for their Governors' misbehavior, asked that the Proprietaries themselves give bond for the observance of the instructions. A letter from the King, dated April 22, 1697, to the various Governors and Proprietaries, including Penn, said that great abuses must result from the insolvency of the sureties on the bonds for taking cargoes to England, or the remissness of past and present Governors, who should duly prosecute such bonds. The letter to Penn warned him that a failure to enforce the laws might lead to a forfeiture of his patent. Subsequently, Penn was notified to sign a bond to obey the instructions.

Capt. Daniell, coming with Acting Commodore Wager to New Castle and Philadelphia in the month following the affair at New Castle, and being entertained by Markham, unpleasantly referred to the losing of the men, although having promised Wager not to do so. After three of Daniell's crew, on March 8, deserted from his vessel in the Patuxent River, going off at night in the barge, Daniell, while offering to entertain Markham in return, if he would pay a visit, wrote to Markham that he (Daniell) supposed that these three men had gone to Pennsylvania, knowing how ready Markham and all under him were to entertain and protect deserters, "to the great prejudice of his Majesty's service and trade, except to your *quaking* subjects, that never did the King or Kingdom any service." Having been informed that deserters from his (Daniell's) ship had appeared publicly daily, and offered themselves to sea captains, Daniell added: "I wonder you should rather endeavour to gratify the men aforesaid than have a regard to his Majesty's service." Markham spiritedly replied on March 30 that the letter was "so rude and indecent that it seems rather penned in the

Failure in Government.

cook room than in the great cabin;" he would secure the men, if found, but why was no notice taken of the fact that they must have passed through the whole length of Maryland? Yet, on a surmise that they had reached Pennsylvania, its inhabitants were vilified. Markham called attention to Daniell's carelessness; when Markham was in the navy, oars and sails were not left in the boats at night, when there was likelihood of any of the men running away. Daniell had penned this sentence: "It will be in vain for any ships to trade here so long as they have encouragement to run to your parts whence they are allowed to go trampuseing where they please." Markham, in his reply, said: "I know not what you mean by trampuseing unless you aimed at French to show your breeding which you have ill set forth in your mother tongue." Markham finished by expressing disinclination to be entertained by Daniell.

Governor Nicholson of Maryland lent a willing ear to what was reported against Pennsylvania, prejudiced as a strong Churchman against Quakers, and doubtless desirous of the achievement of the great reform suggested by Randolph, and hoped for by a party in Pennsylvania, viz: the annexation of at least the Lower Counties, if not of the Province also, to Nicholson's jurisdiction. On March 27, 1697, in reply to the Commissioners for Trade, Nicholson wrote a long letter, which as to Markham and Pennsylvania repeated much that had been said by Randolph, and reported the affair of Day and the loss of Daniell's men.

When Penn heard of this letter, almost simultaneously came stories of the wickedness in the colony. The Quaker Justices, while getting severe against non-Quakers, were showing leniency, almost levity, when called upon to punish immorality in members of their own Society. It looked as if the Society was becoming a nobility or caste, those within which would stand by one another. Penn wrote in 7th month (September), 1697, to the Council, to issue orders for suppressing forbidden trade and piracy and vice and looseness, until some severe laws could be passed, and to let no license be granted to keep public houses except to those who gave good security for the conducting of them, and who were known to be "of sober conversation," and that the County Courts have the approbation, if not the licensing. The result was a proclamation of the 12th of February rather vindicating the conduct of magistrates and people, but urging them to greater efforts, and authorizing the Justices of each of the six counties after the 1st of March to nominate for said county those who alone would be licensed or permitted by the Governor to keep taverns, inns, or drinking places, which "condescension" of the Governor, limiting his right to license, was embodied in a law of 1699, together with a power in three of the Justices to disqualify from keeping drinking places in future those who allowed disorders.

The Governor of Maryland, Nicholson or whoever should be such Governor at any time, was authorized by the Admiralty on June 26, 1697, to appoint Judges, Registers, Marshalls, and Advocates for Admiralty Courts of Maryland, Pennsylvania, and West Jersey on the death or disability of those in office. The Board of Trade summoned Penn in the Fall of 1697. Fortunately, the war with France was over: the question of defence was no longer a complication. Reminding the Lords that Markham had been, not Penn's, but the late Queen's choice, to serve during the war, Penn wrote on 8ber 15, offering to turn out Markham, if he had behaved badly, but, as he ought not to be judged *ex parte,* asking that the Earl of Bellomont be ordered to inquire. Richard Coote, Earl of Bellomont in the peerage of Ireland, had been commissioned on June 18, 1697, as Governor of New York, Massachusetts Bay, and New

Hampshire. Penn was able to bring to Markham's defence the agents upon whose presence in England Nicholson and his party were relying. Francis Jones, before mentioned, was the bearer of a later letter from Nicholson, but, although examined by the Commissioners for Trade, Jones regretted that his application to Nicholson against Day had eventuated in Nicholson's representation against Pennsylvania, and so Jones wrote a letter, dated 9ber 13, addressed to Penn, and read before the Commissioners, correcting some of Nicholson's statements, and saying that Markham, notwithstanding Jones's anger against him, was the best fitted man to administer the colony, having during the five years of Jones's residence or visiting there, governed to the satisfaction of the substantial inhabitants and traders, until some turbulent and discontented people from other colonies, particularly one Snead from Jamaica, had arrived, and started a correspondence with Maryland. Nicholson, on subsequently sending over a witness to England, hoped that he would be examined before Penn could "get at him." Quary, moreover, in a letter avowed having advised Markham to commission Day. Snead attributed the letter to Penn's assistance in Quary's securing most of Charles Sanders's business. Quary explained to Snead that Penn had now the King's friendship, the King writing to Penn "particularly" (personally?) from Flanders, and satisfying him of the King's proceedings there, as if Penn were of the Privy Council. There was also a report that Penn had by letter advised Fletcher to linger in America, Penn having, it was said, no doubt about being able to get the Governorship of Maryland for Fletcher.

In the closing years of that Century and the opening years of the next, there flourished the pirates most celebrated in tradition, and from works of fiction based upon their career. Some indeed were mutineers who had left port on an honest voyage, a few may have gathered or joined the ship's company upon a plain agreement to undertake piracy, which is defined as robbery at sea, and others, after starting on a legal errand, had yielded to the temptation presented by an opportunity to enrich themselves. Hardly ever was a naval officer of rank guilty of such capital offence; but mariners from the merchant service, intrusted with armed vessels as privateers, often made criminal use of their power. It was a legitimate war measure to offer the property at sea of the hostile people as booty to any dare-devil who would go after it. An unprincipled prize-seeker would not respect a neutral; a desperate character would attack the vessels of his own nation: and all this was true often of those who had previously kept within the limits of law. The valuable products of the Indies which led Europeans to establish settlements for trade in those regions, tempted British sailors to the Indian Ocean, to waylay the cargoes being carried from one point to another of those coasts. If justice might ferret out those who attacked their own countrymen, still an Asiatic merchantman might be plundered with comparative impunity. If, indeed, the operations were mostly in distant waters, because more was found there to steal, yet the rovers came to the sparsely settled coasts of America to dispose of their spoil, or to escape punishment, and preyed upon what they found in their path. After the capture of one or two good prizes and distribution of the spoil, the crews were reduced or gradually disbanded, and various detachments, as opportunity presented itself, made their way to the home ports, or to the colonies, many of the individuals with the intention of finding some honest calling, or at least living peaceably upon their gains.

Villagers or farmers unused to fighting among whom any men of physical strength and some ready money came amicably, were not anxious to question any plausible account such men gave of themselves: even officials in England, with all their power, corruptly or in hopes of finding such experienced seamen useful, left those thought guilty undisturbed. Randolph, in 1696, furnished a list of fifteen pirates from the Red Sea who came to Philadelphia from South Carolina in 1692, and he also said that some pirates in the city, when in their cups, had boasted of capturing an eastern princess on the way to marry some great man, and of throwing her overboard after violating her. The original fifteen had come during Lloyd's rule. It was hypocritical in Randolph to speak of them; for he had offered to pardon all such pirates, if they would make up a sum of money to cover the expense of securing afresh the authority to pardon which he had under King James; of course a sum large enough to leave a fee for Randolph. Doing without this pardon, these early pirates had lived unmolested, some marrying and owning houses. Markham, whether under Fletcher or Penn, welcomed other settlers of this kind, as contributing by their money to the prosperity of the colony. Colonial Governors, either for the presents they received, or because they were at the mercy of any large crew, or to secure some one to chase away the privateers or war vessels of France, and sometimes for all three reasons, made friends with mariners of whose previous career they were suspicious, and granted them pardon, assistance, and letters of marque. It was charged that Fletcher made large sums by this course both in New York and Pennsylvania. Markham acknowledged that some small presents had been at the same time made to himself, and that one captain of a privateer left him a legacy. Ex-pirates, ostensibly retired privateersmen, became quickly of such consequence in the various colonies, affiliating in business or social friendship or by intermarriage with the local officeholders, that they seemed intrenched: and, moreover, the leading merchants found that the most profitable ventures by sea were by the employment of captains who would bring goods without explanation; nor were men of saintly record particularly looked for in the supposedly justifiable enterprise of trading with red-handed sea robbers, or even in the desperado's game of robbing them in turn. The magistracy of the various colonies was practically given to the merchants: for scarcely was there an inhabitant financially independent of traders and trade. Penn, to be sure, was situated aloof, but his colony had so little of his presence.

The island of Madagascar, already visited by legitimate traders, had many spots where disorderly crews could hide. Some pirates settled there, building forts, even conquering the natives, among whom they married, and over whom they tyrannized. It is supposed that the first settlers were the followers of Captain Thomas Tew, who, after being commissioned by Governor Fletcher for privateering against the French, started as a pirate for the Red Sea. Whether with the ex-rovers settled in Madagascar, or with those pirates bringing towards it their plunder, there grew up a surreptitious trade from the American colonies, managed in the following way, when trade with that island became suspected or prohibited: a lawful cargo was carried from the colonies to Madeira; there wine and brandy were taken aboard; and thence the vessel proceeded to Madagascar, where barter was made for the goods which the pirates had found; and these were brought back, and commanded high prices.

A book written some years after the death of John, or Henry, Every, or Avery, purporting to give his career, calls him "King of Madagascar," but he was not a "pirate King" in that sense. Every had been mate of a vessel fitted out at Bristol in 1694 in the service of the Spaniards. On May 30 of that year, when off the mouth of the Garonne, he secured command of the ship, and set sail for the Indian Ocean, allowing on the next day the captain and a few faithful ones to go off in the long boat. At Madagascar, Every made a combined fleet with men who had run away with two sloops from the West Indies. A ship belonging to the Great Mogul was captured; a proceeding which nearly caused the extirpation of the East India Company's settlements, for the Great Mogul, not discriminating between one Englishman and another, threatened so to revenge himself. Every got the treasure into his own vessel, which then sailed away from the sloops which had aided him. He reached the Bahamas in April, 1696, and, calling himself Henry Bridgeman, and the ship the "Fancy," secured permission to land at New Providence with his 200 men, on their giving security. In the company was James Brown, who, in an examination later, said that Every, an old acquaintance, and not known by Brown to be a pirate, had let him come as a passenger. Brown had sailed from Boston, Massachusetts, to trade with Madagascar. The company of the "Fancy" scattering, and some coming to the North American colonies, Brown got back to Boston eleven months after leaving that town. The innocency of his voyage outward being suspected, he answered some queries before certain officials, and was let go. He was in Philadelphia and already married to the Lieutenant-Governor's daughter by April 26, 1698, the date of a letter from Randolph to the Commissioners for Trade. Very likely a part of Every's crew is referred to in a story that in the Spring of 1696 thirty pirates, having made 8000*l*. each by robbing vessels in the Red Sea, arrived at New York in a ship from Madagascar, and proceeded unmolested to Pennsylvania. Every himself going to Ireland, he and six of his men were indicted for piracy: he escaped, but the six were hung.

The Lords Justices of England having issued a proclamation for the arrest of Every's companions, and

Snead, who was a County Justice, having seen a copy of it, he with some difficulty induced Markham to have three arrested, viz: Robert Chinton, or Clinton, said to have been Every's chief lieutenant, Edmund Lassall, and Peter Claussen. Whatever may be said of Robert Snead, who had been a carpenter in Jamaica, he was valiant, a quality which apparently had caused him to receive the rank of Captain and a seat on the local bench. It took a brave man to meddle with ex-pirates, and, as he desired authority to hunt out not only these three but others, Markham actually deprived him of the arms which he carried and seemed ready to use, so that Snead rode at least once to his plantation out of town defenceless. Snead's story is that when he first urged Markham to arrest Every's men, Markham's wife and daughter slipped out, and told Chinton, and that various pirates thereafter muttered "informer" as Snead passed along the street. The Council expressed willingness to spend the money to send the three to England for trial. Certain of Snead's colleagues on the bench of Philadelphia County authorized bail. There was a difficulty about trying them, the crimes having been committed on the high seas, where the colonial courts had no jurisdiction, and it was thought that the Governor could not grant a special commission for a court to hear the case without encroaching upon the prerogatives of the Admiralty. The accused appear not to have found bail, and were in prison when on June 16, 1697, Markham received orders from England to secure the persons of all pirates and sea robbers and those reasonably suspected of being such. He then ordered these three to be put in close confinement, and their goods and effects to be seized. With the help of friends, however, the three that very night got out of what the Sheriff called the safest part of the jail. Claussen was caught, but Chinton and Lassall escaped, and, although pursued, said the Sheriff, "with

FAILURE IN GOVERNMENT. 313

horse and foot,'' reached New York, where they were seized but let go. A woman's story of their being among the bushes about a mile out High street on the 17th or 18th, received little attention, probably because they were reported heavily armed. Four of the old pirates who arrived in 1692, were ordered to be arrested, but the Sheriff returned that they could not be found. The Sheriff was John Claypoole, mentioned in a former chapter. Much suspicion was cast by Markham's enemies upon the zeal and sincerity of this Sheriff, who, in February following, was stated by both Churchman and Quaker Justices to be unable to serve on account of lameness and misbehavior. In view of a warrant of June 19, John Matthews, who had been on Every's ship, surrendered himself, claiming to have been captured and impressed by Every, and was committed to prison, where he died in a few days. Within a month, one of the four old pirates, Charles Gosse, who was about to leave the province, was killed in a quarrel with a Frenchman. At the funeral, two days later, there was a small riot. Snead, going as a magistrate to quell it, was assaulted,—violently, it is said,—and, in defending himself, wounded a man. It being supposed that Medlicott, said to have been surgeon's mate to one of the four pirates in a trip to the Red Sea, and at this time in command of a sloop in Delaware River, was intending to carry away the various pirates or privateersmen, Markham made him give bond in 2000*l.* not to do so: nevertheless it is supposed that Chinton and Lassell, and doubtless others, sailed away with him.

By a statute of 27 & 28 Hen. VIII, piracy was to be tried by commissioners under the great seal of England. Quary's commission as Admiralty Judge did not authorize him to try for that offence. So without trial, Claussen, who was a cooper by trade, and had been on a Hamburg vessel captured by Every off the

Isle of France, and forced, it was said, to go with Every, remained in prison for several years: and so did David Evans, arrested about May, 1698, who claimed to have been acquitted of being an associate of Every, because of also being forced to join, and who was committed in default of bail to remain in the province until he produced the record of acquittal.

In 1698, the Councillors were reelected except Pemberton, Pusey, Alricks, and Jones, who respectively were replaced by Biles, Lloyd, Donnaldson, and William Rodeney (now Rodney). Pemberton was chosen Speaker of the Assembly. Among the acts then passed was one for preventing frauds and regulating abuses in trade. It added to the penalties and forfeitures prescribed by Act of Parliament fines by the Governor and Council not exceeding the value of the goods, and furthermore prohibited, except by permit from the Customs officers, the lading or unlading of tobacco by vessels from foreign or other parts, and the carrying of tobacco to other provinces, or the transport of it to outgoing vessels, or for being shipped to another part of the Province or Territories. Markham, so impecunious that he had wished to be also Collector of the Port of Philadelphia, must have been pleased with a duty payable to the Governor for the time being of $8d.$ per ton on incoming vessels of which a majority of the owners were not inhabitants, and of $4d.$ on those of which a majority were inhabitants; and it was directed that the fines or forfeitures not otherwise disposed of were to go $\frac{1}{3}$ to the King's use, $\frac{1}{3}$ to the Governor, and $\frac{1}{3}$ to the person suing therefor. There was a provision to obviate the inability of "most part of the merchants, traders, & owners of ships or vessels within this government being of ye people called Quakers" to register their vessels under the before mentioned Act of 7 & 8 Wm. III, c. 22, that Act requiring an oath. The Frame of Government of 1696 contained a proviso that no person should be excused from swearing who was required to take an oath by the Acts of Parliament relating to trade and navigation. The Councillors and Assemblymen stated in their Vindication, dated 3mo. 30, 1698, that Quakers were allowed to register by affirmation in England; while John Bewley, the Collector of Philadelphia, was inclined to act accordingly, Randolph had, on April 21, threatened him with dismissal in case he did not require an oath by laying hand on the Bible and kissing the Bible. So the Assembly now provided that those who could not conscientiously take an oath, might make an affirmation whenever an oath was required by the Act of 7 & 8 Wm. III. It was also enacted that, in any court held in the Province or Territories upon bill, complaint, or information for breach of the Acts of Trade or Navigation, the trial should be according to the common law and by jury, a procedure entirely foreign to Quary's commission as Admiralty Judge. Such features of the act were complained of by the King's officials, and the Commissioners of Customs raised a question whether Markham should not be removed from office for consenting. Penn, to ward this off, announced that he had negatived the act. His power to veto an act passed by his deputy with consent of the freemen was denied a few years later, but he at least could agree to having the King disallow an act, and this act was formally disallowed in 1699. Penn also called the attention of the Commissioners for Trade to the mention of juries in the Act of Parliament, and expressed the hope that the unskilfulness of the Assemblymen in law would cause them to be excused, as mistaken instead of disobedient.

While the local act was in force, a court held by the colony's Judges undertook to exercise Admiralty powers, and condemned a vessel. This was one of a series of proceedings calculated to supplant the Admiralty judicature appointed by the chief officers of the realm. Desirable as it might be to reform the administration of justice by introducing trial by jury in every branch, no king, no national authority, could tolerate the dwellers in a little corner of an empire interfering with what the national authority sanctioned.

Before, moreover, the Quakers on the local bench had thus excited the displeasure of the rulers of England, Markham's friends and he himself had threatened or put under duress the Surveyor-General of the Customs in a way to prevent perhaps through fear his performance of duty. Because Randolph, in a representation to the Commissioners for Trade in March, 1696–7, had spoken individiously of Patrick Robinson, the Secretary of the Province, as a Scotchman &ct., Robinson, on July 28, 1698, appeared at Charles Read's house, where Randolph was lodging, and, laying hands on Randolph, and pursuing him to his bed room, forced him to give a letter explaining or weakening what he had said. On the next day, Randolph wrote to Markham that certain navigation bonds would be produced when Markham appointed an Attorney-General to prosecute them, and would be put into Markham's hands upon the King's approbation of the appointment of Markham as Governor. Markham, irritated by this impugning of his title, sent a constable, who, with his staff in hand, kept Randolph in the house as a prisoner, until after Quary had had a pretty warm interview with Markham, but Randolph had given up to him the bonds.

Markham had retained in his or ostensibly the Sheriff's custody he goods of the pirates who had escaped, although Quary claimed the custody for the Admiralty. Markham, under the Proprietary's right to wreckage, took into possession certain goods from a French vessel which had been captured but lost at sea; after the Admiralty Court decided that they were lawful prize, Markham refused to hand over what he actually had, or let the Sheriff hand over what the latter had, to John Moore, deputed to receive prize goods by the Commissioners for Prizes, Markham insisting upon waiting for an order from the Proprietary.

The climax in the interference with Admiralty procedure was reached in August and September, 1698. John Adams of Boston shipped a cargo at New York for Philadelphia on board of the "Jacob," of which the master was Francis Basset. Basset, although the surname is English, was only a naturalized subject, Quary calling him a Frenchman. When the "Jacob" arrived at New Castle, the goods were seized, for want of a certificate, and placed in the custody of Robert Webb, deputed to receive them by the Admiralty Court. Adams was one of those merchants, probably like nearly all the others at a new place, who peddled their goods, or sold them at the water's edge, and then departed. With no dwelling-house or store, time was everything to him; paying board in Philadelphia destroyed his profits. So he sought the Governor to have the goods delivered on security at an appraisement, and was referred by him to the Collector. Exhibiting a certificate, which had subsequently come from New York, that a certain notary had seen letters of denization to Basset, Adams was told by Judge Quary that it was insufficient to qualify the captain. Offering to give security to answer at court, but being put off with various difficulties about getting the goods on such terms, meanwhile obliged to pay storage, and incurring other expenses, and fearing that the goods might rot before an Admiralty Court to try the case were constituted, as the Marshall and Advocate had not yet received their commissions, Adams petitioned the Lieutenant-Governor to grant him a replevin. Markham thought that he had no right to meddle in a matter before the Admiralty, but the next day, while Col. Quary was out of town on his way to Maryland, Adams went to Anthony Morris, one of the Justices of the County Court, and secured a writ of replevin. John Claypoole, apparently restored to health, was still Sheriff. He saw a writ to deliver to Adams, upon his giving security to abide the action of the County Court, goods in the hands of Robert Webb, gentleman, without any hint of the matter being connected with the Admiralty. So the Sheriff took security, and when Webb, who had not the use of his limbs, had gone to the King's store by the water side, and unlocked it, the Under Sheriff and his bailiff seized and disarmed Webb, exhibited the replevin, and carried away the goods, which were then delivered to Adams. Webb making complaint, Markham issued a warrant to the Sheriff to take back the goods, and keep them in his custody until further order or trial in such court as the informer should see fit. The Sheriff's deputy was delayed in getting the goods, and Webb started after Col. Quary, whom he found at New Castle, and there drew up a narrative of the affair, which Quary enclosed in a letter to England, commenting fully upon it, and with reflections upon Markham.

We can readily understand how the sentiments of the officials in London rose to something like indignation, as they heard that a colonial Justice of the Peace had sent away the property seized by a Court of high prerogative, and was calling the question before himself—whom Penn styled a "macaronic judge"— and two or three others about as skilled in law. Had it been known to the "big wigs" that this local Justice was by profession a tailor, the thing would have seemed to them particularly preposterous. We, however, who know that Quary, the sole Judge in Admiralty, was also a layman, a merchant by occupation, do not think him fitter to decide than those who composed the County Court: but the precedent would be bad in the near future, when the Crown could employ a learned jurist in Quary's place.

Yet worse was to come: to injury to Admiralty jurisdiction was to be added insult to the King, carrying to an unnecessary extreme the Quaker disregard of worldly pomp and rank. When the County Court, consisting of Morris, Shippen, Richardson, and James Fox, heard the case of replevin by Adams against Webb, the latter produced in his defence the royal letters patent under the seal of the High Court of Admiralty and the Judge's warrant for the seizure. The patent having a picture of the King at its head and the seal pendent in a tin case, David Lloyd, who had advised the granting of the replevin, and was appearing as counsel for Adams, took the document in his hand, and, exposing it contemptuously before those in the court, exclaimed: "What is this? Do you think to scare us with a great box and a little baby? Tis true, fine pictures please children; but we are not to be frightened at such a rate." This is the way Quary quotes the words: Webb swore to exclamations of similar purport. To be sure, the context may have qualified or counteracted them. The rest of the speech is not given, but it reflected strongly upon Admiralty procedure. Ridicule of the King's picture in public, and acquiescence in it by those holding court,—the Judges appear to have failed to stop or rebuke Lloyd,—were not mere matters of bad taste. The governments of this world, even modern republics in relation to the flag, enforce the principle that the honor or dishonor shown to the image or emblem is honor or dishonor to what it represents. There was no strength as far as the Quakers were concerned in the inference of the Crown officials, that those who insulted the King's picture would treat despitefully his person, except that the Quakers would not raise their hats, or make a bow to him: but by people who fought, such dishonorings were incidents of a revolution.

The Judges who heard Lloyd's speech, seeing the importance of the case, ordered a continuance until the next term. We learn from Quary's letter of Oct. 20 that when Markham spoke to the Provincial Council in regard to the matter,—this was in September,—Halliwell and Donnaldson proposed that the Judges be superseded, but that Lloyd closed the debate by declaring that all who encouraged or promoted the setting up of Admiralty courts were greater enemies to the rights and liberties of the people than those who promoted ship money in the time of Charles I. The Council declared that the Governor was not responsible for the act of Justice Morris. On 7mo. 27, Shippen being away on a visit to New England, Morris, Richardson, and Fox wrote to the Lieutenant-Governor and Council that they considered a replevin as a right of the King's subject, whenever any goods or cattle were taken or distrained. Moreover, the Judges suggested that it was as proper for the Sheriff to take security for the production of the goods as for them to remain in the hands of Webb, whom the Judges did not know to be a proper officer to keep them, and who had given no bonds to the Provincial government. Advice was taken how the matter should be decided.

During this episode, a French pirate sent fifty men ashore at Lewes, and plundered every house in the town, and caused an alarm not confined to the Bay. Markham, left by his Councillors to Penn's powers as a Captain-General, and obtaining an expression that any expense should be defrayed by a tax, had drums beaten for volunteers. What numbers enrolled, we do not know: but no vessel could be found to go to fight the pirate, as Markham refused to promise any share of booty. The pirate, after getting provisions by overhauling a ship bringing passengers from Holland, made off, to avoid being caught by the war vessel at New York. The captain of the war vessel, in view of orders to go to England, refused to hunt for the pirate.

There could be no expectation that the English government, after hearing of Lloyd's antics, would allow him to retain any offce, and the operation of the judicial machinery of the empire seemed to require the elimination of such an eccentric as Justice Morris; but it became in the minds of the officials in London imperative that, in the first place, Markham be removed, although not an actor in the more intolerable proceedings. His negligence, although excusable by reason of physical disability and by lack of ways and means, his complacency, and his want of influence over the legislature and judiciary had shown him unfit to preside over a colony. Penn had no man of capacity who could be put in Markham's place, Quakers being out of the question, and difficulties arising from the matter of salary, royal approbation, bonds, &ct. Feeling, moreover, that he himself could manage the stiff-necked freemen better than any possible envoy, Penn decided to go without further procrastination to Pennsylvania, and rule in person. This solution was accepted by the English government. The patient and slowly moving officials could hope that a new order of things would be started at the end of the months that must be allowed for him to pack up, and make the voyage. The events in America during most of the year 1699 fall therefore within the term of Markham's administration.

In 1699, Pemberton went back into the Council in place of Growdon, and Pusey in place of Simcock, and Richard Willson became a member with Rodney for Kent; but, the people of New Castle County having failed at the regular election to make any choice, and refused at a special election to do so, a law was passed, Blunston being Speaker, ordering in such cases a fine of 100*l.* to be imposed upon a county, to be collected by distraint and sale from any four or more of the inhabitants, and to become a county charge for their reimbursement, and also a fine of 50*l.* upon a Sheriff for neglecting his duty in regard to an election, and a fine of 20s. *per diem* on any elected Councillor or Assemblyman absenting himself; and there was also a provision that on neglect or refusal of the counties to elect, or the absence of those chosen, such members of Council or Assembly as met the Governor might act. A tax at the same rate as that of 1696 was voted to pay, first, the balance still due on former appropriations or any by that Assembly to the Lieutenant-Governor, and, second, the necessary charges of government, as the Governor and Council might appoint.

The English government had desired the various colonies to pass an act relating to piracy upon the model of that passed some years before in Jamaica. Pennsylvania neglected the matter until this session, and then passed an act providing that treasons, felonies, piracies, robberies, murders, or confederacies at sea or in harbor, creek, or bay where the Admiral had jurisdiction should be tried as if committed on land, and also authorizing the appointment of three persons by the Governor and Council, to assist the Admiralty Judge or such persons in his absence as the Governor and Council should name, a quorum of which persons to have the powers given to commissioners under the great seal of England by statute of 28 Hen. VIII. This Pennsylvania act made punishable as accessories or confederates all persons entertaining, concealing, &ct. pirates, and not endeavoring to have them apprehended, and also imposed a fine of 5l. on any person refusing to obey an order to assist an officer in seizing a pirate, and a fine of 20l. on any Justice, Sheriff, constable, or other officer neglecting his duty. Owing to differences in phraseology and otherwise from the Jamaica act, the delay in the appointment of those to hold court, and the risks to be run in punishing capitally upon testimony or verdict given without oath, Quary wrote that the law was impracticable and a mere pretence. The latter word was unfair.

After the act was passed, a brigantine at New Castle, richly laden for England, was, the night before intended departure, seized and carried off by fourteen of the crew, putting ashore the remaining four, who would not join them. Numerous inhabitants of New Castle tried to make capital out of this in a petition to the Lieutenant-Governor and Council, presented on August 9, asking for protection, and complaining that there was neither fort, castle, or breastwork, nor militia, arms, or ammunition. The five Councillors who heard this, all Quakers, had the best of the argument, insincere as they were: they pointed out that the forts of Virginia and Maryland were not much more formidable than the fort at New Castle had been; if that was decayed, it was the inhabitants' fault; it would be more dangerous to build forts, if the people would not hold them, than to have none; as for a militia, the petitioners should have proposed it to the Assembly, instead of neglecting their duty to choose Assemblymen.

Captain Kidd is the English pirate whose name has survived as a household word. His bloodthirstiness has been exaggerated in popular song. The deliberate slaughter of prisoners was not so common with the English or French plunderers of ships. The murder of which Kidd was convicted was of one of his crew in an altercation, and may have been in fear of mutiny. William Kidd had distinguished himself as captain of a privateer against the French in the West Indies, before he was placed in command of a galley fitted out by the Earl of Bellomont and others, to sail under two royal commissions, one being to take the enemy's vessels as prizes, and the other to arrest pirates, and bring them for trial, and seize the goods in their possession. Those who fitted him out, were to share in the profits of the booty. One of these partners of Kidd was Somers, the Lord Keeper of the Great Seal of England, whose joining in such an agreement was the ground of one of the charges in the unsuccessful impeachment of him. Kidd sailed from Plymouth, England, in May, 1696, and, coming to New York, and offering no pay but a share in profits, increased his crew, and thence, in September, went to attack pirates at Madagascar. Finding none there or off Malabar, he was pretty much necessitated to plunder, to provide for his men. So great were their depredations, real and reported, that in less than two years the English government issued, on Dec. 8, 1698, a proclamation offering pardon to all guilty of piracy in certain waters who should surrender themselves before April 30, 1699, except Kidd and Every.

Most of Kidd's men had retired from his service after his chief captures. A large number, bringing considerable possessions, took passage on a vessel under Captain Shelley, sent out by New York merchants to trade with Madagascar, in reality with the pirates there. On May 29, Shelley, with his well laden ship, arrived in Delaware Bay, and, having started a few of these passengers to go where they pleased in a sloop, carried to the western shore twenty others, and to Cape May fourteen or sixteen. Quary managed to have a number captured. Two, John Eldridge and Simon Arnold, were taken on the River with chests containing coral, amber, and manufactured Eastern goods, Arabian and Christian gold, and about 7800 Rix dollars. These men, Quary put into the jail at Burlington, New Jersey, as a more secure hold than that in Philadelphia. The Pennsylvania Council deemed illegal and insulting his action in sending outside for confinement those whom he or his deputy Snead had arrested within Penn's jurisdiction. Upon Quary's discovering that Robert Bradinham (called Brandingham in the Minutes of Council), who had been Kidd's surgeon, and William Stanton, also of Kidd's company, were in Philadelphia, Markham gave Quary two constables, who arrested those two. Markham seized what could be found of their money and goods, rejecting Quary's claim to have the same taken into the Admiralty's custody. Markham refused to press a vessel into service, and to give Quary forty men to capture Shelley's ship, anchored near Cape Henlopen. Governor Basse of the Jerseys had a sloop manned, and with it secured in the lower part of the Bay four of those who had landed at Cape May. Three of the four surrendered themselves. The four confessed, but all their goods had been sent away. All of the six who thus came into West Jersey custody were speedily admitted to bail by Quaker Justices there. Arnold's name does not appear in subsequent papers examined.

Kidd sailed back to North America, secreting most of his treasure on its shores or on the way thither, hoping that some quibble or bribe or the friendship of Lord Bellomont would secure immunity from punishment. Making for New York or New England, Kidd in a sloop with about forty men and much booty, came within the Capes of Delaware Bay in June, 1699, close upon the heels of Shelley, the sloop being supposed to be one which Basse had descried. Kidd remained more than ten days. He sent his boats ashore every day, and was supplied with what he needed by the old pirates and other inhabitants at Whorekills, some going constantly aboard Kidd's sloop, and dealing with him, bringing ashore muslins and other East Indian goods. It is not likely that he trusted such people sufficiently to bury anything in the vicinity. Getting into communication with Lord Bellomont, Kidd received from the latter a promise of safety, if innocence should be shown, and was thus induced to land at Boston, where Bellomont was; but Bellomont, smarting under the imputation that he had expected Kidd to turn pirate, and failing to get information where the treasure had been left, and fearing that Kidd would slip away, put Kidd in jail, and then sent him with others accused of piracy to England.

Bradinham and Stanton were not admitted to bail, but remained in the custody of Sheriff Claypoole aforesaid, who on hot days allowed them to walk in the streets with a keeper. This being criticized, the Sheriff, on August 8, was told to keep them close prisoners. On December 22, Bradinham complained in a petition that he was confined in a low room without fire, and for want of money to support him, and asked for a warmer room and a little of his own money in the hands of Markham, who had just been superseded: Markham was thereupon ordered to allow 12s. a week for Bradinham's subsistence; but Bradinham, as will be seen, had money in concealment, in the hands of his friends. Stanton escaped, probably after Penn arrived. Outlawry was proclaimed, and probably it was for this escape that Penn turned the Sheriff out of office. Claussen disappears from notice, probably producing the all-important record of his acquittal.

The narration of the secular affairs of the Province and Territories will now be suspended, leaving the pirates in their fear of a certain kind of suspension; and the contemporary introduction or establishment of certain non-Quaker religious bodies and something of their subsequent history, will be set forth in a chapter bearing the name of the denomination long the most important.

CHAPTER XI.

THE CHURCH OF ENGLAND.

Clause in Penn's patent—The Non-Jurors—Bp. Compton—Starting of Christ Church, Philadelphia—Union congregation of Baptists and others at "Barbados store"—Separation therefrom of the First Presbyterian Church of Philadelphia—Ministers at Christ Church—Services elsewhere—George Keith's career after taking orders—Rev. John Talbot—Assistance from Swedish ministers—Church edifices—Further history of Baptists—Further history of Presbyterians—Consecration of Welton and Talbot as bishops—Their subsequent course—Powers conferred on Bp. Gibson—Various country churches—Enlargement of Christ Church—Rev. George Whitefield—Nazareth, Penna., and the Philadelphia building with free school project—History of Christ Church continued—Calvinistic Methodists in England and Wales organized—Whitefield's subsequent visits to Pennsylvania.

Probably from the time that the English took possession of the town of New Castle, in October, 1664, stipulating that all the conquered should as formerly enjoy the liberty of their conscience in Church discipline, there was always some person on the western shore of Delaware River or Bay who acknowledged belonging to the Church of England; and probably there were very soon quite a number. Except when the contrary is known, the officers appointed by the Crown may be assumed to have been Conformists at home, and even if not zealous, yet ready to enroll themselves at any mission which the English authorities would inaugurate. The possessions in America were supposed to be attached to the see of London, until the Attorney-General and Solicitor-General of England gave the opinion, in 1725 or 1726, that ecclesiastical jurisdiction over America did not belong to any bishop in England, but was solely in the Crown by virtue of the King's supreme headship. Rev. John Yeo appears to have been the first clergyman of the Church who as such officiated in Pennsylvania or Delaware, he coming from Maryland in December, 1677, with his letters of ordination and his license from the Bishop of London, and holding services for some months during the following year. For about eighteen years after this, if there was, indeed, any Anglican presbyter in the region,—Yeo was in Maryland about 1683,—there appears to have been no public use of the Anglican liturgy in Pennsylvania or Delaware, except possibly an isolated ceremony. It is probable that such non-Quakers as were desirous of attending divine worship, or had occasion, for instance a wedding or a baptism, for a clergyman, accepted the ministrations of Swedes, instead of going or sending to another colony. The Charter to Penn contained a requirement, however, that any preacher or preachers approved of by the Bishop of London should be allowed to reside in the province whenever twenty inhabitants expressed a desire to the Bishop that such be sent. This clause was inserted at the request of Dr. Compton, Bishop of London at that time. After the adoption of the Charter, he was intrusted by his fellows of the Committee for Trade and Plantations with the preparation of a bill for establishing the Protestant Church in Pennsylvania. Penn was opposed to anything like an establishment, and the measure came to naught. Penn says in a letter of 1700 (*Penna. Archives*, 1st Series, Vol. I, p. 141): "The Bp. of London at the passing of my pat^t. did what he could to get savings for the church"—perhaps the probate of wills &ct., which was possessed by the bishops in England, and was at one time thought of as an endowment for a mission in America,—"but," he adds, "was opposed by the Earl of Radnor the Pres^t." As to the meaning of the clause in the Charter in regard to the selection of the minister, the learned canonist, Rt. Rev. Dr. Edmund Gibson, Bishop of London from 1723 to 1748, wrote in 1738, that he did not pretend to any more right than that of licensing the person who was to be minister, intimating that he was to be nominated by the inhabitants either as individuals, or representing as vestrymen the individuals; and we find in most cases when the Bishop of London picked out the person to be licensed, that he had been requested to do so, it being generally hard for the people to find a minister, and when Bp. Gibson in 1742, after failure to receive a unanimous recommendation from the vestry of Christ Church, Philadelphia, of anybody to be minister there, issued a license to Rev. Robert Jenney, both the latter and the Bishop explained that it was not an appointment but a recommendation or approbation conditional upon the vestry accepting him.

From the Revolution of 1688 down to the close of George I's reign, the embracing of opportunities for services by Anglican clergymen was interfered with by the peril of countenancing Non-Jurors, i.e. those who had refused to swear allegiance to the new sovereigns. Sancroft, Archbishop of Canterbury, and the other bishops deprived of their sees for such contumacy in William and Mary's time, had many followers in the large body of persons then having ecclesiastical dignity, benefice, or promotion, and, similarly, when oaths were required for further alienation of the Crown from James II's son, a number in a later generation of clergymen sacrificed their livings. Men required for such reasons to leave home were now and then the only

Anglican priests ready for employment on the Delaware. The "Jacobites," as those were called who believed James II or his son the lawful sovereign, omitted the Christian name of the King from the prayers: so did the whole Scottish Episcopal Church down to the time when Seabury was consecrated Bishop of Connecticut; and, Seabury's consecrators having recommended such omission to him, the Protestant Episcopal Church in the United States of America to-day, in praying for the President of the United States, does not give his name.

No question, however, as to who was Bishop of London troubled the Anglican Churchmen in the reign of William or of Anne. The Rt. Rev. Dr. Henry Compton, perhaps best remembered as the builder of St. Paul's Cathedral, and perhaps of really great influence on the course of history through his instruction and religious guidance of the Princesses Mary and Anne, who both ascended the throne, had, in 1675, been translated from the see of Oxford to that of London, had been suspended and soon restored by James II, had taken an active part in the movement against James, even appearing at the head of a troop of horse, when war was breaking out, and had crowned William and Mary in Westminster Abbey. He continued Bishop of London until his death in 1713. Although rather a military prelate, son of an earl who had fallen in battle for Charles I, and himself, in his youth, a pikeman to aid the cause of Charles II, and, before studying divinity, an ensign, he was devout, benevolent, and, except for his violent Protestantism and sincere Orthodoxy, tolerant. He was faithful to his charge, whether over the colonies or in England, and he regretted that he was unable personally to visit America, and he favored the proposal that America have a bishop residing there. He was much interested in the Indians, endeavoring to further their conversion to Christianity, as well as being solicitous, as has been mentioned in the chapter on the Acquisition and Distribution of the Land, that the savage natives should receive payment for the soil of Pennsylvania. He secured from Charles II the grant of a present of £20 to each chaplain that was sent to America by the Bishop. James II's treasury paid to those going during his reign, and, after discontinuance of the practice in William and Mary's hard times, this Bishop brought about a revival of it. Compton, however, was not desirous of the extension of his own Church through the weakening of other evangelical bodies holding the great principles of truth. He had a grand scheme for the union or intercommunion of the Protestants of Europe. He was particularly unlikely to encourage proselyting the Swedes.

Contemporaneously with the yearly efforts to establish the Church of England in Maryland, Sir Thomas Lawrence, Bart., Secretary of that Province, and Francis Nicholson, its Governor, who arrived in August 1694, interested themselves in organizing the Churchmen in Pennsylvania. The latter Churchmen may have sought the others' aid, or may have first been stirred by them, or one of the Maryland clergy may have broached the matter to those two officials and the Churchmen of Philadelphia. In a letter to the Committee of the Privy Council for Trade dated Nov. 15, 1694, and another dated June 14, 1695, Nicholson asks them to hear Sir Thomas Lawrence on the subject. There is no doubt that between those dates, or, more likely, before the earlier one, the movement had started in Philadelphia to build Christ Church. Some slight progress had been made, before the rumor discussed in the Provincial Council of Pennsylvania on June 15, 1695, induced the Churchmen in the capital to sign a petition to the King to be allowed the free exercise of their religion and arms for defence. Robert Suder in a letter to Governor————(Nicholson?), dated Nov.

20, 1698, printed in Bp. Perry's *Historical Collections relating to the American Colonial Church, Vol. II—Pennsylvania,* says that, as soon as the Quaker magistrates heard of the petition, they sent a constable after Suder, and, on his appearing before them, questioned him. When he stated what the petition was for, Shippen, who was one of the Judges, said to the others: "Now they have discovered themselves. They are bringing the priest and the sword amongst us, but God forbid: we will prevent them;" and he directed the Attorney to read the law making it an offence to speak or write against the government. Suder said that he hoped they would not hinder the right of petition. They arrested attorney Griffith Jones, on suspicion of having written the paper, and bound him over from session to session. A part of the unoccupied lot of Quaker—or, rather, Keithian—Griffith Jones, the merchant, was chosen as a site for a house of worship; and Joshua Carpenter, brother of Samuel Carpenter, as trustee to take title. This Griffith Jones, by deed of Nov. 15, 1695, conveyed the site—nearly all of the present church edifice stands on it—to Carpenter on a ground rent of 10*l.* silver money of the Province, redeemable within 15 years for 150*l.* Meanwhile, on October 30, Sir Thomas Lawrence appeared before the Lords of the Committee for Trade, and consideration was given to his memorial, which asked that 1*d.* per *l.* on side trade of tobacco in Penn's dominion be granted with the arrears for maintaining two Protestant (meaning Church of England) divines to be sent thither. The matter being referred to the Commissioners of the Treasury, they thought that the better method would be to grant a salary out of the revenue, and this the Lords of the Committee for Trade, on Nov. 25, agreed to report to the King, but it was several years before a stipend was allowed, and this was for one minister only. Meanwhile and afterwards, through this reign and Anne's, the revived present of £20 to each minister sent to the colonies was given.

The "Case of the Keithian Meeting House," prepared in 1730 (*Penna. Archives,* 1st Series, Vol. I, p. 285), says that the congregation of Christ Church had the use of said meeting-house, and the sacraments were administered therein according to the Established Church "for some years"—which is an exaggeration, unless Christ Church edifice was started before the lot was bought, for the Case adds "until the church (before begun) was finished." With the help of money contributed by Governor Nicholson, as is acknowledged in a letter to him of Jany. 18, 1696-7, Christ Church was finished by that date. The signers of the letter probably included all the Churchmen of the City except Markham. They were, as printed in Perry's *Collections:* (Yeates and Grant heading 2d and 3d columns)

Francis Jones
Saml. Peres
Darby Greene
Enoch Hubord
Thos. Walter
Thos. Curtis
Edwd. Smout
Joshua Carpenter
Wm. Dyre
Addam Birch
John Sibley
Robert Gilham
Jasper Yeates
Jarvis Bywater
Thomas Harris
George Fisher
Fardinando Dowarthy
John Willson

Robt. Quary
Sam. Holt
Edw. Bury
Thos. Stapleford.
John White
John Gibbs
Willm. Grant
Thos. Briscoll
John Herris
John Harrison
Thomas Craven
Anth'y Blany
Charles Sober
Robt. Snead
Jeremiah Price
Jeremiah Hunt
Geo. Thompson
John Moore.

Very few of these—perhaps only Yeates—had ever been Quakers. Dyre was the grandson of the Quaker martyr Mary Dyer, or Dyre, whose husband and children appear not to have adopted her religion. Comparison of the list with certain lists of sympathizers with Keith in the chapter on Religious Dissension, shows how distinct from them were these original Churchmen of Philadelphia, and that the accession of Keithians to the congregation must have been later. Apparently while the Keithian meeting-house was used, a clergyman was secured, pending the licensing of one by the Bishop of London. The name of this clergyman is not known. The congregation soon dismissed him. From him, Markham, who wrote in his favor to the Bishop, learned that there were several persons in the town in a cabal against Markham, because of his countenancing Quakers so much. This is mentioned by Markham in a letter to Penn of March 1, 1696-7.

The moral condition of Penn's dual colony at this period, as shown in the last chapter, called for a missionary; and the only religion presented to the English-speaking people of it was what most Christians looked upon as queer, the largest religious denomination having no ceremonies at all and a certain self-sufficiency, rejecting doctrines, another denomination insisting upon immersion, and refusing to baptize infants, and some religionists keeping Saturday instead of Sunday, and some practising feet-washing. Perry, in the aforesaid *Collections,* prints a letter sent about 1698 to Markham, not from "Gov.," as Perry describes it, but from "Rev." John Danforth, who was Congregationalist Pastor at Dorchester, Massachusetts, asking that "beloved brother" Mr. Benjamin Woodbridge be received on a religious mission, "not to handle such points as are matters of controversies among Protestants." The religion of New England outside of Rhode Island was Calvinistic, and, in the sense that elder was the highest rank in the ministry, Presbyterian, but in the congregational basis of Church polity, was very different from Scotch Presbyterianism. We are apt to be misled by the loose application of the name "Presbyterian" to all non-prelatists except Baptists and Quakers. The few regular—as distinguished from Keithian—Baptists in Philadelphia, with one or two others aloof from the Church of England, had gathered at the Barbados store at Second and Chestnut, where, from about April, 1695, the Baptist minister from Pennypack, Rev. John Watts, is said to have preached every other Sunday, but preceding him, or sometimes in his place, was probably the head of the Baptists at Cohansey, New Jersey, Rev. Thomas Killingworth, spoken of in the chapter on Religious Dissension. On the alternate Sundays, as the Baptists soon afterwards stated, any "Presbyterian minister" who happened to come, was allowed to preach in the room at the Barbados store. We do not know whether Woodbridge did so. He may have brought Rev. Jedidiah Andrews to Philadelphia. In the Spring or Summer of 1698, Andrews, who had been licensed to preach by some authority in Massachusetts, came to minister to those described as Presbyterians. Their claim to that name has been well disputed by Irving Spence in his *Letters on the Early History of the Presbyterian Churches on the Peninsula,* addressed to Rev. Robert M. Laird, printed in 1838, Spence defining a Presbyterian as one who believed in the theory of Church government adopted by the General Assembly of the Scottish Kirk on February 10, 1645. The union congregation at the Barbados store became divided, one part hearing its minister in the morning, and the other hearing opposite views in the afternoon. Thus was started what has received the name of the First Presbyterian Church of Philadelphia. The letter of the Baptists, dated 8, 30, 1698, after the others had expressed themselves unwilling to join in worship with them, is addressed to Mr. Jedidiah Andrews, John Green, Joshua Story, Samuel Richards, "and the rest of those of Presbyterian judgment belonging to the meeting in Philadelphia." The answer, dated Nov. 3, asking a conference, was signed by Andrews, Green, and Richards, and also by David Giffing, Herbert Corry, John Van Lear, and Daniel Green. We have thus probably the names of nearly all the male adults who pronounced for that side. Van Lear was doubtless a Calvinistic Dutchman. In due time, the Budd family became Presbyterians, the chief representatives among them of the Keithian seceders from the Society of Friends. John Budd became an elder.

It would seem that the Anglican clergy of Maryland, although they did not pay, nevertheless sent as missionaries, and superintended, the two or more clergymen who had charge of Christ Church before Portlock, if, indeed, the one who first had charge was not a mere wanderer or visitor, asked to officiate. Perhaps the licenses to these men were for doing work as the Maryland clergy should arrange: it was before the arrival of a Commissary for Maryland. Rev. John Arrowsmith, who, as schoolmaster and chaplain on the way to that province, had an order for the King's allowance on Jany. 18, 1695–6, was in charge of Christ Church, Philadelphia, and its school at the beginning of 1698, but was only a deacon, writing to Governor Nicholson that some of the congregation were desirous of receiving the sacrament, if it could be administered at Easter, and that Mr. Sewell (evidently Rev. Richard Sewell of Maryland) had promised to come for that purpose.

It is supposed that Rev. Thomas Clayton was the first minister appointed for Philadelphia by the Bishop of London. Webster's *History of the Presbyterian Church in America* is wrong in saying that Clayton had been rector of Crofton, Yorkshire, confusing him possibly with the Rev. John Clayton, Rector there from 1687 to 1697, who may have been a relative, and may have employed Thomas Clayton as curate. Two

Thomas Claytons, both of Christ Church College, Cambridge, were graduated from that University, one as A.B. in 1684 and A.M. in 1690, the other as A.B. in 1690 and A.M. in 1694. The younger of these was probably the one in whom we are interested, and who, being on his way to Maryland—he either was not originally sent to Pennsylvania, or was to serve there under the Maryland Commissary or clergy—had order for the King's allowance on Jany. 11, 1697-8, and arrived in Philadelphia before the end of the Summer. He started a movement for Church Unity, writing letters to the Baptists, and to both the Keithians and the Quakers who had disowned Keith, which Quakers Clayton calls "Lloydians." In Bp. Perry's *Collections,* that name is printed "Hoytians," but the original letters have been examined for this present work. Clayton asked for each of the three sects to come over in a body, but he could hardly have expected those as aforesaid designated as followers of Thomas Lloyd to accept such an invitation. Clayton had a long conference with some of the Keithians the night before a great meeting, perhaps their Yearly Meeting, and had hopes of something like a general union, which, however, were frustrated the next day. The reply of the Baptists is printed in Edwards's *History:* but Clayton reports on 9ber 29, 1698, that there was a considerable party among them working vigorously for union. After two letters from the Lloydian Quakers, and when Clayton was engaged on a further answer to them, he was, for some reason, stopped from going further by what he calls an "inhibition from my brethren," apparently some of the Anglican clergy of Maryland. To the Rev. Jedidiah Andrews, the Presbyterian, who threatened to go home during the coming Spring, and whose flock could increase only by accessions from Clayton's, Clayton made a promise to confine himself to his own people so long as he saw himself in no danger of losing a congregagation. Not however sufficiently deferential to Mrs. Markham and her daughter, Clayton lost their attendance, which Andrews gained. Clayton, however, with the assistance of Arrowsmith, was quite successful in building up a congregation. Isaac Norris writes from Philadelphia, 7mo. 11, 1699: "Thomas Clayton, minister of the Church of England, died at Sassafras in Maryland, and here is another from London in his room, happened to come very opportunely."

The new-comer was Rev. Edward Portlock, who appears to have been previously chaplain in the English forces serving in Flanders, Penn speaking in an undated letter to Sir Robert Harley of "the heat of a few churchmen headed by a Flanders camp parson under the protection of the Bishop of London, who, having got a few together," made it their business to inveigh against the Pennsylvania government, inveighing in the pulpit against Quaker principles and such of the latter as concerned the State, as to oaths &ct. Portlock seems to have come to America to take a church at Perth Amboy, but he called himself Minister of Christ Church, Phila., in his receipt to Robert Bradinham, dated March 9, 1699, in 12th year of Wm. III. Portlock on July 12, 1700, wrote that in four years the Church of England had grown from a very small number to 500 sober and devout souls in and about the city. Thomas Story in his *Journal* mentions the circulation, which he says was by "the clergy" of the colony or the neighbouring colonies, of the report of a miracle in Holland, whereby a letter had been unearthed warning to preparation for judgment, and telling parents to baptize their children. The account of this, he says, was read in the churches, and convinced some in favor of water baptism. It is not remarkable that the tale, whatever its source, was credited in an age when Fox, Penn, and others spoke of their marvellous experiences. Portlock left for Maryland before Dec. 31, 1700, but appears to have visited Kent County afterwards. Penn speaks of Portlock before this in the pulpit hypocritically inveighing against him for leniency to pirates, when Portlock himself was intimate with Bradinham, Kidd's surgeon, and actually took a large amount of gold from Bradinham on deposit. It is sorrowful to see that there was often more politics than theology in the minds of adherents of the Church of England during the period of this history.

This chapter will not speak of the Church as a political party, but will deal with its organization, extension, and domestic concerns. Already the reader has seen the clashing of the interests of Quary and Moore, as Crown officials, with the interests of William Penn, and later will find what feelings prominent men of this ecclesiastical affiliation had towards various measures of the civil government, and how, with the exception of the Mennonites and certain Germans, all the non-Quakers, of whom the Churchmen were in various ways the most important, and long the most numerous, opposed the binding of the public with the peace principles of the Society of Friends.

Not imbued with the idea of heading an anti-Penn party, however, was the Bishop's appointee or licensee to succeed Clayton, viz: Rev. Evan Evans, native, it is said, of Wales. Order was issued to him for the royal allowance on July 5, 1700, and he arrived in Philadelphia before November 1 following, and devoted himself not only to the care of the Philadelphia congregation, but also to visiting various points in the country, as Chichester, Chester, and Radnor with the district, northwest of Radnor, spoken of as Montgomery, and one or more points in West Jersey, preaching sometimes in private houses, and baptizing in about three years and a half about five hundred persons. Many of such as were adults had been brought up as Quakers.

Christ Church, Philadelphia, had adopted before Dec. 31, 1700, the plan, growing into use in England, of choosing a "select vestry," instead of all the attendants or all the parishioners managing affairs at meetings in the "vestry," or vesting-room. The number of selected vestrymen, which in most churches has been twelve, has been altered for Christ Church from time to time. In 1717, with which the extant minutes begin, there were twelve besides the two wardens: but at first, although James Logan speaks in a letter as if the governing body amounted to twenty, which would correspond with the number of petitioners specified for toleration in the royal patent, it is doubtful if attention was paid to that, in view of the religious freedom in Penn's dominions, and it seems unlikely that the signers of the following letters from the Vestry were a decided minority. The first, dated Jany. 28, 1700-1, was signed by Evans the Minister, and Robert Quary, Joshua Carpenter, J. Moore, Charles Sober, Edwd. Smout, and Samll. Holt: the second, dated Oct. 27, 1701, was signed by Evans, the Minister, John Thomas, the clerk, and by Holt and Sober, the wardens, and by Quary, Carpenter, Moore, William Hall (who was a physician), Edward Smout, John Crapp, and Thomas Tench (who was some time one of the Council in Maryland).

Following King William's letters under the privy seal of Jany. 31, 1701, Queen Anne, under the privy seal, issued a warrant, dated July 15 in 1st year of her reign, to pay £50 stg. per an. to "such protestant minister as shall be residing within the province of Pennsylvania," and £30 stg. per an. "to such schoolmaster there," out of the duty of 1d. per l. upon tobacco exported thence to other British plantations in America, from the time to which they had been paid under King William's letters, or, in case no payment had been made, then from the date of residence, and to continue during her pleasure.

The Church of England.

George Keith, mentioned in a previous chapter, was admitted to deacon's orders by Bishop Compton on May 12, 1700. In the following year, largely through the efforts of Rev. Thomas Bray, D.D., who had spent a short time in Maryland as the Bishop's Commissary, the Society for the Propagation of the Gospel in Foreign Parts was incorporated by patent dated June 16. Keith was the first missionary appointed by the Society, and, in the Spring of 1702, was sent to America as an itinerant to investigate the opportunities, and to awaken a sentiment for religious ministrations by the Church of England. Thomas Story's *Journal,* before quoted, says that the Bishop of London was unwilling to ordain as priest any one who had fluctuated in opinion like Keith, and so the latter came over unable to administer the communion. Contradicting this are the words of that Bishop's recommendation of Keith to Gov. Nicholson of Virginia, dated Apr. 3, 1702: "He is in the full Orders of our Church, so that you may permit him to preach when & where you please within your Government" (*Virginia Mag. Hist. & Biog.,* Vol. XXIII, p. 145). With Keith was Rev. Patrick Gordon, appointed as missionary to Jamaica on Long Island, but who died a few days after his arrival there. Rev. John Talbot, formerly Rector of Fretherne, Gloucestershire, but at this time Chaplain of the man-of-war "Centurion," in which Keith sailed, joined him in his travels, which extended from Piscataway River in New England to Currituck, North Carolina. They arrived in Philadelphia on Nov. 5, 1702, and preached in Christ Church on the Sunday following, and several times afterwards, at intervals between visits to other places, joining Rev. Evan Evans in having prayers and sermons every day during the Friends Yearly Meeting held in Philadelphia in September, 1703. The work of the two itinerants was very active and very successful. They brought many throughout the middle provinces into the fold of the Church. They saw in Penn's dominions, partly as the result of Evans's labors, the establishment of congregations at Chester, Frankford (the church since called Oxford) in Philadelphia County, New Castle, and Appoquinimy. Talbot preached on Jany. 24, 1702-3, the first sermon in the newly finished St. Paul's Church at Chester. Rev. Henry Nicolls, a Fellow of Jesus College, Oxford, sent to Chester by the aforesaid Society, arrived there on Mch. 1, 1703-4, and, on April 18, a vestry consisting of him and eleven laymen was elected. Keith preached, on Aug. 22, the first sermon in the newly finished St. Mary's at Burlington. Keith's last sermon in Philadelphia was on Sunday, April 2, 1704, after which he went to Virginia to take passage for England. If, indeed, he had not been previously ordained priest, he must have been in the course of a year following, for, in 1705, he received the small living of Edburton, Sussex, which he held until his death in 1716. For a while, at least, his wife had remained a Friend; but his daughters turned with him. He appears to have left no son. From a daughter who married in Virginia was descended George Wythe, a Signer of the Declaration of Independence. Talbot about 1705 settled down to the charge of St. Mary's, Burlington.

On Aug. 14, 1706, Evans gave Gov. John Seymour of Maryland a receipt for the old great seal of that Province, promising to deliver the seal, on safe arrival in England, to Col. Nathaniel Blackiston, Agent of the Province, to carry to the Lords for Trade. David Humphreys's *History of the Society for the Propagation of the Gospel in Foreign Parts,* printed in London in 1730, speaks of Evans's coming to London upon private concerns in 1707. Quary had represented him as too friendly to his namesake John Evans, Penn's Deputy, and to Penn, and to the Quakers. Rev. Mr. Evans was well received, and came back about the beginning of 1709, having received the royal order of £20 on Aug. 9, 1708, and bringing silver communion pieces for Christ Church from Queen Anne. In 1711, the church building was considerably enlarged, the congregation worshipping for some weeks in the Swedish church, although offered the use of the Presbyterian (Dorr's *History of Christ Church*). Evans went again to England about 1714, and appears then to have received the degree of D.D., as he is called "Dr." afterwards. He returned about the end of 1716 (O. S.), when, in addition to Christ Church, he took charge of Radnor and Oxford, preaching at those country churches alternately on Thursdays. Finding the work too much for him, he retired in June, 1718, to accept a living in Maryland. Visiting Philadelphia in October, 1721, he read prayers and preached in Christ Church on Sunday, the 8th, in the morning. At the afternoon service, he was taken with an apoplectic fit, and sank down immediately in the desk, and was carried to his lodging, where he remained speechless until about two o'clock on Wednesday, when he died. He was buried in the church on the 12th, the register giving also the date of his death as if it happened on Tuesday, and his age as sixty years. Rev. John Vicary was at that time the Rector, being the minister licensed for Christ Church next after Evans, and serving about three years from Sep. 4, 1719, and dying in office.

The interest of Governor Gookin in Church affairs will be spoken of in a later chapter. His successor, William Keith, who, by the way, was not a near relation of George Keith, at first did much to facilitate the preaching of the Gospel by Anglican clergymen, taking them with him on his visits to certain points. As Gookin had been, so he was he a member of the Vestry of Christ Church. Keith was defeated for re-election after one year's service, because, said Peter Evans, he took upon him to overrule the other members, and entirely deprived them of their just freedom.

With the Swedish clergy, the Anglican at this period in Pennsylvania were in full communion. Rev. Andreas Rudman, former Pastor of Gloria Dei Church, Weccacoe, was put in charge of the congregation at Oxford in 1705 by the Society for the Propagation of the Gospel aforesaid, and, after Evans left for England, served Christ Church, dying before Evans's return. Rev. Andreas Sandel, Pastor of Gloria Dei, attended meetings of the Anglican clergy in 1713 and 1715, as well as being present at the dedication or opening of the present edifice of Trinity Church, Oxford, on Nov. 5, 1713, and the laying of the corner stone of the present edifice of St. David's, Radnor, on May 9, 1715 (see *Penna. Mag.*, Vol. XXX). Between these dates, a church edifice for St. James's, Bristol, was finished and opened on St. James's Day, with sermon from Rev. Francis Phillips. Of that unworthy clergyman something will be said in connection with Lieut. Gov. Gookin.

The offer of the Presbyterian edifice to Christ Church congregation recalls our attention to the non-Quaker religious denominations in Pennsylvania besides the two National Churches. The dispute before mentioned between the Baptists and Presbyterians of the union congregation in Philadelphia, ended, according to the Baptists' story, in the Presbyterians failing to keep to the offer to hold a conference. On the second Sunday of December in 1698, nine Baptists, viz: John Holmes, John Farmer and wife, Joseph Todd, Rebecca Woosencroft, William Silverstone, William Elton and wife, and Mary Shepherd met at the Barbados store, and "coalesced into a church for the communion of saints, having Rev. John Watts for their assistance." Of these, John Farmer and wife were from the congregation of Rev. Hanserd Knollys in London, and Joseph Todd and Rebecca Woosencroft were from that at Limmington, Hampshire; while the others, with the possible exception of Holmes, had been immersed by Rev. Thomas Killingworth after coming to America. Shortly after this "coalescing," Thomas Bibb and Nathaniel Douglas were members of the Philadelphia congregation. The Presbyterians contending for the place of worship, the Baptists abandoned it to them, and went to Anthony Morris's brewhouse. There the Baptists remained until Mch. 15, 1707, and then, by invitation of the Keithians, moved to the latter's building in 2nd street below Arch. Having perfected their title to the lot, as shown in the chapter on Religious Dissension, and having the adjoining lot, formerly owned by John Holmes, the Baptists, in 1731, replaced the wooden structure with a brick one, used until 1762, when they built a larger edifice, probably partly covering both lots. In the said year 1707, the various Baptist congregations of Philadelphia and vicinity, having, it is thought, previously had annual reunions, formed, or gave disciplinary power to, an Association composed of their delegates. The Baptists were reinforced by the arrival of a number of ministers and ruling elders from South Wales and the West of England in 1710 and afterwards. Rev. Thomas Selby, an Irish minister, who came to the Philadelphia congregation, was excommunicated by the Association in 1712. About this time, all the ministers of the Association had accepted the rite of laying on of hands. Terms of association were adopted in 1742, adding Articles XXIII and XXXI to those published in London by one hundred congregations in 1689, and called the Century Confession. The treatise of discipline has been *"The Glory of a true Church and its Discipline,"* published in London in 1697; and the catechism has been that published in London in 1699.

Contrary to the threat, or, rather expectation, reported by Clayton, the Rev. Jedidiah Andrews did not leave his flock in the Spring of 1699, nor, in fact, until his death in 1747, except during a few months in old age by suspension for "indiscretions," on repentance for which he was restored. There is mention in Rev. Dr. Wm. B. Sprague's *Annals of the American Pulpit* of a notion held by some that Andrews gave up the Independent theory in 1729; but his support of the measures of Irish Presbyterians, and other facts mentioned by Rev. William H. Roberts, D.D., LL.D., in the *Journal of the Presbyterian Historical Society,* Vol. V, No. 5, are inconsistent with his clinging to Independency, or Congregationalism, so late, if he ever clung to it after leaving New England. Moreover, there always were a number of divines in New England, who wholly or largely inclined to the opinion that the true scheme of Church government was that set forth in those chapters of the Westminster Confession which the Synod at Cambridge, Massachusetts, changed in 1648, and the Rev. Peter Hobart, Pastor at Andrews's native town in Andrews's childhood, was one of those called Presbyterians by those who distinguished such from Congregationalists. It is said that Andrews was ordained in Philadelphia, and probably in 1701, when the record of the baptisms performed by him commences. Talbot may have heard of this ordination by Apr. 24, 1702, when he wrote: "The Presbyterians here come a great way to lay hands on one another, . . . In Philadelphia one pretends to be a Presbyterian." This seems to mean claiming the office of presbyter by Apostolic succession through presbyters. The Virginia shores of the Chesapeake and the neighbourhood of New York were in those days "a great way" off from Philadelphia, and nobody who thought the congregation competent to ordain would have made a longer journey. It would seem, therefore, that those taking part in the ordination of Andrews were two

Presbyterians properly so called, viz: Revs. Francis Makemie of Accomac County, Virginia, and Josias Mackie of Norfolk County, Virginia, and also two neighbours of doubtful ecclesiastical antecedents, viz: Revs. Samuel Davis (who had long been in Delaware) and Nathaniel Taylor (perhaps of Maryland, but whose being in New Jersey is suggested in Rev. Dr. William Hill's *History of American Presbyterianism*). Makemie was an Irishman, said confidently in Sprague's *Annals* to have been ordained for colonial work *sine titulo* by his native Presbytery of Laggan, after application, in 1678, for a minister in Barbados, and, in December, 1680, for one in Maryland, in both of which places we find Makemie preaching. If his ordination in Ireland or that of Davis or Taylor in the British Isles is doubted, there were a number of Scotch or Irish Presbyterian ministers in New Jersey or Maryland for several years previous to the English Revolution, who might have ordained each of the three, among such Scotch or Irish ministers being Rev. William Traill, the former Moderator of the aforesaid Laggan Presbytery, who, after that body was broken up, went to Maryland. Rev. Dr. Robert Ellis Thompson, D.D., in his *History of the Presbyterian Churches in the United States,* gives 1682 as the date of Traill's arrival, and 1683 as that of Makemie's. The last named went to Europe in 1704, and, in 1705, brought back Revs. George Macnish and John Hampton, and gathered together the Presbytery of Philadelphia, the Mother Presbytery of the United States. The minutes of the body are preserved from the meeting in Philadelphia in 1706, when Makemie was Moderator, and Andrews, Davis, Wilson, Taylor, Macnish, and Hampton were the other ministers, with John Boyd, a licentiate from Ireland, whom they ordained for Freehold, New Jersey. Andrews and Wilson and possibly Davis were the only ones stationed in Penn's dominions. The congregation in the capital city is seen from the surnames in the early records to have been made up of English Nonconformists, New Englanders, and New York Reformed Dutch, and never in times following could be classified as Scotch Irish, although including persons of that race. It is likely that an important early Presbyterian of Philadelphia, William Allen, a sea captain who married into the Budd family, and was father of the rich Chief Justice of the name, was a Scotch-Irishman, as this sea captain mentions in his will a sister Catherine Cally living in Dungannon in Ireland, and an uncle William Craig at that place. In 1714, a congregation was started in the Great Valley, i.e. in Tredyffrin Township, Chester County, and, in the same year, some Independents formed one at Abington, then in Philadelphia County, and accepted Presbyterianism, calling as Pastor a Welsh Presbyterian, Rev. Malachi Jones, who, on arrival, was admitted to the Presbytery as an ordained minister.

In 1716, the Presbytery agreed to divide into three or four presbyteries, which should unite annually in a Synod. Six ministers were to compose the new Presbytery retaining the name of Philadelphia, viz. Andrews and Jones and Howell Powell or ap Howell, who had been ordained in Wales, and was settled at Cohansey, N. J., and John Bradner, a Scotchman, recently ordained for Cape May, and Joseph Morgan, born and ordained in Connecticut, then at Freehold, N. J., and Robert Orr, then at Hopewell, N. J., who was the only Irishman, he having come from "the old country" as a probationer. Another Presbytery was to bear the name of New Castle, which Isaac Norris in a letter in 1700 called "that Frenchified, Scotchified, Dutchified place," and in this Presbytery were James Anderson, ordained by Irvine Presbytery in Scotland, and who was the minister at New Castle, Daniel McGill, sent from London to a Scotch congregation at

Marlborough, Md., Robert Wotherspoon, who had come as a probationer from Scotland, and was minister at Appoquinimy, Del., David Evans, a Welshman, preaching to his countrymen at the Welsh Tract in New Castle Co. and in the Great Valley, Chester Co., Hugh Conn, a native of Ireland, and graduate of Glasgow, minister at Patapsco, Maryland, and George Gillespie, a native of Glasgow, also educated at the university there, and licensed by Glasgow Presbytery, ordained for the White Clay Creek congregation, and serving that vicinity. Three ministers were to compose a Presbytery of Snow Hill, viz: Davis, who was preaching at Lewes, and Hampton, who was minister for Snow Hill, and John Henry, ordained by Dublin Presbytery, minister for Rehoboth and the lower part of the Eastern Shore: but this Presbytery did not go into operation. To bring the Northern Calvinists into a Presbytery of Long Island were Macnish, then at Jamaica, Long Island, and Samuel Pumry at Newtown, Long Island, a New Englander, ordained by New Englanders, and admitted to the "Mother Presbytery" only a year before. Anderson was soon sent to be the first minister of the Scots congregation in the City of New York. Communion with many of the Connecticut ministers, and some accessions to the Presbytery of Long Island, and accessions of Nonconformists in Maryland and Virginia to the Presbytery of New Castle, seemed to promise a large religious denomination based upon opinion, and drawing strength almost equally from different races. In connection with the Irish, or Scotch Irish, immigration, the further history of Pennsylvania Presbyterianism will be given in a later chapter.

The fact that the Anglican clergymen in the colonies were practically out of the Bishop of London's reach, and unworthy men of the cloth resorted thither, and that the laymen could not be confirmed, unless they went to England, induced many, including Talbot as early as 1703, and Bp. Compton, who suggested a suffragan for Virginia in 1707, to favor the appointment of a bishop for America. Abp. Tenison left £1000 towards providing for two bishops there, the interest, until such were consecrated, to be paid to disabled missionaries of the Society for the Propagation of the Gospel. Petitions for a bishop were sent by the Vestry of Christ Church, Philadelphia, in 1718 and 1719, Talbot, who was often holding service there, joining in the latter of these petitions. In about a year after its date, he went to England, and in April, 1721, he obtained an order from the Lord Chancellor for the interest on Tenison's £1000.

Those in power in Church and State not being likely to provide America with any one invested with the spiritual functions of a bishop, Talbot turned to the Non-Jurors, who, without asking permission of Hanoverian King or Whig Parliament, were keeping up an episcopal succession. One of their bishops was Ralph Taylor, D.D., consecrated on Jany. 25, 1720-1, in Grey's Inn, in the presence of the Earl of Winchelsea and others, by Bps. Hawes, Spinckes, and Gandy. Among the priests of this faction was the Rev. Richard Welton, D.D. (Cantab.), formerly Rector of St. Mary's, White Chapel, who was deprived in 1715 for not taking the oath of allegiance to George I. Talbot, not holding a position in Great Britain, had not been required to take this oath, although, when an English rector, he must have sworn allegiance to William and Mary. Bp. Taylor now consecrated Welton and Talbot himself, Welton no doubt receiving the laying on of hands first. Rawlinson's manuscript list of consecrations by Non-Jurors (*Notes and Queries*, 3rd Series, Vol. I. p. 225) says, without date, and in a misleading place in the list: "Ric. Welton D.D. was consecrated by Dr. Taylor alone in a clandestine manner. — Talbot, M.A., was consecrated by the same person at the same time and as irregularly." The date could scarcely have been later than Oct. 1, 1722, O. S., as Talbot writes from Burlington on Nov. 27, speaking of his six weeks' voyage home. The consecration of these two was disapproved of by Taylor's fellow bishops either before or after it had taken place, and may be described as uncanonical but valid.

Whether either Welton or Talbot ever performed any episcopal function is not proved. The probability is that they administered confirmation, when they could do it in secret, or without attracting much attention, the confirming of a few, who could not otherwise be confirmed, not being likely to be looked upon by those in political or ecclesiastical power as an interference.

Talbot resumed charge of the Burlington church, and on Oct. 23, 1723, was willing, as a member of the convention of the clergy "of this province" (Pennsylvania with the Territories) to concur in the removal of Rev. John Urmston from Christ Church, Philadelphia, which Urmston was supplying in the interim following the death of an appointee of the Bishop of London. Afterwards Talbot occasionally filled that pulpit. Urmston wrote on June 30, 1724, that, after Talbot had been there about three months, some persons threatened **Sir William Keith, the Lieutenant-Governor**, that if such a Jacobite were allowed to officiate, they would complain against both him and the Lieutenant-Governor. So Keith, shutting up the church building, made Talbot leave about the end of February. Urmston adds: "Some of his confidants have discovered that he is in————orders, as many more rebels are. I have heard of no ordinations he has made as yet." Urmston supposed that Talbot would persuade clergymen to be reordained by him, in accordance with the opinion of some Jacobites that all ordinations by the bishops who supplanted the Non-Jurors were illegal. Before or a few days after Urmston's letter was written, Welton came to America, bringing probably for Talbot and himself the episcopal seals, with one of which Talbot's widow sealed her will, and the other being found among Welton's effects at his death. A letter from Gov. Keith dated July 24, mentions reports that some of the Non-Juring clergy of the neighbourhood pretended to the authority and office of bishops, but says that they do not own it, and that he has announced his determination to prosecute all who should attempt "to debauch any of the people with schismatical disloyal principles of that nature." Governor Burnet of New Jersey writes on Aug. 3 that Talbot had had the folly to confess that he is a bishop. Rev. Jacob Henderson of Maryland writes on Aug. 16 that Mr. Talbot had arrived two years before, but his episcopal orders had been kept a great secret until of late, and that, about six weeks before the date of the letter, Dr. Welton had arrived, "as I am credibly informed in the same capacity." Christ Church was reopened for ministrations performed by Welton. Peter Evans, in a letter defending the course of the vestrymen, says that English newspapers had reported that Welton had taken the oaths. Accordingly, the opportunity had been embraced to have services resumed, Welton being asked on July 27 to take charge. In due time, warning from England was sent to the Lieutenant-Governor, who answered, that, as the Vestry was entirely independent of him, he could not be held responsible, and suggested the desirability of some authority to him, instead of allowing a minister to be admitted by a Vestry without license from the Bishop or an induction. Such provision for worship the Vestry, however, only made in an emergency, and to be superseded by the arrival of the Bishop's appointee three months at least after an incumbent's death. Gov. Keith himself, for the marriage ceremony of his daughter in December, 1724, made use of Welton.

Talbot had been reported by Urmston to have put on episcopal robes, and to have demanded obedience from the other clergy, perhaps on the occasion of the convention which agreed to the removal of Urmston, but Talbot, writing on July 2, 1725, to the Bishop of London, denied exercising jurisdiction over the missionaries, and declared that he could prove his innocence by a thousand persons. He was not disturbed, and is stated to have taken the required oath before long.

Welton did not fare so well. A writ of privy seal was sent over to Lieutenant-Governor Keith commanding Welton on his allegiance to return forthwith to England. The notice was served in January, 1725-6, and Welton started, about March 1, on what was often at that period the only way of reaching London, viz: taking a vessel bound directly for Lisbon. While at Lisbon, he died of dropsy in August, 1726, refusing to join in the communion service with the English clergymen there.

To supply the want of sufficient foundation for ecclesiastical jurisdiction by the Bishop of London over America, Bp. Gibson, on Feb. 9 in the 13th year of George I's reign, obtained a royal patent conferring certain powers upon himself during royal pleasure. This was expressly revoked by a patent from George II dated Apr. 29 in the 1st year of his reign (1728), whereby visitatorial power over colonial churches whose service was according to the English liturgy and the right to inflict ecclesiastical punishments, subject to appeal, upon the ministers of such churches, and upon colonial presbyters and deacons in English orders, was conferred upon Bp. Gibson personally, to be exercised by.commissaries by him appointed and removed.

There were several districts of the civilized part of Pennsylvania to which the services of the Church were extended, chiefly by ministers stationed at places before mentioned, often many miles away, during the period from 1700 to 1748, and to those days is traced the collecting of the congregations of St. Peter's in Great Valley, St. Thomas's at Whitemarsh, St. James's at Perkiomen, St. Mary's at Warwick, St. Martin's at Chichester, St. John's at Concord, Bangor (Churchtown) in Lancaster Co., and St. John's, Pequea (Compassville). Some details will be found with a reprint of valuable documents in the edition very recently issued of Henry Pleasants's *History of Old St. David's Church Radnor.* The present edifice of St. Peter's (East Whiteland Township, Chester Co.) in the Great Valley was built in 1744. We are not concerned with the churches and mission stations of Delaware, which, however, multiplied very early, owing somewhat to the non-Quaker predilection of the original settlers.

The lot on which the overcrowded house of worship for Christ Church in Philadelphia was standing, was enlarged by the purchase of ground adjoining on the north by Robert Assheton, Dr. John Kearsley, and Samuel Hasell by deed of July 19, 1725, and, on April 27, 1727, the corner-stone of a western addition to the building was laid by Lieutenant-Governor Gordon. Eventually, about 1738, the whole was embraced in the present symmetrical structure except the steeple, the latter being completed some years later. The main structure, even if not absolutely finished, was in use some time before Whitefield's first visit.

A movement on somewhat the same general principle as Pietism among the Lutherans, which will be spoken of in connection with the German immigration, started within the Church of England in the reign of George II. The nickname "Methodists" given to certain young men, because, in their religious fervor, they undertook to live by rule and method, was accepted by them, and has been retained by their followers in other ideas, inappropriate or insufficient as is the designation. The separation organically of those so called from the Church of which the Wesleys and Whitefield were priests, did not take place during the time of this history; so there are only to be noted the labors of Whitefield in the region so closely associated with two other great leaders in their respective denominations, Penn and Zinzendorf. Whitefield's leadership, strong enough to establish an opposition to John Wesley, differed from that of Penn and Zinzendorf in the absence of any advantages of birth to help Whitefield. His *Life* by Rev. L. Tyerman is authority for most of the following account. George Whitefield was born on Dec. 16, 1714, at Gloucester, England, and entered at Oxford in 1732. As an undergraduate, he joined, becoming the most youthful member, the "Holy Club," as others at the University laughingly styled the coterie gathered by Charles Wesley for acts of devotion, such as receiving the communion every week, and for acts of charity. Whitefield was impressed by the book *The Life of God in the Soul of Man* with the essential need of the new birth, defined to be the vital union with Christ in the heart. Whitefield "experienced that assurance which comes in conversion" about June, 1735, which was several years before the Wesleys experienced it, and he soon became fully persuaded that justification is by faith only, although that doctrine took a small place in his earliest sermons. Whitefield was made deacon by the Bishop of Gloucester on Sunday, June 20, 1736, about two weeks before graduation as B.A., and attracted attention even by his first sermon, and, while a deacon, drew crowds in London and Bristol, people in the latter city hanging upon the rails of the organ loft, and climbing on the leads of the church. Whitefield had spent several months as a missionary in the new colony of Georgia, and been ordained priest at Oxford on Sunday, Jany. 14, 1738–9, by the aforesaid Bishop of Gloucester, acting for Bp. Secker of Oxford, and was on the way a second time to Georgia when he first visited Pennsylvania. He had become the foremost exponent of the views of the Methodists. When the strange effect upon some whom he had moved, the doctrines themselves, and the expressions in his published journals had made the clergy of any place withhold the use of their churches, Whitefield had preached in fields and parks, often to twenty thousand persons, and at least once to thirty thousand; but just before his embarkation for this visit to America, those who appeared in print against him or the excitement which he promoted, were joined by Bishop Gibson.

Whitefield and his friend William Seward arrived in Philadelphia in the evening of Friday, Nov. 2, 1739, on horseback from Lewes, where they had left the ship. The attitude of Bp. Gibson, if it was then known in the colonies, did not prevent his Commissary for Pennsylvania, Rev. Dr. Archibald Cummings, Rector of Christ Church, from receiving Whitefield with civility, nor the people from wishing to hear him. He read prayers, and assisted in the administration of the communion at Christ Church in the morning of the following Sunday, and preached there that afternoon and every day for the rest of that week with increasing congregations, and also in the afternoon of the second Sunday. He dined at Thomas Penn's and at both church wardens', was often visited by the Presbyterian minister, by the Baptist minister, and by Quakers, and twice preached at six in the evening from the court house stairs to several thousand persons. After a trip to New York, Whitefield preached in the yard of Rev. William Tennent's church on the Neshaminy to about three thousand, and from the porch window of the Presbyterian church at Abington, and again several times in Christ Church. On one of the last mentioned occasions, Sunday morning, Nov. 25, after his sermon, the Rev. Richard Peters, Secretary of the Province, who had retired from the work of the ministry, "exclaimed with a loud voice 'That there was no such term as *imputed righteousness* in Holy Scripture; that such a doctrine put a stop to all goodness; and that we were to be judged for our good works and obedience, and were commanded to do and live.' " When he had ended, Whitefield says: "I denied his first proposition, and brought a text to prove that 'imputed righteousness' was a scriptural expression, but, thinking the church an improper place for disputation, I said no more at the time. In the afternoon, however, I discoursed upon the words 'The Lord our Righteousness.' "

When Whitefield was to preach his farewell sermon, in the afternoon of Wednesday Nov. 28, the church not being large enough for those expected, he adjourned to the fields, and preached to ten thousand. The next day, people wept at his door when he departed; twenty gentlemen on horseback accompanied him out of town, and were joined by others, until there were two hundred. At Chester, the minister secured a balcony for him, the church being too small, the court adjourned, and Whitefield spoke to five thousand, of whom about one fifth had come from Philadelphia. Crowds as large in proportion heard him in the Lower Counties.

He was energetically philanthropic as well as, we may say, violently religious. His main purpose in going back to Georgia after his first visit there, and the object of all his begging sermons in England in 1739, and in Pennsylvania in 1739 and 1740, was to carry on a house for the care of poor orphans in Savannah. To buy provisions for this, he had come by way of Philadelphia on his second trip to America. He had received about forty orphans under his care, and, on the five hundred acres donated by the Trustees of the Colony, had started the main building before he came back to Philadelphia. He had favored the allowing of slavery as the only means of developing the colony, but, at the end of 1739, he had seen the miseries of the slaves in Maryland, Virginia, North Carolina, and South Carolina, and he printed a letter to the inhabitants of those colonies, telling them that he thought that God had a quarrel with them for their cruelty to the negroes. The question of the lawfulness of buying slaves was passed over, but it was declared a sin to use them worse than brutes, not only in the barbarity with which they were punished, but in not giving them convenient food to eat or proper raiment, and in obliging them to grind the corn for themselves after a day's work. Whitefield said that he prayed God that the slaves might never get the upper hand, yet, should such a thing be permitted by Providence, "all good men must acknowledge the judgment would be just."

The effect of Whitefield upon the Presbyterians will be noted in the chapter upon the Irish and their Kirk.

The Anglicans of Philadelphia had been divided for several years between the friends of Peters and the Rector respectively, only dissuasion by Peters himself preventing the building of a separate church for him. His action towards Whitefield discrediting the latter, as it did somewhat, and stemming the general assent to his teaching, aroused against the plucky interrupter an "evangelical" party. However, the Rector came to the side inimical to Whitefield, after the latter, during the few months before his return, reiterated and vindicated in print his remark, originally made privately by John Wesley, that "Archbishop Tillotson knew no more about true Chrisianity than Mahomet." So the Rector refused Whitefield the use of Christ Church, when, on coming back, he asked for it.

After ten days' voyage in a sloop bought by Whitefield and Seward, they and a number of Moravians arrived at New Castle from Savannah. On Sunday, April 13, 1740, the day of or day after landing, Whitefield preached in the church, the Rector being ill. It being made known that he would preach there in the afternoon also, the Presbyterian minister at White Clay Creek, or Christiana Bridge, gave up his second meeting for worship, and, with two hundred others, rode to New Castle and heard Whitefield. The next day, Whitefield preached at Wilmington from the balcony of the house where he lodged, to three thousand people. In Philadelphia, a platform was erected for him on Society Hill (near Front and Lombard), and there or at the court house he preached to from five to fifteen thousand persons daily, except when preaching out of town.

Whitefield undertook to found in Pennsylvania a school for negroes, and with it a settlement for persons converted in England by his preaching, and subjected to annoyance on that account. For a site, an agreement was made on April 22, 1740,—Reichel gives the date in new style as May 3—with William Allen to buy from him for 2200*l*. 5000 acres at the Forks of the Delaware, title to be made to Whitefield, and then assigned to Seward, who had some fortune, as security for Seward's advancing the money. Two days afterwards, Whitefield preached in the morning at the German settlement on the Skippack Creek to about five thousand persons, and in the evening, after riding twelve miles to Henry Antes's, to about three thousand, the Moravian Böhler following with an address in German. On that day, Whitefield offered to hire as builders the Moravians who had arrived from Savannah on the sloop with him. The ground being visited, the Moravians, by the cast of the lot, according to their custom, felt directed to engage. Seward, on April 28, left Philadelphia for England, partly to convert some securities into cash, and also to solicit contributions. He was hit on the head at Caerleon, Wales, and died a few days later, Oct. 22, 1740. On Sunday, May 11, Whitefield went twice to Christ Church, Philadelphia, and there heard himself taken to task by the preacher; and, in the afternoon, Whitefield preached as a farewell to nearly twenty thousand hearers. After preaching in New Castle and Chester County, he sailed to Savannah.

After he left, his friends designed a meeting-house for him to preach in, and a school for poor children to be carried on within it. He seems, from two letters written on July 18 from Charleston, to have first heard of this on that day or the night before. One letter is to Mr. I. R. (James Read?), and thanks him for going with friends E——— and B———(perhaps Böhler) to Nazareth, and says later on: "I thank my dear friends for their zeal in building a house, but desire it may not have any particular name or be put to any particular use till my return to Philadelphia. I wish them good luck in the name of the Lord." A foot note to the collection of Whitefield's Works, published in 1771, says that the building "is now the College of Philadelphia." The other letter speaks of private letters received from Philadelphia the night before or that morning, and says: "Philadelphia people are building a house for me to preach in one hundred and six feet long and seventy-four feet wide." An advertisement, dated July, 1740, appeared in a Philadelphia newspaper. After saying that the Almighty had now disposed many Christians to lay aside bigotry and party zeal, and unite their endeavors to promote the interest of the kingdom of Jesus, the advertisement proceeds: "With this view it hath been thought proper to erect a large building for a charity school for the instruction of poor children gratis in useful literature and the knowledge of the Christian Religion and also for a house of public worship the houses of this place being insufficient to contain the great numbers who convene on such occasions, and it being impracticable to meet in the open air at all times of the year because of the inclemency of the weather. It is agreed that the use of the aforesaid school and house of religious worship be under the direction of certain trustees viz: [they were not named] and other persons to be appointed by them [with provision that, upon death of any, the majority of the survivors should fill the vacancy] which trustees before named and hereafter to be chosen are from time to time to appoint fit and able school masters and mistresses and introduce such Protestant ministers as they judge to be sound in principle, acquainted with experimental religion in their own hearts and faithful in their practise without regard to those distinctions or different sentiments in lesser matters which have unhappily divided real Christians. . . . The building is actually begun under the direction of [not named] and the foundation laid on a lot of ground late of Jonathan Price and Mary his wife (who have generously contributed) situate near Mulberry Street in the City of Philada., where materials for the building will be received as also subscriptions for money and work taken in by the underwritten persons. Philad^a July 1740." Jonathan Price and Mary his wife conveyed by deed of Sep. 15, 1740, a lot on the west side of Delaware Fourth Street, 100 ft. south of Mulberry (Arch), 150 ft. front by 198 ft. deep to Edmond Woolley, carpenter, John Coats, bricklayer, John Howell, mariner, and William Price, carpenter: and these and other friends of Whitefield built on it the hall one hundred feet long and seventy feet wide. The roof was not yet on, when the first sermon resounded there. This was preached by Whitefield on Sunday, Nov. 9. By deed of Nov. 14, Woolley, Coats, Howell, and Price covenated to stand seized for Whitefield, Seward (whose death was not then known in America), John Stephen Benezet of Phila., merchant, James Read of Phila., gent., Thomas Noble of New York, merchant, Samuel Hazard of New York, merchant, Robert Eastburne of Phila., blacksmith, Edward Evans of Phila., cordwainer, and Charles Brockden, the Recorder of Deeds of Phila. Co., and for the survivor in fee, they to have power to appoint new trustees, in trust substantially as stated in the advertisement, and to convey as directed by a majority of the trustees. The school was not started by these projectors, probably because Whitefield soon found himself heavily in debt for his Orphan House in Georgia, and obliged to confine himself, in appealing for money, to that or some other pressing object, while Christ Church seems to have been spurred on in the matter of its parochial school. On 6mo. 8, 1747, Woolley and Coats petitioned the Assembly of the Province asking that, as the school was part of the purpose of the said building, and the trust had failed, the building be sold, and the subscriptions paid back. In 1749, by direction of a majority of the surviving trustees, whose action met with Whitefield's approval, Woolley and Coats conveyed the building and lot for 775*l*. 18*s*. 11*d*. 3*far*, with which to pay off certain advances, to James Logan and others, who are usually denominated the founders of the University of Pennsylvania, to be used as a free school for the instruction of children in useful literature and the Christian religion, with the right to establish a seminary of the languages, arts, and sciences, and as a place of worship wherein Mr. Whitefield should be allowed to preach whenever he was in the city, and so desired, and the trustees should introduce such preachers to teach the word of God as should subscribe to the articles of religion appended to the deed of conveyance; which articles declare belief in the Trinity, the Atonement, and Justification by Faith, and end in affirming the IXth, Xth, XIth, XIIth, XIIIth, and XVIIth Articles of the Church of England "as explained by the Calvinists in their literal and grammatical sense." Thus the College of Philadelphia, afterwards the University, came into possession of the building which was its main hall until removal to Ninth Street.

Whitefield's stay in Philadelphia in the Fall of 1740 was for about a fortnight, at the end of a visit to New England and New York.

Two houses had by that time been built at Nazareth, as he named the place for the negro school. Now came a dispute between him and those employed by him. Reichel says that Whitefield, disapproving of one of Böhler's doctrinal opinions, and unable in an argument conducted in Latin to convince him, discharged the Moravians, closing the interview with the words: "Sic jubeo; stet voluntas pro ratione." The Moravians were allowed to stay on the property for some months by Allen's agent; and the whole project failing, largely through Seward's death, Whitefield, after taking title, was glad to assign it to the Moravians. This he did when in England. The further history of the property and an account of the religious people aforesaid and some reflections on the difference between the work of Whitefield and Zinzendorf will appear in a chapter on the Unitas Fratrum and Church Unity. Whitefield was absent from America during the whole time of Zinzendorf's visit. Zinzendorf, after returning to England, declared the opposition of the Moravians to Whitefield, unless he would recant his doctrine of reprobation, and openly preach free grace. This estrangement of two bodies once so sympathetic explains Benjamin Franklin's story of the unwillingness of the trustees of Whitefield's building in Philadelphia to elect any Moravian as successor to the Moravian member who had died.

Dr. Cummings, Rector of Christ Church, Philadelphia, having died on Apr. 23, 1741, Peters, although he warned his friends of the "evangelical" feeling against him, was favored for the Rectorate by the majority of the Vestry, although not by the older members. His stand against Whitefield was portrayed as a merit by Lieut.-Gov. Thomas in a letter of recommendation. Thomas Penn, still a Quaker, tried, out of friendship, to influence the Bishop of London. On the other hand, Peters was opposed by those who wished to keep clear of the Proprietaries, and, in the interests of peace, the neighbouring clergymen protested against such an appointment. Bp. Gibson, to whom on a former occasion, his Quaker kinsman Jeremiah Langhorne had written in favor of Peters, was now as much against Whitefield as formerly, and might have been expected to be glad to reward Peters, but did not yield to such considerations. Watson tells us that in 1741 the Churchmen of Philadelphia manifested some disaffection at the alleged supremacy of the Bishop of London, saying that, as the Bishop declined to license Mr. Peters after they had chosen him (alleging as a reason his living by his lay functions), they would not accept any person whom he might license, claiming that his diocese did not extend to this Province, and Mr. Peters himself alleging that a right of presentation lay in the Proprietaries and Governor. That they came to a better frame of mind was probably due to the policy of the prelate in not filling the vacancy immediately and to the satisfaction given by Rev. Æneas Ross, who devotedly served in the interim, but it argues something for the conscientiousness of Peters, who became a useful member of the Vestry and a liberal contributor under Rev. Robert Jenney. Twenty years later, on Jenney's death, Peters was unanimously appointed Rector by the Vestry, and in 1763 received the approval of Gibson's successor.

Whitefield's early bent towards the doctrine of election &ct. had been strengthened before his first coming to Pennsylvania. The time from which he can be called a Calvinist is fixed by Tyerman as about June, 1739. Whitefield's letter to John Wesley of the 25th of that month, although starting with disapproval of Wesley's encouraging convulsions and other signs in his hearers, goes on to declare the writer shocked by a report that Wesley was about to print a sermon against predestination. Whitefield, as he knew that his opinion of it would be asked, thought silence on both sides desirable. Wesley drew lots, and, as the result was affirmative, printed; moreover he sent at least one copy to America. Whitefield's intercourse with Dissenters, while it never induced him to leave the Church of England, confirmed him in the theology then generally accepted by American Presbyterians and Congregationalists. By the time, in the year 1741, when he went back to England, he was strongly Calvinistic, and deemed it his duty vigorously to oppose the Wesleys, and was printing an answer to John Wesley's sermon on free grace. On March 6, five days before Whitefield arrived, occurred the split in the Kingswood Society, from which John Wesley dates the division of the Methodists. John Cennick, a layman in charge of the school, had preached Calvinism; Wesley told the people that they must choose between him and Cennick, whereupon about one third decided to go with the latter. Whitefield's friends, chiefly Dissenters, built a frame preaching-hall for him in London, close to the Foundry, where John Wesley preached. This Tabernacle, as Whitefield called it, became the headquarters of those who agreed with him. Three Church of England clergymen besides himself, one being a Welsh rector, and three lay preachers held on Jany. 5, 1743, at Waterford, Wales, the first Calvinistic Methodist Conference, and arranged that the ordained clergymen should visit districts as they were able, and that there should be lay preachers as district superintendents and public and private exhorters, and that Howell Harris, a lay preacher, should be their overseer. At the second Conference it was arranged that Whitefield was to be

Moderator whenever in England, there were to be Quarterly Associations, and in every county of South Wales a Monthly Association consisting of an ordained minister and the superintendent of the district or circuit and his exhorters, and all who thought they had a call to be exhorters should be examined by some Monthly Association, and by it appointed to a district. Thus was started a body which became separated from the Church of England, and which has still considerable strength in Wales.

Whitefield, after spending three and a half years in England, and about a year in New England, passed through Philadelphia in the Fall of 1745. He was then offered 800*l.* to preach there six months in the year, but declined and went on to Georgia. He was back, but only for a few days, in August, 1746, but, in the following year, spent part of May and June and a few days of September in Philadelphia. He visited the city several times later at considerable intervals, the last time being a few months before his death, arriving on May 6, 1770, as we learn from the newspaper, and, after a week's trip in the interior, finally leaving on June 15. He wrote during his stay: "To all the Episcopal churches, as well as to most of the other places of worship, I have free access:" and besides the Second and Third Presbyterian, the Methodist, the Swedish at Kingsessing, and St. Paul's, Third Street, he preached in both Christ Church and St. Peter's, then united under the rectorate of his old opposer, Peters. Whitefield died on September 30, 1770, at Newburyport, Mass.

CHAPTER XII.

PENN'S SECOND MARRIAGE AND SECOND VISIT.

Penn's continued financial distress—Death of his first wife and his second marriage—False conveyancing between him and Ford—Opposition to Penn among English Quakers—The Regents' orders to him when about to sail—Logan and the voyage to Pennsylvania—Birth of John Penn "the American"—Quary, Morris, and David Lloyd—Assembly passes laws against pirates and forbidden trade—Proceedings against suspected pirates—The trials in England, and hanging of Kidd—Quaker traders provoked at Penn not curbing the Admiralty court—Tobacco—Election for Councillors and Assemblymen—Lloyd suspended from the Council—Tax for debts of government and impost for Penn—Old Charter surrendered: Penn rules under powers granted by King Charles II—Councillors appointed by Penn—Water Bailiffs—Oaths—Mixed judiciary attempted—"Sweet Singer of Israel"—Assembly at New Castle in October and November, 1700—2000*l.* voted to Penn—Law fixing right to vote and eligibility for Assemblymen—Marriage law—Assembly refuses to contribute to erecting forts on frontier of New York—Bill in Parliament to unite Proprietary governments to the Crown—New Assembly confirms laws passed at New Castle—Modified marriage law—Courts of law and equity—New Frame of Government—New charter for the City—New Council for the Governor—Proposed Charter of Property—Penn returns to England.

William Penn had been unable to extricate himself from the financial embarrassment in which the Revolution of 1688 found him, and which was marked by a change in the secret title to his possessions on the western side of Delaware River and Bay with certain exceptions. The change was effected by a release dated Aug. 30, 1690, of his equity of redemption of the lease held by Ford, and an assignment, dated Sep. 1, of that lease to Thomas Ellwood, in trust to hold it to attend the freehold and inheritance, and a conveyance, by lease and release of Sep. 2 and 3, from Penn of the fee simple to Ford. The right to redeem and annul this was dependent upon the word of Ford. Towards having any money to use in redemption, Penn, since then, was saving nothing out of his income. He estimated in 1705 that, on an average, in the fifteen years between his first and second visits to Pennsylvania, he had spent £400 annually in London "to hinder much mischief against us if not to do us much good." During some years of the time, his Shanagarry estate, by reason of King James's war in Ireland and other causes, was unproductive. Penn, when requesting the following loan, spoke of £450 per annum (probably the rent-roll approximately) totally laid waste (his word was "wasted") in Ireland.

The request for a loan by Pennsylvanians, made under date of 12mo. 4, 1693, mentioned in the chapter on England, was that one hundred persons should lend Penn each on an average 100 pounds (probably sterling in London net above exchange) without interest for four years, on Penn's bond, to draw interest on whatever might remain unpaid at the end of four years. As mentioned, the £10,000 were not raised.

Resuming the project of a secondary settlement on the Susquehanna front, Penn made some sales to persons in London of land to be laid out between the Delaware and Susquehanna. To secure equal opportunities with the Londoners, a number of Pennsylvanians entered into an agreement to buy Susquehanna

Penn's Second Marriage and Second Visit. 369

lands to the value of their respective subscriptions at the same rate as sold or intended to be to the Londoners, and to pay for the pieces, after survey and confirmation, half the price in the March following Penn's arrival in the province to manage the purchase from the Indians, and the other half of the price in the March next following. If Penn came not within two years from date, the agreement was to be void. The date of the articles was the 1st of 1st month, 1696 (1695-6), and on 3, 20, 1696, it was certified that 2824*l*. had been subscribed, Carpenter having subscribed the largest sum, viz: 100*l*., Shippen 80*l*., Morris and Ewer and David Lloyd each 50*l*. Markham afterwards subscribed 50*l*., and later the sum was brought up to 3974*l*., but this was not sufficient to enable Penn to prosecute the undertaking, or even to comply with the condition of leaving the British Isles under the circumstances in which he was, or had caused himself to be.

Losing his first wife on Feb. 23, 1693-4, Penn, after declaring his intention to the Bristol Men's Meeting as early as November 11, 1695, married again, when over fifty-one years of age, and having three children. As he was practically a reigning prince under an emperor, this event was a turning-point in the history of Pennsylvania and Delaware, and is not to be dismissed from consideration, as in the case of a private, even distinguished, man, with the statement that his subsequent home life was happy, and that certain children were born of the union. This adroit politician seems to have taken this step without calculation, and showed no discernment except for personal qualities. Romance would have been more natural in a younger man, or at a longer time after Guli's death. The less sentimental reason often adduced for the seeking of a wife, of being all alone, or of having young children needing a mother, did not exist in his case. His financial circumstances made it so desirable for him to remain single, and practise economy, unless he could get somebody with a great fortune, which benefit to his family and tenantry he was not securing, that we are inclined to believe that he found the justification to himself in the amorous nature which there is evidence for attributing to him. The choice which he made for a second wife has been commended as judicious, and would have been such for a Quaker burgher, but not for an impoverished lord palatine. Hannah Callowhill, whom he married on 1mo. 5, 1695-6, had all the virtues, even in after years inconveniencing herself in kindness to her step-son's family, and she developed very considerable business capacity. She was the only child of Thomas Callowhill, a respected Quaker of Bristol, England, successful as a dealer in linens. As he lived long after her marriage, and left his property to his grandchildren, no direct financial advantage was derived by William Penn, except Callowhill's taking a large share in the mortgage of 1708, and perhaps other Quakers would have made that up. Hannah's family did not belong to the gentry, and she had no influential connections to strengthen Penn with the officials of the Crown, nor did she ally him to any of the great leaders of the Society of Friends, among whom the regard for him was none too strong. Could he have gone to Pennsylvania, and there selected a bride, and made the home for his family among the people whom he had led thither, there would have been at least retrenchment in the cost of living, and, one would have expected, a renewal of popularity with the taxpaying tenantry. If, indeed, he was impelled to what he did by being terribly in love with the lady, the disastrous consequences could call to mind the remark of the ancient chronicler "Thus all the trouble in the world from Eve in the garden and Helen of Troy down to the conquest of Ireland has come from a woman."

Penn's second marriage lowered the prospects in

life of his three children then living, carried him into greater expenditure and deeper embarrassment, dragged his friends and taxpayers into the hardship of assisting him, and finally placed Pennsylvania under a new family with relatively no other wealth than what could be gotten out of it. The three children, over whom a step-mother was placed, were, in order of birth, Springett, Lætitia, and William. The eldest alone was then grown up, but was still single. He was a very satisfactory heir-apparent, serious minded, very much "after his father's heart." Springett died a month after the change in his home. The second son, two years later, married at the age of nineteen. Of the object of young William's "impetuous inclination," his father writes in 1707: "I wish she had brought more wisdom, since she brought so little money, to help the family." The young man, by 1703, when he came to Pennsylvania, jealous of his step-mother and her children, and emancipated from his father, had raised his own set of creditors. Lætitia, who was born in 1678, lived with her father and step-mother until her own marriage, Aug. 20, 1702, with William Aubrey, afterwards seeing her dowry delayed, and her legacy made small. By Hannah Callowhill, William Penn had seven children, being sixty-four years old when the youngest was born.

Unable to meet the interest charges made by Ford, and furthermore obliged to borrow from him, Penn made a new conveyance, dated Sep. 29, 1696, of all right to Ford in fee clear of equity of redemption, Ford making thereupon a separate instrument covenanting to reconvey on payment of £10657. This sum was the balance shown due to him by an account, to which Penn did not object, but which charged Penn with heavy commissions, and compounded the interest on advances every six months or oftener at six per cent, and frequently at eight per cent.

Penn's liberality to the needy, his expenses in soliciting, and the extortion suffered by him were estimated in 1707, in his codicil to his will of 1705, to have lessened his estate £50000. Some of the trouble taken for individuals was pecuniarily profitable; for the custom of the time was for those who had access to kings, cabinet ministers, members of parliament, and officials to exert influence or powers of persuasion for men or measures, and to receive, not wages or salary, but presents if successful. Penn, who on another page has been called a "lobbyist," complained in 1707 that John Hamilton, whom Penn upon promise of a present had helped in England to £1650, would merely deduct forty odd pounds of Penn's debit to Governor Andrew Hamilton, John's father. Much, however, tha Penn did was without tangible, at least without worldly, reward, or the hope of it: and this willingness to do a favor, or habit, as we may say, of doing one, seems to have been what led him in April, 1697, to deviate so far from the straight moral course as to take part in proceedings to deceive the English government in the matter of Ford's taxes. Without such excuse as the alternative of spoiling the province would have been for quibbling, or as danger to Penn's life would have been for prevarication, this is after all the worst thing that is proved against Penn, every accusation equally grave being the proper subject for the decision "not guilty" or the Scotch verdict "not proven." The proceedings in question, which saved Ford £300, probably a years' support of his family, must be mentioned, as they involved the final conveyancing between Penn and Ford, and the settlement of the title to what Penn had in Pennsylvania and Delaware so as to give rights which were never intended, but were afterwards pressed, turning this episode of our history into something like a fable, say by Æsop, about trusting those who would cheat others. Subsequent to the release and covenant of Sep. 29, 1696, which made Penn owner subject to a mortgage, an Act of Parliament had levied a tax upon real and personal estate in England. To make it appear to the taxing officers that Ford was owner of land in America, which was taxable only there, instead of holder of bonds or other personalty or creditor of money due, which was taxable at his residence in England, as the loan to Penn certainly was, Penn, after hesitation, consented to convey to Ford in fee the soil of the Province and Territories, and to let it be supposed that the conveyance was an absolute one, it being agreed between them that the transaction should constitute a mortgaging, that the money owed by Penn to Ford should be paid as the former raised it out of the land, and that meanwhile a paper enabling Penn to demand a reconveyance should be executed by Ford in a form "the better to blind the business upon his affirmation." To carry out the plan, Penn by a writing dated April 1, 1697, released the premises covered by the document of Sept. 29, 1696. Eight days intervened before Penn had anything to show that he longer had any interest in the land, and Penn supposed, as he afterwards wrote, that within that time the officers made the examination. Ford made a lease, under date of April 10, of the Province and Lower Counties to Penn for four years from April 1, 1697, at £630 per annum (the interest on £10500, to which the debt of Sep. 29 had been reduced); and in this lease was a stipulation that Ford would convey the premises to Penn in fee, if he paid him £12714 5s. at the end of three years. A receipt for £159 of that sum was appended.

Penn's bills of exchange drawn on his America collectors and debtors in 1697 were not honored. The 600l. promised to him in consideration of relinquishing the impost were not paid in; nor had any quit rents been forwarded to him in England since 1686. Hoping to get to America in the Summer of 1698, he meanwhile, in 3rd month of that year, went to Ireland, combining with the inspection of his estate there, a preaching tour among Friends' meetings. Thomas Story, who had studied law, and been converted to Quakerism, and who had made Penn's acquaintance about a year before, attended him. As Story tells us in his printed *Journal*, they arrived in Dublin from England on 3mo. 6, 1698. After three months' stay, they returned, and, in the latter part of the Autumn, Story sailed for America, Penn bidding him farewell at Deptford.

Story tells us that while they were in Ireland, "Satan was busy in evil work in London," in that about that time some Quakers, including ministers "setting up in the Society as no small dictators," "being filled with envy" of William Penn, "made unworthy attempts against his character and even in the Yearly Meeting." What was the particular subject of the concern manifested against him in that Meeting, is not mentioned. It may be inferred that William Mead, Penn's old companion in trial, and Thomas Lower had become displeased with him; as Logan, about eight years later, spoke of them as known to be inimical.

At last Penn complied with the imperative call for his presence in America, and followed his often expressed wish to be there.

The Regents of England, commonly called the Lords Justices, at the last interview he had with them before his departure, extracted a promise from him to punish David Lloyd, and to notify them of the fact and character of the punishment. They further, by letter of July 25, 1699, to the Proprietary and Governor of Pennsylvania, required him to see that the Acts of Parliament relating to trade and navigation were put into execution in the country governed by him, and therefore to give constant protection and encouragement to the officers of customs and of the Admiralty. On August 4, the Commissioners for Trade recommended that Markham be removed from the Lieutenant-Governorship, that David Lloyd be superseded as Attorney-General, and removed from all public employment, and that Anthony Morris be removed from his judgeship; and, on August 10, it was further recommended that all pirates seized in Pennsylvania and West Jersey be sent to England for trial, together with the "evidences"—witnesses as well as record of examinations? The Lords Justices, on Aug. 31, formally disallowed the appointment of Markham as Lieutenant-Governor, and gave orders in accordance with these recommendations, and declared void the Pennsylvania law for preventing frauds and other laws on the subject of the customs and the Admiralty contrary to the known laws of England.

Meanwhile Penn had succeeded in making a big sale, by means of which he could transport his family, his deeds of lease and release to the "London Company," mentioned in the chapter on the People, being dated respectively August 11 and 12, 1699; and he had secured as secretary a Quaker then in Bristol, twenty-five years of age, James Logan, who had been a school teacher, and more recently in mercantile business, son of Rev. Patrick Logan, a Scotch clergyman converted to Quakerism. Having prepared a voluminous address to Friends, which was dated at Cowes, Isle of Wight, "weighing anchor," 7mo. 3, 1699, Penn sailed for Pennsylvania in the "Canterbury," accompanied by his wife and his daughter Lætitia and the secretary. Whether the secretary then or afterwards had any thoughts of marrying Lætitia is a matter of conjecture, not of history. The secretary showed himself more of a knight than a Quaker on the voyage. One day a vessel which was not recognized, bore down upon the "Canterbury," and the crew of the latter prepared to make resistance. As Penn retired below, Logan went to the guns. The vessel turned out to be friendly. Logan rejoining Penn, the latter reproached Logan for his readiness to shed blood. Logan retorted, that if Penn had indeed disapproved, he, being Logan's master, should have ordered him below. They landed at Philadelphia on Sunday afternoon, Dec. 10, a crowd, including Quary and Moore, receiving them at the wharf, from whence the Proprietary went to call on Markham, thus superseded, who appears to have been as usual too unwell to leave his house. After addressing a large gathering at the Friends' meeting, concluding with a prayer, Penn took his family and his secretary to Edward Shippen's. There they stayed about a month—apparently boarding, as money was subsequently paid for Shippen's "entertainment" of the Proprietary on his arrival.

Penn secured for a city residence the house, built by Samuel Carpenter, long known as the "slate roof house," at the southeast corner of 2nd and the present Sansom Street. There Hannah Penn had a son, born on January 29, 1699-1700, named John, the only male of the Penn family born in the New World. He was sometimes referred to by his father as "the American," and is distinguished in history as "John Penn the American" from his two nephews named John. Most of the second visit of the first Proprietary to Pennsylvania, however, was spent at Pennsbury manor, Bucks County, Logan being left in the "slate roof house." No wages to Logan were paid at the time, and perhaps the additional housekeeping by Logan was overlooked, when Penn spoke later of having spent in Pennsylvania £1000 per annum, having a wife, child (Lætitia), nurse (the baby not mentioned), three maids, and three or four men.

We learn from two accounts hereafter quoted, a Churchman's "Brief Narrative" and Logan's letter to William Penn Jr., that, a few days after the Proprietary's arrival, he received Colonel Quary and perhaps others of the Churchmen, and, admitting that there were grounds for complaint, declared that it should be his own chief care and endeavor to administer justice impartially without favor or affection in relation to opinions, and to make "everything as even as his two eyes." Quary, when he saw the steps taken by Penn and the change brought about by him in the attitude towards the Crown officers, wrote strongly in commendation of Penn.

Anthony Morris was willing to sacrifice himself to enable Penn to comply with the desire or requirement of the English government; but David Lloyd, "extremely pertinacious and somewhat revengeful," had no consideration for the Proprietary's difficulties, and stoutly opposed the course essential to the latter's interests, apparently on December 21, 1699-1700, when Penn met the Council for the first time after his arrival. Penn answered with much warmth, and enforced his will. On Dec. 22, Morris brought before the Council the papers in the matter of the replevin, and resigned his judgeship, and Penn reprimanded him for issuing the writ, and delivered to Judge Quary, who appeared by request, the inventories of the goods replevied and the bonds given by Adams and his sureties. Penn asked Quary to suggest any expedients for discouraging and punishing piracy and illegal trade, and expressed a hope that the Admiralty and the Proprietary authorities would work hand in hand for that purpose. A month later, Quary reported that the surety refused to hand over the value of the replevied goods, and, the Sheriff who took the bond being no longer in Office, Quary asked for an order that Morris restore the goods. It was unreasonable, Quary said, that the Crown be put to the expense of a suit to recover them. Morris made answer that he had acted in ignorance, not in malice, and had no interest in the goods or in their owner, and, in a similar case, would not again act as he had done. Penn then told Quary that the Admiralty officers should be put in possession of the value without trouble or expense. Quary was asked what further satisfaction he wished from Morris. He replied, that, having no personal animosity, he was satisfied with Morris's submission, in view of the Proprietary's promise. More than this, after making charges against Lloyd, Quary was willing to let them drop, as will be seen.

For passing a sufficient law against piracy and illegal trade, Penn called an Assembly. With a proviso that he was not bound by the Frame of Government of 1696, he issued a writ to the Sheriff of New Castle to supply the omission to choose Councillors and Assemblymen the year before, and summoned the Assemblymen already elected to meet on the 25th of January those to be so chosen. The Sheriff of New Castle on that day returned Richard Halliwell and Robert French as chosen for Councillors, and John Healy, Adam Pieterson, William Guest, and William Houston as chosen for Assemblymen. It happened that the people along Brandywine Creek had no notice of the election, and twenty-nine petitioners asked that there be a new election, but the Proprietary induced all to acquiesce in the choice, by his promising to punish the Sheriff for his neglect, and to pass no other laws than against pirates and illegal trade, and by declaring that the acceptance of the return should not be deemed a precedent. After earnest debate for two weeks, the speical session passed a law against piracy and also a law against illegal trade, the Proprietary consenting to a clause indemnifying all persons who had traded with such pirates as had surrendered themselves under the Jamaica proclamation, and the Assembly consenting to a prohibition of the trade to Madagascar and Natal for three years.

Among the members of Assembly elected in 1699 from Kent County was Markham's son-in-law, the suspected Brown. He was, however, arrested before the special session. Markham having offered to go bail, but objecting to the bond being so worded as to bind his executors, Penn wrote a note on January 27, 1699-00, reminding him that, if he or his estate were to lose anything by Brown running away, it would be the only money paid out as any marriage portion for Markham's only child. A few days later Markham is mentioned as having gone bail in 300*l.* The old pirates who came before Every's crew, Penn had bound over to answer any charges which might be made within one year. Bradinham and Evans and, afterwards, Brown were sent to the Earl of Bellomont, and were taken to England by a man-of-war, with Eldridge and five others, viz: Nicholas Churchill and James Howe, who had both sailed with Kidd, Robert Hickman, Derby Mullens (or Mullig), and Turlagh O'Sullivan, the last named having gone aboard Every's vessel after all the prizes had been taken, and being at the time of arrest occupied in farming in New Jersey. Although Penn, on April 12, examined some of those accused of having dealt with and received goods from Kidd, and some of them were sent to New York, they appear to have been let off. In England, Brown and Evans were acquitted; and let us trust that O'Sullivan was. Perhaps O'Sullivan and Hickman, as to neither of whom has there been mention found in our records, were never indicted. Evans soon afterwards died. Brown may be identical with the "Captain James Brown" selected with others to command ships which the promoters of the South Sea enterprise—later called "Bubble"—were to send against Spanish localities and shipping: at any rate, Brown rejoined his wife, having later three children, instead of an only child, as when sent prisoner: but he did not manage to leave his family provided for at his death. To convict Kidd, it was necessary to get the testimony of some of his companions. So Bradinham received a pardon. Largely on his testimony, Kidd, Churchill, Howe, Mullens, and others were found guilty of piracy. Kidd was also found guilty of murder, and, sentenced for both crimes, was hung. The rope broke, and he was picked up alive, and spoke to the officer, and was hung again, that time effectually. Eldridge was also convicted.

The Quaker traders had welcomed William Penn as a deliverer from a party among the colonists which was building "steeple-houses"—although probably there were no steeples—and enforcing English laws; a party which, moreover, was inimical to himself. When he was seen not to suppress, but to compromise with such a "faction," lending his Proprietary authority and personal influence to the strengthening of the Crown officials, there was disappointment, want of insight into his circumstances, and coldness towards him. Instead of thinking of what he had done for Quakers in general and those in Pennsylvania in particular, the latter were thinking how they were injured in reputation and unsafe, and were probably blaming him for not taking better care of them by means of his supposed influence at Court. Nor was their situation favorable: there was the impossibility of a Quaker making the statement to register a vessel; and the Admiralty jurisdiction on the Delaware was being extended by its officers to every private cause relating to a vessel, even as to charter-parties, wages, bread, beer, sails, smith work, carpenter work done at the quay or dock, &ct.; and in such courts not only were the papers in Latin, but there was simply a decision by Quary, and no jury trial, and the expenses were four times greater than in the courts of common law.

About this time, a change was made in the agriculture of Penn's dominions. The people had been accustomed to wearing English woolens, and the paying for such had caused an exportation of money, as the products of the region were not in sufficient demand by England. To raise an article which would be required, the planters, possibly at Penn's suggestion, began to raise tobacco in considerable quantity.

It was agreed that the Council and Assembly to meet in 1700 should be chosen according to the old Frame of 1683, and should prepare a new Frame of Government. Once more the Councillors were to start with terms of three, two, and one year.

We can conclude that there was a rumor that some member of the Church of England would be a candidate at the election in Philadelphia County, and perhaps the suggestion had been made in Penn's hearing that so important a part of the community was entitled to a seat. This is not told us; but that he bestirred himself to have a body friendly to him chosen, we learn from a contemporary paper among the MSS. of the Society for the Propagation of the Gospel, entitled a "Brief Narrative of the Proceedings of William Penn," printed in Perry's *Collections, Vol. II.* The writer, we learn from Logan's letter of 3mo. 2, 1702, was Quary. He says that Penn appeared at the place of election, exhorted the voters to elect only such as were friends of his government, asserted that no one could vote or be voted for who would swear,—an ambiguous word, as the "Narrative" well says,—and even told those present that there were not over two dozen Churchmen at most. Penn's speech on meeting the new Councillors on April 1, instead of reproving Quakers for narrow-minded sectarianism, as it appears to do, may have referred to the Churchmen, in saying that he was grieved to hear some at the last election at Philadelphia "make it a matter of religion." Logan two years after the election procured certificates of non-Quakers that Penn did not speak about swearing, and inferentially that he did not influence the election. Carpenter, Shippen, and Dr. Griffith Owen, Quakers friendly to Penn, were chosen for three years, two years, and one year respectively by Philadelphia County. In Bucks and Chester, it would have been hard to find a non-Quaker fit to send. Bucks chose Growdon, Biles, and Richard Hough; Chester chose Lloyd, Pusey, and Simcock. Of the Delaware members of the Council, viz: Halliwell, Donnaldson, and Yeates from New Castle, John Walker, Henry Molleston, and Thomas Bedwell from Kent, and Samuel Preston, John Hill, and Thomas Fenwick from Sussex, we know that Preston was a Quaker. Every Assemblyman chosen from the Upper Counties was a Quaker; and perhaps three or four of those chosen by the Lower. The new Assembly organized on May 13, with Blunston again Speaker.

On May 15, Penn and the Council, by unanimous vote, suspended Lloyd from that body, pending his trial on the charge of making the remarks about the great seal, the King's picture, and the Court of Admiralty. Such trial did not take place: for Quary, to whom Penn referred the prosecution of Lloyd before the Quarter Sessions, became disposed, in the absence of orders from England, to overlook Lloyd's offence, and hoped to receive no orders, remarking what a loss it would be if the colony were deprived of its only lawyer except John Moore.

On May 24, a committee composed of all the Councillors and Assemblymen presented to the Proprietary the draft of such a charter as they desired for a Frame of Government. On June 4, he submitted to a subcommittee such a one as he was willing to grant. This the Assembly amended in some particulars; but there was a conflict between the Upper and Lower Counties as to the number of representatives. On the last day of the session, eight laws were passed, one of them levying $1d.$ per $l.$ and $6s.$ per head for the debts of the government. Penn had called the attention of his friends to the "worsting" of his estate by his maintaining his Deputy,—that must mean Blackwell and Markham,—and protested, that, although some said that he, Penn, came to get money, and be gone, he hoped that he or his while they lived would dwell with his people, for his absence had been disastrous to him as well as to the colonists. He broadly hinted that as they treated him, so would he serve them in return. An attempt was made by his friends to secure for him from the Assembly money to be raised by a general tax, but this was voted down, and, instead of it, an impost was laid for his benefit on imported wine, beer, ale, &ct. This, continued during two years, would, it was said, yield him 1000*l.* per an., but Isaac Norris, member from Philadelphia County, thought it to amount to an "unhandsome" gift of less than half of that sum. On June 7, after approving of the laws carried, Penn, despairing of inducing an agreement upon a new charter, put the question to the Assemblymen, with the consent of the Council, would they be ruled by the old Charter? This was carried in the negative. He then asked, should he resume the government as it was after the Act of Union under the letters patent from Charles II. All who voted except four or five of the whole number of Councillors and Assemblymen answered in the affirmative: evidently the necessary six sevenths of the freemen's representatives agreed not merely to amend, but to destroy. It was then unanimously declared that all the laws passed at Chester, and embodied in the Petition of Right of 1693, and all since made, and the one just passed for confirming the laws, should, except as repealed, altered, or supplied, continue in force until twenty days after the rising of the next session. Then the Speaker, on behalf of the Assembly, and Biles, on behalf of the Councillors from the Upper Counties, and Hill and Rodeney, on behalf of those from the Territories, took the old Charter of 1683, constituting the

Frame, and, with the unanimous consent of those present, returned it to the Proprietary, who, in undertaking to rule by the royal letters patent and Act of Union, and bidding farewell to those present, said that he would endeavor to give them satisfaction, and advised them not to be easily displeased one with another, to be slow to anger, and swift to charity.

On June 25, the Proprietary, thus untrammelled as Governor, sent for Shippen, Carpenter, Moll, Turner, Owen, Clark, Pusey, and Growdon to come to his house in Philadelphia. To those appearing, he said that it was not fit that he should be without a Council, and he had chosen them to belong to one. They then signed a qualification, which he had prepared. Those who were absent that day signed subsequently, and Thomas Story was admitted and qualified on the 26th, Penn making him also Master of the Rolls. Of these nine, Moll alone represented the Swedish or Dutch element; all the others belonged to the Society of Friends, except Turner, the Keithian.

A few days before this, one of the commissions being dated June 20, 1700, the Proprietary undertook to appoint Water Bailiffs, commissioning two of the Sheriffs as such, authorizing them to execute upon the river or waters of the Delaware from end to end of their respective counties all writs and other process upon any person or ship or goods from any court of record. The occasion was that a vessel in port had fired through a house in the middle of the quay. Quary was absent, but Moore called the Proprietary's attention to the affair, but the Proprietary found it an accident; nevertheless he perceived the danger of there being no one to enforce law upon the river. Quary, on his return, complained to Penn: if the latter could take the rivers, Quary must lose all authority; for his commission as Judge of Vice Admiralty did not extend to the high seas. Penn told the Sheriffs, one of whom had served only two writs as Water Bailiff, and the other had served none, to forbear acting in such capacity until further order, but Penn contended for his right to make the appointment, offering to have the same decided by the Admiralty in England. This not being taken up, the Proprietary, on leaving, granted the same powers to the Corporation of the City, and in July, 1702, the Attorney-General and Advocate-General in England gave their opinion that the commissioning of a Water Bailiff to act upon the rivers within a county, but not on the high seas, was in fact appointing a Sheriff, and not an interference with the Admiralty. The absence of Quary for months at a time upon private business, besides his attention to duties away from Philadelphia, kept him rather clear of the clashing of the other Churchmen with the Quakers, and, while irritated at times by Penn's meddling with the exercise of Admiralty power, Quary kept on civil terms with Penn throughout the latter's stay.

Randolph, in "Articles of High Crimes and Misdemeanors charged upon the Governors of several Proprieties [Proprietary provinces]," read to the Commissioners for Trade on Mch. 24, 1700-1, says that not long before he wrote, two persons had been tried and condemned in the Lower Counties, the Judges and juries not being sworn, and the condemned had been executed, while in Pennsylvania proper one person had been tried, condemned, and executed, the Judge and jury not being sworn. All this seems to have taken place before the arrival of Penn.

The great change which had taken place within ten years in the character of the immigration made the question of oaths of more practical importance than merely enabling Randolph to pick a flaw, or embarrassing the punctilious Quary, or letting anti-Quakers pretend that they as a class were in greater danger than the other inhabitants. When so moral a community as the Quaker settlers filled at least the Upper Counties, it was safe to take the word of a neighbour solemnly promising to speak the truth; in fact even the promising provided for by the law of 1682 seemed a superfluous formality, for a good Quaker or any right-minded man would, when justice was involved, tell the truth without promising to do so: but there were now coming men of inferior conscience, of indifference to justice and virtue, and glad to find in their not being under oath an excuse for helping an associate. The customs officers, dependent, as they necessarily were, upon the testimony of just such men, doubtless were having increased difficulty in the enforcement of the severe laws, when the testimony was not sworn to: and all citizens might well feel themselves in danger from the animosity of future witnesses who were not reminded of their accountability to God. When a man's liberty or property, and particularly when his life depends upon the story told by some low character, it is necessary to take great precautions against falsehood, and some persons who can not be terrorized by human laws against false witness can be controlled by religious, perhaps what the reader may call superstitious, fears. The "hot Church party" would doubtless have liked to see, mainly, perhaps, for the strangulation of Quakerism, the abolition of all affirmations, but, this being impossible, wanted, for individual protection, the affirmations to have the form and limited use mentioned in the English statute of 7 & 8 Wm. III allowing Quakers to affirm: while, on the other hand, the extreme Quakers in Pennsylvania set themselves against any mention of God in the attestation.

We learn from the aforesaid "Brief Narrative" in Perry's *Collections* that, after the Assembly had adjourned, Penn declared it his pleasure that some of the Churchmen should have a share in the government, and induced three of the Vestry of Christ Church to accept seats on the bench for the County of Philadelphia, the other Justices then appointed being "six strong Foxian Quakers, one Swede, and a sweet Singer of Israell." It can be made out from Logan's letter of 3rd mo. 2, 1702, that Andrew Bankson was the Swede, and that John Moll was the Sweet Singer of Israel. Moll, from Amsterdam, after residing at the Delaware settlement for a number of years, was one of the Labadist grantees of part of Herman's Bohemia manor in 1684, and was mentioned with others in 1692 as living on Bohemia River "peaceably and religiously." The Labadists were the flock of Jean de Labadie, a native of France, who had been a Jesuit, and favored by Richelieu, but became a Reformed minister, and emigrated to Holland after inculcating pietism and mysticism, and ultimately established himself at Altona. Transferring themselves to the region between Delaware Bay and the Chesapeake, some members of his congregation lived together some years as an industrial religious fraternity. The application of the name "Sweet Singers of Israel" to the Labadists is not otherwise known, but seems in line with the fact that Jasper Danckaerts, their leader in Maryland, had translated the Psalms into rhyme in Low Dutch.

When the first quarter session after the appointment of these Justices was held, the first person called upon to give evidence asked that he be sworn. Some may question whether this was done in good faith, but the "Brief Narrative" meets the objection by the statement that oaths had been administered in such court ever since Penn received the government from King Charles II, Judges qualified to administer them being appointed, but the statement that these very Quakers had been on the bench may be incorrect as to Shippen, who was not an old resident. It is more likely that the administration of oaths, since the grant to Penn, had started upon the enacting of Fletcher's law, which had not been repealed, and which, by using the word "may" instead of "shall," had altered the requirement of qualifying by merely promising into a permission to qualify in that manner. On the present occasion, the Episcopalian Justices said that the demand was reasonable, and that they supposed themselves appointed for the purpose of administering oaths to those who were willing to take them. The Quakers interposed, declaring that they could not conscientiously remain where an oath was being taken. The Churchmen urged that it was only fair that others as well as Quakers should have the liberty of giving evidence according to their own way; and finally proposed that the affirmation allowed to the Quakers in England by Act of 7 & 8 William III be used, viz: "I. A. B. do declare in the presence of Almighty God the witness of the truth of what I say." The Quaker Justices declared that this naming of God made the affirmation objectionable, and that, as was perfectly true, the Act of Parliament governed only in the places it named, England, Wales, and Berwick. Penn "outwardly," says the "Narrative," but surely with a sincere wish for harmony, endeavored to induce the Quakers to recede from their position, telling them that he had taken the affirmation in England, and that they could sit on the bench while an oath was being taken, without being concerned in it. The fact was that these of his co-religionists had more radical ideas and stronger wills than his. He could not control them, but was compelled to fight on their side. He had accomplished much in inducing the Quakers in power in the Province, men not at all amenable to fear, and little to expediency, to comply with the requirements of the home government that Morris and Lloyd should cease to hold office. It is clear that the Proprietary had pressed his influence as far as it would go. The attitude of the Assembly further warned him that he was not master of the money-voting power. The

"Narrative" says: "The scene was presently changed by making his personall appearance in the courte laying the whole blame upon the Churchmen, . . . in so much that he must be constrained to ride up & down the country, and shew his letters patent to satisfy the people of his authority . . . ." Possibly, as we have not heard Penn's side in the affair, there was something to call for this in the Churchmen's argument. Declaring that he had palatine powers, which was correct, and claiming that the province had been given to him to relieve his people from oaths, he caused a new commission to be read appointing the six Quakers, the Swede, and the Sweet Singer, and leaving out the Churchmen. Two years later, when the charges embodied in the "Narrative" were heard of in Pennsylvania, four of the Quakers concerned made an affidavit, spoken of in Logan's letter before mentioned, as an answer about turning out the magistrates. The other Quakers were John Jones, who in 1702 was in Barbados, and John Bevan, who, residing in another county, never served. The certificates and affidavits contradicting the "Narrative" have not been found, and their scope and force can not be observed.

Feeling the necessity for a written constitution, for a law of property, and for a tax for the support of the government and the payment of public debts, Penn summoned an Assembly of four from each county chosen on October 1, 1700. Several of the Councillors were elected Assemblymen, and were temporarily excused from service in the Council. Humphrey Morrey, Richard Halliwell, Jasper Yeates,—the two last being non-Quakers,—and Phineas Pemberton, William Biles, and John Blunston, Quakers, entered the Council about this time. Growdon was Speaker of the Assembly. The session was at New Castle, and one hundred and nine laws were passed, Penn duly publishing them under the great seal on November 27. Most of them were re-enactments or slight modifications of the laws in the Petition of Right. An allowance was established for each member of the Assembly of 6s. for each day of attendance, and 3d. per mile travelling, the Speaker's daily allowance being 10s. There was some adjustment of the matter of oaths, thus: the radical Quaker formula of promising to perform official duty was followed in an act directing the attests of several officers, jurors, and attorneys, but a section was added that a magistrate who had no scruples against administering an oath should be allowed to do so to those who were free to take it; a clause to salve the conscience of Quaker Justices was inserted, that the act should be deemed that of the magistrate alone, and so entered on record, but be as valid as if done in the name of the court; Fletcher's law allowing testimony by "solemnly promising" was re-enacted. The promise for the attorneys was so thorough-going as to discourage any conscientious observer of it from practising law. The sum of 2000l. was voted to Penn. It was apportioned among the counties, no two paying the same amount, and was to be raised by assessing on all estates with some exceptions as much as would be required, with a poll tax of 4s. on every person not otherwise rated, to make up the county's share. Although Penn may have been worth this much to the People, and certainly to those who enjoyed civic importance under him, yet the tax was not popular, and was not paid with alacrity, and, before the following July, many, for one reason or another, refused to pay it.

It was also enacted that any person speaking, acting, or writing anything tending to sedition "or disaffection to this government" or disturbance of the peace, or spreading false news tending thereto, should be imprisoned three months, or fined not less than 5l., in the discretion of the Justices of the County Court. This law was repealed by Queen Anne.

Among these laws of November 27, 1700, was one fixing the number of Assemblymen from each county at four, and prescribing the qualification for voters and Assemblymen, as follows: a native born subject of England or one naturalized either in England or the Province (meaning the Lower Counties as well), of age and wealth as in Markham's Frame of 1696, also resident two years before the election. This qualification, confirmed and re-enacted, remained requisite in Pennsylvania until the American Revolution.

Fletcher's marriage law of 1693 allowed marriages in the parties' religious society, or by persons authorized by the Church of England and observing the laws and usages of England, to be without the otherwise required presentation to a religious society or Justice of a certificate of clearness of all engagements, and affixing to the door of a court house or meeting-house a declaration of intention one month before solemnization, which solemnization was to be by taking for husband and wife in presence of twelve witnesses, one being a Justice. As declarations had been put up at night, and taken down in the morning, and banns had been given out where the parties were unknown, one act of Nov. 27, 1700, required the date of affixing to be added by a Justice, and made such affixing necessary also for marriages in a religious society. Penalties were prescribed in case of marriage of a servant without the master's consent. Any person marrying or joining in marriage contrary to the act was to pay 10*l.* to the Proprietary; the "persons so joining others in marriage" were to forfeit 20*l.* to the Proprietary, and pay damages to the party aggrieved. Ecclesiastical canon, however, provided for the marriage of persons of full age, not within the prohibited degrees, if banns had been given out three times. The Vestry of Christ Church under date of Jany. 28, 1700-1, made a representation to the Lords for Trade against royal allowance of this act, as interfering with the free exercise of the Churchmen's religion. The representation made mention also of there being no militia or military commissions outstanding or any gun mounted, while taxes had been imposed to give Penn large sums, also of the law about speaking or writing against the government, and of the interpretation being in the hands of Quakers, there not being one magistrate belonging to the Church of England, and of the attestation tending to deprive the Churchmen of having lawyers, and furthermore of the Quakers being less in number than the non-Quakers. This estimate, very different from Penn's, may have related to the whole dominion, including the Lower Counties; and Penn's, only to Pennsylvania proper.

The one known case of sentence under the aforesaid act was where the master abetted the marriage of his servants. John Keble, planter in Kent County, had procured certain of his servants to be married at his house by an Anglican minister, whom he was entertaining. The minister was prosecuted, and fined 20*l.*, according to the act, and was obliged to keep away from Keble's, to avoid imprisonment for not paying; while Keble's affidavit, put in shape by the Vestry of Christ Church, speaks of himself being prosecuted, and of his suffering distraint to the value of 14*l.* 1*s.* This was resented as an interference with the Church of England; and Bp. Compton objected on Dec. 29, 1701, to the act as making it impossible for any but Quakers to live in the country subject to it, probably not only from the canon's silence as to the master's consent, but because the people of other religious societies, having scarcely a house of worship in any neighbourhood or a minister in the whole dominion, could be married under their own form only as sudden opportunity offered.

The requirements of this law figured in the case of a young Quaker in prison upon the charge of the capital crime of rape. The woman, having made the charge, but being told that a wife could not testify against her husband, was induced to marry the culprit, so as to save his life by disqualifying herself as a witness. No publication of intention one month previously could be made. She went to the prison, and married him there, and a certificate under the hands of thirteen persons was duly made. The law of marriage was deemed violated, but the bridegroom was admitted to bail, as likely to be acquitted, and, in view of the opinion of both of the two lawyers in the colony, was never tried.

Apart from requiring an oath for registering vessels, which Penn was endeavoring to have cured by an Act of Parliament, the Trade and Navigation laws, as we have seen, were very harsh, whether enforced by reason of the cupidity or the sense of duty of the Crown's local representatives for such matters. A particularly hard case was that of the ship "Providence," Capt. John Lumby, owned by residents of Hull. Although entitled to registration as an English vessel, she had sailed without registration papers. Intending to put in to Virginia or Maryland, in stress after five months at sea, but, mistaking the capes of Delaware Bay for those of the Chesapeake, Lumby had brought her within the jurisdiction of Quary, and had begun to break bulk. Moore, the Advocate, acting as informer, she and her cargo had been seized before Penn's visit. The sympathy of the trading community being particularly excited by the affair, disinterested merchants offered to go security for answering in the Court of Admiralty in England, if the voyage were allowed to be continued. After argument and trial, in which Lumby's evidence to excuse himself was not able to be admitted, Quary, as Admiralty Judge, had felt bound to decree condemnation; the law absolutely requiring a register, and, moreover, the waiving of it in any case tending to making the law a dead letter. Quary was liable to removal, if not further punishment, for any neglect to give the King his right. Recognizing that this case was a hard one, Quary did not speedily order a sale, but sent the goods to the King's store, and left the vessel in the captain's care, while a merchant going to England undertook to obtain relief. He appears to have notified Penn, but was reported to have failed. After nine or ten months, the goods beginning to deteriorate, Quary caused an appraisement as low as possible to be made; and the captain, about July, 1700, wishing to buy the ship, Quary arranged that the informer would compound cheaply for his third, and Penn agreed to give his third, leaving the King alone interested in the proceeds of sale. Before the scheme could be carried out, there arrived an inhibition from the High Court of Admiralty in England for the purpose of having the case heard there. The High Court confirmed Quary's judgment of condemnation. On an order from the High Court, Penn had his third appraised, and so the value of the King's third was shown to be greater, making the low appraisement look suspicious. Penn's and the informer's thirds were handed over in kind to them respectively, Penn's going to the owners. The goods left for the King and those delivered to the informer were put up for sale, and the former owners were obliged to let them go, or pay high for them. Quary combatted before the Board of Trade, Penn's subsequent representations (printed with *Penn and Logan Correspondence*) as to Quary's conduct in this matter.

A letter from the King ordering a contribution of £350 sterling towards erecting forts on the frontiers of New York &ct., obliged Penn to summon the prorogued Assembly to meet on August 1, 1701. When the members appeared before him, he apologized for bringing them together at that season of the year, and asked them to give serious consideration to the message from the King. In a few days, the Speaker returned answer, that, by reason of the expenditure by the inhabitants in settling, and the great sums lately assessed in imposts and taxes, and the arrears of quit rents, the present capacity would hardly admit of levying money at that time, and, as it was understood that the adjacent colonies had done nothing, the members hoped that the matter would be postponed, and that representation would be made to the King of their condition and willingness according to ability to answer as far as religious persuasion would permit. Seven members from the Lower Counties, viz: Halliwell, Robert French, Yeates, John Healy, John Brinckloe, John Hill, and Luke Wattson Jr., made a separate address, asking that no contribution be expected for forts abroad, until they were able to build some at home, they being daily threatened with war, but unable to furnish themselves with arms and ammunition, having used up their money "in making tobacco, which hath proved very advantageous for the Kingdom of England," yet the King's Majesty had not taken notice of them "in the way of protection," for they had neither standing militia nor persons empowered to command the people in case of invasion. With such opposition from both elements in the Assembly, Penn could do nothing but dissolve the body. He wrote or had written to the Governor of New York, that, even if he, Penn, were obliged to pay the money out of his own pocket, it should not be wanting for the King's service. The Governor replied that he needed neither men nor money, but Col. Kramer, the engineer whom the New Englanders kept from him.

On 6, 21, 1701, Penn received news by the ship "Messenger" of efforts to procure an act of Parliament uniting all Proprietary governments to the

Crown, a bill for that purpose having been already introduced into the House of Lords. It was thought inevitable that it would pass at the next session, unless Penn went to England to fight it. On the next day, the Council agreed to have Assemblymen chosen on the 4th of September to meet on the 15th.

For his assistance, subscriptions were sought through the gatherings of Friends for the Monthly Meetings, the subscribers to be reimbursed with land near the Susquehanna.

At the meeting of the Assembly, Penn told of the necessity for him to leave, and his resolution to return, and to settle his posterity in Pennsylvania: he asked the members to think of some suitable provision for safety in privileges and property, and to review and perfect the laws, and to give the postponed consideration to the King's letter. It seems as if the mention of property was a slip of the tongue, or at least that what Penn intended was a charter which might protect religious immunities, in anticipation of the possible transfer of the government, and under which, if the government were not taken by the Crown, his own heirs and assigns would not be as near absolute as King Charles's patent made them.

The controversy precipitated in a few days over questions strictly of property has been detailed in the chapter upon the Acquisition and Distribution of the Land.

Penn called the Assemblymen before him on the 29th, and asked what progress had been made in the matter of the King's letter, and expressed wonder that nothing had been sent to him in amendment of the laws, and that the opportunity was not being embraced of securing the freemen in their privileges, he desiring to part with them lovingly, and having no longer than three weeks to stay. Joseph Growdon, the Speaker, reported the resolution of the House,—it had been carried unanimously,—asking to be excused for the present from responding to the King's request, the country having been much drained of late by paying debts and taxes, and it not appearing what other colonies equally concerned had done on like demands; the representatives had been going over the laws; as to privileges,—the authors of the message must have been in bad humor,— they felt that they had sufficient as Englishmen, and were inclined to leave the rest to Providence. Nevertheless, some days later, while certain laws were being considered, Penn had a Charter of Privileges drafted and submitted to the House.

A plea having been set up by certain inhabitants of Philadelphia County against the legality of the tax imposed by the law passed at New Castle, on the ground that New Castle was outside the bounds of the Province granted by Charles II, the magistrates asked that the laws passed at New Castle be confirmed. A bill for that purpose was prepared and sent by the Council to the Assembly, where it was received on October 10th. Thereupon the members from New Castle and Kent and one from Sussex decided to withdraw from attendance, and said, in a paper addressed to the Governor, that the consequences would be fatal to the Lower Counties, if their representatives must come into Pennsylvania to make laws affecting them. Penn told the seceders that he was grieved at the prospect of a division of a union which had cost him 2000 or 3000*l*. They replied that, however the union was intended, the Territories were great sufferers from it, and could not support the burden of the expense. He then said that they were free to break off and act by themselves, when they could do so upon amicable terms. Pleased with his declaration that they were free to break off, and have a distinct legislative body, the seceders went back, but the representatives of Pennsylvania refused, in passing the confirmation, to express any salvo of the privileges of the Lower Counties. Some of the seceders again retired; but Penn again brought them together.

Notifying the Assembly of having written to England to procure the King's approbation of Col. Hamilton, Governor of the Jerseys, as the acting Governor of Pennsylvania and Territories, Penn asked for the nomination of fit persons to administer the government from Penn's departure. The Assembly acknowledged this evidence of his good will, but requested to be excused, leaving the choice to him. He duly notified the Assembly that the support of Hamilton would fall upon the colonists, and not upon the titular Governor, whose Deputy he would be. The House forwarded the request of some inhabitants of the city that the burdens on trade, such as the impost on liquors, be remitted. He replied that he would have accepted an equivalent, but, as the session must close, it was too late; so the House voted that the impost be continued, unless 300*l*. be secured to him before he sailed, payable within six months. This was not secured.

The House had actually, on October 27, sent an answer, in the determination to regulate the resurveying of property, that a certain **Charter of Property** must be passed first, and, dependent upon such action, the bill for the confirmation of the laws: but this stand was not adhered to, and among the laws which received the great seal on October 28 was one confirming ninety-six laws passed at New Castle. In re-enacting the law about marriages, there was an endeavor to appease the Churchmen by leaving out of the proviso the requirement that intentions be published, and substituting a requirement of a month's previous notice to parents, masters, mistresses, or guardians as the only condition upon which the law was not to refer to a marriage in the religious society of the parties. This law was allowed by the Queen.

The law passed on Oct. 28, 1701, for establishing

courts of judicature in the Province and Territories, and under which justice was administered for about five years, provided for county courts holding sessions quarterly, that for Philadelphia beginning the first Tuesday in March, June, September, and December, the county courts trying all criminal cases except for certain offences, and trying all civil cases. They were furthermore authorized to hear and decree all matters of equity, and it may surprise some who speak of a subsequent Governor's Court of Chancery as the first in Pennsylvania, to read that the proceedings in these county courts in equity were to be by bill and answer and "such other pleadings as are necessary in chancery courts, and proper in these parts, with power also for the said justices to force obedience to their decrees in equity by imprisonment or sequestration of lands, as the case may require." It is fair to assume that the facts for equitable relief were found by a jury, and not by a master or a judge. There was to be a Provincial Court, or, in other words, a Supreme Court over the whole Province and Territories, for appeals and for trying treason, murder, and certain other crimes, including burglary and burning of houses. From judgments on appeals there could be appeal to England on deposit of the amount of money involved, or giving security in double the amount. The county Justices with the Register-General or his deputy in each county were to form an Orphans' Court.

The Charter of Privileges involving a Frame of Government proposed by Penn did not satisfy the people of the Lower Counties, but after some emendation was, upon the day of adjournment, executed by the Proprietary in the presence of his Council, and probably of a number of Assemblymen including the Speaker. It was said that less than a majority of the House adopted the Charter. The House was not in actual session when the Speaker appended his signature to a certificate that the Charter had been approved and agreed to, and was thankfully received, and that he signed by order of the Assembly. As thus established, this instrument of October 28, 1701, in connection with Charles II's patent to Penn, was the written constitution of Pennsylvania proper until the Revolutionary War. The provisions will be stated in the next chapter.

The bill relating to property was not agreed upon. On the last day of the session, the House made certain offers, but Penn, rejecting these, summoned the representatives to his residence, expostulated with those who came, told them that he had scarcely half an hour to spend with them, pressed his latest proposal upon them, and advised them to go into his parlor and consider it. They accordingly retired to his parlor, and, in about an hour, sent word in writing that they could not depart from their former concession.

On October 28, 1701, the Assembly was dissolved, and a new Charter for the City of Philadelphia was signed by Penn with several commissions. One of these commissions named as a Council of State to advise the Governor or Deputy-Governor, and in the absence of both to exercise the powers of government, the following "trusty and well beloved friends," viz: Shippen, Guest, Carpenter, Clark, Story, Owen, Pemberton, Samuel Finney (mentioned in chapter on the People), Pusey, and Blunston, the first named to take the Chair on failure of the Lieutenant-Governor to name a President. Four were to be a quorum to advise, and five to be a quorum to exercise the powers of government. The Lieutenant, or Deputy, Governor, could add new members.

Penn had intended to take with him to England one or two Pennsylvanians, and to leave his wife and baby and Lætitia to await his return: but he was obliged to do without advisers or aids from the colony, as neither Hannah nor the daughter could be prevailed upon to stay without him. They went down on a yacht to New Castle, where the whole family embarked on the ship "Dolmahoy." The ship remained a few days afterwards at New Castle. About this time, Quary, sent for by persons in England to promote the abolition of Proprietary governments, found that there was a vessel about to sail from Virginia; so he hastened thither, in hopes of reaching England as soon as Penn. David Lloyd went to New Castle, and submitted to Penn a Charter of Property, which, at the entreaty of several persons, Penn signed and handed over to the Secretary with a paper, dated 8ber 31, explaining that he had not had time to digest the terms, especially as to courts, and postponed the complete passing of the Charter until he could see the state of affairs in England, that he could not give such rights to persons in Pennsylvania alone, this Charter not mentioning the Lower Counties, that he confirmed the part relating strictly to land: he accordingly in this paper ordered Governor Hamilton to have the great seal affixed at the end of six months, if no message were received to the contrary, and promised to execute such Charter or one which counsel in England would advise, as well as a suitable Charter of Property for the Lower Counties, if they wished it.

The "Dolmahoy" went aground in the Bay, but got off without much damage. Logan accompanied his master as far as the Capes, receiving a letter of instructions from him dated on shipboard, 9mo. 3. The remainder of the passage was a swift one, twenty-six days from land to soundings, thirty to Portsmouth. He sent back a message, dated January 8, 1701-2, annulling the Charter of Property, that is ordering the seal not to be put to it, unless within six months he should change his mind. This he did not do.

CHAPTER XIII.

GOVERNMENT BY PENN'S FRIENDS.

The new Frame of Government—The result of Penn's visit a reduction of the People's power.—Political situation of the Churchmen—Parmiter—Quary's military scheme—Andrew Hamilton and his namesake—Changes in the Council—Anne becomes Queen—Pennsylvanians ready to accept Lord Cornbury—War with France and a voluntary militia—Legislative separation from Lower Counties—Failure of bill to abolish Proprietary governments—Disagreement about trying capital cases—Hamilton approved for one year—Queen's order as to oaths—Hamilton's death—Shippen and fellow Councillors—Mompesson—Value of foreign coins—Indians and the traders among them—Approval of a Lieutenant-Governor—Lord Cornbury wanted by Churchmen—The Assemblymen chosen in 1703—Gov. Evans and William Penn Jr. arrive—New Councillors—The legislative separation of Lower Counties confirmed—Penn's reservation of assent to laws declared void—Assembly addresses Queen concerning oaths—Penn's financial circumstances—The Ford claim pressed—Penn asks for a house in Philadelphia and annuity—Penn offers to sell the government—Suggestion to pay Quary, Moore, et al. to leave—Solicitude of Penn's friends as to selling value of the Governorship.

The new Charter of Privileges, or written Constitution, had as its first clause practically the old law for liberty of conscience, and that all persons professing belief "in Jesus Christ the Saviour of the World" should be capable of serving the government on solemnly promising, when required, allegiance to the King, and fidelity to the Proprietor and Governor, and on taking the attests prescribed in the law passed at New Castle as recently amended and confirmed. Four members annually chosen from each county were to form an Assembly, the right to choose or be chosen being limited according to the law passed at New Castle. Two persons for each county were to be chosen triennially, from whom the Governor should select the Sheriff, and two from whom the Governor should select the Coroner, the Sheriff and Coroner serving three years. Criminals should have the same privileges of witnesses and counsel as their prosecutors. No person should answer relating to property before the Governor and Council or elsewhere than in the courts of justice, unless appeals were appointed by law. No person should keep a house of public entertainment unless licensed by the Governor upon recommendation by the county Justices. The estate of any person killing himself should descend as if he had died a natural death. The Charter could be changed or diminished in effect only by the Governor and six sevenths of the Assembly met. A postscript was added allowing within the next three years the representatives of either Pennsylvania or the Lower Counties by a majority vote to withdraw from the Assembly, and establish a separate legislature, that for Pennsylvania to consist of not less than eight members from each county and also two members from the town of Philadelphia.

When we compare the old constitution with this Frame and various other arrangements left by Penn, we can state the great result of his visit to have been a change of the government from one by the People to one by the Proprietary's friends. To be sure, while the City Corporation received somewhat greater powers than what the City's charter signed by Lloyd in 1691 had given, and the right to elect officers and fill vacancies had made the new as well as the old a close corporation, the body was independent, and the members appointed by the charter of the new to serve at first, except Shippen, the Mayor, and Story, the Recorder, and one or two others, could hardly be called Penn's close friends. Not so, however, as to province and county. Logan wrote some years later that Penn, at a time not specified, was inclined for an aristocracy, and had designed to give to an upper element control; but was thwarted by some individuals. If this was the case at the preparation of the Frame of 1701, it is to be inferred that David Lloyd was the chief obstructor. Far from being democratic, what Logan says was made republican, was made monarchic. Under the Frame of 1683, and even under that of 1696, the free men of Pennsylvania and Delaware after a short residence or at least those who had a little property, had been able not only to force or retard legislation, but, except within the sphere of the City charter of 1691, to control, by their delegates in the Provincial Council, the management of all public affairs. Under the Frame of 1701, the Governor had an absolute veto upon laws, and there was no Upper House elected to participate in executive business. All the power left in the People was that a part of the People could choose an Assembly, like the English House of Commons, to do only what the House of Commons at that time could do, viz: propose laws, and offer money. The acting Governor or the Governor-in-Chief behind him was to be supreme, like a local king—that is, a king of that day, no mere figure-head, like a modern constitutional monarch. Furthermore, the advisers of the acting Governor, like the contemporary cabinets of kings, and unlike to-day's Parliamentary ministries, were to be independent of the voters. It also can be said that, beginning with the first Hamilton, and until the close of this history, the Lieutenant-Governors personally had less in common with the inhabitants than those appointed before 1700. Of those earlier ones, Blackwell, to be sure, had been a stranger, but Markham was the leader whom the purchasers from Penn had followed to their new home, and Thomas Lloyd had the respect of the majority of the settlers as a preacher and sufferer for their religion, while the other Commissioners of State and the Assistants were such as the planters, left to their own judgment, might have elected.

One explanation of the change in the constitution, or a contributing motive for it, may have been the idea that only a ruler independent of the People can preserve the liberties of the minority, and Penn must have foreseen that the Quakers, for whose enjoyment of privileges his colony had been started, were about to become the minority in it. He left the government well organized against the Churchmen, likely to include the poorer immigrants of the future, and to bring into coalition with themselves the Lutherans, Presbyterians, and Baptists on the question of war and oaths. With the Quaker landholders preponderating in the Assembly, and with the judiciary filled as he had chosen, nothing contrary to the consciences of his fellow religionists could be imposed, except by the government in London, and, being in England, he might influence those officials to be considerate.

The active Churchmen wished the Province and Territories put under a Governor selected by the Cabinet ministers, and holding directly under the Crown. Quary carried over to England two addresses, one, dated Oct. 25, from eight representatives of the Lower Counties, Yeates, Halliwell, Adam Pieterson, Luke Wattson Jr., William Rodeney, John Brinckloe, John Walker, and John Donnaldson, complaining of Penn's giving no satisfaction about defence. Yeates at least was a Churchman, and in the Lower Counties the non-Quakers were strong. The other address was from the Minister and some of the Vestry of Christ Church, dated Oct. 27, setting forth certain failures of justice under Quaker control of the judiciary. Rather ungratefully, we should say, John Moore signed this: he was both Register-General of Wills and Attorney-General by Penn's appointment, and was drawing, as Attorney-General, a salary directly from Penn.

Except in the case of Moore and of two or three persons sent over by Penn to hold office, the political circumstances of an Episcopalian residing in the Upper Counties at this time were not pleasant. In more cases than among the Quakers, he was one of the poor disqualified from voting, yet obliged to pay a tax. If, however, he had the ability and standing fitting him for office, he was discriminated against by the voters. Everybody was taxed for a gratuity to William Penn, to help pay for his having been a great man at Court, and other parts of his career which did not interest, or were disapproved of by Churchmen, and the net result of which was the maintenance on the Delaware of the political power of men who would not administer, much less require, an oath, and would not authorize, much less take part in, the defence of the colony. It may be said that the Quakers had a right to the country which they had planted, and that the dissatisfied minority should have left: but that course naturally did not commend itself even to such as could afford to remove: they were adhering to the ecclesiastical organization and customs adopted by the Anglo-Saxon race, and Pennsylvania comprised an extensive region, one of the best under the English Crown.

Penn had intended the superseding of Moore as Attorney-General, but the commission for that purpose to Paroculus Parmiter, if signed, was not made use of, it being learned that Parmiter, who was one of Penn's kindred, had been convicted at Bristol, England, of the capital crime of forgery, but pardoned. Penn commissioned Markham on 5, 27, 1703, as Register-General, but Moore claimed a freehold in the office, withheld the official seal, and sued Markham, but, after the latter's death, abandoned or lost the case.

Quary, who remained in England until July, 1702, suggested, but did not succeed in having taken up, the following solution of the problem of defence, viz: that in every colony all freemen and all immigrants be obliged to enroll themselves in a company of militia, the poor as foot soldiers, the rich as dragoons: but that Quakers and others with scruples against bearing arms were to certify their opinion in writing, and, in place of bearing arms, to do an equivalent in some public work, and to furnish their quota agreeable to their estates, said quota to be laid out in providing arms, ammunition, and all warlike stores.

Andrew Hamilton, who met the Council on November 14, 1701, and to whom Logan was instructed to make up an allowance of 200*l*. per annum until royal approbation of the appointment, and 300*l*. thereafter, was a native of Scotland, and had acted as Governor of one or both of the provinces of New Jersey at different times since 1689, and is mentioned in another chapter as having started an inter-colonial postal service. When Quary, before the Board of Trade, made the point against Penn of his leaving Hamilton as acting Governor without the royal approbation, Penn pleaded the necessity of the case. He had obtained the opinion of William Attwood, Chief Justice at New York, that the deputizing by a Governor-in-Chief was good until the King could be informed. Penn explained that he had chosen Hamilton because there was no other non-Quaker at hand fit for the position except Markham, whom the Crown had so lately ordered to be removed from it. Quary said that there were several others, who were, moreover, less liable to objection. Hamilton had been careful of Quaker interests in New Jersey, but was not personally disliked by the Churchmen. He had probably adhered to the episcopally governed clergy both in Scotland and in London, where he is said to have been a merchant.

In the late years of his life, he befriended a young Scotchman, said to have been born in Edinburgh about 1676, who took the name of Andrew Hamilton while residing in the Virginia or Maryland "Eastern Shore," and with such name appears in history, being the greatest lawyer of his day in Pennsylvania. He is said to have emigrated from Scotland in such needs as to have his time sold to a planter, because fleeing from an actual or impending charge of murder, as the result of a fight. Despite all that has been surmised, there was probably nothing interesting about the paternity of the fugitive. He had sufficient education to assist his second employer in teaching school, and, as he at one time bore the name of Trent, he may have been related to William Trent, the Pennsylvania Councillor, or more closely to Maurice Trent, who was early in New Jersey, and afterwards of Leith, Scotland.

Without raising the objection of Hamilton's appointment not having been confirmed, Halliwell, Moore, and Yeates, three of those authorized by a document known as a *"dedimus potestatem"* to administer to the Governor of Pennsylvania the oath required by the Act of 7 & 8 Wm. III, very captiously refused to administer the oath to Hamilton, unless the *dedimus potestatem* were surrendered to them. The Council thought the Secretary or the Master of the Rolls the proper custodian, and, as the document gave to any five of the Council with the Collector of the Port the same power as to those particularly named, Councillors Guest, Samuel Finney, and John Finney with John Bewley, Collector of the Port, administered the oath in presence of

Councillors Carpenter, Clark, and Pusey, who joined in signing the certificate.

The membership of the Governor's Council, a few months after its establishment, was slightly changed by the death of Phineas Pemberton, Penn's staunchest friend in Bucks Co., and the admission, in accordance with Penn's wishes, of John Finney, eldest son of Samuel Finney. On the same day as John Finney, viz: April 21, 1702, Logan qualified as a member.

On the death of William III, March 8, 1701-2, Queen Mary having died previously, her sister Anne, wife of Prince George of Denmark, succeeded to the throne. Staunch as she was for the Anglican Church, she was no enemy to her old acquaintance, Penn, the friend of her father, James II. In a letter of July 14, 1706, unsigned but attributed to Penn, the writer speaks of his own steady and secret (private) and public services to her in many ways, for which not everybody besides himself had the power or talent.

Edward Hyde, by courtesy Viscount Cornbury, son of the Queen's uncle, Henry, 2nd Earl of Clarendon, having been appointed Governor of New York and Commander of the Militia of the Jerseys and Connecticut by the late King, came to Burlington in June, 1702, and was invited to Philadelphia, where he spent the night at Shippen's, and, with a retinue thirty in number, was entertained at the Proprietary's expense at as handsome a dinner, it was said, as his Lordship had seen in America. The next day, he was escorted from Burlington to Pennsbury, and there entertained, about fifty being in company. By his manners, the Quakers were so much pleased with this cousin of the Queen that they thought, that, if proprietary government were abolished, they would be satisfied to have him as Governor. Furthermore, they were becoming indifferent to the bill before Parliament, if only certain privileges could be retained, the more spiritually minded thinking that acts of government were foreign to their profession, and those who loved Penn feeling that his life would be easier, and he probably happier, if he had the Proprietaryship only. Naturally, there was, however, a desire that the reflections upon the Quakers' conduct of affairs should be dispelled, and that the country should not fall under the control of the non-Quaker partisans, who had cast such reflections.

On July 10, 1702, without the receipt of an order from the English government, but preparatory to inviting those inclined to form a militia, in view of the new war against France and Spain, proclamation of Anne's accession was made. On the 24th, the war was proclaimed. In a few days, one company of militia was started. George Lowther, a lawyer from Nottinghamshire, but of a Yorkshire family, was made the captain. But the enrolment was not a success. The Churchmen wished it a failure, so that the English government would think it necessary to take the dominions into its own hands. The Quakers could not join the colors on account of their principles. There was, moreover, an idea that those who joined would be required to proceed to Canada. So, after great efforts, only about a score or two of the poorest men, with only six swords among them, and, we are told, just as deficient in shoes and stockings, mustered for a review.

The Aldermen of the City claimed in 1702 the right to act as Justices in the Court of Common Pleas for both County and City; and, when Hamilton and some lawyers thought them wrong, and Capt. Finney, the head of those commissioned for the County, refused to sit with the Aldermen, the Mayor's Court was held, and all fines for offences in the cognizance of those Aldermen, including fines of keepers of public houses for selling without a license, were claimed. Penn, hearing of this, hoped for some change of feeling, but was inclined to recall the corporation's charter, as certain lawyers thought he could legally, and he was confident that the English government would approve.

Quary making charges against Penn in particular and the Quakers in general, to show their malfeasance as a cause for abolishing their government, and Penn answering, and making counter charges against Quary, there was a fruitless contention, some of the papers in which appear in the printed *Penn and Logan Correspondence.* Quary returned to America with a letter from the Commissioners of Trade, desiring him to acquaint the gentlemen of the Lower Counties of their letter of Oct. 25, 1701, being under consideration for their relief, and to assure them of the Queen's protection and care for their welfare and security. Quary also brought a letter of protection from the Queen requiring all Governors, Lieutenant-Governors, magistrates, and officers civil and military to assist him. Both letters are printed in *Virginia Mag. Hist. & Biog.,* Vol. XXIII.

The people of the Lower Counties did not like the Charter, or Frame of Government of the Province and Territories, granted on Oct. 28, 1701, because, according to Quary, of the toleration of Deists and of the eligibility of Papists to office; and there was a denial of the validity of the Charter, in view of its not having been agreed to by a clear majority of the Assembly. On the day for the first election for Assemblymen under the Charter, none were chosen by the Lower Counties. The Upper Counties, comprising Pennsylvania proper, or the Province strictly so called, chose the required number, viz: Joseph Growdon, John Swift, William Paxon (now Paxson), Jeremiah Langhorne, David Lloyd, Anthony Morris, Samuel Richardson, Griffith Jones (formerly mentioned as a Quaker), Nicholas Pyle, Andrew Job, John Bennet, and John Worrall. These arrived in Philadelphia at the time for organizing the House, and, acting upon the default of the Lower Counties, declared the disunion spoken of in the Charter to have taken place, and accordingly asked for the increase provided for in such case in the number of representatives of Bucks, Chester, and Philadelphia, including two from the City.

At this time, William Penn's title to the government and territory of New Castle &ct. was being strongly questioned in England. Hamilton and the friends of Penn saw that the relations of the two parts of the dual colony required conciliation or at least temporizing: so Hamilton pleaded with the representatives of the Province not to take the radical measure. He pointed out that tobacco, which was the chief commodity sent to England, and was mostly furnished by the Territories, would be so incumbered by a separate legislature at the place of growth as to divert the trade from Philadelphia. The inhabitants of the Territories were very likely, upon the erection of a distinct Assembly for the Province, to remonstrate to the Queen, and pray that they, being thrown off and left destitute, be taken under her immediate protection: and such remonstrance would probably be taken advantage of by the officials in England desirous of weakening Proprietary government, and cause the royal approbation of Penn's appointment of the Lieutenant-Governor to be restricted to Pennsylvania. If the Assemblymen were bent upon a separation from the Lower Counties, it would be better first to wait to see whether, as the result of the questioning of Penn's title to those Counties, the Queen would make the separation, in which case the Pennsylvanians would not incur blame. As to increasing the number of representatives, the Lieutenant-Governor could not see how it could be done until the next election appointed by the Charter, the first of October following. The Assemblymen, nearly all being Quakers, were inclined to insist, declaring that, by the union, the first purchasers from Penn had been unable to have the privileges they had expected. However, it being thought that the Lower Counties might elect representatives, if summoned to do so by writs, writs were issued, and the Assemblymen from Pennsylvania agreed to await the result. The Lower Counties duly chose representatives, but these expressed unwillingness to sit with members chosen under direction of the Charter, which the Lower Counties did not recognize. The Assemblymen from Pennsylvania, coming back to Philadelphia, were willing to join with those chosen by the Lower Counties, but would do so only on the basis of the Charter being in force. Although there was a letter from the English government through Lord Cornbury requiring a contribution to the fortification of the frontiers at Albany, and there seemed a necessity for a law for a militia composed of those without scruples against bearing arms, so as to repel invasion from the sea, Hamilton could only dismiss the legislators. Then the twelve representatives of Philadelphia, Bucks, and Chester certified under hand and seal that they desired the filling up of the body for the Province according to the Charter, with two members from the City, and so that Philadelphia County should have eight members, Bucks nine, and Chester nine. It does not seem as if such disparity for the rural districts was intended by Penn when he said that each county should "not have less than eight persons;" and Griffith Jones, in joining the other representatives, excepted against the extra member from Bucks and Chester.

The bill for the abolition of proprietary governments had failed to pass at the session of Parliament during which Penn decided to go to England to fight the bill: but it was subsequently pressed by the persons connected with the governmental bureaus in London. Penn suggested such modification as would reunite the military government to the Crown, and give to the

Commander-in-Chief the superintendence of the Customs and Admiralty officials, but leave the civil authority as it stood, just as in corporations in England where the King's appointee was Governor, and, moreover, allow appeal to the King on all matters above £300, and, besides, give to the King a veto on all laws. This modification the Lords for Trade rejected, declaring that the original bill "might be very expedient." The Proprietors of the Jerseys had been prevailed upon to surrender their rights of government: but when the question came of taking away such rights against the will of those invested with them, the nobles and knights of the shires in Parliament, accustomed to offices, jurisdictions, and perquisites as freeholds, appear to have felt that such an act would be an invasion of private property. The chance to make a bargain with the Crown was thus left open to the Proprietary of Pennsylvania, to be availed of as will be narrated later.

Although the Act of Assembly directing attests, which was still in force because not yet repealed by the Crown, prescribed the qualifying of Judges and jurors by merely solemnly promising, and the Act relating to the manner of giving evidence, also in force, allowed witnesses to qualify in the same way, the rather shallow Churchman of the legal profession, John Guest, whom Penn had made Chief Justice of the Provincial Court, and ex-merchant Finney, the other Churchman on that bench, were unwilling to condemn a criminal to death on testimony not sworn to, or at least the testimony of persons who had no scruples against oaths, but were unsworn; on the other hand, the other Judges, Shippen, Clark, and Thomas Masters, Quakers, were restrained by conscience from administering oaths. In the absence of Clark, resulting in the impossibility of "three of a kind" holding court, Hamilton issued a commission of jail delivery to Guest and

Finney and Edward Farmer, who also was willing to take and administer oaths; but, the cases for trial being such as involved the death penalty, another horn of the dilemma was reached, viz: Hamilton's confirmation as acting Governor not having been obtained, his commission would not be sufficient foundation for taking away the life of an English subject. So the accused remained in jail, until Clark's return gave the Quakers a quorum commissioned by Penn himself.

The Commissioners for Trade and Plantations objected to the approbation of Hamilton as acting Governor, because he was under the imputation of having encouraged illegal trade in the Jerseys. Finally Penn petitioned Queen Anne that Hamilton be confirmed for one year. She expressed herself in Council as inclined so to gratify the petitioner, and on November 11, 1702, the approbation of Hamilton as Deputy-Governor of the Province and Territories for one year was given, on condition that Penn or others enter the usual security in £2000 for the Governor's observance of the Acts of Parliament relating to trade, and on condition that Penn answer certain questions put to him by the Board of Trade as to oaths or affirmations in Pennsylvania and Territories, and as to the rate at which Spanish dollars were current there, &ct. Penn's answers were laid before the Board on December 1, and were viewed as not altogether satisfactory, but, for the dispatch of business, the Commissioners were willing to let matters proceed. The order giving the approbation having stipulated that it was not to set aside or diminish the Queen's title to the Lower Counties, the Commissioners insisted that Penn sign a declaration to that effect in the form drafted by them. This he did on December 10. The entering of security made further delay, and the final certificate under which Hamilton was authorized to act did not reach Philadelphia before he died.

The Queen in Council ordered on January 21, 1702-3,

that all persons in judicial or other office in Pennsylvania or the Lower Counties, before entering on their duties, take the oath directed by the laws of England, involving allegiance, abhorrence of the doctrine as to excommunicated princes, declaration against foreign princes, non-belief in transubstantiation, &ct. (as in a former chapter), or take the affirmation allowed in England to Quakers, involving the same points as the oaths, and also the subscription to faith in the Trinity and inspiration of the Scriptures; and she further ordered that all persons willing to take an oath in public proceedings be allowed to do so, otherwise the proceedings to be null and void. This order was as far as possible followed: Penn, not on the spot, blamed his colonists for obeying what they had a good defence against. He with his freemen's consent was authorized to make laws which were to be in force until disapproved, and by such laws had covered the case of the qualifying of officers, requiring only a promise of fidelity to the Sovereign and the Proprietary and promise to perform the respective duties. Acts of Parliament did not bind the American settlements, to override local laws or the common law of England, unless the American settlements were mentioned in the Act, and they were not mentioned in the Acts prescribing these tests, or relating to Quakers' affirmations. The order did not arrive in Pennsylvania until one of the criminals whom the special court had failed to try, was on the point of being hung. The Provincial Court, meeting on April 10, 1703, had tried two cases of murder without any oath or affirmation being given, although certain non-Quaker Judges and Moore, the Attorney-General, declined to take part, a substituted prosecuting attorney being secured. A man was convicted of manslaughter, for which, as an offence within "the benefit of clergy," he was burnt in the hand, and another person—some say a woman for killing her child—was convicted of murder, and was sentenced to death. The warrant for the execution was sent to Hamilton at Amboy, East Jersey, but he was too ill to sign it, and, without doing so, died two days later. When this sentencing to death after trial by Quaker jurors not sworn, and not attested in manner prescribed by Parliament, was brought to the attention of the Lords for Trade through Lord Cornbury, Penn took the reasonable ground that a colony and constitution of government made by and for Quakers could not be expected to leave them and their lives and fortunes out of so essential a part of government as juries, otherwise the founders of the country would have stayed at home.

Hamilton's death occurred on 2mo. (April) 26, 1703: his illness had lasted over nine weeks. It may be said that he never settled in Pennsylvania. The Council succeeded to the executive functions.

Edward Shippen, who had occasionally presided over the Council in Hamilton's absence, thus became the highest person in the colony, and so continued for about ten months. He had been converted to Quakerism by or upon marriage with a Quakeress. The disadvantages of having a President and other executives who could not conscientiously administer an oath first arose as to registering vessels. The arrangement hit upon by the Council was that John Bewley, the Collector of the Port, administer the oath in the Council Chamber, and the Secretary certify it, and the seal of the Province be affixed: but Colonel Quary declared such method repugnant to the words of the law, and that he would be obliged to suspend Bewley, if he did this. The Queen's order having then arrived, and the Councillors deciding to comply with it, and that it was necessary as acting Governor to take oath or affirmation under the Acts relating to trade, they sent for Quary, Halliwell, Moore, and Yeates, commissioners under the old *dedi-*

mus potestatem, to administer such oath, but those men adhered to the letter of their commission as authorizing an oath only, and to be taken by one Governor, so that it could not be administered to less than all the members, or at least a quorum, *i.e.* five. The commissioners were supposed to have seized with pleasure upon this legal objection to starting the machinery of justice, and Halliwell is reported, in a letter from Quaker Councillors to Penn, to have boasted that the commissioners had laid the government on its back, and left it sprawling, unable to move hand or foot. Acting under the alternative in the *dedimus,* by which the Council and the Collector of the Port could administer qualifications, Bewley, the Collector, was induced to administer the oath to Guest and Finney. Shippen, Carpenter, Clark, Owen, and Pusey made affirmation for the performance of the same duty. All made oath or declaration acknowledging fidelity, abhorring the Pope's supremacy, &ct. Subsequently Guest and Finney appear to have administered in Council the oath for registering vessels.

Roger Mompesson, a lawyer, who had been Recorder of Southampton, and twice elected to Parliament, secured appointment as Judge of the Admiralty for Pennsylvania and Lower Counties, New Jersey, and New York, coming to America, and making his residence in Philadelphia, in 5mo., 1703, to lead a "simple life," so as to pay debts, for which he was bound, although contracted by his father. Thus Quary was superseded, but he was appointed Surveyor-General of the Customs. Penn hoped that the colony would make sufficient allowance to induce Mompesson to take also the Chief Justiceship of the Provincial Court.

When the Justices of Chester County offered to qualify under the Queen's order, Yeates induced Walter Martin, who had a *dedimus potestatem* for administering the affirmations, to insist upon the declaration

GOVERNMENT BY PENN'S FRIENDS. 419

against the "pretended Prince of Wales", as recently prescribed by Act of Parliament, but those commissioned refused, because the Act did not extend to the Province, and the Queen's order did not mention that oath or the affirmation in its place. In the other counties, and apparently in Chester later, the qualifications mentioned in her order were taken. In the Philadelphia court, Hugh Durborow, a Quaker, called upon to give testimony, refused to use the form speaking of the presence of God. Guest was here reasonable, and, apparently, with him enough Quaker Justices to make a majority favored letting Durborow affirm as he pleased,—for he certainly testified,—although all the non-Quakers wished him committed for contempt of court. In one case in Philadelphia, when some witnesses were about to be sworn, the Quaker Justices left the bench, but Justices Guest, Samuel Finney, Edward Farmer, and Andrew Bankson held court.

The trouble about administering oaths caused the introduction of more non-Quakers into executive and judicial office, and, with the presence in the dominion of a sharp-witted faction watching for questionable proceedings, it was imperative that the government have a non-Quaker chief on the spot. Logan suggested that, pending the appointment of a Lieutenant-Governor, a new Council be commissioned with Mompesson, who was a Churchman, at its head, and Logan later hoped that Penn was making Mompesson Lieutenant-Governor.

The Commissioners for Trade exerted themselves against the Assembly's enhancement of the value of foreign coin, one of the acts of Nov. 27, 1700, having, with slight modification of a former act, made a Peru piece of eight weighing not less than 12 dwt., as well as a Lion or Dog dollar, pass for 6s., and every other piece of eight or dollar weighing 15 dwt., for 7s., with an advance or abatement respectively of 4d. for every pennyweight in excess or shortage; the price of smaller coins being also fixed. A representation for the disallowance of the Act was made to the Queen, pointing out that a piece of eight of the due weight, stated to be 17 dwt. 6 gr., so made current at 7*s.* 10*d.*, was intrinsically worth no more than 4*s.* 6*d.* On July 30, 1703, the Act was disallowed. The English government, at Penn's suggestion that there should be a general standard, was inclined to make the value of these foreign coins in the colonies the same as in England, but this had been prevented, or at least seemed too difficult, the late King having consented to a law of New England fixing a different value there. The next best thing was to make all the other colonies conform to the one: accordingly, on the 18th of June following the disallowance of the Pennsylvania law, the Queen issued a proclamation fixing the value from the 1st of the coming January at the New England rate. Thereby pieces of eight of Seville or Mexico or Pillar pieces, which had been passing in Pennsylvania for eight shillings, were to pass for six shillings only. Subsequently an Act of Parliament confirmed this, to be enforced from May 1, 1709.

After the failure, in Hamilton's time, of the attempt to form a voluntary militia, the consciences of the President and many Councillors restrained them from taking any part in the war. They were free, however, to enforce police authority upon persons within their jurisdiction who might commit injuries, or bring about injuries; and accordingly the Council undertook to watch such suspicious characters as Frenchmen, and particularly those travelling through the Indian country. The danger of the Five Nations casting their lot with the French always existed, except when the English had actually engaged the warriors for a campaign: and, although no breach of the alliance of those tribes with the government of New York actually took place during the period of this history, there was fear that "foolish young men" of the Iroquois, or of their nominal subjects or tributaries, would be stirred up against the settlers of Pennsylvania. Of the traders whom the provincial government distrusted, the treatment was severe. Capt. Le Tort's son James, brought up from infancy in the province, had gone to Canada in time of peace, but, after about two years' stay, returned to Pennsylvania in the Spring of 1703, submitting to various examinations, and appearing to be innocent of evil designs. He and Peter Bezellon, who was under still stronger suspicion, because then a Roman Catholic, coming to Philadelphia in August following, were bound in the heavy bail of £500 stg. each to hold no correspondence with the enemy, and to give all information coming to their knowledge. About a year later, and after a Lieutenant-Governor had taken charge, Le Tort was some time in jail in Philadelphia, and was obliged, for obtaining his liberty, to give security in 1000*l.*; while Nicholas Gateau, the French cook, who had been naturalized, but had tried to leave Philadelphia secretly to escape, he said, his creditors, was also detained in jail, and required to give security in 1000*l.* for good behavior, and not to go out of the jurisdiction, or further from the city than twenty-five miles up or down the Delaware River, or than ten miles back into the country.

On hearing of Hamilton's death, Penn wrote quickly to the Lords for Trade, asking them, in the emergency, to recommend either Markham or John Finney for royal approbation as successor; so that the opportunity of a vessel then lading for America be seized for communicating proper authority to some one in the Province and Territories. The Board aforesaid, while making the reply that it was requisite to make the first application to her Majesty, let Penn see that the feeling against Markham had not changed. Penn not knowing how he was to furnish security for Finney, it appears that Charlewood Lawton, Penn's agent, suggested for the Lieutenant-Governorship, a personal acquaintance, able to furnish his own security, having some political influence, and for some reason willing to accept, viz: John Evans, about twenty-six years old, whose father had been a friend of the Proprietary. It seems from certain expressions in the *Penn and Logan Correspondence* that Evans was a nephew of Rt. Rev. Dr. John Evans, a strong Whig, made Bishop of Bangor on Jany. 2, 1702. Penn quickly took what was within reach. In a few days after the aforesaid letter to the Board, his petition for young Evans was laid before the Queen. The Board, having the matter referred to it, asked for information concerning him. To gain the favor of the Earl of Nottingham, then a Secretary of State, Evans, entitled to a bond of Baron Dartmouth to Evans's father, who had been treasurer of a political fund, released or cancelled the bond. Dartmouth had married a niece of Nottingham. Dartmouth himself was one of the Commissioners for Trade and Plantations. After Penn's explaining that Evans was not under the objection of being a merchant, and, although not a soldier, had seen the army in Flanders, was a gentleman living on his estate, and was a hearty Churchman, and would be recommended by a number of persons, the Board put no obstacles in the way of the approbation. It was given on July 30, 1703. Penn again signed a declaration that the Queen's title to the Lower Counties should not be diminished by her giving the approbation. Evans not only furnished the security for his own behavior, but actually reimbursed Penn for all that had been spent in obtaining approbation for Hamilton. Penn, according to his letter of 12, 9, 1705-6, promised Evans 200*l*. Penna. money per annum until the Assembly would grant a support.

Lord Cornbury, coming to Burlington in August,

1703, after appointment as Governor of New Jersey, was waited upon by Quary and other Philadelphia Churchmen, and was reported to have received an address from vestrymen or attendants of Christ Church requesting him to solicit the Queen for the embracing of Pennsylvania and probably Delaware under his government. He was said to have answered that he would obey the Queen's orders with alacrity when orders to such effect came. Notwithstanding that he was staying at Quary's, Cornbury was again entertained by the Quakers in Philadelphia: but they began to dread his being appointed in place of Penn, seeing that Quary and Moore would probably be Cornbury's advisers as to Pennsylvania affairs, that the royal commission to him as Governor of New Jersey gave him great powers, and required him to administer oaths, including that against the Pretender, and said nothing about affirmations, and that a man of such rank would expect a large salary.

In October, 1703, eight Assemblymen from each county of Pennsylvania, and two from the City of Philadelphia, were chosen; they met, and elected Lloyd as Speaker, and made the disunion of the Province from the Territories an accomplished fact. These Assemblymen were: Nicholas Pyle, John Bennet, Andrew Job, David Lewis, Nathaniel Newlin, Joseph Baker, Robert Carter, Joseph Wood, William Biles, Joseph Growdon, Tobias Dymmoke, Richard Hough, William Paxton, Jeremiah Langhorne, Joshua Hoopes, Thomas Stevenson, Rowland Ellis, Nicholas Waln, Samuel Richardson, Isaac Norris, David Lloyd, Anthony Morris, Samuel Cart, Griffith Jones, Joseph Willcox, and Charles Read.

Although Griffith Jones refused at first to do more in the way of qualifying than promise allegiance to the Crown and fidelity to the government, yet in due time all the twenty-six representatives signed the confession of faith, declarations, test, &ct., as in the Act of Parliament of 1 W. & M. c. 18.

The Council construing the commission to themselves as not giving power to enact laws, the Assembly resolved to adjourn until 3mo. (May) 1, contending for the right to sit upon their own adjournment. The result was that the Assembly adjourned until that date, unless sooner called, and the Council declared it prorogued to the same time: but the dispute gave rise to a project to establish the House's right by a law.

Evans published his commission in Philadelphia on 12mo. 3, 1703-4, having arrived the night before, and duly took the oaths, the least fitted by experience of all the persons selected by the Penns for the office, and, as it turned out, the most discreditable in private life. To intemperance, which was soon the topic of common talk, there was added in time an item of seduction. The great Quaker had been deceived; for William Penn, distracted as he may have been with financial and political troubles in England, and important as it was to fill the vacancy quickly, was too wise knowingly to send as his representative one whose loose living would shock the staid people of the colony, and give a handle to the anti-Proprietary faction. Apart and aloof from the Churchmen were some persons resentful against or distrustful of Penn who were rigid Quakers, and would appeal to the ideal of a land where good men administered good laws.

Yet, as will be shown on a later page, a handle for Penn's enemies was to be given by one very near to him, viz: his eldest surviving son, who came with Evans, and whose debts had driven him across the water, leaving wife and children at home to await future plans. He speedily, in connection with Logan, hired for a city residence "Clark's great house" near the S. W. corner of Third and Chestnut. Mompesson soon joined them, and so did Evans, after boarding first with Al Paxton, and afterwards with John Finney. For information on business, but not guidance in mode of life, Evans and Penn Jr. looked to Logan. Having as Judge jurisdiction as far north as New Hampshire, and being in turn very soon superseded as to Pennsylvania and West Jersey by a new commission reappointing Quary, Mompesson was usually away. He and William Penn Jr. and Bewley, the Collector, were invited to become members of the Council. Mompesson qualified on February 7, and the younger Penn on the 8th, but Bewley declined, because the position might be thought by some to conflict with his position in the Customs. Logan appears to have qualified a second time, immediately after the qualifying of the Proprietary's son, to whom was given precedence at the board over all others. In the course of ten days after Evans's arrival, William Rodeney, William Trent, Richard Hill, and Jasper Yeates became members, and in May, George Roche, and in October, Joseph Pidgeon.

Evans had come ignorant of there being a split in the Assembly, and, when he found it necessary to summon a legislature, he determined, if possible, to effect a reunion. He sent writs to the Lower Counties for the election of four members each, but when the twenty-six already chosen by Pennsylvania proper appeared, they insisted that they were already a separate House. The representatives of the Territories, among whom were Rodeney, Brinckloe, and Hill, thereupon announced their consent to accept the Charter, if its provision were complied with that there be only four representatives from each of the six counties. The representatives from Pennsylvania replied that they were unable to recede from what they had done, including the increase of their number. So it was settled there should be a separate House for the Territories, its members to be chosen by new writs, and to meet in New Castle.

When the Assembly of the Province convened, Evans asked for a salary for himself, and the raising of the £350 fixed by the late King for the building of fortifications in the province of New York. The House, in a very courteous message, expressed anxiety as to the allowance of the laws by the Crown, and referred to the former excuse as to the £350. In a reply, which again urged the relief of the Proprietary by the assumption of the acting Governor's support, and even asked for making good Penn's promise of allowance to Hamilton, Evans angered the members by arguing the insufficiency of the excuse for not voting money to the Queen.

More serious than Evans's wounding of the Assemblymen's sensibilities in contradicting their mind, was that Penn's commission to Evans had reserved the final assent to all laws. This instance of depriving the Deputy of the power to represent the principal had to be brought to the scrutiny of so acute and so ill disposed a lawyer as Lloyd, and nearly caused the Assembly to declare the commission void. The heir-apparent's most important political act while in America was joining with the other Councillors, Mompesson among them, in deciding, in response to the Assembly's question, that the clause was void, but did not invalidate the rest of the commission, and that the bills which the Lieutenant-Governor passed into laws, and to which the great seal was affixed, could not be annulled by the Proprietary without the vote of the Assembly. This declaration was made on 3rd month 23, 1704. Logan, while saying that it was clearly right, explained to Penn that the Councillors would not have made it, had they not seen that the Assembly would do nothing without it.

After the Assembly had voted an address to the Queen congratulating her upon her accession, the obliviousness of the members to their representing any but one religious denomination was shown in entitling another address to her, which they unanimously adopted, "The humble address of the People called Quakers convened in Assembly at Philadelphia." By the prayer with which this Address closed, we see that the Assemblymen, and presumably most of their Quaker constituents, were willing to make affirmation "in the presence of Almighty God." The Address said that, at the time of the grant to Penn, the tract called Pennsylvania was little cultivated, and the few inhabitants were Dutch, Fins, and Swedes, "whose manner of living was of small advantage to the Crown of England;" that, in hopes of enjoying the liberties granted, a considerable colony of Quakers with some of other persuasions came over, and made great improvements, and others differing from them in religious matters had become sharers of the government, which was carried on by the obligation of a solemn attestation under the local laws, without oaths, the taking or administering of which was against the religious persuasion of the Quakers, still the most considerable inhabitants for number and estates; that some of the Quakers who might be serviceable in courts of judicature were excluded by the effect of the royal order in Council of Jany. 21, 1702, requiring the administration of oaths to those willing to take them; that those who wished to introduce oaths had often declared their willingness to take the said solemn affirmation wherever the life of a subject was not in question: therefore those addressing the Queen prayed her to grant that the affirmation prescribed by Act of Parliament to be taken by Quakers might be allowed to all persons and on all occasions instead of an oath. The Assembly drafted a provincial law to this effect, to be adopted when the Queen showed herself favorable. Evans, on the other hand, issued a proclamation declaring the judicial proceedings null and void when carried on without oath.

Penn's financial circumstances were by this time distracting. He had paid, but not promptly, some of the interest on the Ford account accruing since April 1, 1697. Ford, however, had seen by the time of Penn's second arrival in America that there would be a default in paying the redemption money on April 1, 1700, and had determined to stand upon the rights which the face of the papers executed between Penn and himself gave him. "Not having the fear of God before his eyes," as many men and many women have not when making their wills, although such action, if unrecalled, will be the parting act of their lives, Philip Ford made a will dated Jany. 21, 1699, speaking of his having purchased Pennsylvania and Delaware, and giving said land to trustees to sell. He made a proviso that, if in Ford's lifetime or within six months after his death, William Penn paid £11134 8s. 3d., and all arrears still due on April 1 following the date of the will, and all other debts due, the trustees should convey the land to Penn: but this proviso, Ford declared to be a voluntary kindness to Penn, and not the result of any obligation. By April 1, 1700, Penn had not by redeeming prevented such a will from becoming operative, and, on April 1, 1701, the lease had expired with the rent about paid up. Ford died on Jany. 8, 1701 (O. S. ?). His widow and children, beneficiaries of his will, had an account stated with Penn, by which he owed on April 1, 1702, £591 8s. 10d. over and above the principal represented by the redemption price. Although he continued to pay at short intervals small amounts, it was impossible for him to pay the principal.

There was, to be sure, a large amount of indebtedness due apparently from Americans for land, Logan holding bonds in 1705 for about 2000l., but the realization of such must await the debtors' pleasure and ability. Penn appears to have brought home to England no ready money but what was soon called for, nor did he find any considerable balance awaiting him there. Much lobbying against the bill to abolish proprietary government had been done by William Jr. It was an age of fees instead of salaries, and consequently of perquisites, extortion, and corruption. The elder Penn rather complained that the young agent, in his zeal, had promised too much. Apart from anything like bribery of statesmen, the mere attendance upon them involved outlay. The cost of the Proprietary's sojourn in London after return from America, and other expenses to fight the aforesaid bill, to promote the allowance of the laws, and to attend to other affairs of the colony, were said by him to have been over £3000 by July, 1704. Besides there was the money to be paid to make up the income of Lætitia's dowry, and to supplement for William Jr.'s wants the estate of Worminghurst, which, moreover, being absorbed by William Jr., had ceased to be profitable to the family at large. William Jr. was living at his father's expense during the stay in Pennsylvania. The Proprietary was chagrined when he found that he was to maintain two houses, that at Pennsbury, and the Clark house, which the heir-apparent, instead of boarding when not at Pennsbury, hired for a city residence for himself and the Secretary. Little money was coming from Pennsylvania, where the cost of administration took so much of the ordinary receipts. The tax imposed for the Proprietary's benefit was withheld by many; the impost in its second year became inconsiderable, because the previous drought in Barbados lessened the amount of rum coming thence to Pennsylvania to one third as much as had been coming; the subscriptions to the Susquehanna venture to a great extent failed to be paid, and what payments were made were in wheat and flour; partly because of the war, sales of land were pretty much at an end; and quit rents were usually in arrears. When there was any balance to be put into William Penn's hands, such was the scarcity in the colony of cash, and of bills of exchange on England, that, practically, the only way of forwarding the amount was to invest in a cargo, and ship the same at the risk of bad market, storm, and capture. A number of vessels trading from Pennsylvania were taken.

Penn's principal source of revenue had once been his estate in Ireland. He wrote, 12, 24, 1702, that that country had "hardly any money: England severe to her, no trade but hither and at England's mercy for prices, saving butter and meat to Flanders and the West Indies, that we must go and eat out half our rents, or we cannot enjoy them;" and he mentioned that the exchange from Ireland to England was twenty-six per cent.

In these difficulties, as he found that his Governorship was not likely to be taken forcibly from him by Parliament, he thought of making a sale of it to the Crown. While waiting an opportunity for this, or as an alternative, he devised an arrangement for his return to Pennsylvania, asking, in a letter of 2mo. 1, 1703, for "the town"—probably the well-to-do citizens of Philadelphia—to build for him on one of his City lots or his liberty land "a pretty box like Ed. Shippen's," or to purchase Griffith Owen's, Thomas Fairman's, Daniel Pegg's, or any such house, Pennsbury house being too small to hold the entire family including William Penn Jr's; and, in addition to this present, costing, Penn supposed, 500*l.* to 600*l.*, he wished an allowance, perhaps by tax, of 500*l.* a year. There was no response to this.

Penn wrote on May 11, 1703, to the Board of Trade, that, seeing the bent extremely strong to bring all proprietary governments directly under the Crown, he was willing, if there could be a just regard for his and

his people's security in their civil rights according to
the laws and constitution of the country, to resign the
government, saving some few privileges, upon a reasonable pecuniary satisfaction to him. The Commissioners wishing to know his terms, he sent word in the
following month: the Lower Counties—he meant the
soil therof—were to be duly patented to him, all rights
as lord of the soil of the Province to remain, he and
his heirs to have the right to present at each vacancy
two names, from which the Crown should choose the
Governor, also £30,000 to be paid to Penn with a royalty
—presumably perpetual—of $\frac{1}{2}d.$ per pound of tobacco
and per $l.$ of what sums the people paid the Governor!
This was, of course, "an asking price." Yet it must
be remembered that in 1700 he declared that the colony
had then cost him in the clear £24,000, and, a year after
this offer, he wrote to Logan that Pennsylvania had
cost him above £30,000 more than he had gotten out of
it. Penn desired also that he and his heirs should have
some honorary distinction, in recognition of his being
the Founder, such as first Councillor or Chief Justice:
but upon this he did not insist, being ready to content
himself with the rights of landlord. Neither did he
long hold out for the £30,000, but on or before Feb. 9,
1703-4, wrote to the Lord High Treasurer that he was
willing to accept £20,000 for the Governorship.

Harassed by the fault finding of Quary and Moore,
Penn offered to the Commissioners for Trade, about
the time Evans was arriving in Pennsylvania, either
to sell out, or to have the "turbulent Churchmen"
bought out, probably meaning to pay Quary, Moore,
and others to move away. Some of the Commisioners,
perhaps because of the Queen's kind feeling for Penn,
expressed a wish that the latter alternative could take
place; whereupon Penn desired them to promote it, and
assured them that he could find four persons able and
willing to provide for it. Who were the three besides

Shippen, or the two besides Shippen and himself? The aforesaid solution of trouble was not effected. While Lowther had been made Attorney-General of the Province, Moore had, on Bewley's death, obtained from Quary, Surveyor-General of the Customs, the good post of Collector of the Port of Philadelphia, and kept it during the rest of his life. At times hesitating, and at times asking the advice of Logan and others, and generally encouraged by Logan on condition that Quaker rights could be protected, Penn kept alive the project of turning into cash the political authority which had cost him so much.

Not only were Penn's friends who were intrusted with his authority in the Province and Territories particularly bound, in taking care of his interests, so to act as to avoid giving to Parliament any provocation to confiscate his viceroyalty; but, imbued with devotion to him, and seeing his necessities, they undertook, in opposition to the scheme of representative government, the policy of nursing and strengthening every limb of his prerogative, so that the selling value of this piece of property—the powers, revenues, and patronage being recognized as property—should be great when he treated with the Crown.

CHAPTER XIV.

THE ANTI-PROPRIETARY PARTY.

Feelings of various elements of the population—The City magistrates—The Assembly contends with Evans—A Remonstrance ordered to be sent to the Proprietary—The Militia—William Penn Jr. in a row with the City watchmen—Is indicted in Mayor's Court, and leaves the colony—Lloyd writes the Remonstrance and a letter to eminent English Quakers—The Assembly of 1704—A "great fray," in which Evans receives a beating—The Assemblymen's attitude as to Lloyd's Remonstrance—Biles's disrespectful words about Evans—The Ganawese and Shawnees—Some of the former move to Tulpehocken—The Fords bring suit in Chancery, and claim possession of Pennsylvania and Territories—Proprietary's friends carry election of 1705—Legislation—Religious qualification for officers and religious affirmation adopted—Law as to intercourse with Indians—Revenue Act—Change as to Sheriff and Coroner—Assemblymen to be chosen by plurality vote—Unpleasant circumstances of the old Quaker families.

Preceding chapters have mentioned Swedish suspicion, David Lloyd's resentment, Keithian opposition, Custom House officers' interests, and Anglican rivalry, as well as some purchasers' real or supposed, greater or less, suffering in property, such as prompted the struggle with Penn at the close of his second visit. It has also been shown that the Quaker settlers of the general type were democratic, querulous, and self-important, and, with a certain amount of gratitude to

Penn and amenableness to his personal influence, looked upon themselves as partners with him in the great colonial venture. They had left home, and subdued the wilderness, in order to enjoy privileges. A war ending in 1697 and one lasting from 1702 to 1713 took away, either by capture at sea, or scarcity and high price of European articles, or cessation of immigration, much of the money profit of their labor. It is not surprising that persons so situated grudged every shilling for which Penn asked.

The inconvenience of proprietary governments to the empire at large has been mentioned in the chapter on England. To the inhabitants of the locality subjected, such a government might become intolerable. Liberty had flourished in Pennsylvania, because of the enlightened ideas of the Proprietary who founded the colony: but was it fair that those who were maintaining by great hardship civilization in remote regions, and were still bound by their duties to the King, should have a second lord and master? Particularly when, after the first Proprietary must pass away, his successor, coming by birth or purchase, would be neither the King's nor the People's choice?

The opponents of Penn other than the Crown officials with some Churchmen, were not desirous of abolishing his viceroyalty, the basis of the colony's independent and improved jurisprudence; nor was the experience of those colonies of which the Governors were selected by the Crown, in the high salaries and military exactions and ecclesiastical arbitrariness, encouraging for a change. In fact, that Penn was inclined to allow such a change was looked upon as a betrayal. All that his opponents and the majority of the freemen wanted was to cut down expenses, and to minimize his power and more particularly the power of his Deputies.

The City Corporation very soon fell into the hands of those inimical to Penn, Lloyd becoming Recorder in place of Story, and, after Shippen's two terms as Mayor, that office being held by Anthony Morris, Griffith Jones, and Joseph Willcox successively. After the Queen's order, the fact that Lloyd and nearly all of the Aldermen were Quakers, made the Mayor's Court and those Aldermen acting as magistrates the only judiciary representing the religious society opposed to oaths. Thus the favor of many Assemblies was enlisted.

The first Assembly with which Evans came in contact endeavored, by proposing certain laws, to have the City Corporation strengthened, to state the powers of the House, and to confirm property. At the same time, it was unanimously voted to raise 1000*l.*, and to send 100*l.* thereof to agents to be selected, rather in place of Penn, for attending the Attorney-General or Solicitor-General and Board of Trade to obtain the Queen's approbation of the laws: but disputes with the Lieutenant-Governor, recess, and adjournment prevented the perfecting of a bill for raising money, it being the determination of the People's representatives to grant nothing unless satisfaction were received. They were, at the same time, great sticklers for respect to be shown to the House, and some remarks of Councillor Guest in public and private ridiculing it, and speaking of proposed laws as absurd, unreasonable, and monstrous, caused a vote that he should be rebuked; non-compliance with which, by the Lieutenant-Governor, may have added to the ill feeling. Evans and his Councillors deemed preposterous the powers given in the bill relating to the City Corporation, and as not sufficiently careful of the Proprietary's interests the bill for confirming property. These bills were in fact smothered in Council rather than fought. The great contention arose from the bill for the confirmation of the Charter of Privileges, or Frame of Government. This bill declared the Governor unable to prorogue or dissolve the

Assembly. Such power, Evans and his advisers did not consider to have been relinquished by the Proprietary, and therefore did not think the Lieutenant-Governor had any right to bind the Proprietary to forego, although the Assembly offered to limit the length of the sessions, except when the Governor consented. One of several amendments proposed by Evans gave the Council a part in legislation: this was rejected, one of the unanimous resolves of the Assembly on 6mo. 10 being that it would be inconsistent with King Charles's patent and the Charter of 1701, except when the government (the Lieutenant-Governorship) were vested in the Council, which the House was willing should happen on the death of a Lieutenant-Governor, unless there should be some other provision by the Governor-in-Chief. The Assemblymen decided to adjourn, and so to leave the subject to their successors, and asked the Lieutenant-Governor to think over the bills meanwhile. Accordingly, an order was made that the Speaker, who seems to have been regarded as something like the Clerk of a Quaker Meeting, should have the minutes for the year prepared, and take the advice of Biles, Willcox, Morris, Norris, Wood, Jones, and Richardson or as many of them or others of the body as could be conveniently consulted, about the minutes being published. Thus the phraseology of the minutes was left to be perfected later by Lloyd, whose consulting others was practically optional. It was ordered on 6mo. 25 that a representation to the Proprietary be prepared by the Speaker, Norris, and Willcox, and be brought into the House the next day, they to deal plainly with the Proprietary concerning the privileges and immunities which he promised to the People, and how inconsistent and repugnant thereto was his commission to the present Deputy, as well as former orders and proceedings, how the People were wronged and deprived of those privileges, how they were injured in their properties, and what inconveniences had happened from the Proprietary's not passing the bill for regulating fees proposed to him in 1701. Willcox reported on the 26th that the committee of three had made little progress, and could not finish; but Lloyd, as he avows (see *Penn and Logan Correspondence,* Vol. II, p. 407), had written nine articles to be embodied, and, the House resolving that the subject matter be forthwith drawn up, these were proposed, and, although, so near adjournment, some of the members were not paying attention, the articles were read, somewhat amended, and agreed to without one vote in the negative, and the representation was ordered to be drawn according to those heads, and to be perused by the members who were to peruse the minutes. Some time afterwards, certain members, who may be called fickle or weak-kneed, frightened at the turn resulting from their action or complaisance, said that they had not heard the articles, and had had confidence that the committee would be very respectful to the Proprietary—in what member except Norris could they have had such confidence?—and that the whole House would hear and vote upon the Remonstrance before it were sent—but when could that be, the immediate aljournment being final? There can be very little doubt that the interlineation by Lloyd himself, who had control of the minutes, to the effect that the Representation be signed by the Speaker, and sent to the Proprietary by the first opportunity, expressed what was ordered.

Certain proceedings of Evans and some of his Councillors gave the City Corporation some grievances. The militia had increased in Philadelphia to three companies, under Captains Lowther, George Roche, and John Finney, and on 4mo. 13, 1704, gave a military funeral to the old naval veteran, former Lieutenant-Governor Markham. To encourage enlisting, a proclamation was issued by the Governor relieving all who were on the muster rolls from the duties of watch and ward, which the City authorities enforced upon all the citizens. Guest, Samuel Finney, Roche, and Pidgeon, put into the County Court in order to administer oaths, claimed a concurrent jurisdiction with the Mayor's Court in licensing drinking places; and it was only after approval of the County Court was obtained that the Governor issued any license. A third source of complaint was the protection given to a tavern keeper, after conviction in the Mayor's Court for a misdemeanor, the charge apparently having resulted largely from the conduct of William Penn Jr.

Young Penn's natural inclinations for livelier company than the older Quakers, and his knowledge that his Quaker family could not retain the government unless non-Quakers undertook the defence of the region, made him the friend and champion of the militia officers, although he still belonged to the peace-loving Society, and had written to Logan two years before: "as for the poking-iron [sword], I never had courage enough to wear one by my side." One evening, not long after the Governor's proclamation excusing the militia from watch and ward, the City watchmen, as Logan gives the account in a letter to the Proprietary, "meeting with a company at Enoch Story's, a tavern, in which some of the militia officers were, a difference arose, that ended with some rudeness. Next night, the watch coming again to the same place, and thy son happening to be in company, there was something of a fray which ended in the watch retiring." This was a euphemistic way of describing it to the young man's father, if Watson the Annalist has preserved the truth in the statement following: "Penn called for pistols to pistol them, but the lights being put out, one fell upon young Penn, and gave him a severe beating." If he did call for pistols, the case is made out that he was drunk. Before his arrival in the country, his father had written to Logan not to let him be in any public house after the allowed hours. The severe beating may have been confused with that given to Governor Evans after young Penn had left the colony. Isaac Norris wrote that William Penn Jr. was "in company with some extravagants that beat the watch at Enoch Story's." Logan goes on to say: "This with all the persons concerned in it, was taken notice of at the next Mayor's court that sat"—*i.e.* on Sep. 3, Morris being Mayor, and Lloyd being Recorder, and probably gloating over the opportunity to hurt the elder Penn. The grand jury made a virtue of being no respecter of persons; but Logan says that the indignity of a presentment put upon the eldest son of the founder of the Corporation, although no further action was taken, was looked upon as base by most people of moderation, and, in fact, caused some obstreperousness—he says "disorders"—at night, which he acquits William Jr. of instigating. Certainly the act of the Corporation was resented by the heir apparent himself, and afterwards by the Proprietary. Story was proceeded against for entertaining at the house certain servants of William Bevan, whereupon Story's counsel claimed that, under the Queen's order, a certain non-Quaker witness for the prosecution should be sworn. None of the Court being conscientiously able to administer an oath, the witness was allowed to be attested, and Story was convicted. He appealed to the Governor and Council on 7ber 15, and, following the Queen's order, a proclamation was issued setting aside the proceedings, and forbidding all officers from executing any writ founded thereon. William Penn Jr. attended that meeting of the Council, but none later. To show his contempt for the strict Quakers, he drank toasts, and appeared in fashionable clothes when Lady Cornbury made a visit from Burlington to Philadelphia,—this is the way we must translate Logan's statement that William Jr. "indulged himself in the same freedom that others take,"—but he still declared his adherence to Quaker doctrine. He entertained Lord and Lady Cornbury at Pennsbury, and came back to Philadelphia to assist in receiving Governor Seymour of Maryland, and then, having sold Williamstadt manor on the Schuylkill (now Norristown and Norriton township), left America, fated never to return.

Lloyd, consulting Willcox and Jones, wrote, as we are told (*Penn and Logan Correspondence,* Vol. I, p. 331) a "most virulent unmannerly invective" as the Representation, or Remonstrance, to the Proprietary, but, indeed, to make an invective, there was required very little change in the words of the heads agreed upon by the Assembly. These heads were viz: 1st, that the Proprietary's artifices brought all privileges and charters to be defeasible at his will and pleasure; 2nd, that all dissolutions and prorogations and calling Assemblies by writs, as authorized by commissions to the present Deputy and orders to former Deputies and Commissioners, were contrary to the charters granted; 3rd, that the Proprietary had had great sums of money for negotiating the confirmation of laws and good terms for the people, and easing as to oaths, but none of the laws were confirmed, and, by the Queen's order requiring oaths to be administered, the Quakers were disabled to sit in Courts; 4th, that there had been no Surveyor-General since Pennington's death, but great extortions by surveyors and the other officers concerned in property by the Proprietary's refusal to pass the law regulating fees; 5th, that there was likely to be no remedy except where particularly granted by the Proprietary, because the present deputy called it a hardship on him, and the Council urged it as absurd and unreasonable, to expect any enlargement or explanation of what the Proprietary granted; 6th, that there was no remedy against wrong or oppression by the

THE ANTI-PROPRIETARY PARTY. 441

Proprietary, because his Clerk of the Court refused to make out any process, and, by the Justices appointed by the Proprietary, the latter was practically judge of his own case; 7th, that, Sheriffs and other officers commissioned by him being persons of no estates, and their security being given to him, the abused or defrauded persons could reap no benefit; 8th, that the Commissioners of Property neglected and delayed making satisfaction where people had not the full quantity of land; and, 9th, that the Proprietary should not surrender the government, as he had intimated, and should understand how vice was growing of late. Lloyd did not show the Remonstrance to Norris, the other member of the committee of three, but showed it to Richardson, who disapproved of it. Lloyd (*Penn and Logan Correspondence*, Vol. II, p. 408) afterwards said that all but three of the seven members of the committee on minutes approved, and that five Assemblymen examined the fair transcript before it was sent. Lloyd actually signed it when his term as Speaker had been ended by the new election for Assemblymen. He enclosed a copy in a letter, dated 8ber 3, to three prominent Quakers in England, George Whitehead, William Mead, and Thomas Lower, of whom Mead and Lower were known to be unfriendly to Penn, requesting them by "such Christian methods" as they should see fit to oblige William Penn to do the People justice. There was mentioned as also enclosed a copy of the bill which the Assembly wished to pass in relation to oaths, and the persons addressed were desired to solicit the Queen in favor of it. The letter said "I suppose you will have a more ample account by others of the condition this poor province is brought to by the late revels and disorders which young William Penn and his gang of loose fellows he accompanies with are found in, to the great grief of Friends and others in this place." The letter closed with the request for an endeavor to get an able lawyer of sobriety and moderation, but not in Penn's interest, to be commissioned Chief Justice of the Province and Lower Counties and also the Jerseys; a position which could be worth 400 or 500l. per annum besides fees and perquisites. The letter spoke of Mompesson as thought of formerly, but unable to stay, besides "too much in William Penn's interest, and given to drink." This letter with its enclosures was sent on a vessel which was captured by the French, and all were examined, and thrown upon the deck. A fellow passenger other than the one intrusted with them, gathered them up, and, with permission of the French officer, eventually had them put into the hands of Penn, without going to the three Quakers.

The election in October, 1704, resulted in little change in the Assembly, in fact in the loss of two or three who might have restrained the majority. At the same time, in Philadelphia County, John Budd Jr. and Benjamin Wright were chosen to be presented to the Governor for him to select one as Sheriff, that office being held by John Finney, appointed in August, 1703, on the resignation of Thomas Farmer. The Frame of Government having prescribed for the presentation every three years, Evans claimed that this could not be made until 1705, and, accordingly, he allowed John Finney to continue in office. Evans raised an inquiry as to how the Assemblymen were being qualified, but the Council satisfied him that the promise of fidelity prescribed by the law of 1700 was sufficient. He then received and addressed the Assembly without providing a chair for the Speaker, and so, although he himself was standing, gave affront to at least Lloyd, who had been re-elected Speaker. The House presented their former bills for confirmation of the Charter, and confirming property, and one, probably the same as copied for Whitehead, to authorize affirmations. The Assemblymen voted, on 8mo. 27, to add to the Remonstrance the aggrievance of persons by reason of quit rents on the lots in the City, especially the bank lots, and to state the Proprietary's promise of a gift of the site of the great town. No agreement on any bill was reached with the Lieutenant-Governor. He had asked for money to maintain the government by his living in becoming style, and by the exigencies of state being "prevented or timely answered;" but the Assemblymen determined not to give anything until their privileges were confirmed. Penn had endorsed his Lieutenant's stand on the bills in debate during the Summer, and one of Evans's messages said that it was strange that reasonable men could propose such an injury to the Proprietary as the bill of property, without offering an equivalent, such as a settled revenue for the support of government, and the defraying of public charges. The Assembly then offered for that purpose 1200*l*. and an impost on wine, cider, &ct., on condition of confirmation of what the members thought agreeable to the Proprietary's engagement with his People. This was not accepted.

Various other matters had increased the estrangement. A "great fray," too late to be made use of by Lloyd in his letter, took place in the city on the night of November 1, 1704. Jenkins, in his *Family of William Penn,* has shown that this has been confused with the affair in which William Penn Jr. figured, the last named being on the seas at this time. In the catalogue of particulars prepared to accompany the Assembly's letter of 4mo. 10, 1707, is mentioned the Lieutenant-Governor's beating "Solomon Cresson, Constable of this City, when he was doing the Duty of his Office upon the Watch about two years ago," and sending him "to Prison, where he was kept till the Afternoon of the Day following, for no other Cause that we can find, but bidding a lewd Tavern-keeper disperse her Company, where the Governor happened to be about One a Clock at Night, though the Constable knew not of his being there till he called him in, and began to beat him." This evidently gives us the starting of the "great fray," as it is called in the Minutes of the Governor's Council. Evidently Cresson sounded an alarm for help. There came to the scene the chief officers of the City. Deborah Logan has quoted a tradition that, the lights being put out, Joseph Willcox, who was an Alderman, seized one of the roisterers, and beat him. This happened to be the Lieutenant-Governor, suffering in his turn. When Willcox became aware whom he had hold of, he beat him again. The next day, the Attorney-General formally complained to the Governor and Council of the abuse of some gentlemen by the watch, and the support given to the latter by the Mayor, Recorder, and an Alderman, and asked whether, as it was impossible to try them in the Mayor's Court, a trial in another court should be ordered. On examination of the Mayor, Recorder, and Alderman Willcox, it was wisely decided that they had been in no way concerned in the disturbance, except to quell it.

Evans demanded from this Assembly a copy of the Remonstrance sent in the name of the preceding one, and, the members disliking Lloyd's using the word "treachery" and some other harsh expressions, word was sent to the bearer of a copy, who was supposed to be still at New York, to bring it back for further consideration, but he had sailed. Logan says that this Assembly, which declined Evans's demand for a copy, refused to adopt the document as its own, in spite of Lloyd's wily suggestion that such adoption would make it proper to furnish the copy. The statement that the Assembly "disowned the Remonstrance" is true only as to some of its strong language. An address of 3rd month contained the following very careful expression: "Our part is to lament (as we really do) that there should be true occasion for such representation, or, if none, that it should be offered our Proprietary." There was, to be sure, added, without really weakening the effect, "whom we both love and honour." The address, which was the one making the conditional offer of money last mentioned, plainly declared Penn's services to the colony overpaid, if he had failed to secure the royal approbation for the beneficial laws, he having promised to do so, and having promised to make good terms for the People upon a surrender of the government, and having had 2000*l.* voted to him. Assurance was given, rather insultingly, that if said sum was insufficient to negotiate this, so that, as had been mentioned, he felt that he should not be at the expense of a large fee to the Attorney-General, what was right would be done by the House upon receipt of an itemized statement of disbursements. Based on the idea that the quit rents of 1*s.* per 100 acres had been agreed to in view of the Proprietary's extraordinary expenses in being Governor, there was a complaint that it would be hard, if the purchasers, as the Proprietary was understood to expect, must pay Thomas Lloyd's salary as Governor in Penn's absence, which absence was for the service of England, and not of the Province, while the business which took him home in 1684, the boundary dispute, was still unsettled, to the great discouragement of both Province and Lower Counties.

In protest against the disposition and conduct of the preceding and the sitting Assembly, a letter to Penn was prepared about 3, 23, 1705, and signed, says Logan, by "almost all the profession" (meaning Quakers), declaring abhorrence of the Remonstrance, and willingness to bear all the expense of the government, but, however, itself mentioning a number of things which the signers thought honestly their due.

Old William Biles, who was now an Assemblyman from Bucks, was reported to have spoken thus of

Evans: "He is but a boy; he is not fit to be our Governor. We'll kick him out; we'll kick him out." For these words, which he denied using, but which doubtless expressed an opinion and wish common among most of the Quakers, Evans sued Biles for 2000*l.* damages, having the writ served on him the evening that the House adjourned for three weeks. Before the County Court, composed of Evans's friends, Guest, Samuel Finney, Pidgeon, and Edward Farmer, Lloyd, as counsel for Biles, pleaded the privileges of an Assemblyman. The Court overruled this, ordered the defendant to plead over, and, on his refusal, would not grant an imparlance, but gave judgment against him. A jury assessed damages at 300*l.* Evans, on June 20, sent a message to the reconvened Assembly, demanding the expulsion of Biles forthwith. The Assembly replied, that, as the words were not alleged to have been spoken in the House, it could not examine into the fact whether they had been spoken or not, that such words, the House had no intention to justify, but that the Sheriff, in summoning a member the very day he was attending the Assembly, and the Justices, by their action, had committed a breach of privilege: the Governor was begged to allow Biles to wait upon him, and, wherein he found Biles faulty, to accept a submission, which the House unanimously directed should be made. Evans, infuriated, dismissed the Assembly.

Penn thought the arrest of Biles legal, and had strong feeling against him as a leading opponent in Bucks County, and Penn also, even before he knew the phraseology of the Remonstrance, was so incensed at the want of consideration shown him by Lloyd and other Quakers that he desired, by selling the government, to leave them in the lurch, being convinced that the Queen would annul the privileges which his charters gave. He felt that he could get more justice from his enemies than from the leaders of his co-religionists,

THE ANTI-PROPRIETARY PARTY. 447

for whom he had been fighting: and, in fact, Quary and Moore, of the Church party in the Province, had been friendly with his son, and would incline fo the Proprietary rather than the opposite interest. Penn and Quary came into such harmony that the former in 1705 or 1706 submitted to his friends in Pennsylvania the question of admitting Quary to the Governor's Council, but this was not done. In 1707, Logan, managing for Penn, leased Pennsbury to Quary for seven years.

About the first of the year 1705, Penn laid before the Commissioners for Trade and Plantations a draft of an instrument of surrender and the conditions on which it was to be made.

The promise in the treaty of April 30, 1701, mentioned in the chapter on the Red Neighbours, that the Pennsylvania government would befriend the Ganawese and Shawnees, as well as the other Indians, was well observed in comforting them in times of apprehension, and in sending messengers or speaking in treaties to conciliate the Five Nations, who were often reported to be preparing attacks upon the Pennsylvania Indians, and furthermore by Pennsylvania exerting influence upon adjacent governments to restrain their red men and their white men. The Ganawese, after an attack on a party of them by Virginians and the loss of a man, were allowed in 1705 to remove to the Tulpehocken region, and dwell with the Delawares there, Menangy, the leader of the Delawares of those parts, making the request to the provincial government for the permission: but a number continued to reside at Connejaghera, or Conejohela, their location being later described as "above the fort"—Qu. the old Susquehanna Fort at the Falls?—and also as "several miles above Conestoga." These Ganawese were sometimes called Conewages, apparently after the name of the

Creek at the Falls, but the name of Conoy Town was the usual one for the village.

The Fords, after the stating of the account with Penn as to what was owing on April 1, 1702, as mentioned in the last chapter, were disposed to give Penn time to redeem the land of Pennsylvania and the Lower Counties, and postponed the probate of the elder Ford's will, in expectation of the family being provided for by the sums promised to be paid. Perhaps Bridget Ford had more conscience than she has been credited with about calling the original transaction an absolute sale. Probably her advisers thought that nobody at the time would give any more for the property than the redemption price: and the widow and three children were not rich enough to hold that amount of capital in unproductive property to await future profit: otherwise, we, looking back from a time when the region has long been so valuable, must think both Penn and the Fords blind to their respective interests in not quickly effecting a compromise by the allotment of land at Penn's standard price in satisfaction of the amount of the Ford claim. As Penn looked over the accounts carefully, he became convinced that he had been cheated in the method of computing the debt, even that payments made by him or for him to Philip Ford had not been entered. So Penn offered, if the whole account were reopened before Quaker arbitrators mutually chosen, to pay down one half of what they found due, and give security for the payment of the other half. This the Fords refused. They determined, probably for forcing a speedy payment in full, to assert their rights according to the face of the papers, and so brought a bill in Chancery in England to have the agreement to resell to Penn cleared away, and the trusts in Philip Ford's will carried out. The family, moreover, executed a power of attorney, dated January 24, 1704-5, to David Lloyd, Isaac Norris, and John Moore to take possession of Pennsylvania and the Territories, and notified those attorneys in a letter of 1mo. 29, 1705, by which time about four years' interest was said to be due, that, the lease of Pennsylvania and Territories made to William Penn having expired, the latter was only tenant at will, and the attorneys were to warn the holders of land not to pay to Penn's agents any quit rents. Even then the Fords were not anxious to take the property, and Lloyd and Moore, as well as Norris, showed patience and consideration: but the instructions sounded like the death knell of Penn's authority, or perhaps rather the funeral tolling over all government commissioned by him at least since the expiration of the lease.

This letter of attorney and the instructions arrived about 5mo. 10, 1705. They appear to have caused some change in the feelings of the voters, or else it was an ordinary instance of reaction, that a great effort of the Proprietary's friends was successful in carrying the ensuing election for Assemblymen. Shippen, Carpenter, Pusey, and Hill, with Norris, whose sympathies were on that side, took the seats recently held by enemies or those acting as such. David Lloyd was rejected by the ballot of the County of Philadelphia, but, however, was one of the two chosen to represent the People of the city. Growdon, his father-in-law, who had differed with him politically for some time, was one of the friendly, as against three or four "scabbed sheep," as Logan calls them, from Bucks. The result in Chester County had been thoroughly controlled. Growdon was made Speaker.

Much legislation resulted from this harmony with the executive branch. The Attorney-General of England had, on Oct. 13, 1704, reported to the Board of Trade, objections to thirty of the laws of 1700 and 1701, and observations on another, viz: that for taking lands in execution. Penn, to enable the Province to save time by making new laws on the various subjects, obtained and sent over a copy of this report, and possibly also suggested alterations in other laws which he knew would be opposed by the Commissioners for Trade and Navigation. The Province acted in nearly every case, and nearly every substituted law was allowed by the Crown. Some of the laws are in force to-day, for instance that for Defalcation, or set-off against a plaintiff's demand, and that for Taking Land in Execution, allowing a jury to declare the rents for seven years insufficient to pay the debt, and in that case having the Sheriff make sale under a writ called by its Latin words *Venditioni exponas*, and furthermore providing that mortgages be sued out by the writ called *Scire facias* and the premises sold under a writ called *Levari*, a great advance upon the proceedings in chancery for foreclosure, as clung to in other parts of the United States.

Some of the changes made were little more than formal; others were quite radical. A table of consanguinity and affinity was set forth within which marriages should be void, but the Assembly made a departure from English law in not including a deceased wife's sister in the table. Milder punishments for some crimes were substituted for the bloody ones which the Quakers had recently prescribed. Doubtless much to Penn's disappointment, but as a necessary compliance with the sentiment of British officials, the law concerning liberty of conscience was so changed as to protect only those who professed faith in the Trinity, and acknowledged the inspiration of the Scriptures.

A compromise between the Anglican and Quaker friends of Penn was attempted in an act for the qualification of magistrates and manner of giving evidence. It allowed Councillors, Assemblymen, Commissioners, Justices, Clerks, Sheriffs, and other officers to qualify by affirmation when conscientiously unable to take an oath, but required them to subscribe the declarations and professions of faith according to the Act of Parliament of 1 W. & M. for relieving Dissenters who scrupled at taking an oath. As regarded the competency of unsworn persons to testify in court, provision was necessary, owing to the Queen's repeal of the Act passed at New Castle in 1700, and re-enacted in 1701, allowing witnesses to give evidence by "solemnly promising" to speak the truth. To guard against what would be practically, but not etymologically, perjury, such act had ordered that a person convicted of wilful falsehood was to suffer the punishment which the one against whom the false testimony was given "did or should undergo." This the Attorney-General objected to, construing it to mean that a person bearing false witness against any one in a trial for felony was to be hung, even although the person tried were acquitted. The omission of religious words in the affirmation was not animadverted upon by the Attorney-General; nevertheless, as Evans's political influence in England was through the Church, the members of the Assembly, who except Griffith Jones, "not in unity with Friends," and Growdon, not in regular standing, and except John Swift, were all Quakers, were constrained by Evans to prescribe, in the new act aforesaid for qualifications and giving evidence, that the affirmant answer yes or yea to the strange expression in the English act, objected to by radical Quakers some years before as partaking of the nature of an oath, viz: "Dost thou declare or thou shalt declare (English act says "I do declare") in the presence of Almighty God, the witness of the truth of what thou sayest" (English act, "of what I say"). However, consideration was given to the consciences of Quaker Judges, such Judges being allowed to make non-Quakers affirm, if there were no one on the bench free to administer an oath, and moreover the administration of an oath, when there were Judges who scrupled at administering one, being declared the act of the person administering it, and not of the whole bench. Evans was afraid to pass this, and only did so upon the insertion of a proviso that the act should not go into force until the 20th of September. Furthermore, he notified the Board of Trade by letter of Jany. 19, 1705-6, so as to have a decision reached, if possible, before the act should go into force. Attorney-General Northey, to whom the Board referred the act, saw the desirableness of so securing service and testimony for the courts in a Quaker colony, but objected to a provision of the same act admitting the written deposition of a sick or removing person to be evidence in all cases criminal as well as civil. Meanwhile, Samuel Finney and others, we are told by Penn, employed an attorney in England to oppose the act before the Commissioners for Trade. This attorney, who was George Willcocks, pointed out, among other objections, that the form of affirmation was not an express declaration that the party says the truth. The Commissioners agreed to recommend disallowance, unless Penn gave assurance that the Assembly would enact by an additional law that no Judges could sit, unless there were one who could administer an oath, and that all who refused to take oaths be obliged to declare their refusal to be for conscientious scruple, and that only in civil cases should the written deposition be accepted as evidence. Of course, Penn could give no assurance of the action of any Assembly, but only that his Lieutenant could take care by appointing enough Churchmen that rarely would a case be tried before Quakers alone. The act was disallowed by the Queen on Jany. 8, 1707-8. Thus fell, after a short life, about the only Quaker provision made by the Assemblymen chosen in 1705.

That the Indians should neither have grievances, nor hear rumors inciting them to rise against the colonists, an act, drawn up by Logan, and to remain in force for three years, was passed, and, moreover, was not repealed in England. Under its terms, any person killing, wounding, beating, or abusing an Indian was made subject to the same punishment as if the injury were done to a natural born subject of England, and was to be fined in addition; a person spreading stories which might alienate the mind of the Indians was, on conviction by either Christian or Indian evidence, to be heavily fined, and to be imprisoned, and to give security for good behavior; fifty pounds a year were allowed for necessary treaties and messages ordered by the Governor and Council; no one for trading with the Indians was to go into the woods or from his plantation except to an English market town or place, unless to buy corn, venison, provisions, or skins for clothing himself or family, without a license from the Governor by order of the Governor and Council, good for one year, which license was to be granted to any natural born subject of the Crown upon his giving security to trade honestly, and observe the rules and orders made by the Governor and Council for regulating the trade; all skins, furs, and other commodities bought of the Indians by such traders were to be sold within the province.

The majority of those Assemblymen being in the humor to do whatever was for the Proprietary's interest, acts were passed for enforcing the payment of his quit rents, for collecting the arrears of the 2000*l.* voted to him in 1700, and for providing for the Lieutenant-Governor, as well as paying debts and application to such other purposes as the Governor and Assembly might appoint. This last mentioned act levied a tax of $2\frac{1}{2}d.$ per *l.* on all estates over 30*l.* exclusive of household goods and implements of use, and 10*s.* per head on all freemen over twenty-one who had been six months clear of apprenticeship, and were not worth 30*l.*, also an impost for three years on certain liquors imported, and on butter and cheese, except when from Delaware, New Jersey, England, or Ireland, and on negro slaves and servants, except when brought from Delaware or New Jersey.

Some changes in the constitution of the government were made by this Assembly. One was in the direction of democracy. The Sheriffs and Coroners were to be selected as before, but were to serve only one year, and their bonds were to be taken in the Queen's name, and to be for the use of those injured by the acts of those officials. On the other hand, majority rule might cease under the Act for Ascertaining the Number of Assemblymen, and Regulating their Election: they were to be chosen by plurality vote; an arrangement which, whether intended so or not, enabled a well organized minority, such as the Proprietary's friends could have expected to command, to seize this refuge of popular government, or, rather, of the qualified voters' government. Only by the determined rallying of a majority around those whom they trusted, could this be prevented.

The Quakers, except a few individuals, had now fallen politically into a situation as unpleasant as that of the Churchmen a short time before, and more particularly the rural, plainer, more radical families, who might be called the co-adventurers with Penn. Their expectations, whether reasonable or not, of an easy, popularly controlled, and cheap government had been disappointed. Penn, of whose influence they had an exaggerated idea, had failed to abolish oaths permanently, to secure an exemption from tribute on the occasion of war, and to free the disposal of the crops and the obtaining of necessaries from jeopardy and frequent loss under Parliament's policy and Admiralty's administration. There were doubtless some individuals who were interfered with by the religious qualification just established, and there were more who disliked it. There was a disappointment throughout the Society of Friends at Evans's putting off the approval of a law empowering religious societies to receive and dispose of lands for their necessary uses, it being doubted whether, without such law, a Quaker Meeting could legally claim any real estate for a meeting-house or burial ground. As, in England, land granted for pious uses could not be alienated, the Vestry of Christ Church was asked whether it was willing to accept the power to do so, and the Vestry expressed objections to the bill; so that Evans feared that consenting to it might offend "the Bishop" (probably the Bishop of London, in charge of the Church in America, but possibly the aforesaid Bishop of Bangor). There were doubtless a number of landholders, non-Quakers as well as Quakers, frightened about their own possessions by the repeal of the old law about property, and the submission to William Penn, across the seas, of a new bill for confirming grants and patents. As to the chance of governing themselves, most of those pioneers or their sons who would have liked to participate in affairs, could feel themselves crowded out, except as to the Shrievalty or Coronership or membership of the Assembly: the Council contained men who had come since the summer of 1699, one member, George Roche of Antigua, having been appointed within about a year after his arrival, without there being excuse, as in the case of Mompesson and young Penn. With the increasing number of Churchmen in office, the Quakers among the Governor's advisers and most of those chosen to the Assembly in 1705, might be said to be "Pennites" first, and Quakers afterwards. Penn had received, or was collecting, under appropriations, considerable sums of money not convenient for the inhabitants to pay, and now all were being called upon to maintain in style above the sumptuary ideas of the Quakers Penn's personal representative as Governor, who had nothing in common with the earnest Quakers, whom they could neither respect like Blackwell, nor feel as a neighbour towards like Markham, nor even make a bargain with like Fletcher. Too faithful to Penn to abate any of his prerogative, Evans was so obedient to the Queen as to interfere with the enforcement of law and order: and Penn was not showing himself a Roman parent as to the behavior of his son, but resenting as a piece of spite the noticing of it. The Quakers were losing one by one the benefits derived from a seigniory in the hands of one of their persuasion interposed between them and the Crown: the seigniory was likely soon to be surrendered; but if it should not be, but descend to William Penn's heir, then if the heir, who had been displeased with the Pennsylvanians, should forsake the Society of Friends, would any benefit remain?